Taste of Home
QUICK COOKING

ANNUAL RECIPES

Taste of Home

RDA ENTHUSIAST BRANDS, LLC • MILWAUKEE, WI

QUICK COOKING

ANNUAL RECIPES 2020

ITALIAN-STYLE PIZZAS (p. 19)

© 2020 RDA Enthusiast Brands, LLC.
1610 N. 2nd St., Suite 102, Milwaukee WI 53212-3906
All rights reserved. Taste of Home is a registered trademark of RDA Enthusiast Brands, LLC.
Visit: *tasteofhome.com* for other Taste of Home books and products.

International Standard Book Number:
D 978-1-61765-945-4
U 978-1-61765-946-1
Component Number:
D 117800071H
U 117800073H
International Standard Serial Number: 1552-6603

Executive Editor: Mark Hagen
Senior Art Director: Raeann Thompson
Editor: Hazel Wheaton
Art Director: Maggie Conners
Senior Designer: Courtney Lovetere
Designer: Jazmin Delgado
Copy Editor: Amy Rabideau Silvers
Cover Photography: Taste of Home Photo Studio

Pictured on front cover:
Fried Ice Cream Dessert Bars, p. 296; Little Cheddar Meat Loaves, p. 173; All-American Hamburgers p. 272; Weeknight Ravioli Lasagna, p. 95; Shredded Chicken Tostadas, p. 216;

Pictured on back cover:
Bacon Breakfast Casserole, p. 189; Nantucket Cranberry Tart p. 278; Homemade Strawberry Ice Cream, p. 172; Skewered Ginger Shrimp with Plums, p. 237; Red Potatoes with Beans, p. 51.

Printed in USA
1 3 5 7 9 10 8 6 4 2

Introduction 4

30 Days of Quick Cooking 6

Secrets to Quick Cooking 8

Appetizers & Beverages 10

Speedy Sides & Salads 28

Quick Soups & Sandwiches 54

Give Me 5 or Fewer 80

30-Minute Dinners 96

Casseroles & Oven Entrees 124

Lightened-Up Delights 138

Family-Friendly Fare 168

Breakfast & Brunch Favorites 180

Breads in a Jiffy 196

Slow Cooker & Instant Pot 208

Hot off the Grill 228

Potlucks & Parties 246

Holiday & Seasonal Pleasers 262

Delectable Desserts 290

Easy Odds & Ends 308

Indexes 322

LIKE US
facebook.com/tasteofhome

TWEET US
@tasteofhome

FOLLOW US
pinterest.com/taste_of_home

SHARE A RECIPE
tasteofhome.com/submit

SHOP WITH US
shoptasteofhome.com

E-MAIL US
bookeditors@tasteofhome.com

VISIT tasteofhome.com
FOR MORE!

CHAMPION ROAST BEEF SANDWICHES (p. 69)

APRICOTS WITH HERBED GOAT CHEESE (p. 45)

PASTA FAGIOLI SOUP (p. 60)

QUICK SLOPPY JOES (p. 176)

QUICK ICEBOX SANDWICHES (p. 174)

SHARE A HOME-COOKED MEAL EVEN ON YOUR BUSIEST NIGHTS

CHICKEN PICCATA POCKETS (p. 270)

RASPBERRY-COCONUT FRENCH TOAST (p. 184)

THE ULTIMATE FISH TACOS (p. 266)

GRILLED SPICY CORN ON THE COB (p. 230)

No time to cook dinner? Think again! With *Quick Cooking Annual Recipes,* you have the complete resource you need to get meals on the table fast!

MAKE IT FAST, MAKE IT GOOD

Today's families are busier than ever—and family meals can get lost in the rush. But with the help of *Quick Cooking Annual Recipes,* you'll never have to skip a sit-down dinner or resort to takeout meals.

Shared by home cooks from across the country and tested in the *Taste of Home* Test Kitchen, these recipes are just what you need to make meals that satisfy the whole family. Collected from the last year of *Simple & Delicious* magazine as well as some of our best-loved recipes, this volume is the foundation for scrumptious home-cooked meals—even when your schedule is tight.

This edition boasts 498 sure-to-please recipes, from breakfasts to side dishes, appetizers to desserts. There are recipes specially selected to appeal to kids, dishes perfect for holiday celebrations, and chapters dedicated to grilled recipes and party pleasers. We've also packed in countless tips, hints and recipe variations to make everything even easier. With this newest edition of *Quick Cooking Annual Recipes,* you'll have dinner (or breakfast, or lunch...) on the table in a flash!

ICONS IN THIS BOOK

These **fast-fix recipes** are table-ready in just 30 minutes or less.

Dishes that use **five or fewer ingredients** (they may also call for water, salt, pepper, canola or olive oil, and optional items).

Our **healthiest recipes,** these dietician-approved dishes are lower in calories, fat and sodium.

Freezer-friendly items that include directions for freezing and reheating.

Recipes that use a **slow cooker**—one of the most convenient kitchen tools.

Recipes made using a handy **Instant Pot**® electric pressure cooker.

BALSAMIC-GOAT CHEESE GRILLED PLUMS (p. 239)

CHICKEN PARMESAN
SLIDER BAKE
(p. 172)

MAKE TIME FOR HOME-COOKED MEALS WITH THESE
550+ RECIPES & TIPS

IN THIS EDITION
Give Me 5 or Fewer
Every recipe in this chapter calls for just a handful of ingredients, so you can save time in both the kitchen and the grocery store! These recipes are budget-friendly and a breeze to pull together on short notice.

Easy Odds & Ends
In this chapter, we turn the spotlight on homemade sauces and relishes, ultra-convenient sheet pan suppers and dump cakes—the quickest way to satisfy your sweet tooth!

30-Minute Dinners
All these main courses go from pantry to table in just half an hour or less. You'll find tons of recipes that are perfect for the most hectic weeknights. Check out the Asparagus Beef Teriyaki (p. 120), Honey Mustard Pork (p. 123) or Penne with Veggies & Black Beans (p. 115).

Slow Cooker & Instant Pot ®
Whether you like to cook fast or cook slow, this chapter is filled with recipes that use the two most popular kitchen gadgets. Use the slow cooker to make Grandma Edna's Cajun Pork (p. 214) or whip up some Buffalo Shrimp Mac & Cheese (p. 227) in the Instant Pot.

Delectable Desserts
There's always time for dessert—and this chapter has the proof! Whether it's an Easy Fresh Strawberry Pie (p. 301) to make the most of summer berries or a Caramelized Pear & Walnut Bread Pudding (p. 298) just right for cooler weather, you can indulge any time.

Lightened-Up Delights
Every recipe in the book includes nutrition facts, and suggestions from our dietician are scattered through the whole book—look for the HEALTH TIP icon. But we go a step further with this complete chapter of our most diet-conscious dishes, making it easier than ever to choose the healthiest options for your family.

30 DAYS OF QUICK COOKING

To get you started, here's a month of dinners using recipes from this book. Plan with an eye for leftovers—the tenderloin from Day 1 can be used to make the Steakhouse Pizza on Day 4. And if you find a recipe that really works for your family, don't be afraid to repeat!

DAY 1
Garlic Herbed Beef Tenderloin, p. 257

MENU ADD-ONS
• Citrus Peach Carrots, p. 39
• Pressure-Cooker Lemon Red Potatoes, p. 210

DAY 2
Nutty Cheese Tortellini, p. 90

MENU ADD-ONS
• Pull-Apart Garlic Bread, p. 251

DAY 3
Fish Tacos, p. 150

MENU ADD-ONS
• Raspberry Coleslaw, p. 52

DAY 4
Cream of Potato & Cheddar Soup, p. 211

MENU ADD-ONS
• Steakhouse Pizza, p. 135

DAY 5
Makeover Deluxe Grilled Cheese, p. 60

MENU ADD-ONS
• Quick Sausage Tortellini Soup, p. 58

DAY 11
Crumb-Topped Sole, p. 132

MENU ADD-ONS
• Orzo with Caramelized Butternut Squash, p. 45

DAY 12
Kale & Fennel Skillet, p. 38

MENU ADD-ONS
• Creamy Chicken Rice Soup, p. 69

DAY 13
Artichoke Chicken Pesto Pizza, p. 86

MENU ADD-ONS
• Fruit salad

DAY 14
Chicken Parmesan Slider Bake, p. 172

MENU ADD-ONS
• Caesar salad

DAY 15
Rosemary Pork with Cherry Topping, p. 133

MENU ADD-ONS
• Black-Eyed Peas with Collard Greens, p. 32

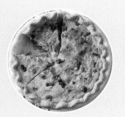

DAY 21
Roadside Diner Cheeseburger Quiche, p. 136

MENU ADD-ONS
• Coleslaw & French fries

DAY 22
Sugar-Glazed Ham, p. 90

MENU ADD-ONS
• Mashed Cauliflower, p. 284

DAY 23
Penne with Veggies & Black Beans, p. 115

MENU ADD-ONS
• Herbed Bubble Bread, p. 207

DAY 24
Chicken Veggie Fajitas, p. 314

MENU ADD-ONS
• Salsa & Tortilla chips

DAY 25
Sensational Spiced Salmon, p. 127

MENU ADD-ONS
• Thai Salad with Cilantro Lime Dressing, p. 44

DAY 6
Mini Meatloaf Sheet-Pan Meal, p. 316

MENU ADD-ONS
• Biscuits or crescent rolls

DAY 7
Cheesy Stuffed Peppers, p. 126

MENU ADD-ONS
• Buttered egg noodles or seasoned pasta

DAY 8
Honey-Glazed Chicken, p. 95

MENU ADD-ONS
• Red Potatoes with Beans, p. 51

DAY 9
Tuscan Portobello Stew, p. 150

MENU ADD-ONS
• Crusty bread

DAY 10
Cranberry Chipotle Chicken Enchiladas, p. 165

MENU ADD-ONS
• Seasoned rice
• Slow-Cooked Black Bean Soup, p. 218

DAY 16
Quinoa with Peas & Onions, p. 31

MENU ADD-ONS
• Tomato Potpie, p. 127

DAY 17
Pork & Green Chile Casserole, p. 135

MENU ADD-ONS
• Tangerine Tossed Salad, p. 48

DAY 18
Orange Tilapia in Parchment, p. 136

MENU ADD-ONS
• Fresh Ginger Carrot Salad, p. 53

DAY 19
Grilled Bacon-Tomato Sandwiches, p. 72

MENU ADD-ONS
• 25-Minute Turkey Chili, p. 226

DAY 20
Deluxe Deep-Dish Pizza, p. 134

MENU ADD-ONS
• Pasta with red sauce

DAY 26
Ham & Cheese Pockets, p. 71

MENU ADD-ONS
• Pasta Fagioli Soup, p. 60

DAY 27
Ham & Scalloped Potatoes, p. 99

MENU ADD-ONS
• Zesty Sugar Snap Peas, p. 53
• Easy Cheesy Biscuits, p. 277

DAY 28
Saturday Afternoon Pot Roast, p. 129

MENU ADD-ONS
• Honey Cornbread, p. 204

DAY 29
Quick Sloppy Joes, p. 176

MENU ADD-ONS
• Roasted Sweet Potato Wedges, p. 48

DAY 30
Creamy Pasta Primavera, p. 146

MENU ADD-ONS
• Antipasto salad

SECRETS TO QUICK COOKING

Being able to pull together a delicious homemade meal quickly every night isn't magic—it comes down to three main factors—planning, shopping and prep. Here are some ideas to help make the most of your time.

REUSE GOOD MEALS

If you find a weekly plan that your family loves, there's no reason to reinvent the wheel. Repeating hit weekly menu plans is a huge timesaver. Just be sure to note what worked well and what needed tweaking.

10 INGREDIENTS YOU SHOULD ALWAYS HAVE ON HAND

Nothing drags out the process of fixing dinner like finding out you're missing ingredients. Even if you don't have a meal planned, you'll be able to pull something together quickly if you have a core set of staples you can count on. Keep these in your pantry or freezer, and you'll always have options.

PANTRY

• Diced tomatoes • Broth or stock • Rice
• Potatoes • Canned beans • Pasta sauce • Pasta

FREEZER

• Ground beef, ground turkey or sausage • Frozen vegetables: corn, peas and/or mixed vegetables • Meatballs

HAVE SNACKS READY!

Use handy single-serving containers to prepare a week's worth of healthy snack packs. You'll always be able to keep hungry kids satisfied without spoiling dinner.

DOUBLE UP

Love a recipe that freezes well? Double it and freeze half for another night. Look for the ❄ icon to identify freezer-friendly recipes in this book (like this Pork & Green Chile Casserole, p. 135).

CHOP ONCE

If you know you need chopped onions in three recipes this week, chop them all at the same time and store in the fridge. Better yet, if you have some time after shopping, prep all the ingredients for the week's meals. Come the weeknight, you're ready to start cooking.

THEME NIGHTS

Make meals fun with family-friendly themes. Choose your favorite cuisines, and everyone will look forward to those nights of the week. Some suggestions: Meatless Mondays, Friday Pizza Night, and Taco/Tex-Mex Tuesday. Try building a night around burgers, grilled cheese or chili—whatever your family's favorites are!

OVERLAP INGREDIENTS

Simplify by using key ingredients more than once. Check out our 30-day meal planner (pp. 6-7). See how that big Sugar-Glazed Ham on Day 22 is used again in the Ham & Cheese Pockets and Ham & Scalloped Potatoes later in the week?

GET THE FAMILY INVOLVED

At dinner, ask your family what they want to eat next week. Kids are more likely to eat healthy if they get to help choose the meal. Keep a list of your family's must-have grocery items on the fridge. Get everyone in the habit of circling an item when it's used up or almost gone—and adding special requests to the list.

FREEZER TIPS

Too often, food vanishes into the freezer, only to be found and discarded a year later. But used correctly, the freezer is a great tool for helping you plan ahead. Here are some simple ways to make the most of your freezer.

- Start with fresh, high-quality food. Food past its prime won't improve upon freezing.

- Freeze chopped onions and fresh herbs in water. Thaw and drain before using.

- Use an ice cube tray to freeze leftover lemon juice, broth, tomato paste, pesto and more in ready-to-use portions. A typical ice cube cup holds about ¼ cup liquid.

- Package food in convenient single-serving portions.

- Freezer burn is a food-quality, not a food-safety issue—and is caused by moisture escaping from the food and freezing on its surface. Remove as much air as possible before sealing freezer bags, and lay them flat while freezing—once frozen, they can be stacked. Cut off any freezer-burnt areas from meat or fish either before or after cooking.

- The door of the freezer is warmer than other areas: Keep nuts, flour, juice and dairy products there.

- Label and date all freezer packages. Put new frozen items in the back of the freezer; rotate older items to the front to be used first.

- Meat-counter meat and poultry can be frozen in their unopened original wrapping for up to 1 month.

FREEZE INGREDIENTS

You can save money by taking advantage of buying big—whether it's a family pack of chicken breasts or the large bag of carrots. But those savings are wasted if you end up throwing unused food away. Instead, separate out what you need for the week and freeze the rest.

Appetizers & Beverages

Whether you're looking to get the party started or want a quick weekend snack to keep your family going between meals, check out these small-plate specials! Appetizers fit for a cocktail party (and cocktails to match!) or bites perfect for a game-day platter—they're all here.

Rosemary & Thyme Lemon Cocktail (p. 25) **Appetizer Blue Cheese Logs** (p. 27)
Marinara-Mozzarella Dip (p. 21) **Creamy Chicken Enchilada Pizza** (p. 27) **Black Russian** (p. 15)

ORANGE RAZZLETINI

This spirited refresher, which mingles orange, raspberry and rum with a splash of Triple Sec, is a wonderful addition to your next holiday event—but there's no need to wait! The citrus and fruit combination is excellent year-round.
—Taste of Home *Test Kitchen*

Takes: 5 min. • **Makes:** 2 servings

Ice cubes
½ cup orange juice
2 oz. raspberry-flavored rum
½ oz. Triple Sec
Optional: Orange zest strips and fresh raspberries

1. Fill a mixing glass or tumbler three-fourths full with ice. Add orange juice, rum and Triple Sec; stir until condensation forms on the outside of the glass.
2. Strain into 2 chilled cocktail glasses. Garnish with orange zest strips and raspberries if desired. Serve immediately.
½ cup: 118 cal., 0 fat (0 sat. fat), 0 chol., 1mg sod., 10g carb. (8g sugars, 0 fiber), 0 pro.

ARTICHOKE SPREAD WITH GARLIC BREAD

ARTICHOKE SPREAD WITH GARLIC BREAD

I've tried several different artichoke dip recipes, but this one is the absolute best! I serve it at nearly every family gathering and there are never any leftovers. It's probably my most-requested recipe.
—Heidi Lacovetto, Phippsburg, CO

Prep: 10 min. • **Cook:** 2 hours
Makes: 16 servings

2 pkg. (8 oz. each) cream cheese, cubed
1 can (14 oz.) water-packed artichoke hearts, drained and quartered
1 cup fresh spinach, torn
¾ cup shredded Parmesan cheese
2 green onions, chopped
1 loaf (16 oz.) frozen garlic bread

Combine the first 5 ingredients in a bowl; transfer to a 1½-qt. slow cooker. Cook, covered, on low, until cheese is melted, 2-3 hours. Meanwhile, prepare the garlic bread according to the package directions. Slice and serve with hot dip.
¼ cup dip with 2 slices garlic bread: 222 cal., 15g fat (8g sat. fat), 35mg chol., 395mg sod., 15g carb. (2g sugars, 1g fiber), 7g pro.

TEST KITCHEN TIP
This recipe makes a thick, spreadable mixture. If you want a thinner consistency—more dip than spread—stir in milk a tablespoon at a time.

BANH MI SKEWERS

I love banh mi sandwiches but wanted to make them easier to serve for a party. These skewers are a fun twist! For quick prep on the day of the party, make the meatballs in advance and freeze them.
—Elisabeth Larsen, Pleasant Grove, UT

Prep: 45 min. + chilling
Cook: 10 min./batch • **Makes:** 12 servings

- 1 cup white vinegar or rice vinegar
- ¼ cup sugar
- ½ tsp. salt
- 1 English cucumber, thinly sliced
- 2 medium carrots, thinly sliced
- 4 radishes, thinly sliced
- 1 cup mayonnaise
- 1 Tbsp. Sriracha chili sauce
- 2 Tbsp. minced fresh cilantro
- 2 green onions, thinly sliced
- 1 Tbsp. soy sauce
- 1 garlic clove, minced
- ¼ tsp. cayenne pepper
- 1½ lbs. ground pork
- 2 Tbsp. canola oil
- 1 French bread baguette (10½ oz.), cut into 24 slices

1. In a large bowl combine vinegar, sugar and salt; whisk until sugar is dissolved. Add cucumber, carrots and radishes; let stand until serving. Combine mayonnaise and chili sauce; refrigerate until serving.
2. In another large bowl, combine cilantro, green onions, soy sauce, garlic and cayenne. Add pork and mix lightly but thoroughly. Shape into 36 balls.
3. In a large skillet, heat oil over medium heat. Cook meatballs in batches until cooked through, turning occasionally.
4. Drain the vegetable mixture. On 12 metal or wooden skewers, alternately thread vegetables, meatballs and baguette slices. Serve with Sriracha mayonnaise.

1 skewer with about 1 Tbsp. sauce: 336 cal., 24g fat (5g sat. fat), 39mg chol., 416mg sod., 16g carb. (2g sugars, 1g fiber), 13g pro.

PEPPERONI PINWHEELS

These golden brown rounds have tons of pepperoni flavor. They are easy to make, look beautiful on an appetizer tray and—best of all— are really good!
—Vikki Rebholz, West Chester, OH

Prep: 20 min. • **Bake:** 15 min.
Makes: 2 dozen

- ½ cup diced pepperoni
- ½ cup shredded part-skim mozzarella cheese
- ¼ tsp. dried oregano
- 1 large egg, separated
- 1 tube (8 oz.) refrigerated crescent rolls

1. Preheat oven to 375°. In a small bowl, combine the pepperoni, cheese, oregano and egg yolk. In another small bowl, whisk egg white until foamy; set aside. Separate crescent dough into 4 rectangles; seal perforations.
2. Spread the pepperoni mixture over each rectangle to within ¼ in. of edges. Roll up jelly-roll style, starting with a short side; pinch the seams to seal. Cut each into 6 slices.
3. Place cut side down on greased baking sheets; brush tops with egg white. Bake for 12-15 minutes or until golden brown. Serve warm. Refrigerate leftovers.

2 each: 122 cal., 8g fat (3g sat. fat), 26mg chol., 291mg sod., 8g carb. (2g sugars, 0 fiber), 4g pro.

BANH MI SKEWERS

GREEK SHRIMP CANAPES

I grew up by the ocean and then moved to a land-locked state. I came up with this recipe to show people in my new home how easy it is to cook seafood. It's become a neighborhood favorite.
—Amy Harris, Springville, UT

Prep: 15 min. • **Cook:** 65 min.
Makes: about 2½ dozen

- 1½ cups olive oil
- ¾ cup lemon juice
- ⅔ cup dry white wine
- ¼ cup Greek seasoning
- 4 garlic cloves, minced
- 1 lb. uncooked shrimp (31-40 per lb.), peeled and deveined
- 2 large cucumbers
- 1 pkg. (8 oz.) cream cheese, softened
  Minced fresh parsley

1. Whisk the first 5 ingredients until blended. Pour 1½ cups marinade into a large bowl. Add shrimp and stir to coat. Cover and refrigerate 45 minutes.
2. Meanwhile, pour the remaining marinade into a 4- or 5-qt. slow cooker. Cook, covered, on high, 45 minutes.
3. Drain the shrimp, discarding the remaining marinade in bowl. Add shrimp to slow cooker. Cook, covered, on high until shrimp turn pink, about 20 minutes, stirring once; drain.
4. Cut each cucumber into ¼-in.-thick slices. Scoop out the centers, leaving bottoms intact. Pipe cream cheese onto each cucumber slice; top with shrimp and parsley.

1 canape: 68 cal., 6g fat (2g sat. fat), 26mg chol., 139mg sod., 1g carb. (1g sugars, 0 fiber), 3g pro.
HEALTH TIP You'll love how light and fresh this slow-cooked appetizer tastes. Slim it down by using reduced-fat cream cheese.

> **TEST KITCHEN TIP**
> If you're in a rush, skip scooping out the centers of the cucumber slices. While creating a shallow indention is helpful, it is not essential.

COLD CHICKEN-CHEESE KABOBS

COLD CHICKEN-CHEESE KABOBS

These appealing kabobs will add pizazz to any party...and you won't even have to get out the grill!
—Sherine Elise Gilmour, Brooklyn, NY

Prep: 20 min. + chilling
Makes: 8 servings

- ½ tsp. salt
- ½ tsp. chili powder
- ⅛ tsp. pepper
- ½ lb. boneless skinless chicken breast, cubed
- ½ cup balsamic vinegar
- 2 tsp. olive oil
- 5 oz. cubed part-skim mozzarella cheese
- 18 cherry or grape tomatoes

1. Combine salt, chili powder and pepper; rub into the chicken cubes. Transfer to a large bowl; add vinegar. Cover and refrigerate for 3-4 hours.
2. In a large skillet, cook the chicken in oil until no longer pink. Cool slightly. Alternately thread the chicken, cheese and tomatoes onto wooden skewers. Serve cold.

1 kabob: 115 cal., 5g fat (2g sat. fat), 27mg chol., 286mg sod., 7g carb. (5g sugars, 1g fiber), 10g pro.

EASY ROAST BEEF ROLL-UPS

For a quick and crowd-pleasing app, you can't beat these flavorful wraps seasoned with salsa. Roll some up for your family and friends!
—Susan Scott, Asheville, NC

....

Takes: 15 min. • **Makes:** 10 servings

- ½ cup sour cream
- ¼ cup mayonnaise
- ¼ cup salsa
- 10 flour tortillas (8 in.), room temperature
- 1 lb. thinly sliced cooked roast beef
- 10 large lettuce leaves
  Additional salsa

Combine the sour cream, mayonnaise and salsa; spread over tortillas. Top with roast beef and lettuce. Roll up tightly and secure with toothpicks; cut in half. Serve with salsa.

1 wrap: 262 cal., 10g fat (3g sat. fat), 26mg chol., 650mg sod., 28g carb. (1g sugars, 0 fiber), 13g pro.

TEST KITCHEN TIP

If your tortillas are difficult to roll without tearing, wrap them in a damp paper towel and warm them in the microwave for 30 seconds, then roll them up and let them cool before assembling the appetizers.

BLACK RUSSIAN

PICTURED ON P. 11

Here's a no-fuss Black Russian that is smooth as silk. Cocktails don't get easier (or tastier) than this!
—*Taste of Home* Test Kitchen

....

Takes: 5 min. • **Makes:** 1 serving

- ¾ to 1 cup ice cubes
- 1 oz. vodka
- 1 oz. Kahlua

Place ice in a rocks glass. Pour vodka and Kahlua into the glass.

¼ cup: 170 cal., 0 fat (0 sat. fat), 0 chol., 2mg sod., 13g carb. (12g sugars, 0 fiber), 0 pro.

EASY ROAST BEEF ROLL-UPS

SKEWERED RAVIOLI WITH CREAMY TOMATO DIPPING SAUCE

I wanted to make an easy appetizer with my favorite pasta—cheese ravioli— but didn't want the mess of frying. I used pesto and bread crumbs for a crust, and broiled them for a little crunch.
—Rebecca Guffey, Apex, NC

Takes: 30 min.
Makes: 10 appetizers (1½ cups sauce)

20 refrigerated cheese ravioli
¼ cup seasoned bread crumbs
4 tsp. grated Parmesan cheese
¼ cup prepared pesto
1 cup marinara sauce
½ cup half-and-half cream

1. Cook ravioli according to package directions; drain and pat dry. In a small bowl, combine bread crumbs and cheese; set aside.
2. Diagonally thread 2 ravioli onto each of 10 soaked wooden appetizer skewers; brush both sides with pesto. Transfer to a foil-lined baking sheet. Sprinkle with bread crumb mixture. Broil 3-4 in. from the heat until browned, 3-5 minutes.
3. Meanwhile, in a small saucepan, combine marinara sauce and cream. Cook and stir over medium-low heat until heated through. Serve with ravioli.

1 appetizer with 2 Tbsp. sauce: 114 cal., 5g fat (2g sat. fat), 14mg chol., 207mg sod., 11g carb. (3g sugars, 1g fiber), 5g pro.

TEST KITCHEN TIP
Feel free to start with frozen or homemade ravioli instead of refrigerated.

CHEESY BRUSCHETTA SPREAD

CHEESY BRUSCHETTA SPREAD

Every bite of this cheesy dip delivers tons of flavor. I have been asked over and over again for the recipe. It's so simple to make and a great appetizer for any time of year.
—Maggie McDermott, Central Square, NY

Prep: 15 min. • **Cook:** 1½ hours
Makes: about 4 cups

1 pkg. (8 oz.) cream cheese, softened
½ cup prepared pesto
¼ tsp. salt
⅛ tsp. pepper
2 cups grape tomatoes
1 carton (8 oz.) fresh mozzarella cheese pearls, drained
Minced fresh basil, optional
French bread slices (½ in. thick), toasted

In a small bowl, mix cream cheese, pesto, salt and pepper until combined. Transfer to a greased 3-qt. slow cooker. Top with tomatoes and mozzarella cheese. Cook, covered, on low until heated though and the cheese begins to melt, 1½-2 hours. If desired, sprinkle with basil. Serve with toasted bread.

2 Tbsp.: 61 cal., 5g fat (3g sat. fat), 13mg chol., 96mg sod., 1g carb. (1g sugars, 0 fiber), 2g pro.

FAST FRUIT SALSA

FAST FRUIT SALSA

We like this refreshing and colorful salsa served with tortilla chips or spooned over grilled chicken. For another fruity option, try stirring in some diced cantaloupe or peaches when they're in season.
—Eileen Miller, Woodridge, IL

....

Takes: 10 min. • **Makes:** 1½ cups

- 1 can (8 oz.) unsweetened crushed pineapple, drained
- 1 can (8 oz.) mandarin oranges, drained and chopped
- ¼ cup chopped red onion
- 1 Tbsp. minced fresh cilantro
  Tortilla chips

In a large bowl, combine the pineapple, oranges, red onion and cilantro. Cover and refrigerate until serving. Serve with tortilla chips.

¼ cup: 48 cal., 0 fat (0 sat. fat), 0 chol., 3mg sod., 13g carb. (12g sugars, 1g fiber), 0 pro.

CHEDDAR BACON TOASTS

Four ingredients are all you need to bake up these golden appetizers. They pair perfectly with a bowl of soup or can be served as an after-school snack.
—Mary Martin, Columbus, KS

....

Takes: 20 min. • **Makes:** 8 servings

- 2 cups finely shredded cheddar cheese
- ¾ cup mayonnaise
- ⅓ cup crumbled cooked bacon
- 1 loaf unsliced French bread (1 lb.)

1. Preheat oven to 425°. In a large bowl, combine the cheese, mayonnaise and bacon. Cut the bread into 24 slices, about ½ in. each. Spread the cheese mixture on 1 side of each slice.

2. Place slices on an ungreased baking sheet. Bake for 8-10 minutes or until golden brown.

3 each: 421 cal., 27g fat (9g sat. fat), 41mg chol., 777mg sod., 31g carb. (1g sugars, 2g fiber), 13g pro.

ITALIAN-STYLE PIZZAS

With prepared pesto and pizza crusts, these tasty treats come together faster than delivery!
—Trisha Kruse, Eagle, ID

Takes: 25 min. • **Makes:** 2 pizzas

- 2 prebaked mini pizza crusts
- ½ cup prepared pesto
- ⅔ cup shredded part-skim mozzarella cheese
- ½ cup sliced sweet onion
- ½ cup thinly sliced fresh mushrooms
- ¼ cup roasted sweet red peppers, drained
- 2 Tbsp. grated Parmesan cheese

Preheat oven to 400°. Place crusts on an ungreased baking sheet; spread with pesto. Layer with mozzarella cheese, onion, mushrooms and peppers; sprinkle with Parmesan cheese. Bake until the cheese is melted, 10-12 minutes.

½ pizza: 429 cal., 23g fat (7g sat. fat), 23mg chol., 820mg sod., 37g carb. (3g sugars, 2g fiber), 19g pro.

CALIFORNIA TURKEY SLIDERS

These child-sized turkey burgers are just right for party starters. If you prefer, use Bibb lettuce or arugula for the avocado.
—Kelly Logan, New Castle, DE

Takes: 30 min. • **Makes:** 8 servings

- 1 lb. ground turkey
- 1 can (10 oz.) diced tomatoes and green chiles, drained
- ¾ tsp. salt
- ¼ tsp. pepper
- 8 slices pepper jack cheese
- 8 bakery dinner rolls, split
- 1 medium ripe avocado, peeled and sliced

1. Combine turkey, tomatoes, salt and pepper, mixing lightly but thoroughly. Shape into eight ½-in.-thick patties.
2. Grill burgers, covered, over medium heat or broil 4 in. from the heat for 5-6 minutes on each side or until a thermometer reads 160°. Top with cheese; cover and grill 1-2 minutes longer or until cheese is melted. Serve on rolls with avocado.

1 slider: 306 cal., 16g fat (6g sat. fat), 77mg chol., 722mg sod., 22g carb. (2g sugars, 3g fiber), 20g pro.

BLACK BEAN TORTILLA PINWHEELS

These savory bites add a Tex-Mex touch to your appetizer plate; serve them up with your favorite salsa. I make these as a weekend snack for my husband—he just loves them!
—Jeannette Sabo, Lexington Park, MD

Prep: 15 min. + chilling
Makes: 50 appetizers

- 1 pkg. (8 oz.) cream cheese, softened
- 1 cup sour cream
- 1 cup shredded Monterey Jack cheese
- ¼ cup chopped green olives with pimientos
- ¼ cup chopped red onion
- ½ tsp. seasoned salt
- ⅛ tsp. garlic powder
- 1 can (15 oz.) black beans, rinsed and drained
- 5 flour tortillas (10 in.)
  Salsa

1. Place beans in a food processor; cover and process until pureed. In a small bowl, combine the cream cheese and sour cream until smooth; stir in the Monterey Jack cheese, olives, onion, seasoned salt and garlic powder. Spread about 3 Tbsp. beans over each tortilla; top with ½ cup cheese mixture.
2. Roll up tightly. Wrap and refrigerate for at least 30 minutes. Unwrap and cut each into 10 slices. Serve with salsa.

1 pinwheel: 64 cal., 4g fat (2g sat. fat), 8mg chol., 123mg sod., 5g carb. (1g sugars, 1g fiber), 2g pro.

ITALIAN STYLE PIZZAS

5i VANILLA BEAN FIZZ

A homemade vanilla bean syrup adds a cozy touch to plain champagne. Once you've made the syrup, save the beans to make vanilla sugar. Just dry them overnight, then place them with a couple cups of sugar in an airtight container. Store at least one week for fragrant, flavorful sugar.
—*Taste of Home* Test Kitchen

Prep: 10 min. + cooling
Makes: 8 servings

- 2 **cups water**
- 1 **cup sugar**
- 4 **vanilla beans, split**
- 4 **cups champagne, chilled**

1. In a small saucepan, bring water and sugar to a boil. Add vanilla beans. Reduce heat; simmer, uncovered, for 10 minutes. Remove from the heat; cool to room temperature. Remove beans.
2. For each serving, pour ¼ cup vanilla syrup into a champagne flute; add ½ cup champagne.
¾ cup: 137 cal., 0 fat (0 sat. fat), 0 chol., 0 sod., 26g carb. (25g sugars, 0 fiber), 0 pro.

SPANAKOPITA SPRING ROLLS

SPANAKOPITA SPRING ROLLS

I turned traditional spanakopita into a hand-held hors d'oeuvre by using won ton wrappers in place of phyllo dough. These are the biggest hit among my friends!
—Jade Randall, Las Vegas, NV

Prep: 15 min. • **Cook:** 5 min./batch
Makes: 14 spring rolls

- 2 **pkg. (10 oz. each) frozen chopped spinach, thawed and squeezed dry**
- 2 **cups (8 oz.) crumbled feta cheese**
- 4 **garlic cloves, minced**
- 2 **tsp. dill weed**
- ¼ **tsp. salt**
- ¼ **tsp. pepper**
- 14 **refrigerated egg roll wrappers**
  Oil for deep-fat frying

1. Mix first 6 ingredients. With a corner of an egg roll wrapper facing you, place about ⅓ cup filling just below the center of wrapper. (Cover the remaining wrappers with a damp paper towel until ready to use.) Fold bottom corner over filling; moisten the remaining wrapper edges with water. Fold side corners toward center over filling. Roll up tightly, pressing at tip to seal. Repeat.
2. In an electric skillet or deep-fat fryer, heat oil to 375°. Fry spring rolls, a few at a time, until golden brown, 3-4 minutes, turning occasionally. Drain on paper towels before serving.
Freeze option: Freeze uncooked spring rolls in freezer containers, spacing them so they don't touch and separating the layers with waxed paper. To use, fry frozen spring rolls as directed, increasing time as necessary.
1 spring roll: 245 cal., 12g fat (4g sat. fat), 20mg chol., 568mg sod., 22g carb. (0 sugars, 3g fiber), 10g pro.

MARINARA-MOZZARELLA DIP

Talk about easy! With three ingredients and two loaves of baguette-style French bread, you have an easy appetizer that will please your family and guests. For variation, try using goat cheese instead of mozzarella.
—Janie Colle, Hutchinson, KS

Prep: 10 min. • **Cook:** 2½ hours
Makes: 12 servings (3 cups)

- 2 cups marinara sauce
- 1 carton (8 oz.) fresh mozzarella cheese pearls, drained
- 2 Tbsp. minced fresh basil
  French bread baguette, thinly sliced and toasted

Pour marinara into a 1½-qt. slow cooker. Cook, covered, on low until hot, about 2 hours. Stir in mozzarella and basil. Cook until the cheese is melted, about 30 minutes longer. Serve with toasted baguette slices.

¼ cup: 76 cal., 5g fat (3g sat. fat), 16mg chol., 219mg sod., 4g carb. (3g sugars, 1g fiber), 4g pro.

> **TEST KITCHEN TIP**
> If the cheese pearls come in a vacuum-sealed package, break them apart as you drop them into the marinara sauce.

CHICKEN & BROCCOLI CUPS

Frozen puff pastry makes these rich and creamy appetizers a snap to prepare. Sometimes, instead of chopping the tomatoes, I put a slice on top of each cup before popping them in the oven.
—Marty Kingery, Point Pleasant, WV

Prep: 15 min. • **Bake:** 25 min.
Makes: 1 dozen

- 2½ cups diced cooked chicken breast
- 1 can (10¾ oz.) reduced-fat reduced-sodium condensed cream of chicken soup, undiluted
- 1 cup frozen chopped broccoli, thawed and drained
- 2 small plum tomatoes, seeded and chopped
- 1 small carrot, grated
- 1 Tbsp. Dijon mustard
- 1 garlic clove, minced
- ¼ tsp. pepper
- 1 sheet frozen puff pastry, thawed
- ¼ cup grated Parmesan cheese

1. Preheat oven to 375°. In a large bowl, combine the first 8 ingredients; set aside.
2. On a lightly floured surface, roll pastry into a 12x9-in. rectangle. Cut lengthwise into 4 strips and widthwise into 3 strips. Gently press the puff pastry squares into muffin cups coated with cooking spray.
3. Spoon chicken mixture into pastry cups. Sprinkle with Parmesan. Bake for 25-30 minutes or until golden brown. Serve warm.

1 serving: 182 cal., 10g fat (3g sat. fat), 23mg chol., 310mg sod., 13g carb. (0 sugars, 1g fiber), 10g pro.

MARINARA-MOZZARELLA DIP

CHOCOLATE-CARAMEL RUM COFFEE

This decadent coffee drink can stand alone or serve as a delightful complement to any chocolate or caramel dessert. Our family loves this drink after a special dinner or just sipping in front of the fireplace.
—Joyce Conway, Westerville, OH

Takes: 25 min. • **Makes:** 8 servings

- 2 cans (12 oz. each) evaporated milk
- ¾ cup rum
- ½ cup chocolate syrup
- ½ cup caramel sundae syrup
- ¼ cup packed brown sugar
- 4 cups hot brewed coffee
- 2 Tbsp. coffee liqueur

COFFEE WHIPPED CREAM
- 1 cup heavy whipping cream
- 6 Tbsp. confectioners' sugar
- 2 Tbsp. coffee liqueur
   Instant espresso powder, optional

1. In a large saucepan, combine the milk, rum, syrups and brown sugar. Cook over medium heat until hot (do not boil). Stir in coffee and liqueur.

2. Meanwhile, in a small bowl, beat cream until it begins to thicken. Add confectioners' sugar; beat until stiff peaks form. Fold in liqueur until combined.

3. Pour coffee mixture into mugs. Garnish each with a large dollop of coffee whipped cream and, if desired, espresso powder.
1 cup coffee with ¼ cup coffee whipped cream: 437 cal., 16g fat (11g sat. fat), 68mg chol., 166mg sod., 50g carb. (43g sugars, 0 fiber), 7g pro.

ZIPPY SHRIMP SKEWERS

These flavorful skewers deliver a mouthwatering kick with minimal effort. Fix them for your next party and watch them disappear.
—Jalayne Luckett, Marion, IL

Prep: 10 min. + marinating
Grill: 5 min. **Makes:** 6 servings

- 2 Tbsp. brown sugar
- 2 tsp. cider vinegar
- 1½ tsp. canola oil
- 1 tsp. chili powder
- ½ tsp. salt

ZIPPY SHRIMP SKEWERS

- ½ tsp. paprika
- ¼ tsp. hot pepper sauce
- ¾ lb. uncooked medium shrimp, peeled and deveined

1. In a large shallow dish, combine the first 7 ingredients; add shrimp. Turn to coat; cover and refrigerate for 2-4 hours.
2. Drain the shrimp and discard the marinade. Thread shrimp onto 6 metal or soaked wooden skewers. Grill, uncovered, on a lightly oiled rack over medium heat or broil 4 in. from the heat until shrimp turn pink, 2-3 minutes on each side.
1 skewer: 57 cal., 1g fat (0 sat. fat), 84mg chol., 199mg sod., 2g carb. (2g sugars, 0 fiber), 9g pro. **Diabetic exchanges:** 1 lean meat.

QUINOA ARANCINI

We love arancini, but they're not the healthiest thing going! I wanted to make a version that we could enjoy guilt-free. I substituted quinoa for rice and tried baking instead of frying. Now we can have them any time.
—Sabrina Ovadia, New York, NY

Takes: 30 min. • **Makes:** 3 servings

1 pkg. (9 oz.) ready-to-serve quinoa or 1¾ cups cooked quinoa
2 large eggs, lightly beaten, divided use
1 cup seasoned bread crumbs, divided
¼ cup shredded Parmesan cheese
1 Tbsp. olive oil
2 Tbsp. minced fresh basil or 2 tsp. dried basil
½ tsp. garlic powder
½ tsp. salt
⅛ tsp. pepper
6 cubes part-skim mozzarella cheese (¾ in. each)
Cooking spray
Warmed pasta sauce, optional

1. Preheat oven to 425°. Prepare quinoa according to the package directions. Stir in 1 egg, ½ cup bread crumbs, Parmesan cheese, oil, basil and seasonings.

2. Divide mixture into 6 portions. Wrap each portion around a cheese cube to cover completely, then shape to form a ball.

3. Place the remaining egg and ½ cup bread crumbs in separate shallow bowls. Dip each quinoa ball in egg, then roll in bread crumbs. Place balls on a greased 15x10x1-in. baking pan; spritz with cooking spray. Bake until golden brown, 15-20 minutes. If desired, serve with pasta sauce.

2 arancini: 423 cal., 19g fat (6g sat. fat), 142mg chol., 1283mg sod., 40g carb. (4g sugars, 5g fiber), 21g pro.

QUINOA ARANCINI

FRUIT ON A STICK

FRUIT ON A STICK

In the summer, my family loves this fun finger food with its smooth, creamy dip.
—Faye Hintz, Springfield, MO

Takes: 15 min.
Makes: 12 servings (1½ cups dip)

- 1 pkg. (8 oz.) cream cheese, softened
- 1 jar (7 oz.) marshmallow creme
- 3 to 4 Tbsp. 2% milk
- 12 fresh strawberries, halved
- 24 cubes cantaloupe
- 3 medium kiwifruit, peeled and cut into eighths

Mix cream cheese, marshmallow creme and milk until smooth. Thread fruit on wooden skewers. Serve with dip.

1 skewer with 2 Tbsp. dip: 149 cal., 7g fat (4g sat. fat), 19mg chol., 77mg sod., 17g carb. (15g sugars, 1g fiber), 2g pro.

ROSEMARY & THYME LEMON COCKTAIL

PICTURED ON P. 11

A bubbly drink means it's time to celebrate! Try dressing up the usual hard lemonade with sprigs of rosemary and thyme for a refreshingly different cocktail any time of year.
—Moffat Frazier, New York, NY

Prep: 5 min. + chilling
Makes: 15 servings

- 5 fresh rosemary sprigs
- 5 fresh thyme sprigs
- 1 bottle (1¾ liters) lemonade

FOR EACH SERVING
- 1½ oz. vodka
  Ice cubes
- 2 oz. carbonated water, chilled

GARNISH
  Lemon zest strips and fresh
  rosemary sprigs

1. In a 2-qt. pitcher, muddle rosemary and thyme; add lemonade. Cover and refrigerate overnight. Strain lemonade; discard herbs.
2. To prepare cocktail: In a mixing glass or tumbler, combine ½ cup lemonade and vodka. Place ice in a highball glass; add lemonade mixture. Top with carbonated water. Garnish with a lemon zest strip and rosemary sprig if desired.

1 cup: 152 cal., 0 fat (0 sat. fat), 0 chol., 8mg sod., 14g carb. (13g sugars, 0 fiber), 0 pro.

MOROCCAN CHICKEN TAGINE POCKETS

I enjoy shredded chicken dishes, Moroccan flavors and pita sandwiches. The addition of the carrot salad laced with dates and pomegranate seeds lends an extra punch and crunch. If you prefer, you can use mini flour tortillas instead of pitas.
—Arlene Erlbach, Morton Grove, IL

Prep: 20 min. • **Cook:** 5 hours
Makes: 14 appetizers

- 1½ lbs. boneless skinless chicken thighs
- 1 cup chunky salsa
- ½ cup pomegranate juice, divided
- ½ cup pitted dates, chopped and divided
- 2 Tbsp. honey
- 1 Tbsp. Moroccan seasoning (ras el hanout)
- 1½ tsp. garlic powder
- 1¼ cups shredded carrots
- 3 Tbsp. mayonnaise
- 2 Tbsp. pomegranate seeds
- 7 miniature pita pockets, halved
  Minced fresh cilantro, optional

1. Place chicken in a greased 3- or 4-qt. slow cooker. Combine the salsa, 6 Tbsp. pomegranate juice, ⅓ cup dates, the honey, Moroccan seasoning and garlic powder; pour over chicken. Cook, covered, on low, until the chicken is tender, 5-6 hours.
2. Meanwhile, combine the carrots, mayonnaise, pomegranate seeds and the remaining dates. Refrigerate, covered, until serving.
3. Remove chicken thighs from slow cooker and cool slightly. Skim fat from cooking juices. Shred chicken with 2 forks. Return chicken and juices to slow cooker. Stir in remaining pomegranate juice and heat through. Serve in pitas with carrot slaw and, if desired, cilantro.

1 pocket: 164 cal., 6g fat (1g sat. fat), 33mg chol., 194mg sod., 17g carb. (7g sugars, 1g fiber), 11g pro.
HEALTH TIP: Using skinless chicken thighs instead of breast meat keeps the chicken tender, juicy and flavorful, and only adds about 20 cal. per serving.

TEST KITCHEN TIP
You'll love the sweet-savory flavor of this make-ahead appetizer. For a lower carb option, serve the chicken filling in lettuce cups.

MOROCCAN CHICKEN TAGINE POCKETS

DILL BLOODY MARYS

DILL BLOODY MARYS

With a nice amount of pepper and just enough dill from the pickle, these Bloody Marys are sure to please. Adding even more garnishes—maybe cheese sticks and bacon—make them more like a meal!
—Jay Ferkovich, Green Bay, WI

....

Takes: 10 min. • **Makes:** 2 servings

SALTED RIM (OPTIONAL)
- ½ tsp. each coarse salt, celery salt, ground cumin, granulated garlic, paprika and ground mustard
- 3 Tbsp. dill pickle juice

BLOODY MARY
- 1½ cups Clamato juice, chilled
- ¼ cup vodka
- 2 Tbsp. dill pickle juice
- 1 Tbsp. Worcestershire sauce
- ¼ tsp. celery salt
- ⅛ to ¼ tsp. pepper
- ⅛ tsp. hot pepper sauce
  Ice cubes
- 2 celery ribs
- 2 pepperoni-flavored meat snack sticks
- 2 dill pickle spears
- 2 each pitted ripe and green olives

1. If desired, to make salted rim, combine spices in a shallow dish. Add 3 Tbsp. pickle juice to another shallow dish. Dip the rims of glasses into the pickle juice, allowing excess to drip off. Dip in salt mixture, pressing lightly. Tap to remove excess.
2. In a small pitcher, combine Clamato juice, vodka, pickle juice, Worcestershire sauce, celery salt, pepper and hot pepper sauce. Pour into glasses filled with ice; garnish with the remaining ingredients.
¾ cup: 224 cal., 9g fat (3g sat. fat), 20mg chol., 1613mg sod., 13g carb. (7g sugars, 1g fiber), 5g pro.

CREAMY CHICKEN ENCHILADA PIZZA

We wanted the taste of our family-favorite chicken enchilada recipe, but we wanted it even faster. This kicked-up pizza is the fun creation we came up with.
—Crystal Jo Bruns, Iliff, CO

Takes: 30 min. • **Makes:** 6 servings

- 1 tube (11 oz.) refrigerated thin pizza crust
- 1 pkg. (8 oz.) cream cheese, softened, cubed
- 1 cup shredded Mexican cheese blend, divided
- 2 tsp. ground cumin
- 1½ tsp. garlic powder
- ½ tsp. salt
- 2 cups ready-to-use fajita chicken strips, cubed
- ½ cup salsa
- ¼ cup green enchilada sauce
  Optional toppings: Shredded lettuce, chopped tomatoes and sliced ripe olives

1. Preheat oven to 400°. Unroll dough and press onto bottom and ½ in. up sides of a greased 15x10x1-in. baking pan. Bake 5 minutes.

2. Meanwhile, in a small saucepan, combine cream cheese, ½ cup cheese, the cumin, garlic powder and salt over medium heat; cook and stir for 5 minutes or until blended. Remove from heat. Add chicken; toss to coat.

3. Spread chicken mixture over crust. Drizzle with salsa and enchilada sauce; sprinkle with remaining cheese. Bake until crust is golden and cheese is melted, 8-12 minutes longer. Serve with toppings of your choice.

1 piece: 428 cal., 25g fat (12g sat. fat), 83mg chol., 1061mg sod., 30g carb. (5g sugars, 1g fiber), 20g pro.

APPETIZER BLUE CHEESE LOGS
PICTURED ON P. 11

Three kinds of cheese and some curry powder make this cheese log a little livelier than most. Swipe it on your favorite cracker with a drizzle of honey for a sensational snack.
—Ethel Johnson, North Saanich, BC

Prep: 15 min. • **Cook:** 5 min. + chilling
Makes: 2 cheese logs

- 1 pkg. (8 oz.) cream cheese, softened
- 1 cup shredded sharp cheddar cheese
- ½ cup crumbled blue cheese
- 1 Tbsp. butter
- 1½ tsp. curry powder
- ½ cup finely chopped pecans
- 2 Tbsp. minced fresh parsley
  Assorted crackers

1. Beat cream cheese until smooth. Fold in cheddar and blue cheeses. Refrigerate, covered, for at least 2 hours.

2. In a small skillet, heat butter over medium heat. Add curry powder; saute 1-2 minutes. Stir in pecans; cook and stir 1 minute. Stir in parsley. Cool slightly. Roll cheese mixture into 2 logs, each about 5 in. long. Roll in spiced pecan mixture; refrigerate. Serve with crackers.

2 Tbsp.: 196 cal., 19g fat (9g sat. fat), 45mg chol., 243mg sod., 2g carb. (1g sugars, 1g fiber), 6g pro.

CREAMY CHICKEN ENCHILADA PIZZA

Speedy Sides & Salads

A great side dish or side salad takes an everyday meal from simply satisfying to extraordinary—so why settle for less? These quick and easy sides are just what you need to fill out your plate, from weeknight family dinners to potlucks and parties.

Grandmother's Orange Salad (p. 40) **Kale & Fennel Skillet** (p. 38) **Sauteed Garlic Mushrooms** (p. 33)
Roasted Asparagus & Tomatoes (p. 42) **Zesty Sugar Snap Peas** (p. 53)

5i

BAKED VIDALIA ONIONS

Served alongside any of a variety of fish and meats, this tender onion dish is a nice change of pace. Folks find it a fun and flavorful side.
—Norma Durham, Rogersville, TN

Prep: 5 min. • **Bake:** 50 min.
Makes: 2 servings

  2 small Vidalia or sweet onions
  4 tsp. butter
  ¼ tsp. salt
     Dash pepper
     Garlic salt to taste, optional

Preheat oven to 350°. Quarter onions halfway through and open slightly. Place each on a 18x12-in. piece of heavy-duty foil. Place 2 tsp. butter in the center of each onion; sprinkle with salt, pepper and, if desired, garlic salt. Fold foil to seal tightly. Bake until the onions are tender, 50-60 minutes. Open foil carefully to allow steam to escape.

1 onion: 148 cal., 8g fat (5g sat. fat), 20mg chol., 376mg sod., 19g carb. (12g sugars, 2g fiber), 2g pro.

PEACH CAPRESE

PEACH CAPRESE

Summer in the Midwest offers a bounty of fresh produce. I wanted to come up with something new from the harvest, and this bright, flavorful salad is the refreshing end result.
—Richard Robinson, Park Forest, IL

Takes: 25 min. • **Makes:** about 6 servings

  2 medium peaches, cut into
     ½-in. pieces
  2 cups grape tomatoes, halved
  1 carton (8 oz.) fresh mozzarella
     cheese pearls, drained
  1 cup chopped peeled mango
  2 Tbsp. minced fresh cilantro
  2 Tbsp. minced fresh basil

DRESSING
  3 Tbsp. balsamic vinegar
  3 fresh basil leaves
  2 tsp. honey
  ¼ tsp. salt
  ⅛ tsp. pepper
  ¼ cup olive oil

Place the first 6 ingredients in a large bowl. For dressing, place vinegar, basil, honey, salt and pepper in blender. While processing, gradually add oil in a steady stream. Pour over the peach mixture; gently toss to coat. Refrigerate until serving. Garnish with additional basil.

¾ cup: 248 cal., 17g fat (7g sat. fat), 30mg chol., 156mg sod., 16g carb. (14g sugars, 2g fiber), 8g pro.

QUINOA WITH PEAS & ONION

Even picky eaters will love this fresh dish. If you have fresh shelled peas on hand, use them in place of the frozen peas.

—Lori Panarella, Phoenixville, PA

Prep: 30 min. • **Cook:** 10 min.
Makes: 6 servings

- 2 cups water
- 1 cup quinoa, rinsed
- 1 small onion, chopped
- 1 Tbsp. olive oil
- 1½ cups frozen peas
- ½ tsp. salt
- ¼ tsp. pepper
- 2 Tbsp. chopped walnuts

1. In a large saucepan, bring water to a boil. Add quinoa. Reduce heat; cover and simmer for 12-15 minutes or until the water is absorbed. Remove from heat; fluff with a fork.

2. Meanwhile, in a large skillet, saute onion in oil until tender. Add peas; cook and stir until heated through. Stir in the cooked quinoa, salt and pepper. Sprinkle with walnuts.

⅔ cup: 174 cal., 6g fat (1g sat. fat), 0 chol., 244mg sod., 26g carb. (2g sugars, 4g fiber), 6g pro. **Diabetic exchanges:** 1½ starch, 1 fat.

Hot & Zesty Quinoa: Omit peas, salt, pepper and walnuts. Prepare quinoa as directed. Saute onion in oil until tender. Add 3 minced garlic cloves; cook 1 minute. Add 2 cans (10 oz. each) tomatoes and green chiles. Bring to a boil over medium heat. Reduce heat; simmer, uncovered, for 10 minutes. Stir in quinoa and ¼ cup chopped marinated quartered artichoke hearts; heat through. Sprinkle with 2 Tbsp. grated Parmesan cheese.

READER REVIEW

"This is my first time having quinoa and it is fantastic! This is perfect when you need to cook up a quick side dish—it's healthy and light and it has a wonderful nutty taste. I will definitely be making this again!"

PINA1551, TASTEOFHOME.COM

HONEYDEW SHRIMP SALAD

A creamy pickle relish dressing deliciously complements this unusual shrimp and fruit medley.

—Lynda Mohan, Scottsdale, AZ

Takes: 10 min. • **Makes:** 4 servings

- 1 lb. cooked medium shrimp, peeled and deveined
- ¼ cup chopped celery
- 1 hard-boiled large egg, chopped
- 2 Tbsp. sunflower kernels
- ⅓ cup mayonnaise
- 4½ tsp. Thousand Island salad dressing
- 1 Tbsp. sweet pickle relish
- ¼ tsp. salt
- ⅛ tsp. pepper
- 1 large honeydew melon, quartered and seeded

In a large bowl, combine the shrimp, celery, egg and sunflower kernels. In a small bowl, combine mayonnaise, salad dressing, pickle relish, salt and pepper. Pour over the shrimp mixture and toss to coat. Spoon onto honeydew quarters.

1 serving: 438 cal., 23g fat (3g sat. fat), 234mg chol., 584mg sod., 34g carb. (30g sugars, 2g fiber), 27g pro.

QUINOA WITH PEAS & ONION

SPECIAL SCALLOPED CORN

Carrots and green pepper make this dish colorful, which grabs attention at a potluck. (For parties, I double the recipe.) The casserole is also a smart idea for when you need to prepare a dish ahead of time; easy baking is all it takes to finish it up.
—J. Brown, Fort Dodge, IA

Prep: 10 min. • **Bake:** 30 min.
Makes: 4 servings

- 1 can (14¾ oz.) cream-style corn
- 2 large eggs
- ½ cup crushed saltines (about 15 crackers)
- ¼ cup butter, melted
- ¼ cup evaporated milk
- ¼ cup shredded carrot
- ¼ cup chopped green pepper
- 1 Tbsp. chopped celery
- 1 tsp. chopped onion
- ½ tsp. sugar
- ½ tsp. salt
- ½ cup shredded cheddar cheese

1. Preheat oven to 350°. In a large bowl, combine the first 11 ingredients. Transfer to a greased 1-qt. baking dish. Sprinkle with cheese.
2. Bake, uncovered, for 30-35 minutes or until a knife inserted in the center comes out clean.

1 serving: 322 cal., 20g fat (12g sat. fat), 157mg chol., 941mg sod., 29g carb. (7g sugars, 2g fiber), 10g pro.

**BLACK-EYED PEAS
WITH COLLARD GREENS**

BLACK-EYED PEAS WITH COLLARD GREENS

Although delicious any time, this dish has special meaning on New Year's Day, when Southerners eat greens for future wealth and black-eyed peas for prosperity.
—Athena Russell, Greenville, SC

Takes: 25 min. • **Makes:** 6 servings

- 2 Tbsp. olive oil
- 1 garlic clove, minced
- 8 cups chopped collard greens
- ½ tsp. salt
- ¼ tsp. cayenne pepper
- 2 cans (15½ oz. each) black-eyed peas, rinsed and drained
- 4 plum tomatoes, seeded and chopped
- ¼ cup lemon juice
- 2 Tbsp. grated Parmesan cheese

In a Dutch oven, heat oil over medium heat. Add garlic; cook and stir 1 minute. Add collard greens, salt and cayenne; cook and stir 6-8 minutes or until greens are tender. Add peas, tomatoes and lemon juice; heat through. Sprinkle servings with cheese.

¾ cup: 177 cal., 5g fat (1g sat. fat), 1mg chol., 412mg sod., 24g carb. (3g sugars, 6g fiber), 9g pro.

CARIBBEAN ISLAND COLESLAW

After trying a similar version of this coleslaw while visiting the island of St. Kitts, I returned home and wanted to make it myself. I've taken it to so many events, and it's always a hit.
—Noreen McCormick Danek, Cromwell, CT

Takes: 15 min. • **Makes:** 10 servings

- 2 pkg. (14 oz. each) coleslaw mix
- 1 cup unsweetened pineapple tidbits
- ½ cup sweetened shredded coconut
- ½ cup golden raisins
- ½ cup finely chopped sweet red pepper
- 1½ cups mayonnaise
- ½ cup unsweetened pineapple juice
- ¾ tsp. salt
- ¼ tsp. celery seed
- ¼ tsp. pepper

Place the first 5 ingredients in a serving bowl. In a small bowl, combine remaining ingredients. Pour over the slaw mix; toss to coat. Refrigerate until serving.
¾ cup: 305 cal., 26g fat (5g sat. fat), 2mg chol., 378mg sod., 19g carb. (14g sugars, 3g fiber), 2g pro.

TEST KITCHEN TIP
Barbecued or jerk chicken would taste even better served with this tropical salad.

SAUTEED GARLIC MUSHROOMS
PICTURED ON P. 29

These tasty mushrooms are so delicious served with steak, chicken or pork. You just can't beat mushrooms, garlic and butter together!
—Joan Schroeder, Mesquite, NV

Takes: 15 min. • **Makes:** 6 servings

- ¾ lb. sliced fresh mushrooms
- 2 to 3 tsp. minced garlic
- 1 Tbsp. seasoned bread crumbs
- ⅓ cup butter, cubed

In a large skillet, saute the mushrooms, garlic and bread crumbs in butter until mushrooms are tender.
½ cup: 109 cal., 10g fat (6g sat. fat), 27mg chol., 123mg sod., 3g carb. (1g sugars, 1g fiber), 2g pro.

CARIBBEAN ISLAND COLESLAW

**CHIPOTLE
SWEET POTATO SALAD**

CHIPOTLE SWEET POTATO SALAD

I love the velvety taste and texture of sweet potatoes. A friend served sweet potatoes cooked with peppers and they tasted delicious together. I took those flavors and developed them into this creamy, smoky potato salad.
—Carolyn Eskew, Dayton, OH

Prep: 20 min. • **Bake:** 25 min. + cooling
Makes: 9 servings

- 3 lbs. sweet potatoes, peeled and cut into ¾-in. pieces (about 7 cups)
- ¼ cup finely chopped sweet onion
- ¼ cup finely chopped celery
- ¼ cup finely chopped seeded fresh poblano pepper
- 1 jalapeno pepper, seeded and finely chopped
- 1 cup mayonnaise
- 2 Tbsp. lime juice
- ½ to 1 tsp. ground chipotle pepper
- ½ tsp. salt
- ¼ tsp. pepper
   Minced fresh cilantro

1. Preheat oven to 425°. Place sweet potatoes in a parchment-lined 15x10x1-in. baking pan; cover tightly with foil. Roast until tender, 25-30 minutes. Cool. Transfer to a large bowl.
2. Add onion, celery, poblano and jalapeno. Combine mayonnaise, lime juice, chipotle pepper, salt and pepper; pour over potato mixture and toss gently to coat. Refrigerate, covered, until serving. Sprinkle with cilantro.

Note: Wear disposable gloves when cutting hot peppers; the oils can burn skin. Avoid touching your face.

¾ cup: 322 cal., 18g fat (3g sat. fat), 2mg chol., 278mg sod., 38g carb. (16g sugars, 5g fiber), 3g pro.

TEST KITCHEN TIP
If you're going to chill this salad for more than a couple of hours before serving, stir in just half of the dressing mixture. Add the rest right before serving for a nice creamy texture.

GREEN BEANS AMANDINE

GREEN BEANS AMANDINE

It's hard to improve on the taste Mother Nature gives to fresh green beans, but my mom has done that for years using this recipe. The crunchy, buttery almonds are a super addition.
—Brenda DuFresne, Midland, MI

Takes: 20 min. • **Makes:** 4 servings

- 1 lb. fresh or frozen green beans, cut into 2-in. pieces
- ½ cup water
- ¼ cup slivered almonds
- 2 Tbsp. butter
- 1 tsp. lemon juice
- ¼ tsp. seasoned salt, optional

1. Place beans and water in a large skillet or saucepan and bring to a boil. Cover and cook until crisp-tender, 10-15 minutes; drain and set aside.
2. In a large skillet, cook almonds in butter over low heat. Stir in lemon juice and, if desired, seasoned salt. Add beans and heat through.

¾ cup: 125 cal., 9g fat (4g sat. fat), 15mg chol., 53mg sod., 10g carb. (3g sugars, 5g fiber), 4g pro. **Diabetic exchanges:** 2 fat, 1 vegetable.

CRANBERRY & ROASTED BEET SALAD

CRANBERRY & ROASTED BEET SALAD

I created this healthy, tasty side dish as a companion to our Christmas dinner. This enticing substitute for cranberry relish is excellent with turkey. Even the kids loved it! Serve the beet blend alone or on a bed of salad greens (as shown).
—Brianna St. Clair, Worland, WY

Prep: 15 min. + chilling
Bake: 45 min. + cooling
Makes: 6 servings

5   medium fresh beets (about 1½ lbs.)
1   medium pear, chopped
¼   cup dried cranberries
2   Tbsp. olive oil
2   Tbsp. balsamic vinegar
2   Tbsp. cranberry juice
1   Tbsp. orange juice
¼   tsp. salt
4   oz. crumbled goat cheese
¼   cup sliced almonds
2   Tbsp. minced fresh parsley
    Fresh arugula or spring mix salad greens, optional

1. Preheat oven to 425°. Scrub beets and trim tops to 1 in. Wrap in foil; place on a baking sheet. Bake until tender, 45-50 minutes. Remove foil; cool completely. Peel beets and cut into ½-in. cubes; transfer to a large bowl. Add pear and cranberries.
2. In a small bowl, whisk oil, vinegar, cranberry and orange juices, and salt; drizzle over the beet mixture. Refrigerate, covered, overnight.
3. Remove from refrigerator 20 minutes before serving. Toss to coat. Top with goat cheese, almonds and parsley. If desired, serve with arugula.

⅔ cup: 212 cal., 11g fat (4g sat. fat), 24mg chol., 278mg sod., 25g carb. (19g sugars, 5g fiber), 6g pro. **Diabetic exchanges:** 2 fat, 1 starch, 1 vegetable.

DID YOU KNOW?
Beet stains are nearly impossible to remove. Protect work surfaces and wear gloves when handling. If you do get beet juice on your hands, lemon juice or a paste of baking soda and water gets the best results.

RICE WITH COLLARD GREENS RELISH

This is a staple in my country of origin, Zimbabwe. It is served with sadza—a cornmeal-based stiff porridge that's used like rice or potatoes.
—Loveness Murinda, Upland, CA

Prep: 15 min. • **Cook:** 20 min.
Makes: 6 servings

- 1 large bunch collard greens (about 2 lbs.)
- ¼ cup finely chopped onion
- 1 garlic clove, minced
- 2 Tbsp. olive oil
- ¾ cup water
- ¾ cup crushed tomatoes
- 1 tsp. curry powder
- ½ tsp. salt
- ⅛ tsp. pepper
- 2 pkg. (8.8 oz. each) ready-to-serve long grain rice

1. Remove and discard center ribs and stems from collard greens. Cut leaves into 1-in. pieces. In a Dutch oven, cook onion and garlic in oil over medium heat until crisp-tender, about 2 minutes.
2. Stir in water, tomatoes, curry powder, salt and pepper. Bring to a boil. Add collard greens in batches; cook and stir until they begin to wilt.
3. Reduce heat; cover and simmer, stirring occasionally, until the greens are tender, 10-15 minutes. Prepare rice according to package directions. Serve with collard greens.

⅔ cup collards with ⅔ cup rice: 239 cal., 7g fat (1g sat. fat), 0 chol., 279mg sod., 38g carb. (2g sugars, 8g fiber), 8g pro.

TOMATOES WITH PARSLEY PESTO

You'll love the summery flavor of this pretty salad. It's a snap to whip up the pesto in the blender then pour it over ripe tomato wedges.
—Donna Hackman, Bedford, VA

Takes: 10 min. • **Makes:** 6 servings

- 1 cup packed fresh parsley
- ¼ cup minced chives
- 1 garlic clove, peeled
- ¼ tsp. salt
  Dash pepper
- 3 Tbsp. olive oil
- 2 Tbsp. red wine vinegar
- 3 medium tomatoes, cut into wedges

1. In a blender, combine the parsley, chives, garlic, salt and pepper. Cover and process until finely chopped. Add oil and vinegar.
2. Transfer to a large bowl; cover and refrigerate until serving. Just before serving, add tomatoes; toss to coat.

4 wedges: 77 cal., 7g fat (1g sat. fat), 0 chol., 9mg sod., 3g carb. (2g sugars, 1g fiber), 1g pro. **Diabetic exchanges:** 1 vegetable, 1 fat.

RICE WITH COLLARD GREENS RELISH

🥕 KALE & FENNEL SKILLET

I love to mix different vegetables and use different herbs and spices to change things up. If you can't find apple sausage, a good mild Italian sausage would substitute just fine.
—Patricia Levenson, Santa Ana, CA

....

Prep: 10 min. • **Cook:** 25 min.
Makes: 6 servings

- 2 Tbsp. extra virgin olive oil
- 1 small onion, thinly sliced
- 1 small fennel bulb, thinly sliced
- ½ lb. fully cooked apple chicken sausage links or cooked Italian sausage links, halved lengthwise and sliced into half-moons
- 2 garlic cloves, minced
- 3 Tbsp. dry sherry or dry white wine
- 1 Tbsp. herbes de Provence
- ⅛ tsp. salt
- ⅛ tsp. pepper
- 1 bunch kale, trimmed and torn into bite-sized pieces

1. In a large skillet, heat olive oil over medium-high heat. Add onion and fennel; cook and stir until onion begins to brown, 6-8 minutes. Add sausage, garlic, sherry and seasonings; cook until sausage starts to caramelize, 4-6 minutes.
2. Add kale; cook, covered, stirring occasionally, until the kale is tender, 15-17 minutes.
Note: Look for herbes de Provence in the spice aisle.

GRANDMA'S POULTRY DRESSING

¾ **cup:** 167 cal., 8g fat (2g sat. fat), 27mg chol., 398mg sod., 16g carb. (6g sugars, 3g fiber), 9g pro. **Diabetic exchanges:** 2 vegetable, 1 lean meat, 1 fat.

GRANDMA'S POULTRY DRESSING

Every family seems to have their own favorite dressing recipe that becomes the standard—this is ours. It came from my grandma, who passed it down to my mother. Now our children have carried it on in their kitchens.
—Norma Howland, Joliet, IL

....

Prep: 20 min. • **Bake:** 40 min.
Makes: 6 cups

- 1 lb. bulk pork sausage
- 1 cup 2% milk
- 7 cups coarse dry bread crumbs
- 1 cup diced celery
- 2 large eggs
- 2 to 3 Tbsp. minced fresh parsley
- 2 Tbsp. diced onion
- ½ tsp. salt or salt to taste

1. Preheat oven to 350°. In a large skillet, brown sausage. Drain sausage, discarding the drippings.
2. Meanwhile, in a small saucepan, heat milk over medium heat until bubbles form around sides of pan. In a large bowl, combine sausage, milk and the remaining ingredients.
3. Transfer to a greased 2-qt. baking dish. Cover and bake until lightly browned, about 40 minutes.
½ **cup:** 352 cal., 12g fat (4g sat. fat), 52mg chol., 826mg sod., 48g carb. (3g sugars, 2g fiber), 12g pro.

CITRUS PEACH CARROTS

The bright flavors of lemon and peach balance the sweet earthiness of carrots in this delicious side.
—*Taste of Home* Test Kitchen

Takes: 15 min. • **Makes:** 4 servings

- 1 lb. fresh baby carrots
- 2 Tbsp. water
- ¼ cup peach preserves
- 2 Tbsp. butter
- 1 tsp. orange juice
- ¼ tsp. grated lemon zest
- ¼ tsp. pepper
- ¼ cup salted roasted almonds, coarsely chopped

1. Place the carrots and water in a microwave-safe bowl. Cover and microwave on high for 4-6 minutes or until crisp-tender; drain.
2. In another microwave-safe bowl, combine the preserves, butter, orange juice, lemon zest and pepper. Cook, uncovered, on high for 30-45 seconds or until the butter is melted. Pour over carrots; sprinkle with almonds and toss to coat.

¾ cup: 193 cal., 10g fat (4g sat. fat), 15mg chol., 177mg sod., 24g carb. (18g sugars, 3g fiber), 3g pro.

TEST KITCHEN TIP
If you don't have roasted almonds, stir in toasted chopped pecans or walnuts for that added crunch and flavor.

CITRUS PEACH CARROTS

COTTAGE CHEESE CANTALOUPE SALAD

This refreshing side is perfect for a light luncheon. For variety, try drizzling a little tangy French salad dressing over the mild combination of cantaloupe, cottage cheese, granola, raisins and nuts.
—Margaret Allen, Abingdon, VA

Takes: 10 min. • **Makes:** 4 servings

- 2 cups 1% cottage cheese
- ½ cup raisins
- ¼ cup chopped walnuts
- 1 medium cantaloupe, quartered and seeded
- ¼ cup reduced-fat granola
- 2 kiwifruit, peeled and sliced
  Leaf lettuce

In a small bowl, combine the cottage cheese, raisins and walnuts. Spoon into cantaloupe wedges. Sprinkle with granola; top with kiwi. Serve immediately on lettuce-lined plates.

1 wedge: 275 cal., 7g fat (1g sat. fat), 5mg chol., 500mg sod., 40g carb. (29g sugars, 4g fiber), 18g pro.

FRIED CABBAGE

When I was young, my family grew our own cabbages, and it was fun to create recipes. This comforting side is great with potatoes, deviled eggs and cornbread.
—Bernice Morris, Marshfield, MO

Takes: 20 min. • **Makes:** 6 servings

- 2 Tbsp. butter
- 1 tsp. sugar
- ½ tsp. salt
- ¼ tsp. crushed red pepper flakes
- ⅛ tsp. pepper
- 6 cups coarsely chopped cabbage
- 1 Tbsp. water

In a large skillet, melt butter over medium heat. Stir in sugar, salt, pepper flakes and pepper. Add cabbage and water. Cook for 5-6 minutes or until tender, stirring occasionally.

1 cup: 59 cal., 4g fat (2g sat. fat), 10mg chol., 251mg sod., 6g carb. (3g sugars, 2g fiber), 1g pro. **Diabetic exchanges:** 1 vegetable, 1 fat.

GRANDMOTHER'S ORANGE SALAD

This slightly sweet gelatin salad is a little bit tangy, too. It adds beautiful color to any meal and appeals to appetites of all ages.
—Ann Eastman, Santa Monica, CA

Prep: 20 min. + chilling
Makes: 10 servings

- 1 can (11 oz.) mandarin oranges
- 1 can (8 oz.) crushed pineapple
  Water
- 1 pkg. (6 oz.) orange gelatin
- 1 pint orange sherbet, softened
- 2 bananas, sliced

1. Drain oranges and pineapple, reserving juices. Set oranges and pineapple aside. Add water to juices to measure 2 cups. Place in a saucepan and bring to a boil; pour over gelatin in a large bowl. Stir until the gelatin is dissolved. Stir in sherbet until smooth.

2. Chill mixture until partially set (watch carefully). Fold in the oranges, pineapple and bananas. Pour into an oiled 6-cup mold. Chill until firm.

1 piece: 161 cal., 1g fat (0 sat. fat), 2mg chol., 55mg sod., 39g carb. (35g sugars, 1g fiber), 2g pro.

ORZO WITH FETA & ARUGULA

ORZO WITH FETA & ARUGULA

In my family, we love salads because they're an interesting way to blend many different flavors. This orzo salad is one of our favorites—it tastes delicious served either warm or cool.
—Laura Adamsky, Decatur, AL

Takes: 30 min. • **Makes:** 6 servings

- 1 cup uncooked orzo pasta
- 6 cups fresh arugula
- ½ cup crumbled feta cheese
- ½ cup sliced almonds, toasted
- ½ cup dried cherries or dried cranberries
- 2 Tbsp. extra virgin olive oil
- ¼ tsp. salt
- ⅛ tsp. pepper
  Lemon wedges, optional

Cook pasta according to the package directions for al dente. Drain orzo; rinse with cold water and drain well. In a large bowl, combine arugula, feta, almonds, cherries, oil, salt and pepper. Add the orzo; toss to coat. If desired, serve with lemon wedges.

1 cup: 279 cal., 11g fat (2g sat. fat), 5mg chol., 198mg sod., 38g carb. (11g sugars, 3g fiber), 8g pro.

TEST KITCHEN TIP
Turn leftovers into lunch by adding sliced grilled chicken.

SIMPLE ORANGE-GLAZED BEETS

In our house, we prefer our beets prepared simply—with a little butter, salt and an orange marmalade glaze.
—Mary Beth Jung, Hendersonville, NC

....

Prep: 10 min. • **Cook:** 30 min.
Makes: 4 servings

- 1 lb. small fresh beets (about 4)
- ⅓ cup orange marmalade
- 1 Tbsp. butter
  Dash salt

1. Scrub beets and trim tops to 1 in. Place in a large saucepan; add water to cover. Bring to a boil. Reduce heat; simmer, covered, 25-30 minutes or until tender. Drain; cool slightly.

2. Peel and cut beets into ¼-in. slices. In same pan, combine marmalade, butter and salt; cook and stir over medium-low heat until blended. Add beets; heat through, stirring to coat.

½ cup: 141 cal., 3g fat (2g sat. fat), 8mg chol., 164mg sod., 29g carb. (25g sugars, 2g fiber), 2g pro.

GARLIC OREGANO ZUCCHINI

This flavorful side dish complements almost any main course. For a colorful variation, use half yellow summer squash.
—Teresa Kraus, Cortez, CO

....

Takes: 15 min. • **Makes:** 4 servings

- 1 tsp. minced garlic
- 2 Tbsp. canola oil
- 4 medium zucchini, sliced
- 1 tsp. dried oregano
- ½ tsp. salt
- ⅛ tsp. pepper

In a large skillet, cook and stir the garlic in oil over medium heat for 1 minute. Add zucchini, oregano, salt and pepper. Cook and stir for 4-6 minutes or until the zucchini is crisp-tender.

1 cup: 90 cal., 7g fat (1g sat. fat), 0 chol., 301mg sod., 6g carb. (3g sugars, 3g fiber), 2g pro. **Diabetic exchanges:** 1½ fat, 1 vegetable.

SIMPLE ORANGE-GLAZED BEETS

MAKEOVER CREAMED CORN

This scrumptious makeover has all the rich feel and flavor of the original, with only about half the calories and about a third of the saturated fat.
—Trisha Kruse, Eagle, ID

Takes: 30 min. • **Makes:** 10 servings

- 4 pkg. (10 oz. each) frozen corn, thawed
- 1 cup half-and-half cream
- ¼ cup butter, cubed
- 2 Tbsp. sugar
- 2 tsp. salt
- ½ tsp. pepper
- ⅓ cup all-purpose flour
- 2 cups fat-free milk
- ½ cup shredded sharp cheddar cheese
  Minced fresh parsley

1. In a Dutch oven, combine the first 6 ingredients. Cook and stir over medium heat until heated through, 8-10 minutes.
2. Combine flour and milk until smooth. Stir into pan. Bring to a boil; cook and stir until thickened, about 2 minutes. Remove from the heat; stir in cheese until melted. Top with parsley.
¾ cup: 234 cal., 9g fat (6g sat. fat), 31mg chol., 574mg sod., 33g carb. (8g sugars, 3g fiber), 8g pro.
HEALTH TIP: To make lighter versions of your favorite recipes that call for cheddar cheese, try using less cheese but switch to sharp cheddar. It's more flavorful, so you'll still get a lot of cheddar goodness.

READER REVIEW

"I made this over the weekend. It was so simple and easy and my family loved it! I will be making it more often! Fantastic!"
STARBUCK7, TASTEOFHOME.COM

ROASTED ASPARAGUS
& TOMATOES

ROASTED ASPARAGUS & TOMATOES

I have a habit of buying too much asparagus when it's in season, but it doesn't go to waste! I toss the spears with cherry tomatoes and goat cheese for this side. Be sure to use good-quality goat cheese—it makes all the difference.
—Holly Battiste, Barrington, NJ

Takes: 30 min. • **Makes:** 4 servings

- 1 lb. fresh asparagus, trimmed
- 1 cup grape tomatoes
- ¼ cup coarsely chopped walnuts
- 1 Tbsp. olive oil
- ¼ tsp. dried oregano
- ¼ tsp. salt
- ¼ tsp. pepper
- 2 Tbsp. crumbled goat cheese
- 1 Tbsp. minced fresh basil

1. Preheat oven to 400°. Place asparagus, tomatoes and walnuts in a greased 15x10x1-in. baking pan. Mix oil, oregano, salt and pepper; add to asparagus mixture and toss to coat.
2. Roast 15-20 minutes or until asparagus is crisp-tender, turning the vegetables occasionally. Sprinkle with cheese. Top with basil before serving.
1 serving: 108 cal., 9g fat (2g sat. fat), 4mg chol., 173mg sod., 5g carb. (2g sugars, 2g fiber), 4g pro. **Diabetic exchanges:** 2 fat, 1 vegetable.

MAKEOVER CREAMED CORN

THAI SALAD WITH CILANTRO LIME DRESSING

THAI SALAD WITH CILANTRO LIME DRESSING

I created this salad to replicate one I tried on a cruise. We love the spice of the Thai chile, but if your family isn't into spice, feel free to leave it out. It will still be delicious!
—Donna Gribbins, Shelbyville, KY

Prep: 35 min. • **Makes:** 22 servings

- 2 medium limes
- 1 bunch fresh cilantro leaves, stems removed (about 2 cups)
- 1 cup sugar
- 1 Thai red chile pepper, seeded and chopped
- 2 garlic cloves, halved
- ½ tsp. salt
- ½ tsp. pepper
- 2 cups canola oil

- 1 head Chinese or napa cabbage, finely shredded
- 1 small head red cabbage, finely shredded
- 1 English cucumber, chopped
- 1 pkg. (10 oz.) frozen shelled edamame, thawed
- 2 medium ripe avocados, peeled and cubed
- 1 cup shredded carrots
- 3 green onions, sliced

1. Finely grate enough zest from limes to measure 1 Tbsp. Cut limes crosswise in half; squeeze juice from limes. Place zest and juice in a blender; add cilantro, sugar, red chile pepper, garlic, salt and pepper. While processing, gradually add oil in a steady stream.

2. In a large bowl, combine cabbages, cucumber, edamame, avocados, carrots and green onions. Drizzle with dressing; toss to coat.

Note: Wear disposable gloves when cutting hot peppers; the oils can burn exposed skin. Avoid touching your face.

1 cup: 271 cal., 23g fat (2g sat. fat), 0 chol., 69mg sod., 16g carb. (11g sugars, 2g fiber), 2g pro.

APRICOTS WITH HERBED GOAT CHEESE

After ending up with bunches of apricots one summer, I created this quick and simple dish. My friends were blown away by its fresh taste and distinctive flavors.
—Wendy Weidner, Ham Lake, MN

Takes: 20 min. • **Makes:** 4 servings

- 3 oz. fresh goat cheese
- 2 tsp. minced fresh basil
- 2 tsp. minced fresh chives
- 2 tsp. 2% milk
- 4 fresh apricots, sliced
- ⅛ tsp. salt
  Dash pepper
- 2 Tbsp. balsamic glaze

Place goat cheese, minced basil, chives and milk in a mini food processor; process until smooth. Arrange apricot slices on a serving platter. Drop goat cheese mixture by teaspoonfuls over top. Sprinkle with salt and pepper; drizzle with balsamic glaze. Garnish with additional basil leaves. Serve immediately.

1 serving: 71 cal., 3g fat (2g sat. fat), 14mg chol., 163mg sod., 9g carb. (6g sugars, 1g fiber), 3g pro. **Diabetic exchanges:** ½ fruit, ½ fat.

TEST KITCHEN TIP
If you can't find fresh apricots, substitute 3 small peaches for the 4 apricots.

APRICOTS WITH HERBED GOAT CHEESE

ORZO WITH CARAMELIZED BUTTERNUT SQUASH & BACON

One year my garden produced a bumper crop of butternut squash, and I made up so many new dishes trying to use up my bounty! This is a tasty, easy side with pretty colors, and it makes plenty to fill your hungry family. To make it into a main, add shrimp or shredded chicken.
—Kallee Krong-McCreery, Escondido, CA

Prep: 20 min. • **Cook:** 20 min.
Makes: 6 servings

- 1½ cups uncooked orzo pasta
- 4 bacon strips, chopped
- 2 cups cubed peeled butternut squash (½-in. cubes)
- ½ cup chopped onion
- 1 cup cut fresh or frozen cut green beans, thawed
- 1 garlic clove, minced
- 1 Tbsp. butter
- 1 tsp. garlic salt
- ¼ tsp. pepper
- ¼ cup grated Parmesan cheese
  Minced fresh parsley

1. In a large saucepan, cook orzo according to the package directions.
2. Meanwhile, in a large skillet, cook bacon over medium heat until crisp, stirring occasionally. Remove with a slotted spoon, reserving the drippings in the pan; drain on paper towels.
3. Cook and stir squash and onion in the bacon drippings until tender, 8-10 minutes. Add beans and garlic; cook 1 minute longer.
4. Drain orzo; stir into the squash mixture. Add butter, garlic salt, pepper and the reserved bacon; heat through. Sprinkle with Parmesan and parsley.

¾ cup: 329 cal., 11g fat (4g sat. fat), 20mg chol., 533mg sod., 47g carb. (4g sugars, 3g fiber), 11g pro.

BLACKBERRY BALSAMIC SPINACH SALAD

This lightly dressed salad is packed with superfoods! When I have time, I make my own vinaigrette from scratch.
—Mary Lou Timpson, Colorado City, AZ

Takes: 15 min. • **Makes:** 6 servings

- 3 cups fresh baby spinach
- 2 cups fresh blackberries, halved
- 1½ cups cherry tomatoes, halved
- ⅓ cup crumbled feta cheese
- 2 green onions, thinly sliced
- ¼ cup chopped walnuts, toasted
- ⅓ cup balsamic vinaigrette

In a large bowl, combine the first 6 ingredients. Divide salad among 6 plates; drizzle with dressing.

1 cup: 106 cal., 7g fat (1g sat. fat), 3mg chol., 230mg sod., 9g carb. (4g sugars, 4g fiber), 3g pro. **Diabetic exchanges:** 1½ fat, ½ starch.

READER REVIEW

"Blackberries were on sale this week, making this salad the perfect addition to my menu. I subbed in goat cheese for the feta because it was what I had available. So good!"

SSTETZEL, TASTEOFHOME.COM

OREGANO GREEN BEANS WITH TOASTED PINE NUTS

OREGANO GREEN BEANS WITH TOASTED PINE NUTS

This super easy side dish is an ideal picnic or potluck recipe. It's a beautiful, surprising dish that leaves guests and family raving. You can substitute any kind of nut for the pine nuts, or even replace them with fresh berries.
—Wolfgang Hanau, West Palm Beach, FL

Prep: 15 min. • **Cook:** 5 hours
Makes: 8 servings

- 2 lbs. fresh thin french-style green beans, cut into 2-in. pieces
- ½ cup water
- 2 Tbsp. minced fresh oregano
- ½ tsp. onion powder
- ½ tsp. salt
- ¼ tsp. celery salt
- ¼ tsp. pepper
- ½ cup pine nuts or sliced almonds, toasted

In a 6-qt. slow cooker, combine all ingredients except pine nuts. Cook, covered, on low until beans are tender, 5-6 hours. Remove with a slotted spoon. Top with pine nuts.

1 cup: 94 cal., 6g fat (0 sat. fat), 0 chol., 191mg sod., 10g carb. (3g sugars, 4g fiber), 3g pro. **Diabetic exchanges:** 1 vegetable, 1 fat.

TEST KITCHEN TIP

Look for green beans labeled as haricots verts. They are thinner and more tender than regular green beans. If you do use regular green beans, increase the cook time by 30-60 minutes.

CABBAGE & RUTABAGA SLAW

This is a favorite crunchy slaw that's a perfect way to use cool-weather veggies. We love it as a side with any spicy main dish.

—Ann Sheehy, Lawrence, MA

Prep: 10 min. + chilling
Makes: 4 servings

- 2 cups diced peeled rutabaga
- 2 cups finely chopped cabbage
- ½ cup finely chopped red onion
- ¼ cup minced fresh Italian parsley
- ½ cup reduced-fat apple cider vinaigrette

Toss together all ingredients. Refrigerate, covered, to allow flavors to blend, about 3 hours.

1 cup: 126 cal., 6g fat (1g sat. fat), 0 chol., 144mg sod., 19g carb. (11g sugars, 3g fiber), 2g pro. **Diabetic exchanges:** 1 vegetable, 1 fat, ½ starch.

BROCCOLI RICE CASSEROLE

This hearty casserole is my usual choice to make for a potluck. With the green of the broccoli and the rich cheese sauce, it's pretty to serve, and it makes a tasty side dish for almost any kind of meat.

—Margaret Mayes, La Mesa, CA

Prep: 10 min. • **Bake:** 25 min.
Makes: 8 servings

- 1 small onion, chopped
- ½ cup chopped celery
- 3 cups frozen chopped broccoli, thawed
- 1 Tbsp. butter

- 1 jar (8 oz.) process cheese sauce
- 1 can (10¾ oz.) condensed cream of mushroom soup, undiluted
- 1 can (5 oz.) evaporated milk
- 3 cups cooked rice

1. Preheat oven to 325°. In a large skillet, saute the onion, celery and broccoli in butter for 3-5 minutes or until crisp-tender. Stir in the cheese sauce, soup and milk until smooth.
2. Place rice in a greased 8-in. square baking dish. Pour cheese mixture over rice; do not stir. Bake, uncovered, for 25-30 minutes or until bubbly.

1 cup: 242 cal., 11g fat (6g sat. fat), 32mg chol., 789mg sod., 28g carb. (5g sugars, 3g fiber), 8g pro.

ZUCCHINI PASTA

The taste of this rich and creamy zucchini pasta dish will have people convinced it's not low-fat, but it is! Garlicky and fresh-flavored, this will be a hit.

—Maria Regakis, Saugus, MA

Takes: 25 min. • **Makes:** 6 servings

- 8 oz. uncooked linguine
- 4 cups coarsely shredded zucchini (about 3 medium)
- 4 tsp. olive oil
- 2 garlic cloves, thinly sliced
- ¼ cup fat-free plain yogurt
- ¾ cup shredded reduced-fat cheddar cheese
- ¾ tsp. salt
- ¼ tsp. pepper

1. Cook linguine according to package directions. In a sieve or colander, drain the zucchini, squeezing to remove excess liquid. Pat dry.
2. In a large nonstick skillet, saute zucchini in oil for 2 minutes. Add garlic; saute 1-2 minutes longer or until the zucchini is tender. Transfer to a large bowl. Add the yogurt, cheese, salt and pepper. Drain linguine; add to the zucchini mixture and toss to coat.

¾ cup: 219 cal., 7g fat (3g sat. fat), 10mg chol., 395mg sod., 32g carb. (4g sugars, 2g fiber), 10g pro. **Diabetic exchanges:** 1½ starch, 1½ fat, 1 vegetable.

CABBAGE & RUTABAGA SLAW

ROASTED SWEET POTATO WEDGES

Sweet potatoes roasted with curry and smoked paprika delight everybody at our table. The mango chutney makes a tangy dip.
—Simi Jois, Streamwood, IL

Takes: 25 min. • **Makes:** 4 servings

- 2 medium sweet potatoes (about 1 lb.), cut into ½-in. wedges
- 2 Tbsp. olive oil
- 1 tsp. curry powder
- ½ tsp. salt
- ½ tsp. smoked paprika
- ⅛ tsp. coarsely ground pepper
  Minced fresh cilantro
  Mango chutney, optional

1. Preheat oven to 425°. Place sweet potatoes in a large bowl. Mix oil and seasonings; drizzle over sweet potatoes and toss to coat. Transfer to an ungreased 15x10x1-in. baking pan.
2. Roast 15-20 minutes or until tender, turning occasionally. Sprinkle with cilantro. If desired, serve with chutney.

1 serving: 159 cal., 7g fat (1g sat. fat), 0 chol., 305mg sod., 23g carb. (9g sugars, 3g fiber), 2g pro. **Diabetic exchanges:** 1½ starch, 1½ fat.

TANGERINE TOSSED SALAD

TANGERINE TOSSED SALAD

I learned to cook from my mother when I was a young girl. I love the combination of sweet tangerines and crunchy caramelized almonds.
—Helen Musenbrock, O'Fallon, MO

Prep: 40 min. • **Makes:** 6 servings

- ½ cup sliced almonds
- 3 Tbsp. sugar, divided
- 2 medium tangerines or 1 navel orange
- 6 cups torn lettuce
- 3 green onions, chopped
- 2 Tbsp. cider vinegar
- 2 Tbsp. olive oil
- ¼ tsp. salt
- ¼ tsp. pepper

1. In a small skillet, cook and stir the almonds and 2 Tbsp. sugar over medium-low heat for 25-30 minutes or until the sugar is melted and the almonds are toasted. Remove from the heat. Peel and section the tangerines, reserving 1 Tbsp. juice.
2. In a large bowl, combine the lettuce, onions, tangerines and almonds. In a small bowl, whisk the vinegar, oil, salt, pepper, reserved juice and remaining sugar. Pour over salad; toss to coat.

1 cup: 138 cal., 9g fat (1g sat. fat), 0 chol., 105mg sod., 14g carb. (11g sugars, 3g fiber), 3g pro. **Diabetic exchanges:** 2 fat, 1 vegetable, ½ starch.

GNOCCHI WITH MUSHROOMS & ONION

Tender potato gnocchi are so delicious with sauteed mushrooms and onions. This is one of my family's go-to side dishes.
—Kris Berezansky, Clymer, PA

Takes: 20 min. • **Makes:** 5 servings

- 1 pkg. (16 oz.) potato gnocchi
- ½ lb. sliced fresh mushrooms
- ¾ cup chopped sweet onion
- ¼ cup butter, cubed
- ¼ tsp. salt
- ¼ tsp. Italian seasoning
- ¼ tsp. crushed red pepper flakes
- Grated Parmesan cheese

1. Cook gnocchi according to package directions. Meanwhile, in a large skillet, saute mushrooms and onion in butter until tender.

2. Drain gnocchi. Add the gnocchi, salt, Italian seasoning and pepper flakes to the skillet; heat through. Sprinkle with cheese.

Note: Look for potato gnocchi in the pasta or frozen foods section.

¾ cup: 287 cal., 11g fat (6g sat. fat), 31mg chol., 583mg sod., 41g carb. (7g sugars, 3g fiber), 8g pro.

TEST KITCHEN TIP
When storing sweet onions, keep them cool, dry and separate. Place in a single layer, wrapped separately in foil or paper towels, in the vegetable bin of the refrigerator.

GNOCCHI WITH
MUSHROOMS & ONION

RED POTATOES
WITH BEANS

RED POTATOES WITH BEANS

You can serve this homey blend of fresh green beans, potato wedges and chopped red onion hot or cold. Either way, it makes a pleasing accompaniment to Mom's meat loaf or almost any other meat.
—Daria Burcar, Rochester, MI

Takes: 20 min. • **Makes:** 6 servings

1⅓ lbs. fresh green beans, trimmed
⅓ cup water
6 small red potatoes, cut into wedges
½ cup chopped red onion
½ cup Italian salad dressing

1. Place the green beans and water in a 2-qt. microwave-safe dish. Cover and microwave on high until tender, 6-8 minutes.
2. Meanwhile, place potatoes in a large saucepan and cover with water. Bring to a boil. Reduce heat; cover and cook until tender, 10-15 minutes. Drain beans and potatoes; place in a bowl. Add onion and dressing; toss to coat.

¾ cup: 138 cal., 3g fat (0 sat. fat), 0 chol., 212mg sod., 23g carb. (5g sugars, 5g fiber), 4g pro. **Diabetic exchanges:** 1 starch, 1 vegetable, ½ fat.

WARM GARLICKY GRAPE TOMATOES

This is one of our favorite quick ways to use up a bumper crop of grape tomatoes (or to take care of an overenthusiastic tomato-shopping spree)!
—Rose Gulledge, Crofton, MD

Takes: 30 min. • **Makes:** 4 servings

2 cups grape tomatoes
3 garlic cloves, minced
1½ tsp. minced fresh basil
½ tsp. salt-free garlic seasoning blend
¼ tsp. salt
⅛ tsp. pepper
1 tsp. olive oil, divided
¼ cup soft whole wheat bread crumbs
¼ cup crumbled feta cheese

1. Preheat oven to 425°. In a small bowl, combine the tomatoes, garlic, basil, seasoning blend, salt and pepper. Add ½ tsp. oil; toss to coat. Transfer to a 3-cup baking dish coated with cooking spray.

APRICOT FLUFF

2. Bake for 15 minutes. Combine bread crumbs and the remaining oil; sprinkle over the top. Sprinkle with cheese. Bake 5-10 minutes longer or until the cheese is softened and the tomatoes are tender.

½ cup: 64 cal., 3g fat (1g sat. fat), 4mg chol., 259mg sod., 8g carb. (2g sugars, 2g fiber), 3g pro. **Diabetic exchanges:** 1 vegetable, ½ fat.

APRICOT FLUFF

When we were both young mothers, my best friend gave me this recipe when I needed to make a dish for a party but didn't have the time (or energy) for something complex. Now, it's a must-have at every barbecue I attend. It's sublime made with peaches and peach gelatin, too.
—Melissa Meinke, Fawn Grove, PA

Prep: 10 min. + chilling
Makes: 10 servings (¾ cup each)

1 cup apricot or peach yogurt
1 pkg. (3 oz.) apricot gelatin
1 carton (8 oz.) frozen reduced-fat whipped topping, thawed
1 pkg. (10½ oz.) miniature marshmallows
3 cups cubed peeled fresh apricots

In a large bowl, add yogurt to gelatin; stir 2 minutes to completely dissolve. Gently stir in the whipped topping, then the marshmallows and apricots. Refrigerate until firm, at least 4 hours.

¾ cup: 225 cal., 3g fat (3g sat. fat), 1mg chol., 57mg sod., 44g carb. (36g sugars, 1g fiber), 3g pro.

READER REVIEW
"I've made this recipe several times over the past few weeks. I have used different gelatin and yogurt flavors. It is delicious however you make it."
RANDCBRUNS, TASTEOFHOME.COM

ROASTED PEPPERS
& CAULIFLOWER

5i ✏️

ROASTED PEPPERS & CAULIFLOWER

Caramelization really enhances the flavors in this easy side dish. The roasted peppers and cauliflower are seasoned just right to go with nearly any main course.
—Cheryl Wilt, Eglon, WV

Prep: 10 min. • **Bake:** 30 min.
Makes: 6 servings

- 1 medium head cauliflower, broken into florets
- 2 medium sweet red peppers, cut into strips
- 2 small onions, cut into wedges
- 2 Tbsp. olive oil
- ½ tsp. salt
- ½ tsp. pepper
- 1 Tbsp. grated Parmesan cheese
- 1 Tbsp. minced fresh parsley

1. Preheat oven to 425°. Place the cauliflower, red peppers and onions in a shallow roasting pan. Add the oil, salt and pepper; toss to coat. Roast, uncovered, for 20 minutes.

2. Stir; roast 10 minutes longer or until vegetables are tender and lightly browned. Transfer to a serving bowl; sprinkle with Parmesan cheese and parsley.
⅔ cup: 88 cal., 5g fat (1g sat. fat), 1mg chol., 243mg sod., 10g carb. (5g sugars, 4g fiber), 3g pro. **Diabetic exchanges:** 2 vegetable, 1 fat.

RASPBERRY COLESLAW

I love the smoky, creamy taste of this coleslaw. If you like your coleslaw on the tangier side, leave out the mayonnaise.
—Diana Martello, Pineville, KY

Prep: 15 min. + chilling
Makes: 6 servings

- 3 cups shredded cabbage
- 1⅓ cups shredded carrots
- 1 cup shredded red cabbage
- ¼ cup smoked almonds, finely chopped
- ½ cup reduced-fat raspberry walnut vinaigrette
- ¼ cup mayonnaise
- ¼ tsp. pepper

In a large bowl, combine the cabbage, carrots, red cabbage and almonds. Whisk together vinaigrette, mayonnaise and pepper; pour over the cabbage mixture. Toss to coat. Refrigerate, covered, at least 1 hour before serving.
⅔ cup: 169 cal., 14g fat (2g sat. fat), 1mg chol., 175mg sod., 11g carb. (5g sugars, 2g fiber), 2g pro.

FRESH GINGER CARROT SALAD

I created this salad as a light alternative to the mayonnaise, raisin and carrot salad my mom used to make. I have a sweet tooth, and this salad satisfies it!
—Lauri Cherian, Scott Depot, WV

....

Prep: 15 min. + chilling
Makes: 6 servings

- 2 cans (8 oz. each) unsweetened crushed pineapple, undrained
- 3½ cups shredded carrots
- 1 cup raisins
- ¾ cup sweetened shredded coconut
- ½ cup chopped walnuts
- 1½ cups fat-free plain yogurt
- 2 tsp. minced fresh gingerroot

Drain crushed pineapple, reserving 3 Tbsp. juice. In a bowl, combine the pineapple, carrots, raisins, coconut and walnuts. Combine the yogurt, ginger and reserved pineapple juice. Pour dressing over the carrot mixture; toss gently to coat. Refrigerate for at least 1 hour.
¾ cup: 291 cal., 11g fat (4g sat. fat), 1mg chol., 112mg sod., 49g carb. (37g sugars, 4g fiber), 6g pro.

FRESH GINGER CARROT SALAD

STRAWBERRY ARUGULA SALAD

We love to make this strawberry salad when there are plenty of fresh greens to pick. I serve it as a side salad, or make it an entree by topping it with chicken.
—Sara Longworth, Worcester, MA

....

Takes: 20 min. • **Makes:** 2 servings

- 2 cups torn fresh arugula or baby spinach
- ¾ cup quartered fresh strawberries
- ¼ cup slivered almonds
- ¼ cup crumbled Gorgonzola cheese
- 2 Tbsp. chopped red onion
- 2 Tbsp. olive oil
- 1 Tbsp. thawed orange juice concentrate
- 1 Tbsp. balsamic vinegar
- 1½ tsp. grated orange zest
- ⅛ tsp. ground ginger

Combine the first 5 ingredients. Whisk the oil, orange juice concentrate, vinegar, orange zest and ginger. Pour over the salad; toss gently to coat.
1¼ cups: 295 cal., 25g fat (5g sat. fat), 13mg chol., 199mg sod., 14g carb. (9g sugars, 4g fiber), 7g pro.

ZESTY SUGAR SNAP PEAS

PICTURED ON P. 29

Lemon-pepper and garlic make these crisp-tender sugar snap peas a flavorful accompaniment to a variety of entrees.
—Taste of Home Test Kitchen

....

Takes: 15 min. • **Makes:** 4 servings

- 1 lb. fresh or frozen sugar snap peas
- ½ cup water
- 1 Tbsp. butter
- 1 garlic clove, minced
- ¾ tsp. lemon-pepper seasoning
- ¼ tsp. salt

In a skillet, bring peas and water to a boil. Reduce heat. Cover and cook until peas are tender, 6-7 minutes. Drain. Add the remaining ingredients. Cook and stir until well-coated, 2-3 minutes.
¾ cup: 74 cal., 3g fat (2g sat. fat), 8mg chol., 267mg sod., 8g carb. (4g sugars, 3g fiber), 4g pro. **Diabetic exchanges:** 1 vegetable, ½ fat.

Quick Soups & Sandwiches

For a satisfying lunch or a light dinner, there's nothing quite like the classic pairing of soup and a sandwich. Turn the page to find a host of recipes that work beautifully on their own or as part of a mix-and-match combo!

Ham & Cheese Pockets (p. 71) **Cheddar French Dip Sandwiches** (p. 63) **Curried Chicken Soup** (p. 72)
Cherry Chicken Croissants (p. 64) **Quick Sausage Tortellini Soup** (p. 58)

BORSCHT WITH GARDEN VEGETABLES

My mother used to make this hearty soup from her garden's bountiful crop of beets and other vegetables.
—Ruth Andrewson, Leavenworth, WA

Prep: 15 min. • **Cook:** 35 min.
Makes: 8 servings (2 qt.)

- 2 cups shredded fresh beets
- 1 cup shredded carrots
- 1 cup chopped onion
- 2 cups water
- ½ tsp. salt
- 2 cans (14½ oz. each) beef broth
- 1 cup shredded cabbage
- 1 Tbsp. butter
- 1 Tbsp. lemon juice
  Optional: Sour cream, chopped chives or fresh dill sprigs

In a saucepan, bring beets, carrots, onion, water and salt to a boil. Reduce the heat; cover and simmer 20 minutes. Add broth, cabbage and butter; simmer, uncovered, 15 minutes. Just before serving, stir in lemon juice. If desired, top each serving with sour cream and chives or dill.

1 cup: 48 cal., 2g fat (1g sat. fat), 4mg chol., 375mg sod., 7g carb. (5g sugars, 2g fiber), 1g pro. **Diabetic exchanges:** 1 vegetable, ½ fat.

BEAN COUNTER CHOWDER

BEAN COUNTER CHOWDER

This hearty chowder is one of our favorite dishes—make it with chicken broth, or use vegetable broth to make it fully vegetarian. Loaded with beans, noodles and bright herbs, it's so comforting on a chilly day.
—Vivian Haen, Menomonee Falls, WI

Takes: 30 min. • **Makes:** 8 servings (2 qt.)

- ½ cup chopped onion
- 1 Tbsp. canola oil
- 2 garlic cloves, minced
- 1 medium tomato, chopped
- 2 cans (14½ oz. each) chicken or vegetable broth
- 1¾ cups water
- ½ tsp. each dried basil, oregano and celery flakes
- ¼ tsp. pepper
- 3 cans (15½ oz. each) great northern beans, rinsed and drained
- 1 cup uncooked elbow macaroni
- 1 Tbsp. minced parsley

1. In a large saucepan, saute onion in oil until tender; Add garlic; cook 1 minute longer. Add the tomato; simmer for 5 minutes. Add the broth, water and seasonings. Bring to a boil; cook for 5 minutes. Add beans and macaroni; return to a boil.
2. Reduce heat; simmer, uncovered, until the macaroni is tender, about 15 minutes. Sprinkle with parsley.

1 cup: 196 cal., 3g fat (0 sat. fat), 2mg chol., 676mg sod., 33g carb. (2g sugars, 9g fiber), 10g pro. **Diabetic exchanges:** 2 starch, ½ fat.

TURKEY SANDWICH WITH RASPBERRY-MUSTARD SPREAD

The tastes and textures in this autumn-themed sandwich are deliciously different and complementary. Crunchy bread, creamy avocado, meaty mushrooms, sweet raspberry, and tangy mustard layered over hearty turkey—it's sure to satisfy any craving!
—Sarah Savage, Buena Vista, VA

Takes: 25 min. • **Makes:** 2 servings

- 1 Tbsp. honey
- 1 Tbsp. spicy brown mustard
- 1 tsp. red raspberry preserves
- ¼ tsp. mustard seed
- 1 Tbsp. olive oil
- 4 oz. fresh mushrooms, thinly sliced
- 1 cup fresh baby spinach, coarsely chopped
- 1 garlic clove, minced
- ½ tsp. chili powder
- 4 slices multigrain bread, toasted
- 6 oz. sliced cooked turkey breast
- ½ medium ripe avocado, sliced

1. Combine the honey, mustard, preserves and mustard seed; set aside.
2. In a large skillet, heat oil over medium-high heat. Add mushrooms; cook and stir until tender, 4-5 minutes. Add spinach, garlic and chili powder; cook and stir until spinach is wilted, 3-4 minutes.
3. Spread half of the mustard mixture over 2 slices of toast. Layer with turkey, the mushroom mixture and avocado. Spread the remaining mustard mixture over the remaining toast; place over top.

1 sandwich: 449 cal., 16g fat (3g sat. fat), 68mg chol., 392mg sod., 40g carb. (14g sugars, 7g fiber), 35g pro.

> **TEST KITCHEN TIP**
> If you don't have mustard seed handy, use stone-ground mustard instead. You can also use apricot or strawberry preserves in place of the raspberry.

SUPER FAST MEXICAN SOUP

We take this spicy soup to rodeos on cool fall nights or sip it by a campfire. For toppings, try minced onions, avocado, cheese, jalapenos, sour cream and salsa.
—Gloria Huse, Simpsonville, SC

Takes: 25 min. • **Makes:** 4 servings

- 2 tsp. olive oil
- 1 lb. boneless skinless chicken thighs, cut into ¾-in. pieces
- 1 Tbsp. reduced-sodium taco seasoning
- 1 cup frozen corn
- 1 cup salsa
- 1 carton (32 oz.) reduced-sodium chicken broth

1. In a large saucepan, heat the oil over medium-high heat. Add chicken; cook and stir 6-8 minutes or until no longer pink. Stir in taco seasoning.
2. Add the remaining ingredients; bring to a boil. Reduce heat; simmer, uncovered, 5 minutes to allow flavors to blend. Skim fat before serving.

1½ cups: 254 cal., 11g fat (3g sat. fat), 76mg chol., 998mg sod., 14g carb. (5g sugars, 1g fiber), 25g pro.

TURKEY SANDWICH WITH RASPBERRY-MUSTARD SPREAD

BROCCOLI CHOWDER

I serve this soothing soup on chilly stay-at-home evenings. Nutmeg seasons the light, creamy broth that's full of tender broccoli florets and diced potatoes.
—Sue Call, Beech Grove, IN

Takes: 30 min.
Makes: 6 servings (1½ qt.)

- 3 cups fresh broccoli florets
- 2 cups diced peeled potatoes
- 2 cups water
- ⅓ cup sliced green onions
- 1 tsp. salt
- ½ tsp. pepper
- 3 Tbsp. butter
- 3 Tbsp. all-purpose flour
- ⅛ tsp. ground nutmeg
- 2 cups whole milk
- ½ cup shredded cheddar cheese

1. In a large saucepan, combine the first 6 ingredients. Bring to a boil. Reduce heat; cover and simmer for 12-14 minutes or until the vegetables are tender.
2. Meanwhile, in another saucepan, melt butter. Stir in flour and nutmeg until smooth. Gradually add milk. Bring to a boil; cook and stir for 2 minutes or until thickened. Stir into the vegetable mixture; heat through. Sprinkle individual servings with cheese.

1 cup: 200 cal., 11g fat (7g sat. fat), 36mg chol., 561mg sod., 19g carb. (5g sugars, 2g fiber), 7g pro.

QUICK SAUSAGE TORTELLINI SOUP

QUICK SAUSAGE TORTELLINI SOUP

I love this soup—it's easy to make and uses common ingredients found in my pantry. You can use any other types of sausage or pasta that you prefer.
—Annalise Lau, Newberg, OR

Prep: 20 min. • **Cook** 15 min.
Makes: 8 servings (3 qt.)

- 3 Italian turkey sausage links, casings removed
- 1 medium onion, chopped
- 4 garlic cloves, minced
- ¼ tsp. crushed red pepper flakes
- 6 cups reduced-sodium chicken broth
- 1 jar (24 oz.) pasta sauce
- 1 can (15 oz.) crushed tomatoes
- 2 Tbsp. tomato paste
- 2 tsp. dried basil
- 2 tsp. balsamic vinegar
- 1 tsp. dried parsley flakes
- 1½ tsp. sugar
- ½ tsp. dried oregano
- ¼ tsp. salt
- ½ tsp. pepper
- 2 cups frozen cheese tortellini
  Shredded Parmesan cheese, optional

1. In a Dutch oven, cook sausage and onion over medium heat until the sausage is no longer pink and the onion is tender, 5-7 minutes, breaking up the sausage into crumbles; drain. Add the garlic and pepper flakes; cook 1 minute longer. Stir in the broth, pasta sauce, crushed tomatoes, tomato paste, basil, vinegar, parsley flakes, sugar, oregano, salt and pepper; bring the mixture to a boil.
2. Add tortellini; cook, uncovered, until the tortellini are tender, 3-5 minutes, stirring occasionally. Serve immediately. If desired, top individual servings with shredded Parmesan cheese.

1½ cups: 192 cal., 5g fat (1g sat. fat), 24mg chol., 1167mg sod., 26g carb. (12g sugars, 4g fiber), 12g pro.

TACO BURGERS

My family loves the taste of tacos, but I've never been a fan of the mess. This recipe delivers the flavor of tacos in the convenience of a burger—and cleanup is a breeze. It really is the best of both, and it makes everyone happy!
—Linda Logan, Warren, OH

Takes: 25 min. • **Makes:** 6 servings

- 1   cup finely crushed corn chips
- 1   envelope taco seasoning
- 1   Tbsp. dried minced onion
- 1   large egg, lightly beaten
- 1½ lbs. ground beef
- 6   slices cheddar cheese
     Sandwich buns, split
     Lettuce leaves
     Tomato slices or salsa

1. In a large bowl, combine the corn chips, taco seasoning, onion and egg. Crumble beef over mixture and mix well. Shape into six patties.

2. Grill, covered, over medium heat or broil 4 in. from the heat for 7-8 minutes on each side or until a thermometer reads 160° and the juices run clear.

3. Top each burger with a cheese slice; heat just until the cheese begins to melt. Serve on buns with lettuce and either tomato slices or salsa.

1 burger: 418 cal., 24g fat (11g sat. fat), 135mg chol., 903mg sod., 20g carb. (0 sugars, 1g fiber), 29g pro.

TACO BURGERS

**MAKEOVER DELUXE
GRILLED CHEESE**

PASTA FAGIOLI SOUP

*My husband enjoys my version of this
dish so much, he doesn't order it at
restaurants anymore. Made with fresh
spinach, pasta and seasoned sausage,
this fast-to-fix soup is a meal by itself.*
—Brenda Thomas, Springfield, MO

Takes: 30 min. • **Makes:** 5 servings

- ½ lb. Italian turkey sausage links,
  casings removed, crumbled
- 1 small onion, chopped
- 1½ tsp. canola oil
- 1 garlic clove, minced
- 2 cups water
- 1 can (15½ oz.) great northern beans,
  rinsed and drained
- 1 can (14½ oz.) diced tomatoes,
  undrained
- 1 can (14½ oz.) reduced-sodium
  chicken broth
- ¾ cup uncooked elbow macaroni
- ¼ tsp. pepper
- 1 cup fresh spinach leaves,
  cut as desired
- 5 tsp. shredded Parmesan cheese

1. In a large saucepan, cook sausage over
medium heat until no longer pink; drain,
remove from pan and set aside. In the
same pan, saute onion in oil until tender.
Add garlic; saute 1 minute longer.
2. Add water, beans, tomatoes, broth,
macaroni and pepper; bring to a boil.
Cook, uncovered, until the macaroni is
tender, 8-10 minutes.
3. Reduce heat to low; stir in sausage
and spinach. Cook until spinach is wilted,
2-3 minutes. Garnish with cheese.
1⅓ cups: 228 cal., 7g fat (1g sat. fat),
29mg chol., 841mg sod., 27g carb.
(4g sugars, 6g fiber), 16g pro.

MAKEOVER DELUXE
GRILLED CHEESE

*With a few simple tricks, we boosted
the fantastic toasty taste of one of our
favorite mouthwatering sandwiches—
and slashed fat, calories and cholesterol
to less than half of the original.*
—*Taste of Home* Test Kitchen

Takes: 15 min. • **Makes:** 2 servings

- 1 small onion, halved and thinly sliced
- 4 slices French bread (½ in. thick)
  Butter-flavored cooking spray
- 1 oz. herbed fresh goat cheese
- ½ small tart apple, thinly sliced
- ½ cup shredded reduced-fat
  cheddar cheese

1. In a small skillet coated with cooking
spray, saute onion until tender; set aside.
2. Place bread slices on a baking sheet;
spritz with butter-flavored cooking spray.
Broil 4 in. from the heat until golden
brown, 2-3 minutes.
3. Spread goat cheese over 2 untoasted
sides of bread slices. Top with apple slices
and the reserved onion; sprinkle with
cheddar cheese. Broil until the cheese
is melted, 2-3 minutes longer. Top with
the remaining toast slices.
1 sandwich: 225 cal., 12g fat (6g sat.
fat), 30mg chol., 400mg sod., 18g carb.
(4g sugars, 2g fiber), 12g pro. **Diabetic
exchanges:** 2 medium-fat meat, 1 starch.

PASTA FAGIOLI SOUP

PORK & BOK CHOY UDON SOUP

PORK & BOK CHOY UDON SOUP

While traveling in Thailand, my husband enjoyed a tasty local soup that street vendors offered for only 50 cents a bowl. We tried many versions, and this comes the closest to his recollection. And we always double the recipe so we have lots of leftovers.
—Donna Noecker, Tulalip, WA

Takes: 25 min. • **Makes:** 6 servings 2¼ qt.

- 6 oz. dried Japanese udon noodles or fettuccine
- 1 small bunch bok choy, coarsely chopped
- 1 pork tenderloin (1 lb.), cut into ¼-in. slices
- 6 cups reduced-sodium chicken broth
- 3 Tbsp. reduced-sodium soy sauce
- 4 tsp. minced fresh gingerroot
- 3 garlic cloves, minced
  Optional: Thinly sliced green onions and Sriracha chili sauce

1. Cook noodles according to the package directions; drain and rinse with water. Meanwhile, in a Dutch oven, combine bok choy, pork, broth, soy sauce, ginger and garlic; bring just to a boil. Reduce heat; gently simmer, uncovered, 5-7 minutes or just until bok choy and pork are tender.
2. Add the noodles to the soup. Serve immediately. If desired, sprinkle with green onions and serve with chili sauce.
1½ cups: 225 cal., 4g fat (1g sat. fat), 42mg chol., 1309mg sod., 24g carb. (5g sugars, 3g fiber), 25g pro.

CHEESE-STUFFED BURGERS FOR TWO

Here's a sandwich that does traditional burgers one better with a surprise pocket of melty cheddar!
—Janet Wood, Windham, NH

Takes: 25 min. • **Makes:** 2 servings

- 1 Tbsp. finely chopped onion
- 1 Tbsp. ketchup
- 1 tsp. prepared mustard
- ¼ tsp. salt
- ⅛ tsp. pepper
- ½ lb. lean ground beef (90% lean)
- ¼ cup finely shredded cheddar cheese
- 2 hamburger buns, split
  Lettuce leaves and tomato slices, optional

1. In a small bowl, combine the first 5 ingredients. Crumble beef over the mixture and mix well. Shape into 4 thin patties. Sprinkle cheese over 2 of the patties; top with the remaining patties and press the edges firmly to seal.
2. Grill, covered, over medium heat for 6 minutes on each side or until a thermometer reads 160° and the juices run clear. Serve on buns with lettuce and tomato if desired.
1 serving: 357 cal., 15g fat (7g sat. fat), 84mg chol., 787mg sod., 25g carb. (4g sugars, 1g fiber), 28g pro. **Diabetic exchanges:** 3 lean meat, 1½ starch, 1½ fat.

CHEDDAR FRENCH DIP SANDWICHES

With leftover roast beef or deli beef, it takes almost no time at all to fix these satisfying hot sandwiches. They are perfect for hectic days.
—Pollyanna Szwej, Bridgeport, NY

Takes: 20 min. • **Makes:** 4 servings

- ¼ cup butter, cubed
- 2 garlic cloves, minced
- 4 ciabatta rolls, split
- 1 cup shredded cheddar cheese
- 1 lb. thinly sliced roast beef
- 1 can (14½ oz.) beef broth

1. In a small skillet, melt butter. Add garlic; saute for 1 minute. Place rolls on a baking sheet; brush the cut sides with the garlic butter. Sprinkle with cheese. Broil 3-4 in. from the heat for 2-3 minutes or until the cheese is melted.
2. In a large saucepan, combine beef and broth; heat through. Using tongs or a slotted spoon, place the beef on the rolls. Serve hot sandwiches with the remaining broth for dipping.

1 sandwich: 664 cal., 27g fat (15g sat. fat), 123mg chol., 1885mg sod., 71g carb. (4g sugars, 4g fiber), 40g pro.

CHEDDAR FRENCH DIP SANDWICHES

SZECHUAN BURGERS WITH BOK CHOY SLAW

This recipe puts a whole new spin on the basic beef burger: a little sweet, a little spice and a lot of flavor. Make the slaw ahead of time to let the flavors combine, then refrigerate until ready to use.
—Amy Fossett, Severn, MD

Prep: 35 min. • **Cook:** 10 min./batch
Makes: 8 servings

- 4 baby bok choy
- ½ cup shredded carrots
- 5 Tbsp. honey, divided
- 3 Tbsp. canola oil
- 3 Tbsp. rice vinegar, divided
- 1 Tbsp. reduced-sodium soy sauce
- ½ tsp. Chinese five-spice powder
- ¼ cup sliced water chestnuts, chopped
- 4 Tbsp. sesame oil, divided
- 2 Tbsp. finely chopped red onion
- 2 Tbsp. chili garlic sauce
- 2 Tbsp. peanut butter
- 1 Tbsp. minced fresh cilantro
- 2 garlic cloves, minced
- 2 tsp. minced fresh gingerroot
- 2 lbs. ground beef
- 8 slices fresh pineapple
- 1 pkg. (12.80 oz.) Hawaiian sweet hamburger buns

1. Trim and discard the root end of the bok choy. Slice leaves into ribbons and thinly slice stalks; transfer to a large bowl. Add carrots, 1 Tbsp. honey, the canola oil, 2 Tbsp. vinegar, the soy sauce and Chinese five-spice powder; toss to coat. Set aside.
2. In another large bowl, combine water chestnuts, 3 Tbsp. sesame oil, red onion, chili garlic sauce, peanut butter, cilantro, garlic, ginger and the remaining 4 Tbsp. honey and 1 Tbsp. vinegar. Add beef; mix lightly but thoroughly. Shape into eight ½-in.-thick patties.
3. Brush pineapple with remaining 1 Tbsp. sesame oil. Heat a grill pan or large skillet over medium-high heat. Cook pineapple until lightly browned, 2-3 minutes on each side. Remove and keep warm.
4. In the same pan, cook the burgers, in batches, over medium heat until a thermometer reads 160°, 5-6 minutes on each side. Serve in buns with bok choy slaw and pineapple.

1 burger: 583 cal., 31g fat (9g sat. fat), 95mg chol., 570mg sod., 49g carb. (29g sugars, 3g fiber), 27g pro.

CHICKEN TOMATILLO SOUP

I had a lot of tomatillos and wanted to make something other than salsa verde, so I combined two favorite recipes, added my own special touches and made chicken tomatillo soup. Feel free to add cayenne pepper or Tabasco sauce to spice it up.
—Katrina Krumm, Apple Valley, MN

Prep: 1 hour • **Cook:** 3¾ hours
Makes: 8 servings (3 qt.)

- 2 Tbsp. olive oil
- 1 medium onion, chopped
- 3 garlic cloves, minced
- 1 carton (32 oz.) reduced-sodium chicken broth
- 1 lb. tomatillos, husks removed and chopped (about 2 cups)
- 2 medium tomatoes, chopped
- 1 medium sweet red pepper, chopped
- 1 lb. boneless skinless chicken breast halves
- 2 Tbsp. taco seasoning
- 1 can (15 oz.) garbanzo beans or chickpeas, rinsed and drained
- 1 can (15 oz.) Southwestern black beans, undrained
- 3 cups fresh or frozen corn, thawed
  Optional toppings: shredded cheddar cheese, minced fresh cilantro and sour cream

1. In a Dutch oven, heat oil over medium-high heat. Add onion; cook and stir until tender, 6-8 minutes. Add garlic; cook 1 minute longer. Stir in broth, tomatillos, tomatoes and red pepper. Bring to a boil; reduce heat. Simmer, covered, until the vegetables are tender, about 15 minutes. Cool slightly; puree in batches in a blender.
2. Place chicken in a 5- or 6-qt. slow cooker; sprinkle with taco seasoning. Pour tomatillo mixture over top. Add garbanzo and black beans. Cook, covered, on low until a thermometer inserted in chicken reads 165°, 3½ to 4 hours.
3. Remove chicken; shred with 2 forks. Return to slow cooker. Add corn. Cook soup, covered, until heated through, about 15-30 minutes longer. Serve with toppings of your choice.

Freeze option: Freeze the cooled soup in freezer containers. To use, partially thaw in refrigerator overnight. Heat through in a saucepan, stirring occasionally and adding a little broth if necessary.

CHERRY CHICKEN CROISSANTS

1¼ cups: 290 cal., 8g fat (1g sat. fat), 31mg chol., 722mg sod., 36g carb. (10g sugars, 8g fiber), 21g pro. **Diabetic exchanges:** 2 starch, 2 lean meat, 1 vegetable, 1 fat.

CHERRY CHICKEN CROISSANTS

I had a similar chicken salad at a restaurant and created my own version. It seems like an odd combination, but the ingredients work really well together. My children love it, and it only takes a few minutes to cut everything up—so easy!
—Katrina Gladdish, Grawn, MI

Takes: 10 min. • **Makes:** 6 servings

- 2 cups diced cooked chicken
- 3 celery ribs, chopped
- ½ cup dried cherries
- ½ cup chopped walnuts
- ½ cup halved green grapes
- 8 bacon strips, cooked and crumbled
- ½ cup mayonnaise
- 6 croissants, split

In a large bowl, combine the first 7 ingredients. Serve on croissants.

1 sandwich: 616 cal., 39g fat (12g sat. fat), 92mg chol., 613mg sod., 41g carb. (18g sugars, 3g fiber), 24g pro.
HEALTH TIP Croissants make these sandwiches special, but you can switch to whole wheat bread and save nearly 100 calories per serving.

TEST KITCHEN TIP
If you don't keep dried cherries on hand, dried cranberries would also taste wonderful.

CHORIZO & CHICKPEA SOUP

Chorizo adds its own spice to the broth of this soup, creating delicious flavor with no need for more seasonings. And while it's cooking, the whole house smells delicious.
—Jaclyn McKewan, Lancaster, NY

Prep: 15 min. • **Cook:** 8¼ hours
Makes: 1½ qt.

- 3 cups water
- 2 celery ribs, chopped
- 2 fully cooked Spanish chorizo links (3 oz. each), cut into ½-in. pieces
- ½ cup dried chickpeas or garbanzo beans
- 1 can (14½ oz.) petite diced tomatoes, undrained
- ½ cup ditalini or other small pasta
- ½ tsp. salt

Place the water, celery, chorizo and chickpeas in a 4- or 5-qt. slow cooker. Cook, covered, on low until the beans are tender, 8-10 hours. Stir in tomatoes, pasta and salt; cook, covered, on high until the pasta is tender, 15-20 minutes.

Freeze option: Freeze cooled soup in freezer containers. To use, partially thaw in refrigerator overnight. Heat through in a saucepan, stirring occasionally; add a little water if necessary.

1 cup: 180 cal., 8g fat (3g sat. fat), 18mg chol., 569mg sod., 23g carb. (3g sugars, 6g fiber), 9g pro. **Diabetic exchanges:** 1½ starch, 1 high-fat meat.

HEALTH TIP Chorizo is very flavorful, but it's also high in fat. Using just a small amount, as in this dish, is a smart way to boost the flavor without creating a high-fat soup.

TUNA ARTICHOKE MELTS

This dressed-up version of a tuna melt elevates a traditional diner favorite to something fancier courtesy of lemon seasoning and artichoke hearts. Serve it on the patio for lunch with a friend!
—Evelyn Basinger, Linville, VA

Takes: 15 min. • **Makes:** 2 servings

- 1 can (6 oz.) light water-packed tuna, drained and flaked
- ⅓ cup coarsely chopped water-packed artichoke hearts, rinsed and drained
- 2 Tbsp. fat-free mayonnaise
- ½ cup shredded reduced-fat Mexican cheese blend, divided
- ¼ tsp. salt-free lemon-pepper seasoning
- ⅛ tsp. dried oregano
- 2 English muffins, split and toasted

1. In a small bowl, combine the tuna, artichokes, mayonnaise, ¼ cup cheese, the lemon-pepper and oregano. Spread over the English muffin halves.

2. Place on a baking sheet. Broil 4-6 in. from the heat for 3-5 minutes or until heated through. Sprinkle with the remaining cheese; broil 1-2 minutes longer or until cheese is melted.

2 muffin halves: 335 cal., 8g fat (4g sat. fat), 47mg chol., 989mg sod., 31g carb. (3g sugars, 2g fiber), 34g pro.

READER REVIEW

"These were delicious! I will definitely make them again. Great for a quick weeknight meal and then I can enjoy any leftover mix for lunch the next day!"

DELORES14, TASTEOFHOME.COM

CHORIZO & CHICKPEA SOUP

CHICKEN CAESAR WRAPS

This classic cold sandwich with tender chicken, Parmesan cheese and chopped Caesar croutons uses just the right amount of dressing. It's a quick and tasty lunch or dinner.
—Nancy Pratt, Longview, TX

Takes: 15 min. • **Makes:** 6 servings

- ¾ cup reduced-fat creamy Caesar salad dressing
- ¼ cup grated Parmesan cheese
- ½ tsp. garlic powder
- ¼ tsp. pepper
- 3 cups cubed cooked chicken breast
- 2 cups torn romaine
- ¾ cup Caesar salad croutons, coarsely chopped
- 6 whole wheat tortillas (8 in.), room temperature

In a large bowl, combine the dressing, cheese, garlic powder and pepper. Add the chicken, romaine and croutons. Spoon ⅔ cup of the chicken mixture down the center of each tortilla; roll up.

1 wrap: 337 cal., 12g fat (2g sat. fat), 57mg chol., 730mg sod., 29g carb. (2g sugars, 4g fiber), 27g pro. **Diabetic exchanges:** 3 lean meat, 2½ starch, ½ fat.

CURRIED BEEF PITA POCKETS

CURRIED BEEF PITA POCKETS

If there's anyone in your family who thinks they won't like the taste of curry, serve this...they might be a curry lover forever!
—Mary Ann Kosmas, Minneapolis, MN

Prep: 5 min. • **Cook:** 30 min.
Makes: 4 servings

- 1 lb. ground beef
- 1 medium onion, chopped
- 1 garlic clove, halved
- 1 Tbsp. curry powder
- ½ cup water
- ½ tsp. salt
- ½ tsp. sugar
- ¼ tsp. pepper
- 1 medium tomato, seeded and diced
- 1 medium zucchini, diced
- 8 pita pocket halves
  Refrigerated tzatziki sauce, optional

1. In a large cast-iron or other heavy skillet, brown ground beef with the onion, garlic and curry. Drain; discard the garlic. Stir in water, salt, sugar and pepper. Cover and simmer for 15 minutes.

2. Add tomato and zucchini; cook just until heated through. Spoon the meat mixture into pita breads. If desired, serve with tzatziki sauce.

2 filled pita halves: 393 cal., 14g fat (5g sat. fat), 70mg chol., 665mg sod., 38g carb. (4g sugars, 3g fiber), 27g pro. **HEALTH TIP** A simple switch to 90% lean ground beef would save 4 grams of fat per serving; to save 8 grams per serving, use 95% lean.

DELI TURKEY LETTUCE WRAPS

I used to make these when I worked at a restaurant in Hawaii. Low-fat, low-carb, high-protein, quick and delicious, they're a great choice before or after a workout. And they're pretty to serve.
—Duncan Omarzu, Astoria, NY

Takes: 25 min. • **Makes:** servings

- 2 tsp. olive oil
- ½ medium red onion, thinly sliced
- 6 oz. sliced deli turkey, chopped
- 6 cherry tomatoes, halved
- 2 tsp. balsamic vinegar
- 6 Bibb or Boston lettuce leaves
- ½ medium ripe avocado, peeled and cubed
- ¼ cup shredded Swiss cheese
- ¼ cup alfalfa sprouts, optional

1. In a large skillet, heat oil over medium-high heat. Add onion; cook and stir until tender, 3-4 minutes. Add the turkey; heat through. Stir in the tomatoes and vinegar just until combined.

2. Serve turkey mixture in lettuce leaves. Top with avocado, cheese and if desired, alfalfa sprouts.

3 lettuce wraps: 270 cal., 16g fat (4g sat. fat), 43mg chol., 799mg sod., 11g carb. (4g sugars, 4g fiber), 22g pro. **Diabetic exchanges:** 3 lean meat, 1½ fat, 1 vegetable.

HEALTH TIP Deli meat is typically lean, like the turkey used in these low-carb wraps, but it's also high in sodium. Switch to leftover cooked turkey or chicken if you want to cut back on salt.

DELI TURKEY LETTUCE WRAPS

CREAMY CHICKEN RICE SOUP

CREAMY CHICKEN RICE SOUP

I created this flavorful soup by making adjustments to a favorite stovetop casserole. We love it for lunch with a crisp roll and fresh fruit.
—Janice Mitchell, Aurora, CO

Takes: 30 min.
Makes: 4 servings (1¼ qt.)

- 1 Tbsp. canola oil
- 1 medium carrot, chopped
- 1 celery rib, chopped
- ½ cup chopped onion
- ½ tsp. minced garlic
- ⅓ cup uncooked long grain rice
- ¾ tsp. dried basil
- ¼ tsp. pepper
- 2 cans (14½ oz. each) reduced-sodium chicken broth
- 3 Tbsp. all-purpose flour
- 1 can (5 oz.) evaporated milk
- 2 cups cubed cooked chicken breast

1. In a large saucepan, heat the oil over medium-high heat; saute carrot, celery and onion until tender. Add garlic; cook and stir 1 minute. Stir in rice, seasonings and broth; bring to a boil. Reduce heat; simmer, covered, until the rice is tender, about 15 minutes.
2. Mix flour and milk until smooth; stir into the soup. Bring to a boil; cook and stir the mixture until thickened, about 2 minutes. Stir in chicken; heat through.
1¼ cups: 312 cal., 9g fat (3g sat. fat), 71mg chol., 699mg sod., 26g carb. (6g sugars, 1g fiber), 29g pro. **Diabetic exchanges:** 3 lean meat, 2 starch, 1 fat.

READER REVIEW
"This is the soup I turn to when I want creamy chicken soup in the winter. I use cornstarch instead of flour for my gluten-free hubby. I love the different basil flavor."

HOMEMADEWITHLOVE,
TASTEOFHOME.COM

CHAMPION ROAST BEEF SANDWICHES

SWEET & SOUR BURGERS

Subtle Asian flavors of ginger and sesame make this burger something special. Be creative with toppings—add any that fit your palate.
—Jessie Apfe, Berkeley, CA

Prep: 20 min. • **Grill:** 15 min
Makes: 4 servings

- 2 Tbsp. soy sauce
- 2 tsp. sesame oil
- 1 Tbsp. sweet-and-sour sauce
- 1 garlic clove, minced
- 1 tsp. minced fresh gingerroot
- ¼ cup chopped green onions
- 1 lb. ground beef
- 4 whole wheat hamburger buns, split
- ⅓ cup mayonnaise
- 4 leaf lettuce leaves
- 4 slices tomato

1. Combine the first 6 ingredients. Add beef; mix lightly but thoroughly. Shape into four ½-in.-thick patties.
2. Grill burgers, covered, over medium heat until a thermometer reads 160°, 6-7 minutes on each side. Grill buns, cut side down, until toasted, 30-60 seconds.
3. Spread the buns with mayonnaise. Top with burgers, lettuce and tomato.

1 burger: 480 cal., 31g fat (8g sat. fat), 71mg chol., 872mg sod., 25g carb. (5g sugars, 4g fiber), 26g pro.

CHAMPION ROAST BEEF SANDWICHES

When I have time, I like to prepare a roast with this much-requested recipe in mind. But when I need a quick meal in a hurry, I use deli roast beef with delicious results.
—Ann Eastman, Santa Monica, CA

Takes: 15 min. • **Makes:** 4 servings

- ½ cup sour cream
- 1 Tbsp. onion soup mix
- 1 Tbsp. prepared horseradish, drained
- ⅛ tsp. pepper
- 8 slices rye or pumpernickel bread
- ½ lb. sliced roast beef
  Lettuce leaves

In a bowl, combine first 4 ingredients. Spread 1 Tbsp. on each slice of bread. Top 4 slices of bread with roast beef and lettuce; cover with remaining bread.
1 sandwich: 318 cal., 11g fat (6g sat. fat), 60mg chol., 1401mg sod., 34g carb. (4g sugars, 4g fiber), 18g pro.

COBB SALAD WRAPS

COBB SALAD WRAPS

Homemade dressing lightens up these refreshing tortilla wraps. The avocado, bacon, blue cheese and tomato deliver the flavors I enjoy most while keeping me on my healthy eating plan.
—Lynne Van Wagenen, Salt Lake City, UT

Takes: 15 min. • **Makes:** 4 servings

2 cups cubed cooked chicken breast
½ cup chopped avocado
4 bacon strips, cooked and crumbled
1 celery rib, thinly sliced
1 green onion, sliced
2 Tbsp. chopped ripe olives
2 Tbsp. crumbled blue cheese
2 Tbsp. lemon juice
1 Tbsp. honey
1½ tsp. Dijon mustard
1 garlic clove, minced
¼ tsp. dill weed
¼ tsp. salt
⅛ tsp. pepper
1 Tbsp. olive oil

4 romaine leaves, torn
4 whole wheat tortillas (8 in.), warmed
1 medium tomato, chopped

1. In a small bowl, combine chicken, avocado, bacon, celery, onion, olives and cheese. In another bowl, combine lemon juice, honey, mustard, garlic, dill weed, salt and pepper. Whisk in the oil. Pour over the chicken mixture; toss to coat.
2. Place romaine on each tortilla; top with ⅔ cup of the chicken mixture. Sprinkle with chopped tomato; roll up.

1 wrap: 372 cal., 14g fat (3g sat. fat), 65mg chol., 607mg sod., 32g carb. (6g sugars, 6g fiber), 29g pro. **Diabetic exchanges:** 3 lean meat, 2 starch, 1 fat.

CAJUN CHICKEN CLUB

It takes just minutes to assemble these sandwiches. Cajun seasoning gives them a zippy flavor.
—J.M. Andrews, Marcellus, NY

Takes: 15 min. • **Makes:** 4 servings

4 boneless skinless chicken breast halves (4 oz. each)
½ to 1 tsp. Cajun seasoning
1 Tbsp. vegetable oil
4 slices Swiss cheese
¼ cup prepared creamy Parmesan salad dressing
4 sandwich rolls, split and toasted
8 tomato slices
8 bacon strips, cooked

1. Flatten the chicken to ⅜-in. thickness; sprinkle with Cajun seasoning. In a large skillet over medium heat, cook chicken in oil for 5 minutes on each side or until juices run clear. Place cheese over chicken. Remove from heat; cover and let stand for 1 minute or until the cheese begins to melt.
2. Spread dressing over both halves of the rolls. Layer the bottom halves with 2 slices of tomato, chicken and 2 strips of bacon; replace tops.

1 serving: 496 cal., 27g fat (11g sat. fat), 51mg chol., 813mg sod., 38g carb. (8g sugars, 2g fiber), 23g pro.

HAM & CHEESE POCKETS

These tasty sandwich pockets will please even picky eaters—they're stuffed with ingredients most kids like.
—Callie Myers, Rockport, TX

Prep: 15 min. + rising • **Bake:** 15 min.
Makes: 10 servings

- 1 loaf (1 lb.) frozen bread dough, thawed
- 2½ cups finely chopped fully cooked ham
- 1 cup shredded Swiss cheese
- 1 large egg yolk
- 1 Tbsp. water

1. Let dough rise according to package directions. Punch down; divide into 10 pieces. On a lightly floured surface, roll each piece into a 5-in. circle.
2. Place 1 circle on a greased baking sheet; top with ¼ cup ham and 2 Tbsp. cheese to within ½ in. of edge. Press filling to flatten. Combine egg yolk and water; brush edges of dough. Fold dough over filling and pinch edges to seal. Repeat with remaining dough and filling. Brush tops with the remaining egg yolk mixture. Bake at 375° until the crusts are golden brown, 15-20 minutes. Serve warm or cold.

1 pocket: 229 cal., 9g fat (3g sat. fat), 50mg chol., 729mg sod., 25g carb. (2g sugars, 1g fiber), 14g pro.

EASY CLAM CHOWDER

This recipe was given to me by an old college friend. Pair steaming bowlfuls with sourdough bread and a green salad.
—Kristy Doty, Riverside, CA

Takes: 30 min. • **Makes:** 8 servings (2 qt.)

- ½ lb. sliced bacon, diced
- 2 large onions, chopped
- 3 cans (6½ oz. each) minced clams
- 3 cups diced unpeeled potatoes
- ½ cup chicken broth
- 1 can (10¾ oz.) condensed cream of celery soup, undiluted
- 1¼ cups milk
- 1 cup heavy whipping cream
- 1 tsp. salt
- ½ tsp. pepper

1. In a Dutch oven, cook the bacon over medium heat until crisp. Using a slotted spoon, remove to paper towels; drain, reserving 2 Tbsp. drippings. Saute onions in the reserved drippings until tender.
2. Drain clams, reserving the juice; set clams aside. Add the potatoes, clam juice and broth to the onions. Cook over medium heat for 15 minutes or until the potatoes are tender. Stir in the clams, soup, milk, cream, salt, pepper and bacon; heat through.

1 cup: 277 cal., 19g fat (10g sat. fat), 59mg chol., 909mg sod., 20g carb. (6g sugars, 2g fiber), 9g pro.

OPEN-FACED TURKEY PHILLIES

This delicious sandwich started as a spin on a traditional Philly cheesesteak, using turkey in place of the beef and with some flavor tweaks to match!
—Lindsey Spinler, Sobieski, WI

Takes: 30 min. • **Makes:** 4 servings

- 1 lb. extra-lean ground turkey
- 2 medium green peppers, julienned
- 2 cups sliced fresh mushrooms
- 1 small onion, halved and sliced
- ½ cup reduced-fat creamy Caesar salad dressing, divided
- ¼ tsp. pepper
- 1 loaf (8 oz.) French bread, halved lengthwise
- 4 slices provolone cheese
  Additional reduced-fat creamy Caesar salad dressing, optional

1. Preheat broiler. In a large skillet over medium-high heat, cook turkey, green peppers, mushroom and onion until the turkey is no longer pink and the vegetables are tender, 8-10 minutes, breaking up turkey into crumbles; drain. Stir in ¼ cup dressing and the pepper.
2. Spread the remaining ¼ cup dressing over cut side of bread. Place on a baking sheet; broil 4-6 in. from heat until lightly toasted, 3-4 minutes. Spread turkey mixture over bread; top with cheese. Broil until the cheese is melted, 1-2 minutes longer. Cut each half into 2 slices. Serve with additional sauce on the side.

1 open-faced sandwich: 481 cal., 22g fat (5g sat. fat), 80mg chol., 1006mg sod., 38g carb. (7g sugars, 3g fiber), 36g pro.

HAM & CHEESE POCKETS

CURRIED CHICKEN SOUP

This started as a favorite recipe that my grandmother made. I added my own touches to the original recipe, including chickpeas, coconut milk and cilantro.
—Deanna Hindenach, Paw Paw, MI

Prep: 25 min. • **Cook:** 45 min.
Makes: 8 servings (2½ qt.)

- 4 tsp. curry powder
- ½ tsp. salt
- ½ tsp. pepper
- ½ tsp. cayenne pepper
- 1 lb. boneless skinless chicken breasts, cut into 1-in. cubes
- 3 medium carrots, chopped
- 1 medium sweet red pepper, chopped
- 1 small onion, chopped
- 2 Tbsp. olive oil
- 1 garlic clove, minced
- 1 can (15 oz.) garbanzo beans or chickpeas, rinsed and drained
- 1 can (14½ oz.) chicken broth
- 1 can (14½ oz.) diced tomatoes, drained
- 1 cup water
- 1 can (13.66 oz.) coconut milk
- ¾ cup minced fresh cilantro

1. In a large shallow dish, combine curry, salt, pepper and cayenne. Add the chicken a few pieces at a time; turn to coat.

2. In a large saucepan over medium heat, cook the chicken, carrots, red pepper and onion in oil for 4 minutes. Add garlic; cook 1-2 minutes longer or until chicken is browned and the vegetables are tender; drain.

3. Stir in the garbanzo beans, broth, tomatoes and water. Bring to a boil. Reduce heat; cover and simmer for 30 minutes. Stir in coconut milk; heat through. Garnish servings with cilantro.

1¼ cups: 270 cal., 16g fat (10g sat. fat), 32mg chol., 555mg sod., 17g carb. (5g sugars, 5g fiber), 16g pro.

GRILLED BACON-TOMATO SANDWICHES

Fresh basil, tangy Italian dressing and melted cheese meld perfectly in this simple sandwich. My family loves them, and they're so easy to prepare, I'm happy to make them any time.
—Betty Snoddy, Franklin, MO

Takes: 20 min. • **Makes:** 2 servings

GRILLED BACON-TOMATO SANDWICHES

- 4 slices Italian bread (½ in. thick)
- 4 slices provolone cheese (1 oz. each)
- 4 slices tomato
- 4 bacon strips, cooked and halved
- 2 tsp. minced fresh basil or ½ tsp. dried basil
- 2 Tbsp. Italian salad dressing

1. Top 2 slices of bread with a slice of cheese each; layer each with 2 tomato slices, 2 bacon strips, half of the basil and another cheese slice. Top with remaining bread. Brush Italian dressing over outside of sandwiches.

2. In a large skillet over medium heat, toast sandwiches for 2-3 minutes on each side or until cheese is melted.

1 sandwich: 471 cal., 26g fat (12g sat. fat), 56mg chol., 1251mg sod., 32g carb. (4g sugars, 2g fiber), 25g pro.

CHICKPEA TORTILLA SOUP

This vegan tortilla soup recipe is healthy, filling and family-friendly! We love how hearty and flavorful it is. We like to play around with the different toppings we add each time it's served.

—Julie Peterson, Crofton, MD

Takes: 30 min. • **Makes:** 8 servings (3 qt.)

- 1 Tbsp. olive oil
- 1 medium red onion, chopped
- 4 garlic cloves, minced
- 1 to 2 jalapeno peppers, seeded and chopped
- ¼ tsp. pepper
- 8 cups vegetable broth
- 1 cup red quinoa, rinsed
- 2 cans (15 oz. each) no-salt-added chickpeas or garbanzo beans, rinsed and drained
- 1 can (15 oz.) no-salt-added black beans, rinsed and drained
- 3 medium tomatoes, chopped
- 1 cup fresh or frozen corn
- ⅓ cup minced fresh cilantro
  Optional: Crushed tortilla chips, cubed avocado, lime wedges and additional chopped cilantro

Heat oil in a Dutch oven over medium-high heat. Add red onion, garlic, jalapeno and pepper; cook and stir until tender, 3-5 minutes. Add the broth and quinoa. Bring to a boil; reduce heat. Simmer, uncovered, until the quinoa is tender, about 10 minutes. Add beans, tomatoes, corn and cilantro; heat through. If desired, serve with optional toppings.

1½ cups: 289 cal., 5g fat (0 sat. fat), 0 chol., 702mg sod., 48g carb. (5g sugars, 9g fiber), 13g pro.

> **TEST KITCHEN TIP**
> You'll love how hearty and filling this is for a meatless soup. Don't skip the lime wedges—the little bit of acid really perks up the soup's warm flavor.

ZESTY TURKEY TOMATO SOUP

This chunky soup is full of flavor and zip! If you don't want as much heat, eliminate the jalapeno pepper. When serving to vegetarians, I omit the turkey and add a small can of garbanzo beans in the last few minutes of cooking.

—Katherine Preiss, Penfield, PA

Takes: 30 min. • **Makes:** 3 cups

- ¼ lb. lean ground turkey
- 1 small zucchini, diced
- 1 small onion, chopped
- 1 can (14½ oz.) reduced-sodium chicken broth
- 1 cup canned Mexican diced tomatoes
- ⅓ cup uncooked whole wheat spiral pasta
- ½ tsp. minced fresh basil
- ¼ tsp. ground cumin
- ⅛ tsp. pepper
- 1 Tbsp. chopped jalapeno pepper
  Shredded fat-free cheddar cheese, optional

1. In a large saucepan, cook the turkey, zucchini and onion over medium heat until meat is no longer pink; drain.

2. Stir in the broth, tomatoes, pasta, basil, cumin, pepper and jalapeno. Bring to a boil. Reduce heat; simmer, uncovered, for 13-15 minutes or until the pasta is tender. Garnish with cheese if desired.

Note: Wear disposable gloves when cutting hot peppers; the oils can burn skin. Avoid touching your face.

1 cup: 143 cal., 4g fat (1g sat. fat), 30mg chol., 719mg sod., 17g carb. (8g sugars, 3g fiber), 11g pro. **Diabetic exchanges:** 1 starch, 1 lean meat.

CHICKPEA TORTILLA SOUP

GOURMET BARBECUE BEEF SANDWICHES

These beef sandwiches were a tradition in my family on winter vacations after a long day of skiing, but they're a hit any time. Serving the savory beef and melty provolone cheese on croissants makes the sandwiches a little more special.
—Katie Anderson, Vancouver, WA

....

Prep: 10 min. • **Cook:** 8 hours 5 min.
Makes: 12 servings

- 1 beef rump roast or bottom round roast (3 to 4 lbs.)
- ½ tsp. salt
- ¼ tsp. pepper
- 1 cup barbecue sauce
- 12 croissants, split
- 12 slices provolone cheese
  Optional ingredients: Tomato slices, lettuce leaves and red onion slices

1. Rub roast with salt and pepper. Place in a 5- or 6-qt. slow cooker. Cook, covered, on low 8-10 hours or until meat is tender.
2. Remove roast; cool slightly. Skim fat from cooking juices. Slice beef; return beef and cooking juices to slow cooker. Add barbecue sauce; heat through. Place croissant bottoms on a baking sheet; top with cheese. Broil 4-6 in. from heat until cheese is melted, 1-2 minutes. Top with beef slices; if desired, serve with optional toppings. Replace croissant tops.

CRABMEAT BOATS

1 sandwich: 511 cal., 25g fat (13g sat. fat), 125mg chol., 805mg sod., 38g carb. (15g sugars, 2g fiber), 33g pro.

TEST KITCHEN TIP
Mix and match favorite toppings for different takes on this slow-cooked sandwich. Try pepper jack cheese with french-fried onions or sharp cheddar with slaw.

CRABMEAT BOATS

I've been making this recipe for more than 40 years. The crab mixture isn't just great as a sandwich—you can also spread it on small rolls and serve them up as an appetizer.
—June Strang, Grand Blanc, MI

....

Prep: 20 min. • **Bake:** 15 min.
Makes: 2 servings

- 2 kaiser rolls, split
- 2 tsp. butter, softened
- 1 can (6 oz.) lump crabmeat, drained
- 4 oz. Swiss cheese, cubed
- 1 celery rib, chopped
- ¼ cup mayonnaise
- 1 tsp. minced fresh parsley
- ¼ tsp. seafood seasoning, optional
- ¼ tsp. paprika

Preheat oven to 400°. Carefully hollow out each roll, leaving a ½-in. shell (save removed bread for another use). Spread inside of rolls with butter. In a large bowl, combine the crabmeat, cheese, celery, mayonnaise, parsley, seafood seasoning if desired, and paprika; divide between rolls. Wrap each in foil and place on a baking sheet. Bake until cheese is melted, 15-20 minutes.

1 sandwich: 661 cal., 44g fat (16g sat. fat), 148mg chol., 863mg sod., 25g carb. (3g sugars, 2g fiber), 38g pro.

RICH SEAFOOD CHOWDER

This creamy, delectable soup is even better the next day. Substitute half-and-half or heavy cream for all or part of the milk to make the soup even richer.
—Anita Culver, Royersford, PA

Prep: 30 min. • **Cook:** 25 min.
Makes: 8 servings (2 qt.)

2 Tbsp. butter
1 small onion, chopped
1 celery rib, chopped
1 medium carrot, shredded
2 Tbsp. all-purpose flour
½ cup 2% milk
3 cups seafood stock
1 medium potato, peeled and diced
1 Tbsp. Worcestershire sauce
1 tsp. salt
½ tsp. pepper
1 lb. uncooked shrimp (41-50 per lb.), peeled and deveined
2 cans (6½ oz. each) chopped clams, drained
2 cans (6 oz. each) lump crabmeat, drained
1 pkg. (8 oz.) cream cheese, cubed
Minced fresh parsley

1. In a Dutch oven, heat the butter over medium-high heat. Add onion, celery and carrot; cook and stir until crisp-tender, 2-3 minutes. Stir in flour until blended; gradually add milk. Bring to a boil; cook and stir until thickened, about 2 minutes.

2. Add stock, potatoes, Worcestershire, salt and pepper; return to a boil. Reduce heat; cover and simmer until potatoes are tender, 10-15 minutes.

3. Add shrimp, clams, crab and cream cheese; cook and stir until the shrimp turn pink and and the cheese is melted, 4-5 minutes. Garnish with parsley.

1 cup: 272 cal., 15g fat (8g sat. fat), 164mg chol., 1076mg sod., 11g carb. (3g sugars, 1g fiber), 24g pro.

TEST KITCHEN TIP
Mix and match your favorite seafood in this chowder; scallops or flaky whitefish work well.

RICH SEAFOOD CHOWDER

PIZZA SLOPPY JOES

SPICY BUFFALO CHICKEN WRAPS

This recipe has a real kick and is one of my husband's favorites. It's ready in a flash, is easily doubled and the closest thing to restaurant Buffalo wings I've ever tasted in a light version.
—Jennifer Beck, Meridian, ID

....

Takes: 25 min. • **Makes:** 2 servings

- ½ tsp. canola oil
- ½ lb. boneless skinless chicken breast, cubed
- 2 Tbsp. Louisiana-style hot sauce
- 1 cup shredded lettuce
- 2 flour tortillas (6 in.), warmed
- 2 tsp. reduced-fat ranch salad dressing
- 2 Tbsp. crumbled blue cheese

1. In a large nonstick skillet, heat oil over medium heat. Cook chicken for 6 minutes; drain. Stir in hot sauce. Bring to a boil. Reduce heat; simmer, uncovered, for 3-5 minutes or until the sauce is thickened and the chicken is no longer pink.
2. Place lettuce on tortillas; drizzle with ranch dressing. Top with chicken mixture and blue cheese; roll up.

1 serving: 273 cal., 11g fat (3g sat. fat), 70mg chol., 453mg sod., 15g carb. (1g sugars, 1g fiber), 28g pro. **Diabetic exchanges:** 3 lean meat, 1½ fat, 1 starch.

READER REVIEW

"Being from the Buffalo area, I'm always happy to try new 'Buffalo chicken' recipes. This one was really great!"

MUFFBEAR74, TASTEOFHOME.COM

PIZZA SLOPPY JOES

If you're tired of the same old sloppy joes, here's a tasty twist. These kid-friendly sandwiches have a definite pizza flavor that families will love, but be sure to serve them with a fork!
—Connie Pettit, Logan, OH

....

Takes: 30 min. • **Makes:** 6 servings

- 1 lb. lean ground beef (90% lean)
- 1 medium onion, chopped
- ¼ cup chopped green pepper
- 1 jar (14 oz.) pizza sauce
- 3 oz. sliced turkey pepperoni (about 50 slices), chopped
- ½ tsp. dried basil
- ¼ tsp. dried oregano
- 6 hamburger buns, split
- 6 Tbsp. shredded part-skim mozzarella cheese

1. In a large nonstick skillet, cook beef, onion and pepper over medium heat until the meat is no longer pink. Drain if necessary. Stir in the pizza sauce, pepperoni and herbs. Bring to a boil. Reduce heat; cover and simmer for 10 minutes.
2. Spoon ⅔ cup of the beef mixture onto each bun; sprinkle with cheese. Place on a baking sheet. Broil 3-4 in. from the heat for 1 minute or until the cheese is melted. Replace tops.

Freeze option: Freeze cooled meat mixture in freezer containers. To use, partially thaw in refrigerator overnight. Heat through in a saucepan, stirring occasionally and adding a little water if necessary. Serve on buns.

1 sandwich: 329 cal., 11g fat (4g sat. fat), 59mg chol., 825mg sod., 29g carb. (8g sugars, 3g fiber), 26g pro.

SPICY BUFFALO CHICKEN WRAPS

DILLY CHICKEN SANDWICHES

DILLY CHICKEN SANDWICHES

The creamy lemon-dill spread adds some summery flavor to tender chicken served between slices of grilled French bread and a layer of lettuce and tomato. The whole family thinks it's about perfect for lunch or for a light dinner.
—Orien Major, Hinton, AB

....

Takes: 30 min. • **Makes:** 4 servings

- 4 boneless skinless chicken breast halves (4 oz. each)
- 6 Tbsp. butter, divided
- 1 garlic clove, minced
- ¾ tsp. dill weed, divided
- 8 slices French bread (½ in. thick)
- ¼ cup cream cheese, softened
- 2 tsp. lemon juice
- 4 lettuce leaves
- 8 slices tomato

1. Flatten chicken to ¼-in. thickness; set aside. In a large skillet, saute garlic and ¼ tsp. dill in 3 Tbsp. butter for 1 minute; Add chicken; cook over medium heat until juices run clear, 3-4 minutes on each side. Remove and keep warm.

2. Spread both sides of bread with the remaining butter. In a large skillet or griddle, grill bread on both sides until golden brown.

3. Meanwhile, combine the cream cheese, lemon juice and the remaining ½ tsp. dill; spread on one side of the grilled bread. Place lettuce, chicken and tomato on 4 slices of bread; top with remaining bread.

1 sandwich: 490 cal., 27g fat (15g sat. fat), 123mg chol., 591mg sod., 32g carb. (2g sugars, 2g fiber), 30g pro.

INDIAN-SPICED BEEFY LETTUCE WRAPS

When I'm short on time but want something with spectacular flavor, this is one of my go-tos. I love Indian flavors and almost always have coconut milk, a jar of mango chutney, and garam masala in my pantry. You can make a Chinese version with hoisin sauce and five-spice powder, too.
—Noelle Myers, Grand Forks, ND

....

Takes: 30 min. • **Makes:** 4 servings

- 1 lb. ground beef
- 1 medium onion, finely chopped
- 2 garlic cloves, minced
- ⅓ cup mango chutney
- 2 Tbsp. soy sauce
- 1 tsp. garam masala
- 1 pkg. (12.70 oz.) Asian crunch salad mix
- ¼ cup canned coconut milk
- 12 Bibb or Boston lettuce leaves
- 1 medium mango, peeled and sliced

1. In a large skillet, cook beef, onion and garlic over medium heat until the beef is no longer pink and onion is tender, about 6-8 minutes, breaking up the beef into crumbles; drain. Stir in chutney, soy sauce and garam marsala; heat through. Add salad mix (reserve the packets); cook and stir until slightly wilted, about 5 minutes.

2. Combine coconut milk and dressing packet until smooth. Spoon beef mixture into lettuce leaves; sprinkle with contents from the toppings packet. Drizzle with coconut milk mixture and top with mango.

3 filled lettuce wraps: 493 cal., 22g fat (8g sat. fat), 74mg chol., 957mg sod., 48g carb. (33g sugars, 5g fiber), 24g pro.

CABBAGE BARLEY SOUP

When my neighbor's garden produced an abundance of cabbage, a group of us had a contest to see who could invent the best cabbage dish. My vegetarian cabbage soup was the unanimous winner.
—Lorraine Caland, Shuniah, ON

Prep: 15 min. • **Cook:** 6¼ hours
Makes: 8 servings (3 qt.)

- 1 cup dried brown lentils, rinsed
- ½ cup medium pearl barley
- 3 medium carrots, chopped
- 2 celery ribs, chopped
- ½ tsp. poultry seasoning
- ¼ tsp. pepper
- 1 bottle (46 oz.) V8 juice
- 4 cups water
- 8 cups shredded cabbage (about 16 oz.)
- ½ lb. sliced fresh mushrooms
- ¾ tsp. salt

1. Place the first 8 ingredients in a 5- or 6-qt. slow cooker. Add cabbage. Cook, covered, on low until the lentils are tender, 6-8 hours.
2. Stir in mushrooms and salt. Cook, covered, on low until mushrooms are tender, 15-20 minutes.

Freeze option: Freeze cooled soup in freezer containers. To use, partially thaw in refrigerator overnight. Heat through in a saucepan, stirring occasionally, adding water if necessary.

1½ cups: 197 cal., 1g fat (0 sat. fat), 0 chol., 678mg sod., 39g carb. (7g sugars, 9g fiber), 11g pro. **Diabetic exchanges:** 2½ starch, 1 lean meat.

TEST KITCHEN TIP
One medium head of cabbage will yield about 8 cups shredded.

HAM & SWISS WITH A TWIST

To satisfy hearty appetites, try this different take on a grilled ham and cheese. The apples give it a sweet taste twist. Try using rye bread as a delicious alternative.
—Marietta Slater, Justin, TX

Takes: 25 min. • **Makes:** 4 servings

- 1 large onion, sliced
- 4 Tbsp. butter, softened, divided
- 8 slices Texas toast
- 2 Tbsp. spicy brown mustard
- ½ lb. thinly sliced deli ham
- 1 medium apple, sliced
- 4 slices Swiss cheese

1. In a large skillet, cook onion in 1 Tbsp. butter over medium heat for 8-10 minutes or until golden brown, stirring frequently.
2. Spread remaining butter over 1 side of each slice of Texas toast. Place slices, buttered side down, on a griddle. Spread with mustard; layer with ham, apple, onion and cheese. Top with another slice of toast, buttered side up. Cook sandwich over medium heat for 3-4 minutes or until it is golden brown. Carefully turn; cook for 2 minutes longer or until the cheese is melted.

1 serving: 510 cal., 26g fat (14g sat. fat), 88mg chol., 1414mg sod., 44g carb. (9g sugars, 3g fiber), 23g pro.

CABBAGE BARLEY SOUP

Give Me 5 or Fewer

You'll be amazed at the dinners you can create with just a handful of ingredients. Each recipe in this chapter calls for no more than five ingredients (not counting salt and pepper, oil and optional items). Save on time, save on budget—and savor the compliments you'll receive!

Enchilada Chicken (p. 85) **Nutty Cheese Tortellini** (p. 90) **Zucchini-Parmesan Bake** (p. 93)
Avocado Egg Salad Toast (p. 85) **Maple-Roasted Chicken & Acorn Squash** (p. 83)

RIBS WITH PLUM SAUCE

I found the recipe for this tangy-sweet basting sauce when a surplus of plums sent me searching for new ideas to use the fruit. In summer, I finish the ribs on the grill, brushing on the sauce, after first baking them in the oven.
—Marie Hoyer, Hodgenville, KY

Prep: 10 min. • **Bake:** 1½ hours
Makes: 6 servings

- 5 to 6 lbs. pork spareribs
- ¾ cup reduced-sodium soy sauce
- ¾ cup plum jam or apricot preserves
- ¾ cup honey
- 2 to 3 garlic cloves, minced

1. Preheat oven to 350°. Cut ribs into serving-size pieces; place with bone side down on a rack in a shallow roasting pan. Cover and bake for 1 hour or until ribs are tender; drain.
2. In a small bowl, combine remaining ingredients; brush some sauce over ribs. Bake at 350° or grill over medium heat, uncovered, 30 minutes longer, turning and basting occasionally.
1 serving: 948 cal., 53g fat (20g sat. fat), 213mg chol., 2005mg sod., 61g carb. (57g sugars, 0 fiber), 55g pro.

SCALLOPS IN SAGE CREAM

SCALLOPS IN SAGE CREAM

I wanted to show off the ocean freshness of the scallops I bought on the dock from a local fisherman, so I used simple ingredients to showcase them. The sage cream sauce is delicate but brightens up this special dish.
—Joan Churchill, Dover, NH

Takes: 20 min. • **Makes:** 4 servings

- 1½ lbs. sea scallops
- ¼ tsp. salt
- ⅛ tsp. pepper
- 3 Tbsp. olive oil, divided
- ½ cup chopped shallots
- ¾ cup heavy whipping cream
- 6 fresh sage leaves, thinly sliced
  Hot cooked pasta, optional

1. Sprinkle scallops with salt and pepper. In a large skillet, cook scallops in 2 Tbsp. oil for 1½-2 minutes on each side or until firm and opaque. Remove and keep warm.
2. In the same skillet, saute shallots in the remaining oil until tender. Add the cream; bring to a boil. Cook and stir for 30 seconds or until slightly thickened.
3. Return the scallops to the pan; heat through. Stir in sage. Serve with pasta if desired.
1 serving: 408 cal., 28g fat (12g sat. fat), 117mg chol., 441mg sod., 9g carb. (1g sugars, 0 fiber), 30g pro.

SAUSAGE SPINACH SALAD

Want a fast way to turn a salad into a hearty meal? Add sausage. The mustard dressing also goes with smoked salmon or chicken.

—Deborah Williams, Peoria, AZ

....

Takes: 20 min. • **Makes:** 2 servings

- 4 tsp. olive oil, divided
- 2 fully cooked Italian chicken sausage links (3 oz. each), cut into ¼-in. slices
- ½ medium onion, halved and sliced
- 4 cups fresh baby spinach
- 1½ tsp. balsamic vinegar
- 1 tsp. stone-ground mustard

1. In a large nonstick skillet, heat 1 tsp. oil over medium heat. Add the sausage and onion; cook and stir until sausage is lightly browned and onion is crisp-tender.
2. Place spinach in a large bowl. In a small bowl, whisk balsamic vinegar, mustard and remaining oil. Drizzle over spinach and toss to coat. Add sausage mixture; serve immediately.

2½ cups: 244 cal., 16g fat (3g sat. fat), 65mg chol., 581mg sod., 8g carb. (3g sugars, 2g fiber), 17g pro. **Diabetic exchanges:** 2 lean meat, 2 vegetable, 2 fat.

READER REVIEW

"When I made this, I put the spinach in the skillet when the sausage and onions were just about fully cooked. I continued sauteing until the spinach was cooked down. Delicious!"

MURPHYNJ, TASTEOFHOME.COM

MAPLE-ROASTED CHICKEN & ACORN SQUASH

PICTURED ON P. 81

When I became a new mother, my mom helped me find comforting and simple recipes to have on hand. This terrific roast chicken was a happy discovery.

—Sara Eilers, Surprise, AZ

....

Prep: 15 min. • **Bake:** 35 min.
Makes: 6 servings

- 1 medium acorn squash
- 4 medium carrots, chopped (about 2 cups)
- 1 medium onion, cut into 1-in. pieces
- 6 bone-in chicken thighs (about 2¼ lbs.)
- ½ cup maple syrup
- 1 tsp. salt
- ½ tsp. coarsely ground pepper

1. Preheat oven to 450°. Cut squash lengthwise in half; remove and discard seeds. Cut each half crosswise into ½-in. slices; discard ends. Place squash, carrots and onion in a greased 13x9-in. baking pan; top with chicken, skin side down. Roast 10 minutes.
2. Turn chicken over; drizzle with maple syrup and sprinkle with salt and pepper. Roast 25-30 minutes longer or until a thermometer inserted in chicken reads 170°-175° and the vegetables are tender.

1 serving: 363 cal., 14g fat (4g sat. fat), 81mg chol., 497mg sod., 36g carb. (23g sugars, 3g fiber), 24g pro. **Diabetic exchanges:** 3 lean meat, 2 starch, 1 vegetable.

SAUSAGE SPINACH SALAD

5i ⏱

LEMON FETA CHICKEN

This bright, Greek-inspired chicken is a busy-day lifesaver! My husband and I prepare the dish often, and it's a hit every single time.
—Ann Cain, Morrill, NE

....

Takes: 25 min. • **Makes:** 4 servings

- 4 boneless skinless chicken breast halves (4 oz. each)
- 2 to 3 Tbsp. lemon juice
- ¼ cup crumbled feta cheese
- 1 tsp. dried oregano
- ¼ to ½ tsp. pepper

1. Preheat oven to 400°. Place the chicken in a 13x9-in. baking dish coated with cooking spray. Pour lemon juice over the chicken; sprinkle with feta cheese, oregano and pepper.
2. Bake, uncovered, for 20-25 minutes or until a thermometer reads 165°.
1 chicken breast half: 143 cal., 4g fat (1g sat. fat), 66mg chol., 122mg sod., 1g carb. (0 sugars, 0 fiber), 24g pro.
Diabetic exchanges: 3 lean meat.

PARMESAN PORK MEDALLIONS

5i 🥕 ⏱

PARMESAN PORK MEDALLIONS

I was so happy to find this recipe. I have served it countless times for family and friends. It takes very little prep time and adapts easily to serve any number.
—Angela Ciocca, Saltsburg, PA

....

Takes: 20 min. • **Makes:** 2 servings

- ½ lb. pork tenderloin
- 2 Tbsp. seasoned bread crumbs
- 1 Tbsp. grated Parmesan cheese
- ¼ tsp. salt
  Dash pepper
- 2 tsp. canola oil
- ¼ cup sliced onion
- 1 garlic clove, minced

1. Cut pork into 4 slices; flatten to ¼-in. thickness. In a large shallow dish, combine the bread crumbs, cheese, salt and pepper. Add pork, 1 slice at a time, and turn to coat.
2. In a large skillet over medium heat, cook the pork in oil until no longer pink, 2-3 minutes on each side. Remove and keep warm.
3. Add onion to the pan; cook and stir until tender. Add garlic, cook 1 minute longer. Serve with pork.
2 slices: 220 cal., 9g fat (2g sat. fat), 65mg chol., 487mg sod., 8g carb. (1g sugars, 1g fiber), 25g pro. **Diabetic exchanges:** 3 lean meat, 1 fat, ½ starch.

AVOCADO EGG SALAD TOAST

After purchasing far too many unripe avocados for an event, I had a surplus of ripe ones each day in my kitchen for the week after! I was making some egg salad sandwiches for lunch and had the great idea to use avocado instead of mayo to bind it. Not only was this version unbelievably delicious, the healthy fats in the avocado make this a much better option that the traditional mayo-laden version.
—Shannon Dobos, Calgary, AB

Takes: 20 min. • **Makes:** 4 servings

    1 medium ripe avocado,
       peeled and cubed
    6 hard-boiled large eggs, chopped
    1 green onion, finely chopped
    1 tsp. lemon juice
    ¼ tsp. salt
    ⅛ tsp. pepper
    4 large slices sourdough bread,
       halved and toasted

In a large bowl, mash avocado to desired consistency. Gently stir in eggs, green onion, lemon juice, salt and pepper. Spread over toast. Serve immediately.
2 pieces : 367 cal., 15g fat (4g sat. fat), 280mg chol., 671mg sod., 41g carb. (4g sugars, 4g fiber), 18g pro.

ENCHILADA CHICKEN
PICTURED ON P. 81

We enjoy southwestern flavors and this six-ingredient recipe never gets boring. The chicken sizzles in the skillet before being baked and comes out tender and juicy every time.
—Nancy Sousley, Lafayette, IN

Prep: 15 min. • **Bake:** 20 min.
Makes: 4 servings

    4 boneless skinless chicken breast
       halves (6 oz. each)
    2 tsp. salt-free Southwest chipotle
       seasoning blend
    1 Tbsp. olive oil
    ¼ cup enchilada sauce
    ½ cup shredded sharp cheddar cheese
    2 Tbsp. minced fresh cilantro

Preheat oven to 350°. Sprinkle chicken with seasoning blend. In an ovenproof skillet, brown the chicken in oil. Top with the enchilada sauce, cheese and cilantro. Bake for 18-20 minutes or until a thermometer reads 170°.
1 chicken breast half : 265 cal., 11g fat (5g sat. fat), 109mg chol., 252mg sod., 2g carb. (0 sugars, 0 fiber), 38g pro.
Diabetic exchanges: 5 lean meat, 1 fat.

AVOCADO EGG SALAD TOAST

SAUSAGE & SAUERKRAUT

from the heat for 6-8 minutes on each side or until fish flakes easily with a fork; baste frequently with molasses mixture. Serve with the reserved molasses mixture.

1 serving: 583 cal., 43g fat (7g sat. fat), 85mg chol., 96mg sod., 20g carb. (15g sugars, 0 fiber), 29g pro.

ARTICHOKE CHICKEN PESTO PIZZA

Garlicky pesto perfectly complements the mild flavors of chicken and artichoke in this delicious pizza. It's a quick and easy crowd-pleaser that also delivers a touch of elegance.
—Trisha Kruse, Eagle, ID

Takes: 15 min.
Makes: 8 servings

- 1 prebaked 12-in. pizza crust
- ½ cup prepared pesto
- 2 cups cubed cooked chicken breast
- 2 jars (6½ oz. each) marinated artichoke hearts, drained
- 2 cups shredded part-skim mozzarella cheese
    Optional: Grated Parmesan cheese and minced fresh basil

Preheat oven to 425°. Place crust on an ungreased 12-in. pizza pan. Spread with pesto. Arrange chicken and artichokes over top; sprinkle with cheese. Bake until golden brown, 10-12 minutes. If desired, top with Parmesan cheese and minced fresh basil.

1 slice: 381 cal., 20g fat (6g sat. fat), 45mg chol., 880mg sod., 28g carb. (2g sugars, 4g fiber), 23g pro.

READER REVIEW

"Fantastic recipe. So easy to put together and so yummy! I buy ready-made pesto from our market's salad bar to make it even easier."

FERRYAL, TASTEOFHOME.COM

SAUSAGE & SAUERKRAUT

Three young children involved in different activities keep me running. I created this for those extra-busy nights. It delivers flavor—and makes life a little easier, too.
—Mary Lyon, Spotsylvania, VA

Takes: 30 min. • **Makes:** 4 servings

- 6 medium red potatoes, cubed
- 2 Tbsp. canola oil
- 1 small onion, halved and sliced
- 1 lb. smoked sausage, cut into ¼-in. pieces
- 1 pkg. (16 oz.) sauerkraut, rinsed and well drained
- ¼ tsp. pepper

In a large skillet, saute the potatoes in oil for 5-6 minutes or until lightly browned. Stir in onion; saute for 3-4 minutes or until tender. Add the sausage, sauerkraut and pepper. Cook, uncovered, over medium heat for 4-5 minutes or until heated through, stirring occasionally.

1½ cups: 567 cal., 38g fat (14g sat. fat), 76mg chol., 2043mg sod., 36g carb. (7g sugars, 6g fiber), 20g pro.

GLAZED SALMON

After I grilled this for my boss and her husband, I was swamped with calls asking for the recipe. My boss said she'd never tasted such delicious salmon. And it takes only minutes to prepare!
—Naomi Mahoney, Oakville, ON

Takes: 20 min. • **Makes:** 4 servings

- ½ cup olive oil
- ⅓ cup molasses
- 2 tsp. minced garlic
- 1½ tsp. grated lemon zest
- 4 salmon fillets (6 oz. each)

1. In a small bowl, combine the oil, molasses, garlic and lemon zest; reserve half the mixture for serving.
2. Grill salmon, uncovered, on a lightly oiled grill over medium heat or broil 4 in.

ARTICHOKE CHICKEN PESTO PIZZA

EASY CHILI VERDE

EASY CHILI VERDE

I love chili verde and order it whenever I can at restaurants. A few years ago I figured out how to make an easy, tasty version at home. There are never leftovers when I make it for my family.
—Julie Rowland, Salt Lake City, UT

Prep: 10 min. • **Cook:** 5 hours
Makes: 12 servings (3 qt.)

- 1 boneless pork shoulder roast (4 to 5 lbs.), cut into 1-in. pieces
- 3 cans (10 oz. each) green enchilada sauce
- 1 cup salsa verde
- 1 can (4 oz.) chopped green chiles
- ½ tsp. salt
  Hot cooked rice
  Sour cream, optional

In a 5-qt. slow cooker, combine pork, enchilada sauce, salsa verde, green chiles and salt. Cook, covered, on low until the pork is tender, 5-6 hours. Serve with rice. If desired, top with sour cream.
1 cup: 287 cal., 17g fat (5g sat. fat), 90mg chol., 729mg sod., 5g carb. (1g sugars, 0 fiber), 27g pro.

BEEF STEAKS WITH BLUE CHEESE

I double these juicy steaks whenever I'm serving them to company. My guests often ask for the recipe, and they're surprised at how simple it is to make.
—Gloria Nerone, Mentor, OH

Takes: 20 min. • **Makes:** 2 servings

- 2 beef tenderloin steaks (1½ in. thick and 8 oz. each)
- 2 oz. blue cheese, crumbled
- 2 Tbsp. butter, softened
- 2 slices white bread, crusts removed and cut into cubes
- 1 Tbsp. olive oil
- 2 Tbsp. grated Parmesan cheese

1. Preheat broiler; broil steaks 4-6 in. from the heat for 5-8 minutes on each side or until meat is browned and cooked to desired doneness (for medium-rare, a thermometer should read 135°; medium, 140°; medium-well, 145°).
2. Meanwhile, in a bowl, combine blue cheese and butter; set aside. In a skillet, saute bread cubes in oil until golden brown. Sprinkle with Parmesan cheese. Top steaks with blue cheese mixture and sprinkle with croutons; broil 1 minute longer or until cheese is slightly melted.
1 steak: 686 cal., 42g fat (20g sat. fat), 155mg chol., 649mg sod., 16g carb. (2g sugars, 1g fiber), 58g pro.
HEALTH TIP Serving size counts when considering nutrition information. An 8-oz. steak is generous, as is the amount of blue cheese topping. Make this recipe work for you by using 4- or 6-oz. steaks and just half the topping mixture.

CHICKEN CORDON BLEU IN PASTRY

Baking chicken breasts in a flaky dough makes them turn out moist and delicious every time. This fancy-yet-simple dish is nice to serve family as well as guests.
—*Taste of Home* Test Kitchen

Takes: 30 min. • **Makes:** 4 servings

- 1 tube (8 oz.) refrigerated crescent rolls
- ¼ cup spreadable chive and onion cream cheese
- 4 thin slices deli ham
- 4 boneless skinless chicken breast halves (4 oz. each)
- 4 slices Swiss cheese

1. Preheat oven to 375°. Separate dough into 4 rectangles on an ungreased baking sheet; seal perforations. Spread 1 Tbsp. cream cheese lengthwise down the center of each rectangle. Place ham widthwise over dough. Arrange chicken halves in center of each rectangle. Wrap the ham around chicken. At each long end, pinch the dough together around chicken, forming points.

2. Bake until a thermometer inserted in the chicken reads 170°, about 15 minutes. Top each with slice of Swiss cheese; bake until the cheese is melted and the pastry is golden brown, about 5 minutes longer.

1 serving: 428 cal., 26g fat (12g sat. fat), 66mg chol., 807mg sod., 24g carb. (5g sugars, 0 fiber), 21g pro.

ORANGE-PECAN SALMON

I first made this baked salmon for a friend's luncheon, and everyone loved it. It was especially nice that I could pop it in the oven just before they arrived and still serve lunch within minutes.
—Pat Neaves, Lee's Summit, MO

Prep: 10 min. + marinating
Bake: 20 min. • **Makes:** 4 servings

- 1 cup orange marmalade
- ½ cup reduced-sodium soy sauce
- ¼ tsp. salt
- ¼ tsp. pepper
- 4 salmon fillets (6 oz. each)
- 1 cup chopped pecans, toasted

1. In a small bowl, combine marmalade, soy sauce, salt and pepper. Pour ⅔ cup of the marinade into a large shallow dish. Add the salmon and turn to coat. Refrigerate up to 30 minutes. Set aside the remaining marinade.

2. Preheat the oven to 350°. Drain and discard marinade from salmon. Place the salmon in a greased 11x7-in. baking dish. Bake, uncovered, 20-25 minutes or until fish flakes easily with a fork.

3. In a small saucepan, bring the reserved marinade to a boil; cook and stir until slightly thickened. Stir in pecans; serve with salmon.

1 fillet with 3 Tbsp. sauce: 582 cal., 32g fat (5g sat. fat), 85mg chol., 1137mg sod., 44g carb. (37g sugars, 3g fiber), 33g pro.

READER REVIEW

"When I saw this recipe I couldn't wait to try it. My husband and I think it's wonderful! Such a good flavor. Thank you for sharing this recipe."

ROSEMARY SWOPE,
TASTEOFHOME.COM

CHICKEN CORDON BLEU IN PASTRY

SUGAR-GLAZED HAM

An old-fashioned sugar glaze gives ham a pretty, golden brown coating just like Grandma used to make. The mustard and vinegar complement the brown sugar and add tangy flavor. Be prepared to serve seconds!
—Carol Strong Battle, Heathsville, VA

Prep: 5 min. • **Bake:** 1¾ hours
Makes: 14 servings

- 1 fully cooked bone-in ham (5 to 7 lbs.)
- 1 cup packed brown sugar
- 2 tsp. prepared mustard
- 1 to 2 Tbsp. cider vinegar

1. Preheat oven to 325°. Place ham on a rack in a shallow roasting pan. Using a sharp knife, score surface of ham with ¼-in.-deep cuts in a diamond pattern. Cover and bake 1½-2 hours or until a thermometer reads 130°.
2. Meanwhile, in a small bowl, combine the brown sugar, mustard and enough vinegar to make a thick paste. Remove ham from oven. Spread sugar mixture over ham. Bake ham, uncovered, 15-30 minutes longer or until a thermometer reads 140°.

4 oz. ham: 284 cal., 16g fat (6g sat. fat), 57mg chol., 1110mg sod., 15g carb. (15g sugars, 0 fiber), 20g pro.

NUTTY CHEESE TORTELLINI

NUTTY CHEESE TORTELLINI

I plant Italian flat-leaf parsley in a long terra-cotta planter so I always have some on hand. It adds bright, fresh flavor to this pasta dish.
—Barbara Penatzer, Vestal, NY

Takes: 20 min. • **Makes:** 3 servings

- 1 pkg. (9 oz.) refrigerated cheese tortellini
- ½ cup butter, cubed
- ½ cup minced fresh parsley
- ⅓ cup chopped walnuts, toasted
- ¼ cup shredded Parmesan cheese
   Coarsely ground pepper to taste

Cook the tortellini according to the package directions; drain and keep warm. In the same pan, melt butter. Stir in the tortellini, parsley and walnuts; toss to coat. Sprinkle with cheese and pepper.

1 cup: 650 cal., 48g fat (25g sat. fat), 123mg chol., 677mg sod., 42g carb. (3g sugars, 3g fiber), 17g pro.

READER REVIEW

"I prepared this dish for dinner tonight and it is scrumptious! I toasted the walnuts before mixing them in with the tortellini. My dad went back for seconds!"

M1OF3, TASTEOFHOME.COM

CRANBERRY MAPLE CHICKEN

Tart cranberries and a hint of maple syrup make a sweet sauce for these easy chicken breast halves. They're a quick but lovely main course for weeknights and other occasions.
—Kim Pettipas, Oromocto, NB

Takes: 30 min. • **Makes:** 6 servings

- 2 cups fresh or frozen cranberries
- ¾ cup water
- ⅓ cup sugar
- 6 boneless skinless chicken breast halves (4 oz. each)
- ½ tsp. salt
- ¼ tsp. pepper
- 1 Tbsp. canola oil
- ¼ cup maple syrup

1. In a small saucepan, combine the cranberries, water and sugar. Cook over medium heat until the berries pop, about 15 minutes.
2. Meanwhile, sprinkle chicken with salt and pepper. In a large nonstick skillet, cook chicken in oil over medium heat until the juices run clear, 4-5 minutes on each side. Stir syrup into the cranberry mixture; serve with chicken.

1 chicken breast half with 3 Tbsp. sauce: 236 cal., 5g fat (1g sat. fat), 63mg chol., 253mg sod., 24g carb. (22g sugars, 1g fiber), 23g pro.

PARMESAN CHICKEN BREASTS

Rich and cheesy breading locks in this chicken's natural juices, making it tender and tempting every time. Because it can be made in advance, I rely on it often during the week and when entertaining.
—Kathie Landmann, Lexington Park, MD

Takes: 30 min. • **Makes:** 6 servings

- 1 cup grated Parmesan cheese
- 2 cups soft bread crumbs
- ½ cup butter, melted
- 6 boneless skinless chicken breast halves (6 oz. each)
- ½ cup Dijon, yellow or country-style mustard

Preheat oven to 425°. Combine cheese, bread crumbs and butter. Coat chicken breasts with mustard, then dip into the crumb mixture. Place breaded chicken in a 13x9-in. baking pan. Bake until a thermometer inserted in chicken reads 165°, about 15 minutes.

1 chicken breast half: 391 cal., 24g fat (13g sat. fat), 119mg chol., 1047mg sod., 10g carb. (1g sugars, 1g fiber), 33g pro.

BAKED BREADED COD

These fish fillets are quick to fix...and they bake in hardly any time! Brushed with ranch salad dressing and coated with seasoned stuffing crumbs and parsley, the cod fillets are moist and flavorful.
—*Taste of Home* Test Kitchen

Takes: 20 min. • **Makes:** 2 servings

- 1 cup seasoned stuffing croutons, crushed
- 1 Tbsp. minced fresh parsley
- 2 cod fillets (6 oz. each)
- 1 Tbsp. reduced-fat ranch salad dressing
  Refrigerated butter-flavored spray

1. Preheat oven to 400°. In a shallow bowl, combine crushed croutons and parsley. Drizzle cod with salad dressing, then coat with crumb mixture. Spritz with butter-flavored spray.
2. Place in an 11x7-in. baking dish coated with cooking spray. Bake, uncovered, for 10-15 minutes or until the fish flakes easily with a fork.

1 serving: 244 cal., 5g fat (1g sat. fat), 75mg chol., 423mg sod., 15g carb. (0 sugars, 1g fiber), 33g pro. **Diabetic exchanges:** 4 lean meat, 1 starch, ½ fat.

CRANBERRY MAPLE CHICKEN

BLUE CHEESE-STUFFED STEAKS FOR TWO

For a fast, fancy dinner for two, try this tender beef with a mild blue cheese stuffing. Tomatoes sauteed in garlic make a colorful and flavorful accompaniment.
—Teddy Devico, Warren, NJ

Takes: 30 min. • **Makes:** 2 servings

- 5 garlic cloves, peeled
- 1 Tbsp. canola oil
- 2 cups grape tomatoes
- 2 boneless beef top loin steaks (8 oz. each)
- ¼ cup crumbled blue cheese
- ¼ tsp. salt
- ⅛ tsp. pepper

1. In a large skillet, saute garlic in oil until tender. Cover and cook over low heat for 5-7 minutes or until golden and softened. Add tomatoes; cook and stir until the tomatoes just begin to burst. Remove from the skillet; set aside and keep warm.
2. Cut a pocket in the thickest part of each steak; fill with blue cheese. Sprinkle with salt and pepper.
3. In the same skillet, cook steaks over medium heat 4-5 minutes on each side or until meat reaches desired doneness (for medium-rare, a thermometer should read 135°; medium, 140°; medium-well, 145°). Serve with the tomato mixture.
Note: Top loin steak may be labeled as strip steak, Kansas City steak, New York strip steak, ambassador steak or boneless club steak in your region.

1 steak with 1 cup tomato mixture: 463 cal., 23g fat (8g sat. fat), 113mg chol., 644mg sod., 10g carb. (4g sugars, 2g fiber), 53g pro

EASY LAZY LASAGNA

One day when I craved lasagna, I devised this simple recipe and it worked out beautifully. Celebrate weeknights, too!
—Carol Mead, Los Alamos, NM

Takes: 30 min. • **Makes:** 2 servings

- 1 cup spaghetti sauce
- ¾ cup shredded part-skim mozzarella cheese
- ½ cup 4% cottage cheese
- 1½ cups cooked wide egg noodles
- 2 Tbsp. grated Parmesan cheese
  Chopped fresh parsley, optional

1. Warm the spaghetti sauce; stir in mozzarella and cottage cheeses. Fold in noodles. Pour into 2 greased 2-cup baking dishes. Sprinkle with Parmesan cheese.
2. Bake, uncovered, at 375° until bubbly, about 20 minutes. If desired, top with chopped parsley.
1 lasagna: 399 cal., 16g fat (8g sat. fat), 68mg chol., 1120mg sod., 37g carb. (12g sugars, 3g fiber), 25g pro.

EASY LAZY LASAGNA

ROSEMARY-THYME LAMB CHOPS

My father loves lamb, so I make this dish whenever he visits. It's the perfect main course for holidays or get-togethers.
—Kristina Mitchell, Clearwater, FL

Takes: 30 min. • **Makes:** 4 servings

- 8 lamb loin chops (3 oz. each)
- ½ tsp. pepper
- ¼ tsp. salt
- 3 Tbsp. Dijon mustard
- 1 Tbsp. minced fresh rosemary
- 1 Tbsp. minced fresh thyme
- 3 garlic cloves, minced

1. Sprinkle lamb chops with pepper and salt. In a small bowl, mix Dijon mustard, rosemary, thyme and garlic.
2. Grill the chops, covered, on an oiled rack over medium heat 6 minutes. Turn; spread herb mixture over chops. Grill 6-8 minutes longer or until meat reaches desired doneness (for medium-rare, a thermometer should read 135°; medium, 140°; medium-well, 145°).
2 lamb chops: 231 cal., 9g fat (4g sat. fat), 97mg chol., 493mg sod., 3g carb. (0 sugars, 0 fiber), 32g pro. **Diabetic exchanges:** 4 lean meat.

PROSCIUTTO-PEPPER PORK CHOPS

Here's a dish that's easy, fast and—most importantly—delicious. Serve these cheesy chops with a pasta salad for a light and satisfying meal.
—Donna Prisco, Randolph, NJ

Takes: 20 min. • **Makes:** 4 servings

- 4 boneless pork loin chops (4 oz. each)
- ⅛ tsp. garlic powder
- ⅛ tsp. pepper
- 2 tsp. canola oil
- 4 thin slices prosciutto or deli ham
- ½ cup julienned roasted sweet red peppers
- 2 slices reduced-fat provolone cheese, cut in half

1. Sprinkle pork chops with garlic powder and pepper. In a large nonstick skillet, cook chops in oil over medium heat, until a thermometer inserted in pork reads 145°, 4-5 minutes on each side.

2. Top each pork chop with prosciutto, red peppers and cheese. Cover and cook for 1-2 minutes or until cheese is melted. Let stand 5 minutes before serving.

1 pork chop: 237 cal., 12g fat (4g sat. fat), 72mg chol., 483mg sod., 1g carb. (1g sugars, 0 fiber), 28g pro. **Diabetic exchanges:** 4 lean meat, ½ fat.

ZUCCHINI-PARMESAN BAKE
PICTURED ON P. 81

When my garden produces zucchini, I turn to this recipe. The mild zucchini works beautifully with the sharp tang of the Parmesan cheese. Mix in some summer squash for a color contrast.
—Shannon Davis, Mason, MI

Takes: 30 min. • **Makes:** 6 servings

- 3 large eggs
- ½ cup canola oil
- 3 cups shredded zucchini (about 1 lb.)
- 1 cup reduced-fat biscuit/baking mix
- ½ cup shredded Parmesan cheese

1. Preheat oven to 375°. In a large bowl, whisk eggs and oil until blended. Stir in the remaining ingredients.

2. Transfer mixture to a greased 10-in. ovenproof skillet. Bake 25-30 minutes or until golden brown.

1 piece: 314 cal., 24g fat (4g sat. fat), 111mg chol., 387mg sod., 17g carb. (2g sugars, 1g fiber), 8g pro.

PROSCIUTTO-PEPPER PORK CHOPS

**HERBED PORK WITH
MUSHROOM SAUCE**

HERBED PORK WITH MUSHROOM SAUCE

Preseasoned pork tenderloin delivers flavorful, quick and satisfying meals without a big mess or leftovers. I've used all flavors of tenderloin for this recipe—the sauce goes with them all!
—Jolene Roszel, Helena, MT

Takes: 30 min. • **Makes:** servings

- 2 Tbsp. olive oil, divided
- 1 peppercorn pork tenderloin (1 lb.) or flavor of your choice, cut into ¾-in. slices
- ½ cup sliced fresh mushrooms
- ¼ cup chopped onion
- 2 Tbsp. all-purpose flour
- 1 cup reduced-sodium beef broth

1. In a large skillet, heat 1 Tbsp. oil over medium heat. Brown pork on both sides. Remove from pan.
2. In same pan, heat the remaining oil over medium-high heat. Add mushrooms and onion; cook and stir until tender, 4-5 minutes.
3. In a small bowl, mix flour and broth until smooth. Stir into mushroom mixture. Bring to a boil; cook and stir until sauce is thickened. Return pork to pan. Cook until a thermometer reads 145°.

3 oz. cooked pork with ¼ cup sauce: 208 cal., 11g fat (2g sat. fat), 55mg chol., 785mg sod., 7g carb. (1g sugars, 0 fiber), 21g pro.

HONEY-GLAZED CHICKEN

When I was young, my oldest sister served this for her Sunday dinners. The tradition continues—I make it twice a month at my house, and my four daughters also serve it to their families as a favorite dish. It has an old-fashioned flavor, and the chicken is crisp and golden brown.
—Pat Dube, Phoenix, AZ

Prep: 5 min. • **Bake:** 1 hour
Makes: 6 servings

- ¼ cup butter, melted
- ¼ cup orange juice
- ¼ cup honey
- ½ tsp. salt
- 1 broiler/fryer chicken (3 to 4 lbs.), cut up

1. In a shallow bowl, combine the butter, orange juice, honey and salt. For basting, remove ⅓ cup and set aside. Dip chicken pieces in remaining butter mixture; place in a well-greased 13x9-in. baking dish.
2. Bake, uncovered, at 350° for 1 hour or until juices run clear, basting occasionally with reserved butter mixture.

4 oz. cooked chicken: 408 cal., 24g fat (10g sat. fat), 125mg chol., 348mg sod., 13g carb. (12g sugars, 0 fiber), 33g pro.

WEEKNIGHT RAVIOLI LASAGNA

My husband and I love lasagna, but it's time-consuming to build and we always end up with too much. Using frozen ravioli solves everything.
—Pamela Nicholson, Festus, MO

Prep: 15 min. • **Bake:** 45 min.
Makes: 6 servings

- 1 jar (24 oz.) pasta sauce
- 1 pkg. (25 oz.) frozen meat or cheese ravioli
- 1½ cups shredded part-skim mozzarella cheese
- 3 cups fresh baby spinach

1. Preheat oven to 350°. In a small saucepan, heat sauce 5-7 minutes over medium heat or just until simmering, stirring occasionally.
2. Spread ½ cup sauce into a greased 11x7-in. baking dish. Layer with half the ravioli, 1½ cups spinach, ½ cup cheese and half the remaining sauce; repeat layers. Sprinkle with remaining cheese.
3. Bake, uncovered, 45-50 minutes or until edges are bubbly and cheese is melted. Let stand for 5 minutes before serving.

1 cup: 344 cal., 10g fat (5g sat. fat), 26mg chol., 850mg sod., 45g carb. (10g sugars, 5g fiber), 17g pro. **Diabetic exchanges:** 3 starch, 2 medium-fat meat.

WEEKNIGHT RAVIOLI LASAGNA

30-Minute Dinners

Get a satisfying, crowd-pleasing meal on the table fast—without resorting to takeout! All these recipes take 30 minutes or less from fridge to plate, and will make your family believe you're a magician in the kitchen.

Turkey Dinner Muffins (p. 111) **Penne with Veggies & Black Beans** (p. 115) **Crab-Topped Fish Fillets** (p. 102)
Nacho Pie (p. 114) **Tuna Potato Supper** (p. 98)

TUNA POTATO SUPPER

Tuna lovers will find this a real treat. My husband and I enjoy it as a nice change from the ordinary baked potato.
—Rosella Peters, Gull Lake, SK

Takes: 25 min. • **Makes:** 2 servings

- 2 large baking potatoes
- 1 can (6 oz.) light water-packed tuna, drained and flaked
- 1 celery rib with leaves, finely chopped
- 1 green onion, chopped
- ⅓ cup creamy cucumber salad dressing
- ⅛ tsp. each salt and pepper
- ¼ cup shredded Colby-Monterey Jack cheese

1. Scrub and pierce potatoes; place on a microwave-safe plate. Microwave, uncovered, on high until tender, turning once, 7-9 minutes. Cool slightly. Cut a thin slice off the top of each potato and discard. Scoop out the pulp, leaving a thin shell.
2. In a bowl, mash the pulp. Stir in the tuna, celery, onion, salad dressing, salt and pepper. Spoon into the potato shells. Sprinkle with cheese. Place on a baking sheet. Broil 4-6 in. from the heat until cheese is melted, 5-6 minutes.

1 potato: 598 cal., 25g fat (6g sat. fat), 38mg chol., 866mg sod., 63g carb. (0 sugars, 6g fiber), 30g pro.

TERIYAKI GLAZED CHICKEN

TERIYAKI GLAZED CHICKEN

I love to experiment with food. We're able to buy sweet onions grown on Maui, so I stir-fry them with chicken and carrots for a tasty teriyaki meal.
—Kel Brenneman, Riverdale, CA

Takes: 30 min. • **Makes:** 4 servings

- 1 lb. boneless skinless chicken breast halves, cut into strips
- 3 Tbsp. canola oil, divided
- 4 medium carrots, julienned
- 1 medium sweet onion, julienned
- ½ cup soy sauce
- ¼ cup packed brown sugar
  Hot cooked rice
  Sesame seeds, toasted, optional
  Sliced green onions, optional

1. In a large skillet or wok, stir-fry the chicken in 2 Tbsp. oil until no longer pink, 6-8 minutes. Remove chicken and set aside. In the same skillet, stir-fry carrots in the remaining oil for 2 minutes. Add onion; stir-fry until vegetables are tender, 2-4 minutes longer.
2. Combine the soy sauce and brown sugar; add to skillet. Bring to a boil. Return chicken to skillet. Boil until the sauce is slightly thickened, about 5 minutes. Serve with rice. Sprinkle with sesame seeds and green onions if desired.

1 serving: 324 cal., 13g fat (2g sat. fat), 63mg chol., 1922mg sod., 23g carb. (20g sugars, 3g fiber), 28g pro.

HEALTH TIP Using reduced-sodium soy sauce will decrease sodium to about 1,200 milligrams per serving, but that's still high. To cut even more, replace some of the soy sauce with reduced-sodium broth or water.

HAM & SCALLOPED POTATOES

I fix this saucy skillet dish often, especially when I'm running late, because it takes so little time to prepare. The recipe won first prize in a recipe contest in our local paper some years back.

—Emma Magielda, Amsterdam, NY

Takes: 30 min. • **Makes:** 4 servings

- 4 medium potatoes, peeled and thinly sliced
- 2 Tbsp. butter
- ⅓ cup water
- ½ cup 2% milk
- 2 to 3 Tbsp. onion soup mix
- 3 Tbsp. minced fresh parsley
- 1 cup cubed Velveeta
- 1 cup cubed fully cooked ham

1. In a large skillet, cook the potatoes in butter until lightly browned. Add water; bring to a boil. Reduce heat; cover and simmer for 14-15 minutes or until tender.
2. Meanwhile in a small bowl, combine milk, soup mix and parsley; stir in cheese. Pour over the potatoes. Add ham; cook and stir gently over medium heat until the cheese is melted and the sauce is bubbly.

1 serving: 353 cal., 17g fat (10g sat. fat), 56mg chol., 1170mg sod., 36g carb. (6g sugars, 2g fiber), 16g pro.

CREAMY TOMATO FETTUCCINE WITH ZUCCHINI

My husband and kids all loved this pasta so much, they ate every last bite and made me write the recipe down to share it. Sometimes I serve it with gnocchi instead of fettuccine.

—Emily Mathews, Cumming, GA

Takes: 30 min. • **Makes:** 4 servings

- 8 oz. uncooked fettuccine
- 2 Tbsp. olive oil
- 3 shallots, thinly sliced
- 1 medium zucchini, halved and thinly sliced
- 2 medium tomatoes, seeded and chopped
- 3 oz. thinly sliced hard salami, julienned
- ½ cup tomato sauce or 1 Tbsp. tomato paste
- ½ cup heavy whipping cream
- ½ cup grated Parmesan cheese
- ¼ cup toasted pine nuts
- ¼ cup minced fresh basil

1. Cook fettuccine according to the package directions. Meanwhile, in a Dutch oven, heat oil over medium heat. Add shallots; cook and stir until tender. Add zucchini, tomatoes and salami. Cook until the zucchini is tender.
2. Stir in tomato sauce and cream. Bring to a boil. Reduce heat; cook and stir until slightly thickened. Remove from heat; stir in cheese, half the pine nuts and half the basil. Drain fettuccine; add to Dutch oven. Toss to coat. Sprinkle with the remaining pine nuts and basil. Serve immediately.

1 cup: 586 cal., 34g fat (12g sat. fat), 63mg chol., 779mg sod., 54g carb. (7g sugars, 5g fiber), 21g pro.

HAM & SCALLOPED POTATOES

HONEY WALLEYE

Our state is known as the Land of 10,000 Lakes, so fishing is a favorite recreational activity here. This recipe is a quick way to prepare the fresh walleye hooked by the anglers in our family.
—Kitty McCue, St. Louis Park, MN

Takes: 20 min. • **Makes:** 6 servings

- 1 large egg
- 2 tsp. honey
- 2 cups crushed Ritz crackers (about 45 to 50)
- ½ tsp. salt
- 1½ lbs. walleye fillets
- ⅓ to ½ cup canola oil
  Optional: Lemon wedge and minced fresh parsley

1. In a shallow bowl, beat egg; add honey. In a shallow dish, combine crackers and salt. Dip fish in the egg mixture, then in the cracker mixture; turn until coated.
2. In a cast-iron or other heavy skillet, cook fillets in oil over medium heat until golden and fish flakes easily with a fork, 3-5 minutes on each side. If desired, top with parsley and serve with lemon wedges.

3 oz. cooked fish: 389 cal., 22g fat (3g sat. fat), 133mg chol., 514mg sod., 23g carb. (5g sugars, 1g fiber), 25g pro.

PORK CHOPS & PIEROGIES

This dish uses the classic taste combo of pork and apples for a different way to use pierogi. It all comes together in one skillet for meal-in-one convenience.
—Greta Igl, Menomonee Falls, WI

Takes: 25 min. • **Makes:** 2 servings

- 8 frozen potato and onion pierogi
- 2 bone-in pork loin chops (¾ in. thick)
- ½ tsp. salt, divided
- ½ tsp. pepper, divided
- 4 Tbsp. butter, divided
- 1 medium sweet onion, sliced and separated into rings
- 1 medium Golden Delicious apple, cut into ¼-in. slices
- ¼ cup sugar
- ¼ cup cider vinegar

1. Cook pierogi according to package directions. Sprinkle pork chops with ¼ tsp. salt and ¼ tsp. pepper. In a large skillet, cook chops in 2 Tbsp. butter over medium heat until juices run clear; remove and keep warm.
2. In the same skillet, saute onion in the remaining butter for 3 minutes. Add apple; saute until almost tender. Stir in sugar, vinegar, and remaining salt and pepper. Bring to a boil. Reduce heat; simmer, uncovered, 5 minutes. Drain pierogi. Add chops and pierogi to skillet; stir to coat.

1 serving: 730 cal., 33g fat (18g sat. fat), 154mg chol., 1207mg sod., 72g carb. (45g sugars, 5g fiber), 36g pro.

GROUND BEEF SPAGHETTI SKILLET

I remember my grandma making this stovetop supper many times—we loved granny's spaghetti! My husband and I now enjoy making this for our supper. You can also easily substitute ground turkey for the ground beef.

—Jill Thomas, Washington, IN

Takes: 30 min. • **Makes:** 4 servings

- 1 lb. ground beef
- 1 medium green pepper, chopped
- 1 small onion, chopped
- 2 garlic cloves, minced
- 1½ cups water
- 1 can (14½ oz.) diced tomatoes, undrained
- 1 can (8 oz.) tomato sauce
- 1 Tbsp. chili powder
- 1 Tbsp. grape jelly
- ½ tsp. salt
- 6 oz. uncooked thin spaghetti, halved

1. In a Dutch oven, cook beef, green pepper, onion and garlic over medium heat until the beef is no longer pink and the vegetables are tender, 8-10 minutes, breaking up the beef into crumbles; drain.
2. Add water, tomatoes, tomato sauce, chili powder, jelly and salt. Bring to a boil. Stir in spaghetti. Reduce heat; simmer, covered, until the spaghetti is tender, 6-8 minutes.

1½ cups: 431 cal., 15g fat (5g sat. fat), 70mg chol., 843mg sod., 47g carb. (10g sugars, 5g fiber), 28g pro.

TEST KITCHEN TIP
Chili powder adds a subtle southwestern flavor to this spaghetti dish. If you like, play that up by garnishing each serving with your favorite taco toppings like a dollop of sour cream and chopped green onions.

GROUND BEEF SPAGHETTI SKILLET

CRAB-TOPPED FISH FILLETS

DINNER IN A BAG

I get a head start on this family-pleasing dinner by assembling ready-to-grab pantry kits. I measure the dry macaroni and spice mixture into separate containers, storing in a paper bag with canned tomatoes.
—Darlene Brenden, Salem, OR

Takes: 30 min. • **Makes:** 4 servings

- 1 lb. ground beef
- 2 cans (14½ oz. each) stewed tomatoes
- ¼ cup dried minced onion
- 1 tsp. salt
- 1 tsp. chili powder
- ¼ to ½ tsp. pepper
- ¼ tsp. sugar
- 1 cup uncooked elbow macaroni

1. In a large skillet, cook beef over medium heat until no longer pink; drain. Add the tomatoes, seasonings and sugar; bring to a boil. Reduce heat and simmer for 5 minutes.

2. Stir in macaroni; cover and simmer for 15 minutes. Uncover; simmer until the macaroni is tender and sauce is thickened.

1 cup: 289 cal., 11g fat (5g sat. fat), 56mg chol., 858mg sod., 25g carb. (8g sugars, 2g fiber), 24g pro.

READER REVIEW

"We've made this for years, and call it 'easy goulash'— it's a great go-to meal when you haven't anything in mind. I love the idea of having all the ingredients together ready to go. Thanks for the tip!"

TAMI, TASTEOFHOME.COM

CRAB-TOPPED FISH FILLETS

Elegant but easy, this recipe is perfect for company. Toasting the almonds gives them a little more crunch, which is a delightful way to top the fish fillets.
—Mary Tuthill, Fort Myers Beach, FL

Takes: 30 min. • **Makes:** 4 servings

- 4 sole or cod fillets or fish fillets of your choice (6 oz. each)
- 1 can (6 oz.) crabmeat, drained and flaked, or 1 cup imitation crabmeat, chopped
- ½ cup grated Parmesan cheese
- ½ cup mayonnaise
- 1 tsp. lemon juice
- ⅓ cup slivered almonds, toasted
  Paprika, optional

1. Preheat oven to 350°. Place fillets in a greased 13x9-in. baking dish. Bake, uncovered, for 18-22 minutes or until fish flakes easily with a fork.

2. In a large bowl, combine the crab, cheese, mayonnaise and lemon juice.

3. Drain cooking juices from baking dish; spoon crab mixture over the fillets. Broil 4-5 in. from the heat for 5 minutes or until topping is lightly browned. Sprinkle with almonds and paprika if desired.

1 fillet: 429 cal., 31g fat (6g sat. fat), 128mg chol., 1063mg sod., 3g carb. (0 sugars, 1g fiber), 33g pro.

DINNER IN A BAG

SAUSAGE-TOMATO
COCONUT CURRY

SAUSAGE-TOMATO COCONUT CURRY

Made in one pan, this tasty and satisfying recipe easily can be altered for vegetarian diets by using a different protein, such as chickpeas, instead of the sausage.
—Jessie Apfe, Berkeley, CA

Takes: 30 minutes • **Makes:** 4 servings

- 2 Tbsp. olive oil
- 1 pkg. (12 oz.) fully cooked roasted garlic chicken sausage links or flavor of your choice, cut into ½-in. slices
- 1 medium onion, chopped
- 2 Tbsp. red curry paste
- 1 garlic clove, minced
- 1 can (14½ oz.) fire-roasted diced tomatoes, undrained
- 1 can (13.66 oz.) coconut milk
- 2 cups chopped fresh spinach
- ¼ tsp. salt
- ⅛ tsp. pepper
- 3 cups hot cooked rice

1. In a large skillet, heat olive oil over medium-high heat. Add the sausage and onion; cook and stir until onion is tender and sausage is browned, 3-5 minutes. Add red curry paste and garlic; cook 1 minute.
2. Stir in the tomatoes and coconut milk. Bring to a boil and reduce heat. Simmer, uncovered, until sauce starts to thicken, 7-10 minutes. Add spinach, salt and pepper; cook and stir until the spinach begins to wilt. Serve with rice.

1¼ cups curry with ¾ cup rice: 560 cal., 30g fat (18g sat. fat), 70mg chol., 1139mg sod., 49g carb. (7g sugars, 2g fiber), 22g pro.

TEST KITCHEN TIP
Fire-roasted diced tomatoes add a subtle smokiness that helps build flavor, but they aren't essential—if you only have plain diced tomatoes on hand, feel free to use them!

SAUSAGE & SWISS CHARD PASTA

I whipped up lunch with fresh produce from the farmers market and the result was amazing.
—Kate Stiltner, Grand Rapids, MI

Takes: 30 min. • **Makes:** 6 servings

- 12 oz. uncooked orecchiette or small tube pasta (about 2½ cups)
- 1 Tbsp. olive oil
- ½ lb. bulk Italian sausage
- ½ cup chopped red onion
- 1 medium fennel bulb, chopped
- ½ lb. baby portobello mushrooms, chopped
- 3 garlic cloves, minced
- 1 bunch Swiss chard, trimmed and chopped
- ½ tsp. salt
- ¼ tsp. pepper
- ¾ cup grated Parmesan cheese, divided
- ½ cup pine nuts or chopped walnuts, toasted

1. Cook pasta according to package directions for al dente. Heat oil in a skillet over medium heat. Cook Italian sausage and onion until the sausage is no longer pink, 3-4 minutes, breaking sausage into crumbles. Add fennel, mushrooms and garlic; cook until tender, 6-8 minutes. Add Swiss chard; cook and stir until wilted, 4-5 minutes longer.
2. Drain pasta; reserve 1 cup pasta water. Combine pasta, sausage mixture, salt, pepper and ½ cup Parmesan cheese, adding enough pasta water to coat pasta and create a creamy texture. Serve with remaining cheese and pine nuts.

1⅓ cups: 487 cal., 25g fat (6g sat. fat), 34mg chol., 726mg sod., 51g carb. (5g sugars, 4g fiber), 19g pro.

HEALTH TIP Lighten up this dish by using turkey Italian sausage, and add fiber with whole wheat orecchiette instead of white pasta.

CRAB-STUFFED PORTOBELLOS

Fans of portobello mushrooms will want to make these delectable treats filled with a tasty blend of crabmeat, cheese and sweet red pepper again and again.
—Pat Ford, Southampton, PA

Takes: 25 min. • **Makes:** 2 servings

- 2 large portobello mushrooms
- 2 Tbsp. olive oil
- 1 garlic clove, minced
- 1 can (6 oz.) crabmeat, drained, flaked and cartilage removed
- 5 tsp. mayonnaise
- 2 roasted sweet red pepper halves, drained
- 2 slices provolone cheese

1. Remove and discard stems from mushrooms. Place caps on a greased baking sheet. Combine oil and garlic; brush over mushrooms. Broil 4-6 in. from the heat for 4-5 minutes or until tender.
2. In a small bowl, combine crab and mayonnaise. Place a red pepper half on each mushroom; top with crab mixture. Broil for 2-3 minutes or until heated through. Top with cheese slices; broil 1-2 minutes longer or until the cheese is melted.

1 serving: 414 cal., 30g fat (8g sat. fat), 103mg chol., 1014mg sod., 7g carb. (4g sugars, 1g fiber), 25g pro.

SAUSAGE & SWISS CHARD PASTA

CHIPOTLE CITRUS-GLAZED TURKEY TENDERLOINS

This simple skillet recipe makes it easy to cook turkey on a weeknight. The combination of sweet, spicy and smoky flavors from the orange, peppers and molasses is amazing.
—Darlene Morris, Franklinton, LA

Takes: 30 min.
Makes: 4 servings (½ cup sauce)

- 4 **turkey breast tenderloins (5 oz. each)**
- ¼ **tsp. salt**
- ¼ **tsp. pepper**
- 1 **Tbsp. canola oil**
- ¾ **cup orange juice**
- ¼ **cup lime juice**
- ¼ **cup packed brown sugar**
- 1 **Tbsp. molasses**
- 2 **tsp. minced chipotle peppers in adobo sauce**
- 2 **Tbsp. minced fresh cilantro**

1. Sprinkle turkey with salt and pepper. In a large skillet, brown the turkey in oil on all sides.
2. Meanwhile, in a small bowl whisk the juices, brown sugar, molasses and chipotle peppers; add to skillet. Reduce heat and simmer for 12-16 minutes or until the turkey reaches 165°. Transfer turkey to a cutting board; let rest for 5 minutes.
3. Simmer glaze until thickened, about 4 minutes. Slice turkey and serve with glaze. Top with cilantro.

4 oz. cooked turkey with 2 Tbsp. glaze: 274 cal., 5g fat (0 sat. fat), 56mg chol., 252mg sod., 24g carb. (22g sugars, 0 fiber), 35g pro.

PORK WITH MUSTARD SAUCE

Back when I was a girl, I couldn't wait until I was grown up and could start cooking for my own family. Now that I am, this is one of my favorite recipes. The tender meat and the rich mustard sauce are delectable together.
—Irma Pomeroy, Enfield, CT

Takes: 30 min. • **Makes:** 4 servings

- 1 **lb. pork tenderloin**
- 2 **Tbsp. butter**
- ½ **cup beef broth**
- ¾ **tsp. dried tarragon**
- ½ **cup heavy whipping cream**
- 1 **Tbsp. Dijon mustard**
  Salt and pepper to taste
  Hot cooked noodles, optional

1. Cut tenderloin into 8 pieces. Slice each piece again, but do not cut all the way through; open each piece and flatten by pounding slightly with a meat mallet.
2. In a large skillet over medium-high heat, cook the pork in butter until the meat is no longer pink, 5-6 minutes on each side. Remove to a serving dish and keep warm; discard the pan drippings.
3. In the same skillet, cook broth and tarragon over high heat until reduced by half. Reduce heat; stir in cream and mustard. Season with salt and pepper. Spoon over the pork. Serve with noodles, if desired.

2 slices pork with 3 Tbsp. sauce: 292 cal., 21g fat (12g sat. fat), 119mg chol., 311mg sod., 2g carb. (1g sugars, 0 fiber), 24g pro.

PORK WITH MUSTARD SAUCE

MEATLESS TACO SALAD

This colorful salad blends together all your favorite taco ingredients—minus the ground beef. And you won't miss the meat at all! The guacamole dressing is thick and creamy.

—Kimberly Dray, Pflugerville, TX

Takes: 20 min. • **Makes:** 2 servings

- ⅓ cup guacamole
- ¼ cup sour cream
- 2 Tbsp. chopped green pepper
- 1 Tbsp. chopped green onions
- 1 Tbsp. prepared Italian salad dressing
- ¼ tsp. chili powder
- ¼ tsp. pepper
- 3 cups shredded lettuce
- 8 cherry tomatoes, halved
- ½ cup canned kidney beans, rinsed and drained
- ¼ cup sliced ripe olives
- ½ cup crushed corn chips
- ½ cup shredded cheddar cheese

In a small bowl, combine the first 7 ingredients; set aside. In a large bowl, combine lettuce, tomatoes, beans and olives. Arrange the lettuce mixture on a serving plate; top with the guacamole mixture. Sprinkle with crushed corn chips and cheese.

1 serving: 486 cal., 33g fat (12g sat. fat), 35mg chol., 849mg sod., 34g carb. (7g sugars, 9g fiber), 16g pro.

MEATLESS TACO SALAD

PORK CHOPS WITH CUMIN RICE

Cumin lends a real southwestern flair to this satisfying main dish. The tender baked chops pick up extra flavor from the well-seasoned rice. Sometimes I use celery instead of green pepper and boneless skinless chicken breasts instead of the pork chops.

—Loyse Keith, Enumclaw, WA

Takes: 30 min. • **Makes:** 2 servings

- 2 bone-in pork chops (¾ in. thick)
- ¼ tsp. salt
- ¼ tsp. pepper
- 1 Tbsp. vegetable oil
- 1 tsp. chicken bouillon granules
- 1 cup hot water
- ½ cup uncooked long grain rice
- 2 Tbsp. chopped onion
- 2 Tbsp. chopped green pepper
- 2 tsp. Worcestershire sauce
- ½ tsp. ground cumin

1. Preheat oven to 350°. Sprinkle pork chops with salt and pepper. In a small ovenproof skillet, brown chops in oil for 2-3 minutes on each side. Remove and keep warm.
2. Dissolve bouillon in water; pour mixture into skillet and stir to loosen the browned bits. Stir in rice, onion, green pepper, Worcestershire sauce and cumin.
3. Place chops over the rice. Cover and bake for 15-20 minutes or until the meat juices run clear and the rice is tender. Let stand for 5 minutes before serving.

1 pork chop with ¾ cup rice: 581 cal., 26g fat (8g sat. fat), 111mg chol., 850mg sod., 43g carb. (1g sugars, 1g fiber), 40g pro.

SWISS MUSHROOM CHICKEN

Everyone enjoys these golden chicken breasts topped with ham, melted Swiss cheese and fresh mushrooms. This dish is easy to prepare but looks and tastes special enough for company.
—Jan Baxter, Humarock, MA

Takes: 20 min. • **Makes:** 4 servings

- 4 boneless skinless chicken breast halves (4 oz. each)
- 1 large egg
- 1 cup crushed butter-flavored crackers (about 25 crackers)
- ¾ tsp. salt
- ½ lb. fresh mushrooms, sliced
- 2 Tbsp. butter, divided
- 4 slices deli ham or thinly sliced hard salami
- 4 slices Swiss cheese

1. Preheat broiler. Flatten chicken to ¼-in. thickness. In a shallow bowl, lightly beat egg. Combine cracker crumbs and salt in another shallow bowl. Dip the chicken in the egg, then roll in the crumb mixture; set aside.

2. In a large ovenproof skillet, saute the mushrooms in 1 Tbsp. butter until tender; remove and set aside. In the same skillet, cook the chicken over medium heat in the remaining butter for 3-4 minutes on each side or until no longer pink.

3. Top each chicken breast half with a ham slice, mushrooms and a cheese slice. Broil 4-6 in. from the heat for 1-2 minutes or until the cheese is melted.
1 chicken breast half: 343 cal., 21g fat (10g sat. fat), 119mg chol., 956mg sod., 18g carb. (3g sugars, 1g fiber), 20g pro.

CURRIED PORK & GREEN TOMATOES

CURRIED PORK & GREEN TOMATOES

When the tomatoes are green in the garden, my husband and sons are thrilled to know this dish will appear on our weekly menus. I've passed the recipe on more times than I can count.
—Coleen Frederick, Redwater, AB

Takes: 30 min. • **Makes:** 4 servings

- 1 large onion, finely chopped
- 2 Tbsp. butter
- 4 large fresh green tomatoes, cubed
- ¼ cup all-purpose flour
- 1 to 2 tsp. curry powder
- ½ tsp. salt
- ¼ tsp. pepper
- ¼ tsp. sugar
  Pinch ground cardamom, optional
- 2 cups chicken broth
- 2 cups cubed cooked pork
  Hot cooked rice

In a medium skillet, saute onion in butter. Add tomatoes; cover and simmer for 10-12 minutes or until tender. Combine flour, curry, salt, pepper, sugar and, if desired, cardamom; slowly stir into the tomatoes. Add broth and pork; simmer, uncovered, until the sauce thickens, 3-5 minutes. Serve over rice.
1½ cups: 275 cal., 13g fat (6g sat. fat), 79mg chol., 879mg sod., 17g carb. (6g sugars, 2g fiber), 24g pro.

EASY SAUSAGE & VEGETABLE SKILLET

This is an old recipe that has been passed down in our family through my sister-in-law. When I was a child, she did most of the cooking in our house, and this was my favorite meal.
—Ruby Williams, Bogalusa, LA

Takes: 25 min. • **Makes:** 2 servings

- ½ lb. Italian sausage links
- 1 Tbsp. canola oil
- 1 cup cubed yellow summer squash (¾-in. pieces)
- ½ cup chopped green onions
- 2 garlic cloves, minced
- 1½ cups chopped fresh tomatoes
- 2 tsp. Worcestershire sauce
- ⅛ tsp. cayenne pepper

1. In a large skillet, cook sausage over medium heat in oil until a thermometer reads 160°; drain.
2. Cut sausage into ½-in. slices. Add the sausage slices, squash and onions to the skillet; cook for 3-4 minutes or until vegetables are tender. Add garlic; cook 1 minute longer. Stir in the tomatoes, Worcestershire sauce and cayenne pepper; heat through.

1 serving: 304 cal., 22g fat (6g sat. fat), 45mg chol., 607mg sod., 14g carb. (7g sugars, 3g fiber), 14g pro.

READER REVIEW

"I was amazed how healthy and delicious this meal was. Great for company— just be sure to double the recipe so you have enough for your family, too!"
HORSESAREMYTHING, TASTEOFHOME.COM

EASY SAUSAGE & VEGETABLE SKILLET

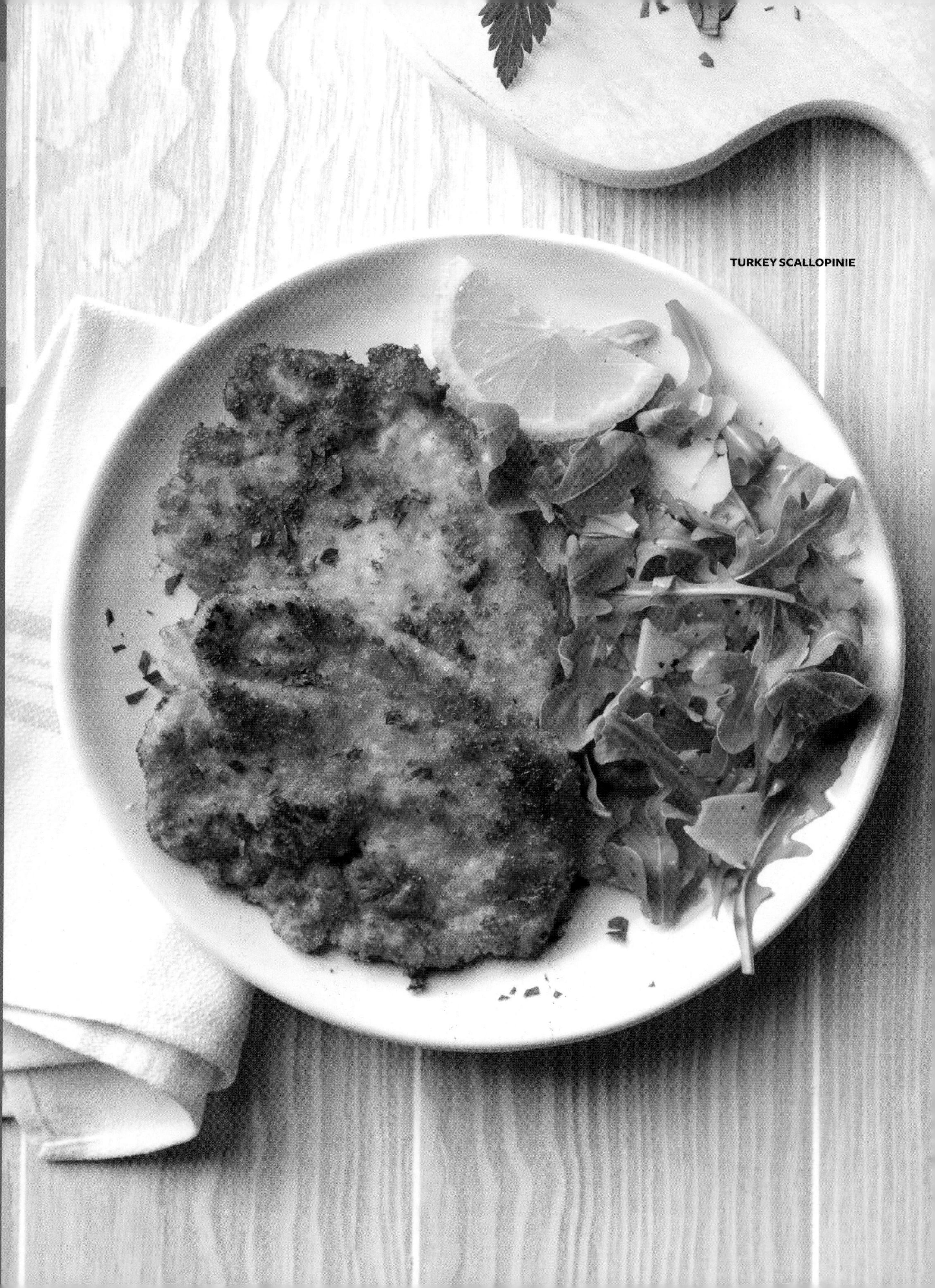

TURKEY SCALLOPINIE

TURKEY SCALLOPINI

Quick-cooking turkey breast slices make it easy to prepare a marvelous meal in just minutes. I've also flattened boneless skinless chicken breast halves in place of the turkey.

—Karen Adams, Cleveland, TN

Takes: 20 min. • **Makes:** 4 servings

- 1 pkg. (17.6 oz.) turkey breast cutlets
- ¼ cup all-purpose flour
- ⅛ tsp. salt
- ⅛ tsp. pepper
- 1 large egg
- 2 Tbsp. water
- 1 cup soft bread crumbs
- ½ cup grated Parmesan cheese
- ¼ cup butter, cubed
  Minced fresh parsley

1. Flatten turkey to ¼-in. thickness. In a shallow bowl, combine the flour, salt and pepper. In another bowl, beat egg and water. In a third shallow bowl, combine bread crumbs and cheese.
2. Dredge turkey in the flour mixture, then dip in the egg mixture and coat with crumbs. Let stand for 5 minutes.
3. Melt butter in a large skillet over medium-high heat; cook the turkey for 2-3 minutes on each side or until the meat is no longer pink and the coating is golden brown. Sprinkle with parsley.

4 oz. cooked turkey: 358 cal., 17g fat (10g sat. fat), 169mg chol., 463mg sod., 12g carb. (1g sugars, 0 fiber), 38g pro.

TURKEY DINNER MUFFINS

PICTURED ON P. 97

I love experimenting in the kitchen. That's how I created these muffins that use up leftovers from a turkey dinner. Team them with a bowl of soup and some fresh fruit for a complete meal.

—Margaret Berardi, Bridgeport, CT

Takes: 30 min. • **Makes:** 10 muffins

- 1¾ cups all-purpose flour
- 3 Tbsp. sugar
- 3 tsp. baking powder
- ½ tsp. salt
- ¼ tsp. poultry seasoning
- 1 large egg
- ¾ cup turkey gravy

GINGERED PORK TENDERLOIN

- ⅓ cup canola oil
- ¾ cup diced cooked turkey
- 2 Tbsp. jellied cranberry sauce

1. Preheat oven to 400°. In a bowl, combine the flour, sugar, baking powder, salt and poultry seasoning. In another bowl, combine egg, gravy and oil; mix well. Stir into the dry ingredients just until combined. Fold in the turkey.
2. Fill greased muffin cups two-thirds full. Top each with ½ tsp. cranberry sauce. Bake 15-18 minutes or until a toothpick inserted in the center comes out clean. Cool for 5 minutes before removing from pans to wire racks. Serve warm.

1 muffin: 198 cal., 9g fat (1g sat. fat), 31mg chol., 352mg sod., 23g carb. (5g sugars, 1g fiber), 6g pro.

GINGERED PORK TENDERLOIN

Ginger, onions and garlic pack a flavorful punch and make an inspired pairing with the mild flavor of pork tenderloin. These tasty medallions smothered in golden caramelized onions are a simple and satisfying main dish.

—Rebecca Evanoff, Holden, MA

Takes: 30 min. • **Makes:** 4 servings

- 2 large onions, thinly sliced
- 4 tsp. olive oil
- ¼ cup water
- 4 tsp. minced fresh gingerroot
- 2 garlic cloves, minced
- ½ cup apple jelly
- 1 pork tenderloin (1 lb.)
- ¼ tsp. salt
  Hot cooked rice pilaf or rice, optional

1. In a large skillet, saute onions in oil for 5-6 minutes. Stir in water, ginger and garlic. Bring to a boil. Reduce heat; cover and simmer until the onions are tender, stirring occasionally, 8-12 minutes. Reduce heat; stir in the apple jelly until melted.
2. Meanwhile, cut tenderloin into 8 slices; flatten each to ½-in. thickness. Sprinkle with salt. In a large skillet coated with cooking spray, brown pork over medium heat, 2-3 minutes on each side. Top with the onion mixture; cover and cook until the meat juices run clear, 5-7 minutes. If desired, serve with rice.

2 slices: 304 cal., 8g fat (2g sat. fat), 64mg chol., 196mg sod., 34g carb. (27g sugars, 1g fiber), 24g pro.

SOUTHWESTERN BEEF & RICE SKILLET

SOUTHWESTERN BEEF & RICE SKILLET

If your family likes stuffed peppers, this deconstructed version is a snap to make on weeknights. Serve this kicked-up skillet dish with warm flour tortillas and a side of guacamole. If you like things even spicier, leave some jalapeno pepper seeds in the dish and enjoy the heat!
—Pat Hockett, Ocala, FL

Takes: 30 min. • **Makes:** 4 servings

- 1   **lb. lean ground beef (90% lean)**
- 1   **medium onion, chopped**
- 1   **medium green pepper, chopped**
- 1   **jalapeno pepper, seeded and finely chopped**
- 1½ **cups uncooked instant rice**
- 1   **can (14½ oz.) diced tomatoes with mild green chiles**
- 1½ **cups beef broth**
- 1   **tsp. ground cumin**
- ¼   **tsp. salt**
- ¼   **tsp. pepper**
- 1   **cup shredded Mexican cheese blend**

1. In a large skillet, cook beef, onion, green pepper and jalapeno over medium heat until the meat is no longer pink and the vegetables are tender, breaking up beef into crumbles, 8-10 minutes; drain.
2. Add the rice, tomatoes, broth and seasonings. Bring to a boil, then reduce heat. Simmer, covered, until the liquid is absorbed, about 5 minutes. Fluff with a fork. Remove from heat; sprinkle with cheese. Let stand, covered, until the cheese is melted.

1½ cups: 482 cal., 19g fat (8g sat. fat), 96mg chol., 962mg sod., 41g carb. (5g sugars, 4g fiber), 33g pro.
HEALTH TIP Use instant brown rice instead of white, switch to reduced-sodium broth, skip the added salt and sprinkle with just ¼ cup sharp cheddar instead of 1 cup of the mild blend. The result: 400 calories, 13g fat and 540mg sodium per serving.

SPRINGTIME PENNE

With ham and asparagus in a creamy sauce, this simple pasta is tasty enough for even your pickiest guests. It's wonderful for Easter, or to use up leftover ham any time.
—Cheryl Newendorp, Pella, IA

Takes: 20 min. • **Makes:** 5 servings

- 3 cups uncooked penne pasta
- 1 lb. fresh asparagus, cut into 1-in. pieces
- 1 large onion, chopped
- ¼ cup butter
- ½ lb. cubed fully cooked ham
- ½ cup heavy whipping cream
- ¼ tsp. pepper
- ⅛ tsp. salt
  Shredded Parmesan cheese, optional

1. Cook pasta according to package directions.
2. Meanwhile, in a large skillet, saute asparagus and onion in butter until asparagus is crisp-tender, 5-8 minutes. Add the ham, cream, pepper and salt; bring to a boil. Reduce heat; cook over low heat for 1 minute.
3. Drain pasta. Add to the asparagus mixture; toss to coat. If desired, top with shredded Parmesan cheese.

1½ cups: 389 cal., 21g fat (12g sat. fat), 75mg chol., 617mg sod., 37g carb. (4g sugars, 3g fiber), 16g pro.

HEALTH TIP Although this pasta dish tastes light and fresh, it does contain butter and cream. To slim this dish down—to just under 300 calories per serving—use just 2 Tbsp. butter and substitute half-and-half in place of the heavy whipping cream.

TARRAGON CHICKEN WITH APPLES FOR TWO

When friends served us this delicious chicken, I knew I had to have the recipe. The original version called for whipping cream, which is a little high in fat for me. I substituted 1% milk and found that it was just as good but not quite as rich.
—Karen Moffatt, Lake Cowichan, BC

Takes: 30 min. • **Makes:** 2 servings

- 2 boneless skinless chicken breast halves (4 oz. each)
- 3 tsp. butter, divided
- ⅛ tsp. salt
  Dash pepper
- 1 medium tart apple, peeled and sliced
- ¼ cup unsweetened apple juice
- ¼ cup 2% milk
- ½ tsp. cornstarch
- 1½ tsp. water
- 1½ tsp. minced fresh tarragon or ½ tsp. dried tarragon
  Hot cooked long grain and wild rice, optional

1. In a large nonstick skillet, brown the chicken in 2 tsp. butter for 3-4 minutes on each side. Sprinkle with salt and pepper; remove and keep warm. In the same skillet, cook apples in the remaining butter for 6-8 minutes or until tender; remove and keep warm.
2. Add apple juice to the pan; cook and stir over medium heat for 4 minutes or until the juice is reduced by half. Add milk. Return chicken to pan; cook for 3 minutes or until chicken juices run clear.
3. Combine cornstarch and water until smooth; stir into the pan juices. Bring to a boil; cook and stir for 2 minutes or until thickened.
4. Add the apples and tarragon; heat through. Serve with rice if desired.

1 serving: 236 cal., 9g fat (5g sat. fat), 80mg chol., 259mg sod., 14g carb. (12g sugars, 1g fiber), 24g pro. **Diabetic exchanges:** 3 lean meat, 1 fruit, 1 fat.

SPRINGTIME PENNE

EASY TURKEY SCHNITZEL

Our family lived in Europe for 11 years and this was by far our sons' favorite recipe. In Germany and Austria, schnitzel is typically served with french fries on the side and lemon wedges for squeezing onto the breaded cutlets. In Europe I used veal, but now that we're back home, turkey slices are a fine substitute.
—Sue Jurack, Mequon, WI

Takes: 25 min. • **Makes:** 4 servings

- ¼ cup 2% milk
- ½ cup all-purpose flour
- 2 large eggs, lightly beaten
- ¾ cup seasoned bread crumbs
- 1 lb. turkey slices (¼ in. thick)
- 2 Tbsp. butter
- 2 Tbsp. canola oil

1. Place the milk, flour, eggs and bread crumbs in 4 separate shallow bowls. Dip the turkey slices into milk, then coat with flour. Dip into eggs and coat with bread crumbs. Place on waxed paper; let stand for 5-10 minutes.
2. In a large skillet, brown the turkey over medium-high heat in butter and oil for 2 minutes on each side or until juices run clear.
1 serving: 424 cal., 18g fat (5g sat. fat), 194mg chol., 475mg sod., 28g carb. (2g sugars, 1g fiber), 36g pro.

NACHO PIE

PICTURED ON P. 97
In place of ground beef and mozzarella cheese, consider topping this zesty pie with lean ground sausage and cheddar cheese. It tastes just as good.
—LaVerna Mjones, Moorhead, MN

Takes: 30 min. • **Makes:** 6 servings

- 4 cups nacho tortilla chips, coarsely crushed
- 1 lb. ground beef
- ½ cup chopped onion
- 1 can (16 oz.) chili beans, undrained, warmed
- 1 can (8 oz.) tomato sauce
- 1 cup shredded part-skim mozzarella cheese

QUICK CILANTRO CHICKEN

1. Preheat oven to 375°. Place chips in a lightly greased 9-in. pie plate and set aside.
2. In a large skillet, cook beef and onion over medium heat until meat is no longer pink; drain. Spoon over chips. Top with beans, tomato sauce and cheese.
3. Bake, uncovered, until heated through and the cheese is melted, 7-8 minutes.
1 serving: 462 cal., 24g fat (7g sat. fat), 59mg chol., 841mg sod., 40g carb. (3g sugars, 6g fiber), 26g pro.

QUICK CILANTRO CHICKEN

If you're a fan of cilantro, you'll definitely like this chicken dish. The cilantro adds herbal flavor, melding with the tangy lemon juice and caramelized onions.
—Mary Pipkin, Melba, ID

Takes: 30 min. • **Makes:** 4 servings

- 1 lb. boneless skinless chicken breasts, cut into 1-in. cubes
- ½ tsp. salt
- ½ tsp. ground cumin
- ¼ tsp. pepper
- 4 Tbsp. butter, divided
- 2 large onions, sliced
- ½ cup lemon juice
- ¼ cup minced fresh cilantro
  Hot cooked rice, optional

1. Sprinkle chicken with salt, cumin and pepper. In a skillet over medium heat, cook and stir the chicken in 2 Tbsp. butter until no longer pink. Remove and keep warm.
2. In the same skillet, saute onions in the remaining butter until tender and golden brown. Return chicken to pan. Stir in the lemon juice and cilantro; bring to a boil. If desired, serve with rice.
1 cup: 260 cal., 14g fat (8g sat. fat), 93mg chol., 469mg sod., 9g carb. (6g sugars, 2g fiber), 24g pro.

PENNE WITH VEGGIES & BLACK BEANS

Chock-full of zucchini, tomato, sweet pepper and carrot, this hearty pasta dish puts your garden harvest to good use.
—Vickie Spoerle, Carmel, IN

Takes: 25 min. • **Makes:** 2 servings

- ¾ cup uncooked penne pasta
- ⅓ cup sliced zucchini
- ⅓ cup sliced fresh carrot
- 4 medium fresh mushrooms, sliced
- ½ small green pepper, thinly sliced
- ½ small onion, thinly sliced
- 1 small garlic clove, minced
- ¼ tsp. each dried basil, oregano and thyme
- ¼ tsp. salt
- ⅛ tsp. pepper
- 2 tsp. olive oil, divided
- 1 cup canned black beans, rinsed and drained
- ¼ cup chopped seeded tomato
- 2 Tbsp. shredded Parmesan cheese
- 2 tsp. minced fresh parsley

1. Cook the pasta according to package directions. Meanwhile, in a large nonstick skillet, saute the zucchini, carrot, mushrooms, green pepper, onion, garlic and seasonings in 1 tsp. oil until vegetables are crisp-tender. Stir in the beans.
2. Drain pasta; add to the vegetable mixture. Add tomato and the remaining oil; toss gently. Sprinkle with Parmesan cheese and parsley.
1⅓ cups: 300 cal., 7g fat (2g sat. fat), 4mg chol., 643mg sod., 47g carb. (6g sugars, 8g fiber), 14g pro.

CHEDDAR BROCCOLI QUINOA

For the longest time, my family didn't catch on that I didn't serve meat on Mondays—the meals were so good, they didn't miss the meat! Quinoa is an excellent protein substitute. I serve this with a tossed salad.
—Marietta Slater, Justin, TX

Takes: 30 min. • **Makes:** 4 servings

- 2 cups vegetable broth
- 1 cup quinoa, rinsed
- 2 cups chopped fresh broccoli
- 2 Tbsp. butter
- ¼ cup chopped onion
- ¼ cup chopped green pepper
- 1 cup shredded cheddar cheese, divided
- ½ tsp. salt
- ¼ tsp. pepper

1. In a large saucepan, bring broth to a boil. Add the quinoa. Reduce heat; simmer, covered, until liquid is absorbed, 12-15 minutes, adding broccoli during the last 5 minutes of cooking. Remove from heat; fluff with a fork.
2. Meanwhile, in a small skillet, heat butter over medium-high heat. Add onion and green pepper; cook and stir until tender, 5-7 minutes. Stir in the quinoa mixture, ½ cup cheese, salt and pepper. Sprinkle with the remaining ½ cup cheese. Cover and let stand until the cheese is melted.
1¼ cups: 350 cal., 18g fat (9g sat. fat), 43mg chol., 876mg sod., 34g carb. (3g sugars, 5g fiber), 14g pro.

PENNE WITH VEGGIES & BLACK BEANS

CHEESY HAMBURGER SUPPER

I have wonderful memories of eating this comforting all-in-one meal while growing up. Our whole family loved the flavor and there were rarely any leftovers.
—Andrea Brandt, Newton, KS

Takes: 30 min. • **Makes:** 4 servings

- 1 lb. ground beef
- 1½ cups water
- ½ tsp. poultry seasoning
- ¼ tsp. pepper
- 1 envelope brown gravy mix
- 1 medium onion, sliced and separated into rings
- 1 medium carrot, sliced
- 2 medium potatoes, sliced
- 1 cup shredded cheddar cheese

1. In a large skillet, cook beef over medium heat until no longer pink; drain. Stir in water, poultry seasoning and pepper. Bring to a boil. Stir in gravy mix. Cook and stir until slightly thickened, about 2 minutes.

2. Arrange onion, carrot and potatoes over beef. Reduce heat; cover and simmer until vegetables are tender, 10-15 minutes. Sprinkle with cheese. Cover and cook until the cheese is melted, 3-5 minutes longer.

1 serving: 412 cal., 19g fat (11g sat. fat), 86mg chol., 796mg sod., 30g carb. (6g sugars, 3g fiber), 30g pro.

CREAMY CURRIED CHICKEN

CREAMY CURRIED CHICKEN

This is a big hit in our house—my young son and daughter just gobble it up! With its irresistible blend of curry and sweet coconut milk, it'll become a favorite with your family, too.
—Tracy Simiele, Chardon, OH

Takes: 30 min. • **Makes:** 4 servings

- 1½ cups uncooked instant rice
- 1 lb. boneless skinless chicken breasts, cut into 1-in. pieces
- 2 tsp. curry powder
- ¾ tsp. salt
- ¼ tsp. pepper
- ½ cup chopped onion
- 1 Tbsp. canola oil
- 1 can (13.66 oz.) coconut milk
- 2 Tbsp. tomato paste
- 3 cups fresh baby spinach
- 1 cup chopped tomato

1. Cook rice according to the package directions. Meanwhile, sprinkle the chicken with curry, salt and pepper. In a large skillet, saute the chicken and onion in oil until the chicken is no longer pink.

2. Stir in coconut milk and tomato paste. Bring to a boil. Reduce heat; simmer, uncovered, for 5 minutes or until thickened. Add spinach and tomato; cook 2-3 minutes longer or until the spinach is wilted. Serve with rice.

1 cup chicken mixture with ¾ cup rice: 508 cal., 27g fat (19g sat. fat), 63mg chol., 541mg sod., 39g carb. (6g sugars, 4g fiber), 29g pro.

TANGY SWEET & SOUR MEATBALLS

A tangy sauce, pineapple and green pepper transform pre-made meatballs into something special. Serve over rice for a satisfying main dish.
—Ruth Andrewson, Leavenworth, WA

Takes: 30 min. • **Makes:** 6 servings

- 1 can (20 oz.) pineapple chunks
- ⅓ cup water
- 3 Tbsp. vinegar
- 1 Tbsp. soy sauce
- ½ cup packed brown sugar
- 3 Tbsp. cornstarch
- 30 frozen fully cooked Italian meatballs (about 15 oz.)
- 1 large green pepper, cut into 1-in. pieces
  Hot cooked rice

Drain pineapple, reserving the juice. Set pineapple aside. Add water as needed to the juice to measure 1 cup; pour juice into a large skillet. Add ⅓ cup additional water, the vinegar, soy sauce, brown sugar and cornstarch; stir until smooth. Cook over medium heat until thick, stirring constantly. Add pineapple, meatballs and green pepper. Simmer, uncovered, until heated through, about 20 minutes. Serve with rice.

5 meatballs: 389 cal., 19g fat (8g sat. fat), 30mg chol., 682mg sod., 47g carb. (36g sugars, 2g fiber), 11g pro.

GREEK VEGGIES EGG WRAPS

This tasty vegetable and egg scramble makes a perfect "breakfast for dinner."
—*Taste of Home* Test Kitchen

Takes: 20 min. • **Makes:** 4 servings

- 1 cup sliced sweet onion
- 1 cup julienned green pepper
- 1 Tbsp. butter
- 8 large eggs, beaten
- 1 Tbsp. minced fresh basil
- ½ tsp. dried oregano
- ¼ tsp. salt
- ⅛ tsp. pepper
- 4 whole pita breads, warmed
- 1 large tomato, sliced
- ½ cup crumbled feta cheese

In a large skillet, saute onion and green pepper in butter for 3 minutes or until tender. Add the eggs, basil, oregano, salt and pepper; cook and stir over medium heat until the eggs are completely set. Spoon onto pita bread. Top with tomato and cheese.

1 serving: 402 cal., 16g fat (7g sat. fat), 440mg chol., 765mg sod., 41g carb. (6g sugars, 3g fiber), 21g pro.

TANGY SWEET & SOUR MEATBALLS

SKILLET TACOS

BLUEBERRY-DIJON CHICKEN

Blueberries and chicken may seem like a strange combination, but prepare to be dazzled! I add a sprinkling of minced fresh basil as the finishing touch.
—Susan Marshall, Colorado Springs, CO

Takes: 30 min. • **Makes:** 4 servings

    4   boneless skinless chicken breast
        halves (6 oz. each)
    ¼   tsp. salt
    ¼   tsp. pepper
    1   Tbsp. butter
    ½   cup blueberry preserves
    ⅓   cup raspberry vinegar
    ¼   cup fresh or frozen blueberries
    3   Tbsp. Dijon mustard
        Optional: Minced fresh basil
          or tarragon

1. Sprinkle chicken with salt and pepper. In a large skillet, cook chicken in butter over medium heat until a thermometer reads 165°, 6-8 minutes on each side. Remove and keep warm.
2. In the same skillet, combine preserves, vinegar, blueberries and mustard, stirring to loosen any browned bits from pan. Bring to a boil; cook and stir mixture until thickened. Serve with chicken. Sprinkle with basil if desired.

1 chicken breast with 2 Tbsp. sauce: 325 cal., 7g fat (3g sat. fat), 102mg chol., 522mg sod., 27g carb. (25g sugars, 0 fiber), 34g pro.

READER REVIEW
"Holy smokes! This was awesome! It is one of the best recipes I have tried in a long time. That it was simple and quick was an added bonus."
JUSTMBETH, TASTEOFHOME.COM

SKILLET TACOS

If you like Mexican food, you'll be whipping up these fast, healthy skillet tacos often.
—Maria Gobel, Greenfield, WI

Takes: 30 min. • **Makes:** 2 servings

    1   Tbsp. olive oil
    ¼   lb. lean ground turkey
    2   Tbsp. chopped onion
    2   Tbsp. chopped green pepper
    1   can (8 oz.) tomato sauce
    ½   cup uncooked elbow macaroni
    ½   cup water
    ¼   cup picante sauce
    2   Tbsp. shredded reduced-fat
        cheddar cheese
    ¼   cup crushed baked tortilla
        chip scoops
    ¼   cup chopped avocado
        Optional: Iceberg lettuce wedges
          and sour cream

1. Heat olive oil in a large nonstick skillet over medium-high heat; add turkey, onion and green pepper and cook until the vegetables are tender and the turkey is no longer pink.
2. Stir in the tomato sauce, macaroni, water and picante sauce. Bring to a boil. Reduce heat; cover and simmer until the macaroni is tender, 10-15 minutes.
3. Divide between 2 plates; top with cheese, tortilla chips and avocado. Serve with lettuce and sour cream if desired.
1 cup: 337 cal., 17g fat (4g sat. fat), 44mg chol., 861mg sod., 30g carb. (4g sugars, 5g fiber), 19g pro.

BLUEBERRY-DIJON CHICKEN

ASPARAGUS BEEF TERIYAKI

ASPARAGUS BEEF TERIYAKI

This simple, savory creation is made in the time it takes to steam a pot of rice. About 20 minutes and—boom!—you're dishing dinner.
—Kari Shifflett, Lake Mills, IA

....

Takes: 30 min. • **Makes:** 4 servings

- ½ cup teriyaki marinade
- 2 Tbsp. water
- 1 Tbsp. cornstarch
- ¼ tsp. pepper
- 2 Tbsp. sesame oil, divided
- 1 beef sirloin tip steak (1 lb.), thinly sliced
- 1 large sweet onion, chopped
- 1 medium green pepper, thinly sliced
- 1 medium sweet red pepper, thinly sliced
- ½ lb. fresh asparagus, trimmed and cut into 1-in. pieces
- 1 garlic clove, minced
- 3 cups hot cooked rice
  Soy sauce
  Sesame seeds

1. In a small bowl, mix marinade, water, cornstarch and pepper until smooth.

2. In a skillet, heat 1 Tbsp. sesame oil over medium-high heat. Add beef and stir-fry until no longer pink, 6-8 minutes. Remove from pan.

3. Stir-fry the onion, green pepper, red pepper and asparagus in remaining 1 Tbsp. oil until vegetables are crisp-tender, 4-5 minutes. Add garlic; cook 1 minute longer.

4. Stir cornstarch mixture and add to pan. Bring to a boil; cook and stir 1-2 minutes or until sauce is thickened. Return beef to pan; heat through. Serve over rice; drizzle with soy sauce and top with sesame seeds.

2 cups stir-fry with ¾ cup rice: 444 cal., 13g fat (3g sat. fat), 72mg chol., 1266mg sod., 50g carb. (11g sugars, 3g fiber), 30g pro.

FLOUNDER ZUCCHINI BUNDLES

A lovely hint of lemon carries the flavors of this colorful meal in one. My husband, not typically a fish eater, enjoys this recipe!
—Isabelle Rooney, Summerville, SC

....

Takes: 30 min. • **Makes:** 4 servings

- 8 flounder fillets (3 oz. each)
- ¼ tsp. lemon-pepper seasoning
- 1 medium lemon, thinly sliced
- 1 medium zucchini, cut into ¼-in. slices
- 12 cherry tomatoes, halved
- ¼ tsp. dill weed
- ¼ tsp. dried basil

Preheat oven to 425°. For each bundle, place 2 fillets on a double thickness of heavy-duty foil (18x15 in.); sprinkle with lemon-pepper. Top with lemon slices, zucchini and tomatoes. Sprinkle with dill and basil. Fold foil around fish and seal tightly. Place on a baking sheet. Bake 15-20 minutes or until fish flakes easily with a fork.

1 serving: 159 cal., 2g fat (0 sat. fat), 80mg chol., 160mg sod., 5g carb. (2g sugars, 1g fiber), 29g pro. **Diabetic exchanges:** 4 lean meat, 1 vegetable.

SOUTHWEST TORTILLA-TURKEY SKILLET

I wanted to cut back on red meat, but my husband thought ground turkey was dry. The taco seasoning and jalapeno juice in this recipe give the turkey added flavor and moistness—and he loves it!
—Lindsay Ludden, Omaha, NE

....

Takes: 25 min. • **Makes:** 2 servings

- ½ lb. ground turkey
- ¾ cup black beans, rinsed and drained
- ½ cup water
- ⅓ cup sliced ripe olives
- 2 Tbsp. reduced-sodium taco seasoning
- 1 Tbsp. juice from pickled jalapeno slices
- 1 flour tortilla (10 in.), cut into 1-in. pieces
- ½ cup shredded reduced-fat Mexican cheese blend
- 2 Tbsp. pickled jalapeno slices
- 2 Tbsp. reduced-fat sour cream

1. In a large skillet, cook turkey over medium heat until no longer pink; drain. Stir in the beans, water, olives, taco seasoning and juice from jalapenos. Bring to a boil. Reduce heat; simmer, uncovered, for 6-7 minutes or until thickened.
2. Stir in tortilla pieces. Sprinkle with cheese and jalapeno. Remove from the heat and cover for 1-2 minutes or until cheese is melted. Serve with sour cream.
1½ cups: 496 cal., 21g fat (8g sat. fat), 91mg chol., 1502mg sod., 41g carb. (6g sugars, 6g fiber), 39g pro.

TORTILLA-TURKEY SKILLET

EASY SALISBURY STEAK

This meat dish can be made in 25 minutes or made ahead of time and reheated with the gravy in the microwave. I often double the recipe and freeze one batch of cooked steaks and gravy for an even faster meal on an especially busy night.
—Carol Callahan, Rome, GA

....

Takes: 25 min. • **Makes:** 4 servings

- ⅓ cup chopped onion
- ¼ cup crushed saltines
- 1 large egg white, lightly beaten
- 2 Tbsp. 2% milk
- 1 Tbsp. prepared horseradish
- ¼ tsp. salt, optional
- ⅛ tsp. pepper
- 1 lb. lean ground beef (90% lean)
- 1 jar (12 oz.) beef gravy
- 1¼ to 1½ cups sliced fresh mushrooms
- 2 Tbsp. water
  Hot cooked noodles, optional

1. In a large bowl, combine the onion, saltines, egg white, milk, horseradish, salt (if desired) and pepper. Crumble beef over the onion mixture. Shape into 4 oval patties.
2. In a large skillet over medium heat, cook patties for 5-6 minutes on each side or until no pink remains and a thermometer reads 160°.
3. Remove patties and keep warm. Add gravy, mushrooms and water to skillet; cook for 3-5 minutes or until heated through. Serve with patties and noodles if desired.
1 serving: 248 cal., 12g fat (0 sat. fat), 66mg chol., 205mg sod., 9g carb. (0 sugars, 0 fiber), 25g pro. **Diabetic exchanges:** 3 meat, ½ starch, ½ vegetable.

HERBED PORK MEDALLIONS

This effortless entree tastes just as good as it looks. The pork slices have a nice blend of seasonings and they broil in just minutes. This dish is special enough to serve to company.
—Jodie Arkin, Waconia, MN

Takes: 20 min. • **Makes:** 6 servings

- 1½ lbs. pork tenderloin
- 2 Tbsp. butter, melted
- ¼ tsp. garlic powder
- ½ tsp. salt
- ½ tsp. dried tarragon
- ½ tsp. dried thyme
- ½ tsp. paprika
- ⅛ tsp. pepper
- ⅛ tsp. cayenne pepper
- 1 Tbsp. honey

1. Preheat broiler. Cut pork into ½-in. slices and pound to flatten. Combine butter and garlic powder; brush over pork. Combine the seasonings; sprinkle over the pork.
2. Broil pork 4-6 in. from the heat for 4 minutes on each side. Brush with the honey; broil 1 minute longer or until the meat juices run clear.

4 oz. pork: 177 cal., 8g fat (4g sat. fat), 73mg chol., 280mg sod., 3g carb. (3g sugars, 0 fiber), 23g pro.

CHICKEN SKILLET SUPPER

Our children are all grown up now so I'm usually cooking for just two. I keep my eye out for recipes I can cut down or are already reduced. This one was worth sharing.
—Delia Kennedy, Deer Park, WA

Takes: 30 min. • **Makes:** 2 servings

- ½ lb. boneless skinless chicken breasts, cut into ½-in. pieces
- 1 Tbsp. vegetable oil
- 1 small onion, chopped
- ½ cup chopped green pepper
- 1 can (14½ oz.) diced tomatoes, drained
- 1 can (7 oz.) whole kernel corn, drained
- 2 Tbsp. salsa
- ½ tsp. ground cumin
  Hot cooked pasta

In a large skillet, stir-fry the chicken in oil until no longer pink. Add the onion and green pepper; cook until tender. Stir in tomatoes, corn, salsa and cumin. Bring to a boil. Simmer, uncovered, for 5 minutes or until thickened. Serve with pasta.

1½ cups: 299 cal., 10g fat (2g sat. fat), 63mg chol., 1025mg sod., 25g carb. (15g sugars, 7g fiber), 27g pro.

HURRY-UP HAM & NOODLES

The rich-tasting dish is ready to serve in almost the time it takes to cook the noodles. I've made it for luncheons and potlucks, but mostly I make it on days when I'm in a hurry to get something on the table.
—Lucille Howell, Portland, OR

Takes: 25 min. • **Makes:** 4 servings

- 5 to 6 cups uncooked wide egg noodles
- ¼ cup butter, cubed
- 1 cup heavy whipping cream
- 1½ cups chopped fully cooked ham
- ½ cup grated Parmesan cheese
- ¼ cup thinly sliced green onions
- ¼ tsp. salt
- ⅛ tsp. pepper

1. Cook noodles according to package directions. Meanwhile, in a large skillet, melt butter over medium heat. Gradually whisk in cream. Bring to a boil, stirring constantly; cook and stir until thickened, about 2 minutes longer.
2. Add ham, cheese, onions, salt and pepper; cook, uncovered, until heated through. Drain noodles; add to the ham mixture. Toss to coat; heat through.

1½ cups: 619 cal., 43g fat (25g sat. fat), 193mg chol., 1154mg sod., 38g carb. (3g sugars, 1g fiber), 22g pro.

HURRY-UP HAM & NOODLES

SOUTHERN SHRIMP & GRITS

We sometimes call this dish "breakfast shrimp." Serve it for brunch, dinner or when company's coming. It's down-home comfort food at its finest!
—Mandy Rivers, Lexington, SC

....

Takes: 30 min. • **Makes:** 4 servings

- 2 cups reduced-sodium chicken broth
- 2 cups 2% milk
- ⅓ cup butter, cubed
- ¾ tsp. salt
- ½ tsp. pepper
- ¾ cup uncooked old-fashioned grits
- 1 cup shredded cheddar cheese

SHRIMP
- 8 thick-sliced bacon strips, chopped
- 1 lb. uncooked medium shrimp, peeled and deveined
- 3 garlic cloves, minced
- 1 tsp. Cajun or blackened seasoning
- 4 green onions, chopped

1. In a large saucepan, bring the broth, milk, butter, salt and pepper to a boil. Slowly stir in the grits. Reduce heat. Cover and cook for 12-14 minutes or until thickened, stirring occasionally. Stir in the cheese until melted. Set aside and keep warm.
2. In a large skillet, cook chopped bacon over medium heat until crisp. Remove to paper towels with a slotted spoon; drain, reserving 4 tsp. drippings. Saute shrimp, garlic and Cajun seasoning in the drippings until the shrimp turn pink. Serve with grits and sprinkle with onions.

1 cup grits with ½ cup shrimp mixture: 674 cal., 42g fat (22g sat. fat), 241mg chol., 1845mg sod., 33g carb. (7g sugars, 1g fiber), 41g pro.

SOUTHERN SHRIMP & GRITS

HONEY MUSTARD PORK

Dijon mustard and honey create a sweet and subtly tangy sauce that perfectly complements lean pork tenderloin.
—Janet Les, Chilliwack, BC

....

Takes: 30 min. • **Makes:** 4 servings

- 1 lb. pork tenderloin, cut into thin strips
- 1 Tbsp. canola oil
- 1 cup reduced-sodium beef broth, divided
- ¼ cup honey
- 1 Tbsp. Dijon mustard
- 1 Tbsp. cornstarch
- 2 Tbsp. cold water
  Hot cooked long grain and wild rice, optional

1. In a large nonstick skillet, brown pork in oil on all sides. Add ½ cup broth. Bring to a boil. Reduce heat; cover and simmer for 10 minutes or until the meat is tender. Remove pork with a slotted spoon and keep warm.
2. Stir in the honey, mustard and the remaining broth. Combine cornstarch and water until smooth. Gradually stir into the pan. Bring to a boil; cook and stir for 2 minutes or until thickened. Return pork to the pan; heat through. Serve with rice if desired.

1 serving: 242 cal., 7g fat (2g sat. fat), 64mg chol., 246mg sod., 20g carb. (18g sugars, 0 fiber), 23g pro. **Diabetic exchanges:** 3 lean meat, 1 starch, 1 fat.

READER REVIEW
"I really enjoyed this meal. The ratio of mustard and honey was perfect and it wasn't too much of either. Just a really balanced sauce with lots of great flavor."
DMWILMOTH, TASTEOFHOME.COM

Casseroles & Oven Entrees

Nothing says home cooking like a scrumptious meal from the oven!
These oven-baked main dishes and comforting casseroles are just
the thing for sit-down dinners with friends and family.

Cornmeal Oven-Fried Chicken (p. 128) **Tuna Noodle Casserole** (p. 128) **Mushroom-Blue Cheese Tenderloin** (p. 130) **Deluxe Deep-Dish Pizza** (p. 134) **Saturday Afternoon Oven Pot Roast** (p. 129)

CHEESY STUFFED PEPPERS

This is my favorite summertime dinner. When I can get peppers and tomatoes fresh from my garden, there's nothing better than this!
—Betty DeRaad, Sioux Falls, SD

Prep: 20 min. • **Bake:** 20 min.
Makes: 6 servings

- 6 medium green peppers
- 1½ lbs. ground beef
- 1 medium onion, chopped
- ½ tsp. salt
- 2 cups shredded cheddar cheese
- 2½ cups chopped tomatoes (3 medium)
- 1½ cups cooked rice

1. Preheat oven to 350°. Cut tops off peppers and remove seeds. In a Dutch oven, cook peppers in boiling water for 6-8 minutes or until crisp-tender.
2. Meanwhile, brown beef, onion and salt in a skillet; drain. Cool slightly. Stir in the cheese, tomatoes and rice.
3. Drain the peppers and stuff with the meat mixture. Place in a baking dish. Bake, uncovered, for 20 minutes or until heated through.

1 serving: 419 cal., 21g fat (13g sat. fat), 96mg chol., 509mg sod., 26g carb. (7g sugars, 4g fiber), 31g pro.

MAKEOVER TATER-TOPPED CASSEROLE

MAKEOVER TATER-TOPPED CASSEROLE

I love Tater Tots, and I always loved my casserole recipe...but I wanted it to be healthier. The experts at Taste of Home slashed the fat in this dish, while keeping the Tater Tots my family loves!
—Scott Woodward, Shullsburg, WI

Prep: 15 min. • **Bake:** 55 min.
Makes: 8 servings

- 1 lb. lean ground beef (90% lean)
- ½ lb. extra-lean ground turkey
- 1 pkg. (16 oz.) frozen mixed vegetables, thawed and drained
- ¾ cup french-fried onions
- 1 can (10¾ oz.) reduced-fat reduced-sodium condensed cream of celery soup, undiluted
- 1 can (10¾ oz.) reduced-fat reduced-sodium condensed cream of chicken soup, undiluted
- ½ cup fat-free milk
- 4 cups frozen Tater Tots, thawed

1. Preheat oven to 350°. In a large skillet, cook beef and turkey over medium heat until no longer pink. In a 13x9-in. baking dish coated with cooking spray, layer the meat mixture, mixed vegetables and french-fried onions.
2. In a small bowl, combine soups and milk; spread over the onions. Top with Tater Tots. Bake, uncovered, until golden brown, 55-60 minutes.

1 cup: 340 cal., 14g fat (4g sat. fat), 44mg chol., 657mg sod., 33g carb. (4g sugars, 4g fiber), 22g pro.

CHICKEN CORDON BLEU PUFFS

I love the flavors of chicken cordon bleu, but wanted a faster weeknight version, so I pulled this recipe together one evening. We loved it so much I had to make it again the next week!
—Angela Keller, Newburgh, IN

Prep: 30 min. • **Bake:** 20 min.
Makes: 8 servings

- 2 **Tbsp. butter**
- 2 **Tbsp. all-purpose flour**
- 1 **cup 2% milk**
- 1 **Tbsp. grated Parmesan cheese**
- 1 **tsp. lemon juice**
- ¾ **tsp. seasoned salt**
- ½ **tsp. Dijon mustard**
- 2 **cups cubed rotisserie chicken**
- 4 **slices deli ham, chopped**
- ½ **cup shredded Swiss cheese**
- 1 **pkg. (17.3 oz.) frozen puff pastry, thawed**

1. Preheat the oven to 400°. In a small saucepan, melt butter over medium heat. Stir in flour until smooth; gradually whisk in milk. Bring to a boil, stirring constantly; cook and stir until thickened, 2-3 minutes. Stir in the Parmesan cheese, lemon juice, seasoned salt and mustard; remove from heat. Stir in the chicken, ham and Swiss cheese.

2. On a lightly floured surface, unfold the puff pastry. Roll each pastry out into an 11-in. square. Cut each square into quarters. Place the quarters in 8 greased jumbo muffin cups, pressing gently onto the bottoms and up sides, allowing the corners to point up. Divide the chicken mixture among cups. Bring the pastry corners together and pinch to seal. Bake until golden brown, 20-25 minutes.

1 puff: 454 cal., 25g fat (8g sat. fat), 53mg chol., 542mg sod., 38g carb. (2g sugars, 5g fiber), 20g pro.

SENSATIONAL SPICED SALMON

A sweet and spicy rub gives this quick salmon entree fantastic flavor. Paired with a green veggie and rice, it's a delightful weeknight dinner that's special enough for company.
—Michele Doucette, Stephenville, NL

Takes: 25 min. • **Makes:** 4 servings

- 2 **Tbsp. brown sugar**
- 4 **tsp. chili powder**
- 2 **tsp. grated lemon zest**
- ¾ **tsp. ground cumin**
- ½ **tsp. salt**
- ¼ **tsp. ground cinnamon**
- 4 **salmon fillets (4 oz. each)**

Combine the first 6 ingredients; rub over salmon. Place in an 11x7-in. baking dish coated with cooking spray. Bake, uncovered, at 350° until fish flakes easily with a fork, 15-20 minutes.

1 fillet: 244 cal., 13g fat (3g sat. fat), 67mg chol., 392mg sod., 9g carb. (7g sugars, 1g fiber), 23g pro. **Diabetic exchanges:** 3 lean meat, ½ starch.

TOMATO POTPIE

I have shared this treasured family recipe with many friends over the years. It should be made with the best tomatoes of the summer and early fall. We eat it as a main dish, but it can also be served as a side. The tomatoes should be about 1 inch deep in the pan before you add the topping ingredients.
—Jeanne McKinnie, Spokane, WA

Prep: 20 min. • **Bake:** 30 min.
Makes: 6 servings

- 2 **large tomatoes, cut into ½ in. slices**
- 1 **tsp. sugar**
- ½ **tsp. salt**
- ¼ **tsp. pepper**
- 2 **Tbsp. finely chopped onion**
- 2 **Tbsp. finely chopped green pepper**
- 1 **cup biscuit/baking mix**
- 1 **large egg, lightly beaten**
- ½ **cup 2% milk**
- ¾ **cup shredded sharp cheddar cheese**

1. Preheat oven to 350°. Place tomatoes in a greased 9-in. pie plate. Sprinkle with sugar, salt and pepper; top with onion and green pepper. In a small bowl, combine the biscuit mix, egg and milk until just until moistened; stir in the cheese. Pour batter over the vegetables.

2. Bake until bubbly and golden brown, 30-35 minutes.

1 piece: 171 cal., 8g fat (4g sat. fat), 47mg chol., 521mg sod., 19g carb. (4g sugars, 1g fiber), 7g pro.

CHICKEN CORDON BLEU PUFFS

TUNA NOODLE CASSEROLE

Families are sure to love the creamy texture and comforting taste of this traditional tuna casserole that goes together in a jiffy. I serve it with a green salad and warm rolls for a nutritious and delicious supper.
—Ruby Wells, Cynthiana, KY

Prep: 10 min. • **Bake:** 30 min.
Makes: 4 servings

- 1 can (10¾ oz.) reduced-fat reduced-sodium condensed cream of celery soup, undiluted
- ½ cup fat-free milk
- 2 cups cooked yolk-free wide noodles
- 1 cup frozen peas, thawed
- 1 can (6 oz.) light water-packed tuna, drained and flaked
- 1 jar (2 oz.) diced pimientos, drained
- 2 Tbsp. dry bread crumbs
- 1 Tbsp. butter, melted

1. Preheat oven to 400°. In a large bowl, combine soup and milk until smooth. Add the noodles, peas, tuna and pimientos; mix well.
2. Pour into a 1½-qt. baking dish coated with cooking spray. Bake, uncovered, for 25 minutes. Toss bread crumbs and butter; sprinkle over the top. Bake until golden brown, about 5 minutes longer.
1 cup: 238 cal., 5g fat (2g sat. fat), 27mg chol., 475mg sod., 32g carb. (6g sugars, 4g fiber), 15g pro. **Diabetic exchanges:** 2 starch, 2 lean meat, ½ fat.

CORNMEAL OVEN-FRIED CHICKEN

CORNMEAL OVEN-FRIED CHICKEN

A crunchy coating of cornmeal and Parmesan really perks up fried chicken. It's a crisp, tasty, mess-free variation on regular fried chicken.
—Deborah Williams, Peoria, AZ

Prep: 20 min. • **Bake:** 40 min.
Makes: 6 servings

- ½ cup dry bread crumbs
- ½ cup cornmeal
- ⅓ cup grated Parmesan cheese
- ¼ cup minced fresh parsley or 4 tsp. dried parsley flakes
- ¾ tsp. garlic powder
- ½ tsp. salt
- ½ tsp. onion powder
- ½ tsp. dried thyme
- ½ tsp. pepper
- ½ cup buttermilk
- 1 broiler/fryer chicken (3 to 4 lbs.), cut up and skin removed
- 1 Tbsp. butter, melted

1. Preheat oven to 375°. In a large shallow dish, combine the first 9 ingredients. Place buttermilk in a shallow bowl. Dip chicken in the buttermilk, then in the bread crumb mixture, a few pieces at a time; turn pieces to coat.
2. Place in a 13x9-in. baking pan coated with cooking spray. Bake for 10 minutes; drizzle with butter. Bake until the juices run clear, 30-40 minutes longer.
3 oz. cooked chicken: 244 cal., 9g fat (3g sat. fat), 82mg chol., 303mg sod., 11g carb. (1g sugars, 1g fiber), 27g pro. **Diabetic exchanges:** 3 lean meat, 1 starch, ½ fat.

TEST KITCHEN TIP
No buttermilk? Then place 1½ tsp. of white vinegar or lemon juice in a measuring cup and add enough milk to measure ½ cup. Stir, then let stand for 5 minutes.

SATURDAY AFTERNOON OVEN POT ROAST

This pot roast will be a welcome sight on your dinner table and will leave your house smelling heavenly. If your cooking liquid evaporates too quickly, add more broth to the Dutch oven.
—Colleen Delawder, Herndon, VA

Prep: 40 min. • **Bake:** 3 hours
Makes: 8 servings

- 1 boneless beef chuck roast (2½ lbs.)
- 1 tsp. salt
- ½ tsp. pepper
- 1 Tbsp. olive oil
- 1 Tbsp. butter
- 4 cups sliced sweet onion
- 1 can (6 oz.) tomato paste
- 4 garlic cloves, minced
- 1 tsp. dried thyme
- ½ tsp. celery seed
- ½ cup dry red wine
- 1 carton (32 oz.) reduced-sodium beef broth
- 6 medium carrots, cut into 1½ in. pieces
- ½ lb. medium fresh mushrooms, quartered

1. Preheat oven to 325°. Sprinkle roast with salt and pepper.
2. In a Dutch oven, heat oil and butter over medium-high heat; brown the roast on all sides. Remove from pot. Add onion to the same pot; cook and stir over medium heat until tender, 8-10 minutes. Add tomato paste, garlic, thyme and celery seed; cook and stir 1 minute longer.
3. Add wine, stirring to loosen browned bits from pot; stir in broth. Return roast to pot. Arrange the carrots and mushrooms around roast; bring to a boil. Bake pot roast, covered, until meat is fork-tender, 2½-3 hours. If desired, skim the fat and thicken cooking juices for gravy.

4 oz. cooked beef with ½ cup vegetables and ¼ cup gravy: 339 cal., 17g fat (6g sat. fat), 98mg chol., 621mg sod., 14g carb. (7g sugars, 2g fiber), 32g pro.

SATURDAY AFTERNOON OVEN POT ROAST

MUSHROOM-BLUE CHEESE TENDERLOIN

1 serving: 438 cal., 29g fat (14g sat. fat), 135mg chol., 1377mg sod., 4g carb. (1g sugars, 1g fiber), 38g pro.

ANGEL HAIR SHRIMP BAKE

Shrimp and pasta blend beautifully with herbs, salsa and three kinds of cheese in this hearty layered casserole. Whatever the occasion, bake up a dish of luscious shrimp goodness to share.
—Susan Davidson, Elm Grove, WI

Prep: 25 min. • **Bake:** 25 min.
Makes: 8 servings

- 1 pkg. (9 oz.) refrigerated angel hair pasta
- 1½ lbs. uncooked medium shrimp, peeled and deveined
- ¾ cup crumbled feta cheese
- ½ cup shredded Swiss cheese
- 1 jar (16 oz.) chunky salsa
- ½ cup shredded Monterey Jack cheese
- ¾ cup minced fresh parsley
- 1 tsp. dried basil
- 1 tsp. dried oregano
- 2 large eggs
- 1 cup half-and-half cream
- 1 cup plain yogurt
  Chopped fresh parsley, optional

1. Preheat oven to 350°. In a greased 13x9-in. baking dish, layer half each of the pasta, shrimp, feta cheese, Swiss cheese and salsa. Repeat layers. Sprinkle with the Monterey Jack cheese, parsley, basil and oregano.

2. In a small bowl, whisk the eggs, cream and yogurt; pour over casserole. Bake, uncovered, until a thermometer reads 160°, about 25-30 minutes. Let stand for 5 minutes before serving. If desired, top with chopped parsley.

1¼ cups: 340 cal., 13g fat (7g sat. fat), 203mg chol., 593mg sod., 25g carb. (5g sugars, 1g fiber), 27g pro.

READER REVIEW
"This angel hair shrimp bake is a must to make! Every year on my friend's birthday she requests I make this dish for her, as it's one of her favorites!"
SUTRAMA, TASTEOFHOME.COM

MUSHROOM-BLUE CHEESE TENDERLOIN

This is a simple entree, but it tastes fabulous. I double the mushroom-Roquefort sauce because it always disappears very quickly.
—Eric Schoen, Lincoln, NE

Prep: 10 min. + marinating
Bake: 45 min. + standing
Makes: 10 servings (1½ cups sauce)

- 1 cup reduced-sodium soy sauce
- ¾ cup Worcestershire sauce
- 1 beef tenderloin roast (3½ to 4 lbs.)
- 4 garlic cloves, minced
- 1 Tbsp. coarsely ground pepper
- 1 can (10½ oz.) condensed beef broth, undiluted

SAUCE
- ½ lb. sliced fresh mushrooms
- ½ cup butter, cubed
- 2 garlic cloves, minced
- 1 cup (4 oz.) crumbled blue cheese
- 1 Tbsp. Worcestershire sauce
- ¼ tsp. caraway seeds
- 4 green onions, chopped

1. If desired, tie tenderloin with bakers twine. In a shallow dish, combine soy sauce and Worcestershire sauce; add the beef and turn to coat. Cover; refrigerate for 2 hours, turning occasionally.

2. Preheat oven to 425°. Drain beef, discarding marinade. Rub the beef with garlic and pepper; place in a shallow roasting pan. Add broth to the pan. Bake, uncovered, for 45-55 minutes or until meat reaches desired doneness (for medium-rare, a thermometer should read 135°; medium, 140°; medium-well, 145°). Let stand for 10 minutes; remove twine before slicing.

3. Meanwhile, in a small saucepan, saute mushrooms in butter until tender. Add garlic; cook 1 minute longer. Add cheese, Worcestershire sauce and caraway seeds; cook and stir over low heat until cheese is melted. Stir in onions; heat through. Serve sauce with beef.

**ANGEL HAIR
SHRIMP BAKE**

CRUMB-TOPPED SOLE

CRUMB-TOPPED SOLE

Looking for a low-carb supper that's ready in a pinch? This buttery sole fits the bill. The moist fillets are covered with a rich but easy sauce and topped with golden bread crumbs.
—*Taste of Home* Test Kitchen

Takes: 15 min. • **Makes:** 4 servings

- 3 Tbsp. reduced-fat mayonnaise
- 3 Tbsp. grated Parmesan cheese, divided
- 2 tsp. mustard seed
- ¼ tsp. pepper
- 4 sole fillets (6 oz. each)
- 1 cup soft bread crumbs
- 1 green onion, finely chopped
- ½ tsp. ground mustard
- 2 tsp. butter, melted
  Thinly sliced green onions, optional

1. Preheat the broiler. Combine the mayonnaise, 2 Tbsp. cheese, mustard seed and pepper; spread over tops of fillets. Place on a broiler pan coated with cooking spray. Broil 4 in. from heat until fish flakes easily with a fork, 3-5 minutes.
2. Meanwhile, in a small bowl, combine bread crumbs, onion, ground mustard and the remaining cheese; stir in butter. Spoon over fillets; spritz topping with cooking spray. Broil until golden brown, 1-2 minutes longer. Sprinkle with green onions, if desired.

1 fillet: 267 cal., 10g fat (3g sat. fat), 94mg chol., 378mg sod., 8g carb. (1g sugars, 1g fiber), 35g pro. **Diabetic exchanges:** 5 lean meat, 1 fat, ½ starch.

READER REVIEW
"I made this with cod and thought it was delicious. It was so easy to prepare!"
FEEN, TASTEOFHOME.COM

ROSEMARY PORK WITH CHERRY TOPPING

Thirty years ago, my new mother-in-law asked me to do something with a large frozen pork loin being served to 18 guests at a Christmas Eve buffet. I assembled some fragrant ingredients and this is the result.
—Sheila Brown, Canton, MI

Prep: 35 min. + chilling.
Bake: 20 min. + cooling
Makes: 12 servings

- 2 pork tenderloins (1 lb. each)
- 1 Tbsp. olive oil
- 1 tsp. salt
- ½ tsp. pepper
- 3 garlic cloves, thinly sliced
- 2 fresh rosemary sprigs

TOPPING
- 2 Tbsp. olive oil
- ¾ cup dried cherries
- ¾ cup shelled pistachios
- 3 garlic cloves, thinly sliced
- 1½ tsp. minced fresh rosemary
  Horseradish mayonnaise or honey mustard
  Croissants, optional

1. Preheat oven to 425°. Rub pork with oil; sprinkle with salt and pepper. Cut slits in pork and insert garlic. Place on a rack in a shallow roasting pan; top with rosemary sprigs. Bake until a thermometer reads 145°, 12-15 minutes. Remove roast from oven; tent with foil. Cool the tenderloins completely; discard rosemary. Refrigerate, covered, overnight.

2. Meanwhile, for the topping, heat oil in a large skillet over medium heat. Add cherries, pistachios, garlic and rosemary. Cook and stir until the pistachios turn green, 4-5 minutes; cool slightly. Transfer to a food processor; pulse until coarsely chopped. Refrigerate, covered, overnight.

3. Thinly slice pork. Serve with pistachio topping and horseradish mayonnaise or honey mustard. If desired, serve the slices on croissants.

1 serving: 197 cal., 10g fat (2g sat. fat), 42mg chol., 261mg sod., 11g carb. (7g sugars, 1g fiber), 17g pro.

> **TEST KITCHEN TIP**
> The cherry mixture is like a dry, loose chutney. If you serve these as sandwiches, you'll definitely want the mayonnaise or honey mustard to help the topping stay put.

TURKEY SQUASH CASSEROLE

I combined two recipes to come up with this casserole, and it suits my family's tastes perfectly. Using ground turkey adds to the convenience.
—Mildred Sherrer, Fort Worth, TX

Prep: 20 min. • **Bake:** 35 min.
Makes: 6 servings

- 1 lb. ground turkey
- 1 Tbsp. canola oil
- 2 cups sliced yellow summer squash
- 1 medium onion, chopped
- 2 large eggs
- 1 cup evaporated milk
- 1 cup shredded part-skim mozzarella cheese
- 6 Tbsp. butter, melted
- ½ tsp. salt
- ¼ tsp. pepper
- 1 cup crushed saltines (about 30 crackers)

1. Preheat oven to 375°. In a large skillet, cook turkey in oil over medium heat until the meat is no longer pink. Add the squash and onion. Cook until the vegetables are crisp-tender; drain.

2. In a small bowl, combine eggs, milk, cheese, butter, salt and pepper. Stir into the turkey mixture. Transfer to a greased 8-in. square baking dish. Sprinkle with the cracker crumbs.

3. Bake, uncovered, for 35-40 minutes or until heated through.

1 cup: 459 cal., 33g fat (15g sat. fat), 177mg chol., 670mg sod., 17g carb. (7g sugars, 2g fiber), 23g pro.

ROSEMARY PORK WITH CHERRY TOPPING

OLD-FASHIONED CHICKEN POTPIE

Although this uses leftover chicken, I serve it sometimes as a special company dinner. I think my husband may enjoy it more than he enjoyed the original roasted bird with all the fixings.
—Marilyn Hockey, Lisle, ON

Prep: 30 min. • **Bake:** 30 min.
Makes: 6 servings

⅓ cup butter
⅓ cup all-purpose flour
1 garlic clove, minced
½ tsp. salt
¼ tsp. pepper
1½ cups water
⅔ cup milk
2 tsp. chicken bouillon granules
2 cups cubed cooked chicken
1 cup frozen mixed vegetables

PASTRY
1⅔ cups all-purpose flour
2 tsp. celery seed
1 pkg. (8 oz.) cream cheese, cubed
⅓ cup cold butter

1. Preheat oven to 425°. In a saucepan, melt butter. Stir in flour, garlic, salt and pepper until blended. Gradually stir in water, milk and bouillon. Bring to a boil; boil and stir for 2 minutes. Remove from the heat. Stir in chicken and vegetables; set aside.
2. For the pastry, combine the flour and celery seed in a bowl. Cut in cream cheese and butter until crumbly. Work mixture by hand until dough forms a ball. On a lightly floured surface, roll two-thirds of the dough into a 12-in. square. Transfer to an 8-in. square baking dish. Pour filling into crust. Roll the remaining dough into a 9-in. square; place over filling. Trim, seal and flute edges. Cut slits in pastry.
3. Bake for 30-35 minutes or until crust is golden brown and filling is bubbly.
1 serving: 591 cal., 38g fat (22g sat. fat), 141mg chol., 860mg sod., 39g carb. (4g sugars, 3g fiber), 23g pro.

DELUXE DEEP-DISH PIZZA

DELUXE DEEP-DISH PIZZA

You don't have to be in Chicago to get delicious deep-dish flavor. My recipe makes it easy, using frozen bread dough. Load it up with your favorite toppings—and keep a knife and fork handy!
—Jenny Leighty, West Salem, OH

Prep: 20 min. • **Bake:** 25 min.
Makes: 8 servings

1 loaf (1 lb.) frozen bread dough, thawed
¾ cup pizza sauce
1 pkg. (3½ oz.) sliced pepperoni
1 cup sliced fresh mushrooms
½ cup chopped green pepper
¼ cup chopped sweet onion
¼ cup mild pickled pepper rings
2 cups (8 oz.) shredded part-skim mozzarella cheese
1 Tbsp. dried oregano

1. Preheat oven to 400°. On a lightly floured surface, roll dough into a 14x10-in. rectangle. Transfer to a greased 13x9-in. baking dish. Build up edges slightly.
2. Spread sauce over the dough. Layer with the remaining ingredients.
3. Bake until the crust is golden brown and the cheese is melted, 25-30 minutes.
1 piece: 325 cal., 14g fat (6g sat. fat), 30mg chol., 830mg sod., 33g carb. (4g sugars, 3g fiber), 16g pro.

TEST KITCHEN TIP
Be patient when rolling out frozen bread dough. The dough is quite elastic and will not want to hold its shape at first. Try covering the dough and letting it rest for 10 minutes halfway through rolling.

PORK & GREEN CHILE CASSEROLE

I work at a local hospital and another job part time, so I'm always on the lookout for good, quick recipes. A friend brought this zippy casserole to a picnic at my house, and I had to have the recipe.
—Dianne Esposite, New Middletown, OH

Prep: 20 min. • **Bake:** 30 min.
Makes: 6 servings

- 1½ lbs. boneless pork, cut into ½-in. cubes
- 1 Tbsp. canola oil
- 1 can (15 oz.) black beans, rinsed and drained
- 1 can (10¾ oz.) condensed cream of chicken soup, undiluted
- 1 can (14½ oz.) diced tomatoes, undrained
- 2 cans (4 oz. each) chopped green chiles
- 1 cup quick-cooking brown rice
- ¼ cup water
- 2 to 3 Tbsp. salsa
- 1 tsp. ground cumin
- ½ cup shredded cheddar cheese
  Sliced jalapeno pepper, optional

1. Preheat oven to 350°. In a large skillet, brown pork in oil; drain. Stir in the beans, soup, tomatoes, chiles, rice, water, salsa and cumin.

2. Pour into an ungreased 2-qt. baking dish. Bake, uncovered, until bubbly, about 30 minutes. Sprinkle with cheese; let stand 5 minutes before serving. If desired, serve with jalapeno slices.

Freeze option: Sprinkle cheese over cooled unbaked casserole. Cover and freeze. To use, partially thaw in refrigerator overnight. Remove from refrigerator 30 minutes before baking. Bake as directed, increasing the time as necessary to heat through and for a thermometer inserted in center to read 165°. If desired, serve with jalapeno slices.

1 serving: 390 cal., 15g fat (6g sat. fat), 81mg chol., 814mg sod., 29g carb. (3g sugars, 6g fiber), 32g pro.

STEAKHOUSE PIZZA

One of my first jobs was in a steakhouse. This recipe brings up memories and celebrates two favorite foods: steak and pizza. Onion rings and an iceberg salad would make this a true steakhouse meal!
—Lisa Benoit, Cookeville, TN

Prep: 35 min. • **Bake:** 10 min. + standing
Makes: 8 servings

- 1 loaf (1 lb.) frozen pizza dough, thawed
- 1 pkg. (8 oz.) frozen spinach and artichoke cheese dip, thawed
- ¾ cup grape tomatoes, halved
- 1 boneless beef top loin steak (1 lb.), thinly sliced
- 1½ tsp. Montreal steak seasoning
- ⅓ cup torn fresh basil
- 3 Tbsp. pine nuts
- 2 bacon strips, cooked and crumbled
- ⅓ cup prepared ranch salad dressing
- 1 Tbsp. prepared horseradish

1. Preheat oven to 400°. Press dough to fit a greased 14-in. pizza pan. Pinch edges to form a rim. Bake until the edges are lightly browned, 10-12 minutes. Let cool 10 minutes.

2. Spread with dip; top with tomatoes. Toss steak with steak seasoning; place over tomatoes. Bake on a lower oven rack until steak reaches desired doneness and crust is golden brown, 10-12 minutes. Let stand 10 minutes. Sprinkle with basil, pine nuts and bacon. Combine ranch dressing and horseradish; serve with pizza.

Note: Top loin steak may be labeled as strip steak, Kansas City steak, New York strip steak, ambassador steak or boneless club steak in your region.

1 slice: 290 cal., 12g fat (2g sat. fat), 28mg chol., 434mg sod., 27g carb. (2g sugars, 1g fiber), 18g pro.

PORK & GREEN CHILE CASSEROLE

ORANGE TILAPIA IN PARCHMENT

Sweet orange juice and spicy cayenne pepper give this no-fuss dish fabulous flavor. A bonus? Cleanup is a breeze.
—Tiffany Diebold, Nashville, TN

Takes: 30 min. • **Makes:** 4 servings

- ¼ cup orange juice
- 4 tsp. grated orange zest
- ¼ tsp. salt
- ¼ tsp. cayenne pepper
- ¼ tsp. pepper
- 4 tilapia fillets (6 oz. each)
- ½ cup julienned carrot
- ½ cup julienned zucchini

1. Preheat oven to 450°. In a small bowl, combine the first 5 ingredients; set aside. Cut parchment or heavy-duty foil into four 18x12-in. lengths; place a fish fillet on each. Top with carrot and zucchini; drizzle with orange juice mixture.
2. Fold parchment over the fish. Working from the bottom inside corner, fold up about ¾ in. of the paper and crimp both layers to seal. Repeat, folding edges up and crimping, until a half-moon-shaped packet is formed. Repeat for remaining packets. Place on baking sheets.
3. Bake until fish flakes easily with a fork, 12-15 minutes. Open packets carefully to allow steam to escape.

1 packet: 158 cal., 2g fat (1g sat. fat), 83mg chol., 220mg sod., 4g carb. (2g sugars, 1g fiber), 32g pro. **Diabetic exchanges:** 5 lean meat.

ROADSIDE DINER CHEESEBURGER QUICHE

ROADSIDE DINER CHEESEBURGER QUICHE

This unforgettable quiche tastes just like its burger counterpart. Easy and appealing, it's perfect for guests and fun for the whole family.
—Barbara J. Miller, Oakdale, MN

Prep: 20 min. • **Bake:** 50 min. + standing
Makes: 8 servings

- 1 sheet refrigerated pie crust
- ¾ lb. ground beef
- 2 plum tomatoes, seeded and chopped
- 1 medium onion, chopped
- ½ cup dill pickle relish
- ½ cup crumbled cooked bacon
- 5 large eggs
- 1 cup heavy whipping cream
- ½ cup 2% milk
- 2 tsp. prepared mustard
- 1 tsp. hot pepper sauce
- ½ tsp. salt
- ¼ tsp. pepper
- 1½ cups shredded cheddar cheese
- ½ cup shredded Parmesan cheese
  Optional garnishes: Mayonnaise, additional pickle relish, crumbled cooked bacon, and chopped onion and tomato

1. Preheat oven to 375°. Unroll crust into a 9-in. deep-dish pie plate; flute edges and set aside.
2. In a large skillet, cook the beef over medium heat until no longer pink; drain. Stir in the tomatoes, onion, relish and bacon. Transfer to prepared crust.
3. In a large bowl, whisk the eggs, cream, milk, mustard, pepper sauce, salt and pepper. Pour liquid over the beef mixture. Sprinkle with cheeses.
4. Bake at 375° until a knife inserted in center comes out clean, 50-60 minutes. If necessary, cover edges with foil during the last 15 minutes to prevent overbrowning. Let stand for 10 minutes before cutting. Garnish quiche with any of the optional ingredients as desired.

1 piece: 502 cal., 35g fat (19g sat. fat), 236mg chol., 954mg sod., 24g carb. (8g sugars, 1g fiber), 23g pro.

DEVILED CHICKEN THIGHS

I make this dish when I invite my neighbor over for supper—it's just enough for the two of us. The tasty chicken thighs are tender and moist, and the cashews give them a bit of crunch.
—Bernice Morris, Marshfield, MO

Takes: 30 min. • **Makes:** 2 servings

- 1 tsp. butter, softened
- 1 tsp. cider vinegar
- 1 tsp. prepared mustard
- 1 tsp. paprika
  Dash pepper
- 2 boneless skinless chicken thighs (about ½ lb.)
- 3 Tbsp. soft bread crumbs
- 2 Tbsp. chopped cashews

1. Preheat oven to 400°. In a large bowl, combine the butter, vinegar, mustard, paprika and pepper. Spread over chicken thighs. Place in a greased 11x7-in. baking dish. Sprinkle with bread crumbs.
2. Bake, uncovered, for 15 minutes. Sprinkle with cashews. Bake until chicken juices run clear and the topping is golden brown, 7-12 minutes longer.

1 chicken thigh: 246 cal., 14g fat (4g sat. fat), 81mg chol., 189mg sod., 6g carb. (1g sugars, 1g fiber), 23g pro. **Diabetic exchanges:** 3 lean meat, 1 fat, ½ starch.

TATER-TOPPED ITALIAN CASSEROLE

I made this recipe for a friend who liked it so much, she asked me for the recipe so she could make it for some of her friends. It's super easy to make and doesn't take many ingredients. The best thing—since it's gluten-free I can eat it too!
—Jackie Hannahs, Cedar Springs, MI

Prep: 20 min. • **Bake:** 40 min.
Makes: 6 servings

- 1 lb. bulk Italian sausage
- 1 small green pepper, chopped
- 1 small onion, chopped
- 2 cups spaghetti sauce
- 2 cups (8 oz.) shredded part-skim mozzarella cheese, divided
- 4 cups frozen Tater Tots

1. Preheat oven to 375°. In a large skillet, cook sausage, pepper and onion over medium heat for 8-10 minutes or until the sausage is no longer pink, breaking up sausage into ½-in. pieces; drain. Stir in the sauce.
2. Transfer to a greased 8-in.-square baking dish. Sprinkle with 1¼ cups cheese. Arrange Tater Tots over the cheese. Bake for 35-40 minutes or until the topping is golden brown. Sprinkle with the remaining cheese; bake 5 minutes longer or until the cheese is melted.

1⅓ cups: 552 cal., 36g fat (14g sat. fat), 77mg chol., 1556mg sod., 34g carb. (9g sugars, 4g fiber), 27g pro.

DEVILED CHICKEN THIGHS

Lightened-Up Delights

Eating healthier meals doesn't mean going light on flavor. These delectable recipes are perfect if you're looking for quick, easy dishes that will help keep your numbers down while keeping your family satisfied.

Pan-Fried Scallops with White Wine Reduction (p. 141) **Creamy Pasta Primavera** (p. 146) **Cumin Quinoa Patties** (p. 149) **Easy Beef Stroganoff** (p. 151) **Tarragon Tuna Salad** (p. 154)

STIR-FRIED SHRIMP & MUSHROOMS

After a tiring but beautiful day of fishing, this is a worthy way to serve our famous Key West pink shrimp.
—Jeanne Wolfort, Summerland Key, FL

Takes: 15 min. • **Makes:** 4 servings

- 4 garlic cloves, minced
- 2 tsp. canola oil
- 1 lb. uncooked shrimp (31-40 per lb.), peeled and deveined
- 3 cups sliced fresh mushrooms
- 1 cup sliced green onions
- ¼ cup chicken broth
  Hot cooked rice
  Lemon slices

In a large skillet or wok, saute garlic in oil for 1 minute. Add shrimp, mushrooms and onions; stir-fry for 1 minute. Stir in the broth; cook 2 minutes longer or until the shrimp turn pink. Serve with rice; garnish with lemon.

1 serving: 132 cal., 3g fat (1g sat. fat), 168mg chol., 258mg sod., 5g carb. (2g sugars, 1g fiber), 20g pro. **Diabetic exchanges:** 3 lean meat, 1 vegetable, ½ fat.
HEALTH TIP This dish is a great option for guests who follow a gluten-free diet. Just make sure your brand of chicken broth doesn't contain gluten (some do).

ZESTY STEAK SALAD

ZESTY STEAK SALAD

Stir-fried steak and veggies give this hearty salad a cozy kick. Add any of your favorite salad ingredients, like shredded cheese, croutons, sliced mushrooms or chopped cucumber.
—Leah Carrell, Quitman, TX

Takes: 20 min. • **Makes:** 4 servings

- 1 lb. beef top sirloin steak, cut into strips
- ⅓ cup Worcestershire sauce
- 1 medium onion, julienned
- 1 medium green pepper, julienned
- 1 Tbsp. butter
- 6 cups shredded lettuce
- 6 to 9 cherry tomatoes, halved
  Salsa, optional

1. In a large bowl, combine the sirloin steak and Worcestershire sauce; cover and refrigerate.
2. Meanwhile, in a large skillet, saute onion and green pepper in butter until crisp-tender, 3-4 minutes. Add cold sirloin; stir-fry until the meat is no longer pink. Spoon the meat and vegetables over lettuce; garnish with tomatoes. Serve with salsa if desired.

1 serving: 218 cal., 8g fat (4g sat. fat), 54mg chol., 314mg sod., 11g carb. (5g sugars, 2g fiber), 26g pro. **Diabetic exchanges:** 3 lean meat, 1 vegetable, ½ fat.

TURKEY ENCHILADA STACK

As a child, my husband was one of the pickiest kids around, but my mother-in-law could always get him to dig in to this enchilada dish. So I knew it was a winner!
—Ashley Wolf, Alabaster, AL

Takes: 20 min. • **Makes:** 4 servings

- 1 lb. lean ground turkey
- 2 cans (8 oz. each) no-salt-added tomato sauce
- 3 tsp. dried minced onion
- ½ tsp. garlic powder
- ½ tsp. pepper
- ¼ tsp. salt
- 4 whole wheat tortillas (8 in.)
- ⅔ cup shredded reduced-fat cheddar cheese
  Optional: Shredded lettuce, chopped tomatoes and reduced-fat sour cream

1. In a large skillet, cook turkey over medium heat until the meat is no longer pink; drain. Stir in tomato sauce, minced onion, garlic powder, pepper and salt; heat through.
2. In a 2½-qt. round microwave-safe dish coated with cooking spray, layer 1 tortilla, about ¾ cup of the meat mixture and a scant 3 Tbsp. of cheese. Repeat layers 3 times. Cover and microwave on high until the cheese is melted, 4-5 minutes. Let stand for 5 minutes before cutting. Serve with toppings as desired.

1 piece: 404 cal., 16g fat (5g sat. fat), 103mg chol., 582mg sod., 31g carb. (9g sugars, 3g fiber), 29g pro. **Diabetic exchanges:** 4 lean meat, 2 starch, 1 fat.

PAN-FRIED SCALLOPS WITH WHITE WINE REDUCTION

PICTURED ON P. 139

I learned the art of reduction from a cooking class—the flavor is fabulous! Despite the fancy title, this special-occasion entree is easy to prepare.
—Katherine Robinson, Glenwood Springs, CO

Takes: 30 min. • **Makes:** 8 servings

- 2 lbs. sea scallops
- 1 tsp. salt
- ¼ tsp. pepper
- 2 Tbsp. olive oil

WHITE WINE REDUCTION

- ½ cup white wine or chicken broth
- ⅓ cup orange juice
- ¼ cup finely chopped onion
- 1 tsp. dried oregano
- 1 tsp. Dijon mustard
- 1 garlic clove, minced
- 3 Tbsp. cold butter, cubed

1. Sprinkle scallops with salt and pepper. In a large skillet, saute scallops in oil until firm and opaque. Remove and keep warm.
2. Add the wine to the skillet, stirring to loosen browned bits from pan. Stir in the orange juice, onion, oregano, mustard and garlic. Bring to a boil; cook and stir until reduced by half, 2-3 minutes. Remove from the heat; stir in butter until melted. Serve with scallops.

4 scallops with 2 Tbsp. sauce: 181 cal., 9g fat (3g sat. fat), 49mg chol., 524mg sod., 5g carb. (1g sugars, 0 fiber), 19g pro. **Diabetic exchanges:** 3 lean meat, 2 fat.

Scallops with Citrus Herb Sauce: Omit white wine reduction. Cook scallops as directed. Wipe skillet clean if necessary. Saute 3 minced garlic cloves in 2 Tbsp. butter until tender; stir in ⅓ cup dry sherry. Cook until the liquid is almost evaporated; stir in 2 Tbsp. lemon juice, ½ tsp. minced fresh oregano and ½ tsp. minced fresh tarragon. Serve with scallops.

TURKEY ENCHILADA STACK

TILAPIA WITH CUCUMBER RELISH

My husband isn't big on fish, but he enjoys this mild-tasting tilapia. The relish adds garden-fresh flavor and pretty color to the lightly browned fillets.
—Mary VanHollebeke, Wyandotte, MI

Takes: 15 min. • **Makes:** 4 servings

- ⅔ cup chopped seeded cucumber
- ½ cup chopped radishes
- 1 Tbsp. tarragon vinegar
- 1 tsp. olive oil
- ½ tsp. salt, divided
- ¼ tsp. pepper, divided
- ⅛ tsp. sugar
- ⅛ tsp. paprika
- 4 tilapia fillets (6 oz. each)
- 1 Tbsp. butter

1. In a small bowl, combine cucumber and radishes. In another small bowl, whisk the vinegar, oil, ¼ tsp. salt, ⅛ tsp. pepper and sugar. Pour over the cucumber mixture; toss to coat evenly. Combine paprika and the remaining salt and pepper; sprinkle over fillets.

2. In a large nonstick skillet coated with cooking spray, melt butter. Add fish; cook for 3-4 minutes on each side or until the fish flakes easily with a fork. Serve with cucumber relish.

1 fillet with ¼ cup relish: 181 cal., 6g fat (3g sat. fat), 90mg chol., 384mg sod., 1g carb. (1g sugars, 0 fiber), 32g pro.
Diabetic exchanges: 4 lean meat, 1 fat.

READER REVIEW

"We seriously love this recipe! It's my favorite way to prepare tilapia and it's so simple to make. Even my 5- and 2-year-old boys love it!"

CRYOPHALLION, TASTEOFHOME.COM

SOUTHWESTERN BEEF BARLEY STEW

SOUTHWESTERN BEEF BARLEY STEW

Hearty and easy to fix, this thick stew has a comforting, chili-like flavor. It's my best barley recipe. I'm sure you'll agree that it's a tasty dish!
—Lisa Kolenicn, Regina, SK

Takes: 30 min. • **Makes:** 3 servings

- ½ lb. lean ground beef (90% lean)
- ½ cup sliced celery
- ⅓ cup chopped onion
- 1⅓ cups water
- 2 tsp. reduced-sodium beef bouillon granules
- 1½ tsp. chili powder
- ¼ tsp. pepper
- ½ cup quick-cooking barley
- 1 can (14½ oz.) diced tomatoes, undrained

1. In a large saucepan, cook the beef, celery and onion over medium heat until the meat is no longer pink and vegetables are tender; drain.

2. Stir in the water, bouillon, chili powder and pepper. Bring to a boil. Stir in the barley. Reduce heat; cover and simmer for 10-12 minutes or until the barley is tender. Stir in tomatoes; heat through.

1⅓ cups: 269 cal., 7g fat (3g sat. fat), 37mg chol., 456mg sod., 33g carb. (6g sugars, 9g fiber), 20g pro.

CHICKEN THIGHS WITH SHALLOTS & SPINACH

What could be better than an entree that comes with its own creamy vegetable side? This healthy supper makes an eye-catching presentation and goes together in no time flat.
—Genna Johannes, Wrightstown, WI

Takes: 30 min. • **Makes:** 6 servings

- 6 boneless skinless chicken thighs (about 1½ lbs.)
- ½ tsp. seasoned salt
- ½ tsp. pepper
- 1½ tsp. olive oil
- 4 shallots, thinly sliced
- ⅓ cup white wine or reduced-sodium chicken broth
- 1 pkg. (10 oz.) fresh spinach, trimmed
- ¼ tsp. salt
- ¼ cup reduced-fat sour cream

1. Sprinkle chicken with seasoned salt and pepper. In a large nonstick skillet, heat oil over medium heat. Add the chicken; cook until a thermometer reads 170°, about 6 minutes on each side. Remove from pan; keep warm.

2. In the same pan, cook and stir shallots until tender. Add wine; bring to a boil. Cook until the wine is reduced by half. Add spinach and salt; cook and stir just until the spinach is wilted. Stir in sour cream; serve with chicken.

Freeze option: Before adding sour cream, cool chicken and spinach mixture. Freeze in freezer containers. To use, partially thaw in refrigerator overnight. Heat through slowly in a covered skillet, stirring occasionally, until a thermometer inserted in chicken reads 170°. Stir in sour cream.

1 chicken thigh with ¼ cup spinach mixture: 223 cal., 10g fat (3g sat. fat), 77mg chol., 360mg sod., 7g carb. (2g sugars, 1g fiber), 23g pro. **Diabetic exchanges:** 3 lean meat, 1½ fat, 1 vegetable.

CHICKEN THIGHS WITH SHALLOTS & SPINACH

SPICY CHICKEN STEW

Cook pasta according to the package directions; drain and rinse in cold water. Transfer to a large bowl. Add the shrimp, coleslaw mix, onions and cilantro. Drizzle with dressing; toss to coat. Cover and refrigerate until serving.

1⅓ cups: 260 cal., 3g fat (0 sat. fat), 147mg chol., 523mg sod., 36g carb. (6g sugars, 2g fiber), 22g pro. **Diabetic exchanges:** 2 starch, 2 lean meat, 1 vegetable.

HEALTH TIP Substitute whole wheat pasta and you'll boost the fiber to 5 grams per serving.

ALMOND-TOPPED FISH

A co-worker gave me this recipe, but I didn't try it until recently. What a mistake it was to wait! Once you've tried this tender fish, you'll never go back to fried. It's easier than dipping, coating and frying—and the flavor is outstanding.
—Heidi Kirsch, Waterloo, IA

Takes: 30 min. • **Makes:** 4 servings

- 1 Tbsp. butter
- 1 small onion, thinly sliced
- 4 cod or haddock fillets (6 oz. each)
- 1 tsp. seasoned salt
- ½ tsp. dill weed
- ¼ tsp. pepper
- ¼ cup grated Parmesan cheese
- ¼ cup reduced-fat mayonnaise
- 1 Tbsp. minced fresh parsley
- 1 Tbsp. lemon juice
- 2 Tbsp. sliced almonds, toasted

1. Preheat oven to 400°. Place butter in a 13x9-in. baking dish; place in hot oven until melted. Spread butter to cover the bottom of the dish; cover with onion.

2. Arrange fish over the onion; sprinkle with salt, dill and pepper. Combine the Parmesan cheese, mayonnaise, parsley and lemon juice; spread over the fish.

3. Bake, uncovered, until the fish flakes easily with a fork, 18-20 minutes. Sprinkle with almonds.

1 fillet: 220 cal., 9g fat (2g sat. fat), 74mg chol., 658mg sod., 5g carb. (2g sugars, 1g fiber), 29g pro. **Diabetic exchanges:** 4 lean meat, 2 fat.

SPICY CHICKEN STEW

SPICY CHICKEN STEW

When you're craving cozy Mexican flavors, try this slightly spicy stew that couldn't be easier to make. Round out the meal with a fresh tossed salad.
—*Taste of Home* Test Kitchen

Takes: 30 min. • **Makes:** 6 servings

- 2 lbs. boneless skinless chicken thighs, cut into ½-in. pieces
- 2 tsp. minced garlic
- 2 Tbsp. olive oil
- 1 can (15 oz.) garbanzo beans or chickpeas, rinsed and drained
- 1 can (14½ oz.) diced tomatoes with onions, undrained
- 1 cup lime-garlic salsa
- 1 tsp. ground cumin
- ⅓ cup minced fresh cilantro
  Sour cream, optional

In a Dutch oven, cook chicken and garlic in oil for 5 minutes. Stir in the beans, tomatoes, salsa and cumin. Cover and simmer until the chicken is no longer pink, about 15 minutes. Stir in cilantro. Top with sour cream if desired.

1½ cups: 359 cal., 17g fat (4g sat. fat), 101mg chol., 622mg sod., 18g carb. (5g sugars, 4g fiber), 31g pro.

SHRIMP & NOODLE BOWLS

It'll look as if you got takeout, but this dish comes from your kitchen! Convenience items reduce the prep time.
—Mary Bergfeld, Eugene, OR

Takes: 25 min. • **Makes:** 6 servings

- 8 oz. uncooked angel hair pasta
- 1 lb. cooked small shrimp
- 2 cups broccoli coleslaw mix
- 6 green onions, thinly sliced
- ½ cup minced fresh cilantro
- ⅔ cup reduced-fat sesame ginger salad dressing

ALMOND-TOPPED FISH

CAJUN SHRIMP

CAJUN SHRIMP

These zippy shrimp bring a lot of pizazz to the table. Use as much or as little cayenne pepper as you'd like, depending on your family's tastes. We love this dish served alongside rice pilaf.

—Donna Thomason, El Paso, TX

Takes: 10 min. • **Makes:** 4 servings

- 2 **tsp. paprika**
- 1 **tsp. dried thyme**
- ½ **tsp. salt**
- ¼ **tsp. ground nutmeg**
- ¼ **tsp. garlic powder**
- ⅛ to ¼ **tsp. cayenne pepper**
- 1 **Tbsp. olive oil**
- 1 **lb. uncooked shrimp (31-40 per lb.), peeled and deveined**

In a large nonstick skillet, saute paprika, thyme, salt, nutmeg, garlic powder and cayenne in oil for 30 seconds, stirring constantly. Add shrimp; saute for 2-3 minutes or until the shrimp turn pink, stirring occasionally.

3 oz. cooked shrimp: 131 cal., 5g fat (1g sat. fat), 138mg chol., 430mg sod., 2g carb. (0 sugars, 1g fiber), 19g pro. **Diabetic exchanges:** 3 lean meat, ½ fat.

CREAMY PASTA PRIMAVERA
PICTURED ON P. 139

This pasta dish is a wonderful blend of crisp, colorful vegetables and a creamy Parmesan cheese sauce.

—Darlene Brenden, Salem, OR

Takes: 30 min. • **Makes:** 6 servings

- 2 **cups uncooked gemelli or spiral pasta**
- 1 **lb. fresh asparagus, trimmed and cut into 2-in. pieces**
- 3 **medium carrots, shredded**
- 2 **tsp. canola oil**
- 2 **cups cherry tomatoes, halved**
- 1 **garlic clove, minced**
- ½ **cup grated Parmesan cheese**
- ½ **cup heavy whipping cream**
- ¼ **tsp. pepper**

1. Cook pasta according to the package directions. In a large skillet over medium-high heat, saute asparagus and carrots in oil until crisp-tender. Add tomatoes and garlic; cook 1 minute longer.

2. Stir in cheese, cream and pepper. Drain the pasta; toss with the asparagus mixture.

1⅓ cups: 275 cal., 12g fat (6g sat. fat), 33mg chol., 141mg sod., 35g carb. (5g sugars, 3g fiber), 10g pro. **Diabetic exchanges:** 2 starch, 2 fat, 1 vegetable.

HEALTH TIP Using a small amount of a single rich ingredient, like heavy cream, is a smart way keep a dish tasting indulgent while cutting calories.

NECTARINE CHICKEN SALAD

When guests are coming for lunch or dinner in the warm summer months, I serve this attractive, colorful salad. The dressing is refreshingly tart. A neighbor shared the recipe with me years ago and I've passed it on many times.
—Cathy Ross, Van Nuys, CA

Takes: 15 min. • **Makes:** 4 servings

- ¼ cup lime juice
- 1 Tbsp. sugar
- 1 Tbsp. minced fresh thyme or 1 tsp. dried thyme
- 1 Tbsp. olive oil
- 1 garlic clove, minced
- 6 cups torn mixed salad greens
- 1 lb. boneless skinless chicken breasts, cooked and sliced
- 5 medium ripe nectarines, thinly sliced

1. In a jar with a tight-fitting lid, combine the lime juice, sugar, thyme, oil and garlic; shake well.
2. On a serving platter, arrange salad greens, chicken and nectarines. Drizzle with dressing. Serve immediately.

1½ cups: 266 cal., 7g fat (1g sat. fat), 63mg chol., 76mg sod., 27g carb. (21g sugars, 5g fiber), 26g pro.
Diabetic exchanges: 3 lean meat, 1½ starch, 1 vegetable, 1 fat.

TRIPLE-CITRUS STEAKS WITH JICAMA & MANGO

This is a recipe I made up several years ago—it's now one of our family favorites. It's easy to make and is a colorful addition to the table!
—Sherry Little, Sherwood, AR

Prep: 30 min. + marinating
Cook: 15 min. • **Makes:** 4 servings

- 1 medium orange
- 1 medium lemon
- 1 medium lime
- 4 Tbsp. honey
- 1¼ tsp. salt, divided
- 4 beef flat iron steaks or top sirloin steaks (6 oz. each) and ¾ in. thick
- ½ cup water
- 1 cup julienned peeled jicama
- 1 medium mango, peeled and cubed

1. Cut orange, lemon and lime crosswise in half; squeeze juice from fruits. Stir in honey and salt. Pour ⅓ cup marinade into a bowl or shallow dish. Add the steaks and turn to coat. Refrigerate at least 3 hours, turning once. Cover and refrigerate the remaining marinade.
2. Drain steaks, discarding the marinade. Heat a large skillet over medium heat. Cook steaks until the meat reaches the desired doneness (for medium-rare, a thermometer should read 135°; medium, 140°; medium-well, 145°), 6-8 minutes on each side. Remove and keep warm.
3. Add water and the reserved marinade. Bring to a boil; cook until liquid is reduced to 3 Tbsp., 10-12 minutes. Add jicama and mango; heat through. Serve with steaks. If desired, garnish with additional orange, lemon or lime slices.

1 serving: 412 cal., 18g fat (7g sat. fat), 109mg chol., 609mg sod., 29g carb. (24g sugars, 3g fiber), 34g pro.

NECTARINE CHICKEN SALAD

SASSY CHICKEN & PEPPERS

This quick chicken dinner tastes like a naked taco and is bursting with fresh flavors. And it can all be prepared in the same pan for easy cleanup.
—Doris Heath, Franklin, NC

Takes: 25 min. • **Makes:** 2 servings

- 2 boneless skinless chicken breast halves (4 oz. each)
- 2 tsp. taco seasoning
- 4 tsp. canola oil, divided
- 1 small onion, halved and sliced
- ½ small green bell pepper, julienned
- ½ small sweet red pepper, julienned
- ¼ cup salsa
- 1 Tbsp. lime juice

1. Sprinkle chicken with seasoning. In a small nonstick skillet, cook the chicken in 2 tsp. oil over medium heat until the juices run clear, 4-5 minutes on each side. Remove and keep warm.
2. Saute onion and peppers in remaining oil until crisp-tender; stir in salsa and lime juice. Spoon the mixture over chicken.

1 serving: 239 cal., 12g fat (1g sat. fat), 63mg chol., 377mg sod., 8g carb. (4g sugars, 1g fiber), 24g pro. **Diabetic exchanges:** 3 lean meat, 2 fat, 1 vegetable.

SMOKED SAUSAGE WITH PASTA

SMOKED SAUSAGE WITH PASTA

Loaded with sausage, mushrooms, tomatoes and basil flavor, this quick recipe satisfies the toughest critics. It's one of my husband's favorite dishes, and he has no idea it's lower in fat!
—Ruth Ann Ruddell, Shelby Township, MI

Takes: 30 min. • **Makes:** 4 servings

- 4 oz. uncooked angel hair pasta
- ½ lb. smoked turkey kielbasa, cut into ½-in. slices
- 2 cups sliced fresh mushrooms
- 2 garlic cloves, minced
- 4½ tsp. minced fresh basil or 1½ tsp. dried basil
- 1 Tbsp. olive oil
- 2 cups julienned seeded plum tomatoes
- ⅛ tsp. salt
- ⅛ tsp. pepper
  Grated Parmesan cheese, optional

Cook pasta according to the package directions. Meanwhile, in a large nonstick skillet, saute the sausage, mushrooms, garlic and basil in oil until the mushrooms are tender. Drain pasta; add to the sausage mixture. Add tomatoes, salt and pepper; toss gently. Heat through. If desired, top with additional fresh basil and grated Parmesan cheese.

1 cup: 232 cal., 7g fat (2g sat. fat), 35mg chol., 639mg sod., 27g carb. (5g sugars, 2g fiber), 15g pro. **Diabetic exchanges:** 2 lean meat, 1½ starch, 1 vegetable, ½ fat.

READER REVIEW

"This was very tasty! I added julienned bell peppers and used a can of Italian tomatoes. This will definitely go into my rotation for dinner."
ANGELIC0W, TASTEOFHOME.COM

ONE-POT SALSA CHICKEN

This skillet recipe is a colorful and healthy main dish that can be on the table in just over an hour. The subtle sweet-spicy flavor is a nice surprise.
—Ann Sheehy, Lawrence, MA

Prep: 20 min. • **Cook:** 45 min.
Makes: 6 servings

- 2 Tbsp. canola oil
- 2 lbs. boneless skinless chicken thighs, cut into 1-in. pieces
- 1 tsp. pepper
- ½ tsp. salt
- 2 medium sweet potatoes, peeled and chopped
- 1 jar (16 oz.) medium salsa
- 2 medium nectarines, peeled and chopped
- 2 Tbsp. Tajin seasoning
- 1 cup uncooked instant brown rice
- 1 cup water
- ¼ cup minced fresh parsley
  Minced fresh chives

1. In a Dutch oven, heat oil over medium-high heat. Sprinkle chicken with pepper and salt. Brown the chicken in batches; return to pot. Add sweet potatoes, salsa, nectarines and seasoning. Bring to a boil; reduce heat. Cover and simmer until the potatoes are almost tender, about 15 minutes.
2. Stir in rice and water; bring to a boil. Reduce heat. Cover and simmer until the potatoes are tender, about 10 minutes. Stir in parsley. Serve in bowls; sprinkle with chives.

1⅔ cups: 432 cal., 16g fat (3g sat. fat), 101mg chol., 1254mg sod., 39g carb. (13g sugars, 4g fiber), 31g pro.

ONE-POT SALSA CHICKEN

CUMIN QUINOA PATTIES

PICTURED ON P. 139

These easy-to-make veggie burgers deliver amazing taste, and the crunch from the quinoa makes for a truly extraordinary texture. Pan-frying them brings it to the next level. The mixture can be made ahead of time, and it freezes very well.
—Beth Klein, Arlington, VA

Takes: 30 min. • **Makes:** 4 servings

- 1 cup water
- ½ cup quinoa, rinsed
- 1 medium carrot, cut into 1-in. pieces
- 1 cup canned cannellini beans, rinsed and drained
- ¼ cup panko (Japanese) bread crumbs
- 3 green onions, chopped
- 1 large egg, lightly beaten
- 3 tsp. ground cumin
- ¼ tsp. salt
- ⅛ tsp. pepper
- 2 Tbsp. olive oil
  Optional: Sour cream, salsa and minced fresh cilantro

1. In a small saucepan, bring water to a boil. Add quinoa. Reduce heat; simmer, covered, until the liquid is absorbed, 12-15 minutes. Remove from heat; fluff with a fork.
2. Meanwhile, place carrot in a food processor; pulse until coarsely chopped. Add the beans; process until chopped. Transfer mixture to a large bowl. Mix in the cooked quinoa, bread crumbs, green onions, egg and seasonings. Shape mixture into 8 patties.
3. In a large skillet, heat olive oil over medium heat. Add patties; cook until a thermometer reads 160°, 3-4 minutes on each side, turning carefully. If desired, serve with optional ingredients.

2 patties: 235 cal., 10g fat (1g sat. fat), 47mg chol., 273mg sod., 28g carb. (2g sugars, 5g fiber), 8g pro. **Diabetic exchanges:** 2 starch, 1½ fat, 1 lean meat.

FISH TACOS

A cool sauce with just a bit of zing tops these crispy fish tacos. This recipe is a delicious guilt-free dish that doesn't break the bank.
—Lena Lim, Seattle, WA

Prep: 30 min. • **Cook:** 20 min.
Makes: 8 servings

- ¾ cup reduced-fat sour cream
- 1 can (4 oz.) chopped green chiles
- 1 Tbsp. fresh cilantro leaves
- 1 Tbsp. lime juice
- 4 tilapia fillets (4 oz. each)
- ½ cup all-purpose flour
- 1 large egg white, beaten
- ½ cup panko (Japanese) bread crumbs
- 1 Tbsp. canola oil
- ½ tsp. salt
- ½ tsp. each white pepper, cayenne pepper and paprika
- 8 corn tortillas (6 in.), warmed
- 1 large tomato, finely chopped
  Additional fresh cilantro leaves, optional

1. Place the sour cream, chiles, cilantro and lime juice in a food processor; cover and process until blended. Set aside.
2. Cut each tilapia fillet lengthwise into 2 portions. Place the flour, egg white and bread crumbs in separate shallow bowls. Dip tilapia in the flour, then the egg white, then the crumbs.

TUSCAN PORTOBELLO STEW

3. In a large skillet over medium heat, cook tilapia in oil in batches until fish flakes easily with a fork, 4-5 minutes on each side. Combine the seasonings; sprinkle over fish.
4. Place a portion of fish on each tortilla; top with about 2 Tbsp. of the sour cream mixture. Sprinkle with tomato. If desired, top with additional cilantro.
2 tacos: 190 cal., 5g fat (1g sat. fat), 30mg chol., 269mg sod., 23g carb. (3g sugars, 2g fiber), 16g pro. **Diabetic exchanges:** 2 lean meat, 1½ starch, ½ fat.

TUSCAN PORTOBELLO STEW

This heart-healthy, one-skillet meal is quick and easy to prepare yet elegant enough for company. I take this to my school's potlucks, where it is devoured by teachers and students alike!
—Jane Siemon, Viroqua, WI

Prep: 20 min. • **Cook:** 20 min.
Makes: 4 servings

- 2 large portobello mushrooms, coarsely chopped
- 1 medium onion, chopped
- 3 garlic cloves, minced
- 2 Tbsp. olive oil
- ½ cup white wine or vegetable broth
- 1 can (28 oz.) diced tomatoes, undrained
- 2 cups chopped fresh kale
- 1 bay leaf
- 1 tsp. dried thyme
- ½ tsp. dried basil
- ½ tsp. dried rosemary, crushed
- ¼ tsp. salt
- ¼ tsp. pepper
- 2 cans (15 oz. each) cannellini beans, rinsed and drained

In a large skillet, saute the mushrooms, onion and garlic in oil until tender. Add the wine. Bring to a boil; cook until liquid is reduced by half. Stir in the tomatoes, kale and seasonings. Bring to a boil. Reduce heat; cover and simmer for 8-10 minutes. Add beans; heat through. Discard bay leaf.
1¼ cups: 309 cal., 8g fat (1g sat. fat), 0 chol., 672mg sod., 46g carb. (9g sugars, 13g fiber), 12g pro. **Diabetic exchanges:** 2 starch, 2 vegetable, 1½ fat, 1 lean meat.

TEX-MEX PORK CHOPS

These easy, flavorful chops won a contest for me! Salsa, cumin and green chiles give them the kick they need to earn the name Tex-Mex.
—Jo Ann Dalrymple, Claremore, OK

Takes: 20 min. • **Makes:** 6 servings

    Butter-flavored cooking spray
1 small onion, chopped
6 boneless pork loin chops (5 oz. each)
1 cup salsa
1 can (4 oz.) chopped green chiles
½ tsp. ground cumin
¼ tsp. pepper

1. In a large skillet coated with butter-flavored cooking spray, saute onion until tender. Add pork chops; cook over medium heat until a thermometer reads 145°, 5-6 minutes on each side.
2. Combine the salsa, chiles, cumin and pepper; pour over pork. Bring to a boil. Reduce heat; cover and simmer until heated through.

1 serving: 223 cal., 8g fat (3g sat. fat), 68mg chol., 433mg sod., 9g carb. (3g sugars, 5g fiber), 32g pro. **Diabetic exchanges:** 4 lean meat, 1 vegetable.

EASY BEEF STROGANOFF

PICTURED ON P. 139

I lightened up my mother-in-law's wonderful stroganoff to come up with this recipe. My family calls it "special noodles" in my house!
—Jennifer Riordan, St. Louis, MO

Takes: 30 min. • **Makes:** 6 servings

4½ cups uncooked yolk-free noodles
1 lb. lean ground beef (90% lean)
½ lb. sliced fresh mushrooms
1 large onion, halved and sliced
3 garlic cloves, minced
1 Tbsp. reduced-fat butter
2 Tbsp. all-purpose flour
1 can (14½ oz.) reduced-sodium beef broth
2 Tbsp. tomato paste
1 cup reduced-fat sour cream
¼ tsp. salt
¼ tsp. pepper
    Chopped fresh parsley, optional

1. Cook noodles according to the package directions. Meanwhile, in a large saucepan, cook the beef, mushrooms and onion over medium heat until the meat is no longer pink. Add garlic; cook 1 minute longer. Drain. Remove and keep warm.
2. In the same pan, melt butter. Stir in flour until smooth; gradually add broth and tomato paste. Bring to a boil; cook and stir until thickened, about 2 minutes.
3. Carefully return the beef mixture to the pan. Add sour cream, salt and pepper; cook and stir until heated through (do not boil). Drain the noodles; serve with beef mixture. If desired, top with chopped parsley.

Note: This recipe was tested with Land O'Lakes light stick butter.

⅔ cup beef mixture with ¾ cup noodles: 333 cal., 11g fat (5g sat. fat), 58mg chol., 329mg sod., 33g carb. (7g sugars, 3g fiber), 25g pro. **Diabetic exchanges:** 2 starch, 2 lean meat, 1 fat.

TEX-MEX PORK CHOPS

LENTIL TACO CUPS

LENTIL TACO CUPS

My trusty muffin tin never fails to help me put fun and easy hand-held mains on the table for my family on busy weeknights. These festive vegetarian cups are so flavorful, nobody misses the meat.
—Shauna Havey, Roy, UT

Prep: 25 min. • **Bake:** 15 min.
Makes: 6 servings

- 12 mini flour tortillas
- 1 can (15 oz.) lentils, drained
- ¾ cup pico de gallo
- ½ cup enchilada sauce
- 2 Tbsp. taco seasoning
- 2 cups shredded Mexican cheese blend, divided

CREMA
- 1 cup sour cream
- ½ cup minced fresh cilantro
- 1 Tbsp. lime juice
- ¼ tsp. sea salt
  Shredded lettuce, sliced ripe olives and chopped tomatoes

1. Preheat oven to 425°. Press warm tortillas into 12 greased muffin cups, pleating sides as needed. In a large bowl, combine lentils, pico de gallo, enchilada sauce and taco seasoning. Stir in 1½ cups cheese. Divide the lentil mixture among cups. Sprinkle with the remaining cheese.

2. Bake until heated through and cheese is melted, 12-15 minutes. Meanwhile, for the crema, combine sour cream, cilantro, lime juice and sea salt. Serve cups with crema, lettuce, olives and tomatoes.
2 taco cups: 303 cal., 20g fat (11g sat. fat), 43mg chol., 793mg sod., 17g carb. (3g sugars, 5g fiber), 14g pro.

CACCIATORE CHICKEN BREASTS

This easy recipe is my lightened-up version of a traditional chicken cacciatore. You can serve the tasty sauce and chicken over rice or noodles. If you want to lower the sodium, use garlic powder instead of garlic salt.
—JoAnn McCauley, Dubuque, IA

Takes: 30 min. • **Makes:** 2 servings

- ½ medium onion, sliced and separated into rings
- ½ medium green pepper, sliced
- 1 Tbsp. olive oil
- 2 boneless skinless chicken breast halves (5 oz. each)
- ¾ cup canned stewed tomatoes
- 2 Tbsp. white wine or chicken broth
- ¼ tsp. garlic salt
- ¼ tsp. dried rosemary, crushed
- ⅛ tsp. pepper

1. In a large skillet, saute onion and green pepper in oil until crisp-tender. Remove and keep warm. Cook chicken over medium-high heat until the juices run clear, 4-5 minutes on each side. Remove and set aside.

2. Add the tomatoes, wine, garlic salt, rosemary and pepper to the skillet. Stir in the onion mixture and heat through. Serve with chicken.
1 chicken breast half with ¾ cup sauce: 272 cal., 10g fat (2g sat. fat), 78mg chol., 462mg sod., 12g carb. (7g sugars, 2g fiber), 30g pro. **Diabetic exchanges:** 4 lean meat, 2 vegetable, 1½ fat.

CREAMY CHICKEN & THYME

Thyme gives this simple chicken dish its distinctive taste. I lightened up the original recipe by using reduced-fat sour cream, but you'd never guess based on its rich, creamy flavor.
—Harriet Johnson, Champlin, MN

Takes: 30 min. • **Makes:** 4 servings

- 4 boneless skinless chicken breast halves (4 oz. each)
- 1 can (14½ oz.) reduced-sodium chicken broth
- 1 Tbsp. all-purpose flour
- ½ cup reduced-fat sour cream
- ½ tsp. dried parsley flakes
- ¼ tsp. salt
- ¼ tsp. dill weed
- ¼ tsp. dried thyme
- ⅛ tsp. onion salt
- ⅛ tsp. pepper
  Hot cooked egg noodles, optional

1. Place chicken breasts in a large nonstick skillet. Add ½ cup of broth. Cover and simmer until juices run clear, 10-12 minutes, turning once. Remove chicken from pan; keep warm. Add remaining broth to skillet and bring to a boil; reduce heat to low.

2. In a small bowl, combine flour and sour cream. Whisk into the pan. Stir in parsley, salt, dill weed, thyme, onion salt and pepper. Simmer, uncovered, until slightly thickened, about 5 minutes. If desired, serve with hot cooked noodles.
1 serving: 167 cal., 5g fat (2g sat. fat), 66mg chol., 575mg sod., 4g carb. (3g sugars, 0 fiber), 27g pro. **Diabetic exchanges:** 3 lean meat, ½ fat.

CHICKEN ORZO SKILLET

CHICKEN ORZO SKILLET

As a busy homemaker with a home-based business, I try to make quick and healthy dinners for my husband and two young children. I combined two recipes to come up with this family favorite.
—Kathleen Farrell, Rochester, NY

....

Takes: 30 min. • **Makes:** 6 servings

- 1 cup uncooked orzo pasta
- 1 lb. boneless skinless chicken breasts, cubed
- 3 tsp. olive oil, divided
- 3 garlic cloves, minced
- 2 cans (14½ oz. each) stewed tomatoes, cut up
- 1 can (15 oz.) cannellini beans, rinsed and drained
- 1½ tsp. Italian seasoning
- ½ tsp. salt
- 1 pkg. (16 oz.) frozen broccoli florets, thawed

1. Cook orzo according to package directions. Meanwhile, in a large nonstick skillet, cook chicken in 2 tsp. oil until no longer pink, 6-7 minutes. Remove and keep warm.

2. In the same skillet, cook garlic in remaining oil for 1 minute or until tender. Stir in the tomatoes, beans, Italian seasoning and salt. Bring to a boil. Stir in broccoli and chicken; heat through. Drain orzo; stir into chicken mixture.

1½ cups: 342 cal., 5g fat (1g sat. fat), 42mg chol., 589mg sod., 49g carb. (9g sugars, 7g fiber), 25g pro. **Diabetic exchanges:** 3 vegetable, 2 starch, 2 lean meat, ½ fat.

TARRAGON TUNA SALAD
PICTURED ON P. 139

It's surprising how just a few herbs can brighten up tuna salad. Made with reduced-fat mayonnaise, this version gets its zip from mustard.
—Billie Moss, Walnut Creek, CA

....

Takes: 10 min. • **Makes:** 4 servings

- 2 cans (6 oz. each) light water-packed tuna, drained and flaked
- 1 cup chopped celery
- ¼ cup chopped sweet onion
- ⅓ cup reduced-fat mayonnaise
- 2 Tbsp. minced fresh parsley
- 1 Tbsp. lemon juice
- 1 tsp. minced fresh tarragon or ¼ tsp. dried tarragon
- ½ tsp. Dijon mustard
- ¼ tsp. white pepper
  Lettuce leaves, optional

In a small bowl, combine tuna, celery and onion. Combine the mayonnaise, parsley, lemon juice, tarragon, mustard and pepper. Stir into the tuna mixture. Serve on lettuce leaves if desired.

⅔ cup: 151 cal., 7g fat (1g sat. fat), 38mg chol., 373mg sod., 4g carb. (2g sugars, 1g fiber), 17g pro. **Diabetic exchanges:** 2 lean meat, 1½ fat.

PECAN PORK CHOPS

A delicate butter and brown sugar glaze makes a tasty topping for these broiled pork chops.
—*Taste of Home* Test Kitchen

Takes: 15 min. • **Makes:** 8 servings

- 8 boneless pork loin chops (4 oz. each)
- ¼ cup packed brown sugar
- 2 Tbsp. cornstarch
- ¼ tsp. salt
- ⅛ tsp. ground mustard
- 2 Tbsp. butter, softened
- 2 tsp. cider vinegar
- 3 Tbsp. chopped pecans

1. Broil pork chops 4-5 in. from the heat for 4 minutes. Meanwhile, in a small bowl, combine sugar, cornstarch, salt and mustard. Stir in the butter and vinegar until smooth.

2. Turn chops over and broil for 2 minutes longer. Spoon about 2 tsp. of the sugar mixture over top of each pork chop. Broil 2-3 minutes longer or until a thermometer inserted in the pork reads 145°.

3. Top each chop with 1 tsp. pecans. Place back under the broiler; broil until pecans are toasted, about 1 minute longer. Let stand for 5 minutes before serving.

1 pork chop: 229 cal., 11g fat (4g sat. fat), 62mg chol., 130mg sod., 9g carb. (7g sugars, 0 fiber), 22g pro.

STEAK FRITES SALAD

All the ingredients in this salad work perfectly together. It has the right amount of indulgence and healthy to create the ideal main dish.
—Cameron Stell, Los Angeles, CA

Prep: 45 min. • **Cook:** 20 min.
Makes: 6 servings

- 4 Tbsp. olive oil, divided
- 1 medium red onion, sliced
- 6 fresh asparagus spears, cut into 2-in. pieces
- 6 baby red potatoes, quartered
- 1 tsp. salt, divided
- ½ tsp. pepper, divided
- 1 beef flank steak (2 lbs.)
- 6 cups fresh arugula
- 1 cup grape tomatoes, halved
- ⅓ cup shaved Parmesan cheese

DRESSING
- ¼ cup red wine vinegar
- 2 Tbsp. olive oil
- 1 tsp. Dijon mustard

1. Preheat oven to 425°. In a large heavy skillet, heat 1 Tbsp. oil over medium heat. Add onion; cook and stir until softened, 6-8 minutes. Reduce heat to medium-low; cook 30-40 minutes or until deep golden brown, stirring occasionally. Add the asparagus; cook and stir until crisp-tender, 3-5 minutes. Remove and keep warm.

2. Meanwhile, place the potatoes on a rimmed baking sheet; drizzle with 2 Tbsp. oil. Sprinkle with ½ tsp. salt and ¼ tsp. pepper; toss to coat. Roast until golden brown and tender, 20-25 minutes, turning once.

3. Sprinkle steak with the remaining ½ tsp. salt and ¼ tsp. pepper. In the same skillet, heat remaining 1 Tbsp. oil over medium-high heat. Cook steaks until meat reaches desired doneness (for medium-rare, a thermometer should read 135°; medium, 140°; medium-well, 145°), 8-10 minutes on each side. Let stand 10 minutes before thinly slicing across the grain.

4. In a large bowl, combine arugula, potatoes, tomatoes, asparagus mixture and Parmesan cheese. In a small bowl, whisk dressing ingredients until blended. Drizzle over salad; toss to coat. Divide among 6 plates; top with steak.

1 serving: 413 cal., 26g fat (7g sat. fat), 75mg chol., 587mg sod., 12g carb. (2g sugars, 2g fiber), 33g pro.

PECAN PORK CHOPS

FETA TOMATO-BASIL FISH

I rely on my husband to supply the main ingredient in this fuss-free dish! He fills our freezer after his annual summer fishing trip.

—Alicia Szeszol, Lindenhurst, IL

Takes: 20 min. • **Makes:** 4 servings

- ⅓ cup chopped onion
- 1 garlic clove, minced
- 2 tsp. olive oil
- 1 can (14½ oz.) Italian diced tomatoes, drained
- 1½ tsp. minced fresh basil or ½ tsp. dried basil
- 1 lb. walleye, bass or other whitefish fillets
- 4 oz. crumbled feta cheese

1. In a saucepan, saute onion and garlic in oil until tender. Add tomatoes and basil. Bring to a boil. Reduce heat; simmer, uncovered, for 5 minutes.

2. Meanwhile, broil the fish 4-6 in. from the heat for 5-6 minutes. Top each fillet with tomato mixture and cheese. Broil 5-7 minutes longer or until the fish flakes easily with a fork.

1 serving: 241 cal., 8g fat (4g sat. fat), 113mg chol., 660mg sod., 12g carb. (7g sugars, 2g fiber), 28g pro. **Diabetic exchanges:** 4 lean meat, 1 vegetable, 1 fat.

LEMON MUSHROOM CHICKEN

LEMON MUSHROOM CHICKEN

There's so much flavor in this dish. The best part? It doesn't seem light at all!

—Carrie Palmquist, Canova, SD

Takes: 30 min. • **Makes:** 4 servings

- 4 boneless skinless chicken breast halves (4 oz. each)
- ¼ cup plus 2 tsp. all-purpose flour, divided
- ½ tsp. salt
- ¼ tsp. pepper
- 2 Tbsp. butter
- ⅓ cup plus 3 Tbsp. reduced-sodium chicken broth, divided
- ½ lb. sliced fresh mushrooms
- 1 Tbsp. lemon juice

1. Flatten chicken to ½-in. thickness. In a large shallow dish, combine ¼ cup flour, salt and pepper. Add the chicken, 1 piece at a time; turn to coat.

2. In a large nonstick skillet over medium heat, cook the chicken in butter for 5-6 minutes on each side or until no longer pink. Remove and keep warm.

3. Add ⅓ cup broth to the pan, stirring to loosen any browned bits. Bring to a boil. Add mushrooms; cook and stir for 3-5 minutes or until tender.

4. Combine the remaining flour and broth until smooth; stir into the mushroom mixture. Bring to a boil; cook and stir until thickened, about 2 minutes. Stir in lemon juice. Serve with chicken.

1 chicken breast half with ¼ cup sauce: 213 cal., 9g fat (4g sat. fat), 78mg chol., 368mg sod., 8g carb. (1g sugars, 1g fiber), 26g pro. **Diabetic exchanges:** 3 lean meat, 1½ fat, ½ starch.

TURKEY SAUSAGE WITH PASTA

You'll be craving what's good for you when this turkey dish is on the menu. It's got the perfect blend of turkey sausage, pasta, fresh veggies and cheesy goodness.
—Mary Tallman, Arbor Vitae, WI

....

Takes: 30 min. • **Makes:** 6 servings

- 1 lb. Italian turkey sausage links, casings removed
- 1 large onion, chopped
- 1 large green pepper, chopped
- 1¼ cups sliced fresh mushrooms
- 2 garlic cloves, minced
- 2 cans (14½ oz. each) diced tomatoes, undrained
- 1 tsp. Italian seasoning
- 1 tsp. chili powder
- 6 cups uncooked spiral pasta
- ½ cup shredded part-skim mozzarella cheese

1. Crumble sausage into a large nonstick skillet. Add the onion, green pepper and mushrooms. Cook over medium heat until meat is no longer pink. Add garlic; cook 1 minute longer. Drain.

2. Stir in tomatoes, Italian seasoning and chili powder. Bring to a boil. Reduce heat; simmer, uncovered, for 10 minutes.

3. Meanwhile, cook pasta according to the package directions; drain. Serve the sausage mixture over pasta; sprinkle with cheese.

1 cup sausage mixture with 1 cup pasta: 396 cal., 10g fat (3g sat. fat), 51mg chol., 679mg sod., 54g carb. (9g sugars, 5g fiber), 24g pro.

GARLIC SHRIMP SPAGHETTI

Served with a salad and garlic bread toast, this simple and satisfying recipe makes a tasty dinner.
—June Foote, Spring Hill, FL

....

Takes: 25 min. • **Makes:** 6 servings

- 1 pkg. (8 oz.) spaghetti
- 2 Tbsp. cornstarch
- ½ cup water
- 1 can (14½ oz.) chicken broth
- 4 garlic cloves, minced
- ⅛ tsp. cayenne pepper
- 2 Tbsp. olive oil
- 1½ lbs. peeled and deveined cooked shrimp (31-40 per lb.)
- 2 Tbsp. lemon juice
- ¼ tsp. grated lemon zest
- ¼ cup minced fresh parsley

1. Cook spaghetti according to package directions. Meanwhile, in a small bowl, combine the cornstarch, water and broth until smooth; set aside.

2. In a large skillet, saute garlic and cayenne in oil until the garlic is tender. Stir the broth mixture and gradually add to the pan. Bring to a boil; cook and stir until thickened, about 2 minutes.

3. Reduce heat; add the shrimp, lemon juice, zest and parsley. Cook until heated through, 2-4 minutes. Drain spaghetti. Transfer to a large bowl. Add the shrimp mixture; toss to coat.

1½ cups: 320 cal., 7g fat (1g sat. fat), 172mg chol., 444mg sod., 33g carb. (2g sugars, 1g fiber), 29g pro. **Diabetic exchanges:** 3 lean meat, 2 starch, 1 fat.

HEALTH TIP Shrimp is naturally high in cholesterol, but that doesn't mean it's off the menu if you're following a heart-healthy diet. The cholesterol in shrimp is different than the blood cholesterol you're trying to manage. Cut back on saturated and trans fats to keep blood cholesterol in check.

TURKEY SAUSAGE WITH PASTA

COD WITH SWEET PEPPERS

This quick and delicious dish is a family favorite. I like to use three or four different colors of peppers.
—Judy Grebetz, Racine, WI

Takes: 25 min. • **Makes:** 4 servings

- 1 medium onion, halved and sliced
- 1 cup reduced-sodium chicken broth
- 1 Tbsp. lemon juice
- 3 garlic cloves, minced
- 1½ tsp. dried oregano
- ½ tsp. grated lemon zest
- ¼ tsp. salt
- 4 cod fillets (6 oz. each)
- ¾ cup julienned green pepper
- ¾ cup julienned sweet red pepper
- 2½ tsp. cornstarch
- 1 Tbsp. cold water
- 1 medium lemon, halved and sliced

1. In a large nonstick skillet, combine the first 7 ingredients. Bring to a boil. Reduce heat; cover and simmer until the onion is tender, 6-8 minutes.

2. Arrange fish and peppers over the onion mixture. Cover and simmer until the fish flakes easily with a fork and the peppers are tender, 6-9 minutes. Remove fish and vegetables and keep warm.

3. Combine the cornstarch and water until smooth; gradually stir into the pan juices. Bring to a boil; cook and stir until thickened, about 2 minutes. Spoon over fish and vegetables. Serve with lemon.

1 fillet with ⅓ cup pepper mixture: 168 cal., 1g fat (0 sat. fat), 65mg chol., 398mg sod., 10g carb. (4g sugars, 2g fiber), 29g pro. **Diabetic exchanges:** 4 lean meat, 1 vegetable.

HERB-GLAZED TURKEY SLICES

HERB-GLAZED TURKEY SLICES

In the mood for turkey, but don't have time to prepare a whole bird? Here's the perfect solution! These savory slices and the easy-to-prepare herb glaze offer the goodness of turkey without the hassle.
—*Taste of Home* Test Kitchen

Takes: 20 min. • **Makes:** 4 servings

- 1 pkg. (17.6 oz.) turkey breast cutlets
- 1 Tbsp. canola oil
- ½ cup chicken broth
- ½ cup apple juice
- 1 Tbsp. honey
- 1 Tbsp. Dijon mustard
- ½ tsp. salt
- ¼ tsp. each dried basil, dried rosemary, crushed and garlic powder
- 1 Tbsp. cornstarch
- 1 Tbsp. water

1. In a large skillet, brown turkey slices on each side in oil. In a small bowl, combine the broth, apple juice, honey, mustard, salt, basil, rosemary and garlic powder; pour over turkey. Bring to a boil. Reduce heat; cover and simmer for 8 minutes or until the turkey is no longer pink.

2. Combine the cornstarch and water until smooth; stir into skillet. Bring to a boil; cook and stir for 2 minutes or until thickened.

4 oz. cooked turkey: 213 cal., 4g fat (1g sat. fat), 78mg chol., 570mg sod., 11g carb. (8g sugars, 0 fiber), 31g pro. **Diabetic exchanges:** 4 lean meat, 1 fat, ½ starch.

MAKEOVER TRADITIONAL LASAGNA

This recipe is so good it's become our family's Christmas Eve tradition. It gets requested for birthdays, too!
—Shelly Behan, Littleton, CO

Prep: 45 min. • **Bake:** 70 min. + standing
Makes: 12 servings

- 1 lb. extra-lean ground beef (95% lean)
- 1 pkg. (14 oz.) breakfast turkey sausage links, casings removed and crumbled
- 3 cans (8 oz. each) no-salt-added tomato sauce
- 1 can (6 oz.) tomato paste
- 2 garlic cloves, minced
- 2 tsp. sugar
- 1½ tsp. Italian seasoning
- ½ tsp. pepper
- 9 whole wheat lasagna noodles
- 3 large eggs, lightly beaten
- 2 cups 2% cottage cheese
- 1 carton (15 oz.) reduced-fat ricotta cheese
- ½ cup grated Parmesan cheese
- 3 Tbsp. minced fresh parsley
- 1½ cups shredded part-skim mozzarella cheese
- 6 slices provolone cheese
  Additional minced fresh parsley

1. Preheat oven to 350°. In a large skillet, cook beef and sausage over medium heat until meat is no longer pink; drain. Add the tomato sauce, tomato paste, garlic, sugar, Italian seasoning and pepper. Bring to a boil. Reduce heat; cover and simmer for 15 minutes. Meanwhile, cook noodles according to package directions; drain.

2. In a small bowl, combine the eggs, cottage cheese, ricotta cheese, Parmesan and parsley. Spread 1 cup of the meat sauce into a 13x9-in. baking dish coated with cooking spray. Layer with 3 noodles, half of the cheese mixture, 1⅓ cups sauce and ½ cup mozzarella cheese. Repeat layers. Top with the remaining noodles and sauce.

3. Cover and bake for 55-60 minutes or until bubbly. Top with provolone and the remaining mozzarella cheese. Bake, uncovered, 15-20 minutes longer or until cheese is melted. Let stand for 15 minutes before cutting. Sprinkle with additional fresh parsley.

1 piece: 361 cal., 15g fat (7g sat. fat), 133mg chol., 634mg sod., 23g carb. (9g sugars, 3g fiber), 32g pro.

MAKEOVER TRADITIONAL LASAGNA

SPINACH & SHRIMP FRA DIAVOLO

This 20-minute dish is spicy, garlicky, saucy, and loaded with delicious shrimp. Plus, with the addition of spinach, you're also getting a serving of veggies. You can substitute arugula or kale for the spinach if you'd like.

—Julie Peterson, Crofton, MD

Prep: 20 min. • **Cook:** 30 min.
Makes: 4 servings

- 2 Tbsp. olive oil
- 1 medium onion, chopped
- 5 garlic cloves, minced
- ½ to 1 tsp. crushed red pepper flakes
- 1 cup dry white wine
- 1 can (14½ oz.) diced tomatoes, undrained
- 1 can (8 oz.) tomato sauce
- 3 Tbsp. minced fresh basil or 1 Tbsp. dried basil
- 1 tsp. dried oregano
- ¼ tsp. salt
- ¼ tsp. pepper
- 1 lb. uncooked shrimp (26-30 per lb.), peeled and deveined
- 3 cups finely chopped fresh spinach Grated Parmesan cheese, optional

PORK CHOPS WITH PARMESAN SAUCE

Tender skillet chops make a speedy weeknight meal. These ones are finished with a creamy and flavorful Parmesan sauce. Here's a new family favorite!
—*Taste of Home* Test Kitchen

Takes: 20 min. • **Makes:** 4 servings

- 4 boneless pork loin chops (4 oz. each)
- ½ tsp. salt
- ¼ tsp. pepper
- 1 Tbsp. butter
- 2 Tbsp. all-purpose flour
- 1 cup fat-free milk
- ⅓ cup grated Parmesan cheese
- 2 Tbsp. grated onion
- 3 tsp. minced fresh parsley
- ¼ tsp. dried thyme
- ¼ tsp. ground nutmeg

1. Sprinkle the pork chops with salt and pepper. In a large nonstick skillet, cook the chops in butter over medium heat until the meat juices run clear; remove and keep warm.
2. Combine flour and milk until smooth; stir into the pan. Bring to a boil; cook and stir for 2 minutes or until thickened. Stir in the remaining ingredients; heat through. Serve with chops.

1 pork chop with ¼ cup sauce: 244 cal., 11g fat (5g sat. fat), 69mg chol., 475mg sod., 7g carb. (3g sugars, 0 fiber), 27g pro.
Diabetic exchanges: 3 lean meat, ½ starch, ½ fat.

1. In a large skillet, heat oil over medium-high heat. Add onion; cook and stir until tender, 8-10 minutes. Add garlic and pepper flakes; cook 1 minute longer. Stir in wine. Bring to a boil; cook until the liquid is reduced by half. Stir in tomatoes, tomato sauce, basil, oregano, salt and pepper. Cook and stir until the sauce is slightly thickened, about 10 minutes.
2. Add shrimp and spinach; cook and stir until the shrimp turn pink and the spinach is wilted, 3-5 minutes. If desired, sprinkle with cheese.

1½ cups: 235 cal., 9g fat (1g sat. fat), 138mg chol., 727mg sod., 14g carb. (6g sugars, 4g fiber), 22g pro. **Diabetic exchanges:** 3 lean meat, 2 vegetable, 1½ fat.

SPINACH & SHRIMP
FRA DIAVOLO

APPLES & ONION TOPPED CHOPS

APPLES & ONION TOPPED CHOPS

My husband and I are trying to lose weight, and it's a challenge to find healthy dishes that are flavorful, quick and appealing to us and our daughter. This one fits the bill on all counts!
—Beverly McLain, Endicott, NY

Takes: 30 min. • **Makes:** 4 servings

- 4 tsp. canola oil, divided
- 4 boneless pork loin chops (5 oz. each)
- 3 cups sweet onion slices
- 2 medium Granny Smith apples, peeled and sliced
- ½ cup water
- 2 Tbsp. brown sugar
- 1 Tbsp. cider vinegar
- 1 tsp. garlic powder
- ½ tsp. salt
- ¼ to ½ tsp. pepper
- ¼ tsp. dried rosemary, crushed

1. In a large nonstick skillet heat 2 tsp. canola oil over medium-high heat; cook chops until browned, about 3 minutes on each side. Remove from skillet; set aside and keep warm.
2. In same skillet, cook and stir onion in the remaining 2 tsp. canola oil for 7 minutes or until onions are golden brown. Add the apple slices; cook and stir 3 minutes longer.
3. Combine the water, brown sugar, vinegar, garlic powder, salt, pepper and rosemary. Stir into skillet. Bring to a boil. Return meat to pan. Reduce heat; cover and cook until the apples are crisp-tender and a thermometer inserted into chops reads 160°, 8-10 minutes.
1 serving: 326 cal., 13g fat (3g sat. fat), 68mg chol., 340mg sod., 24g carb. (17g sugars, 3g fiber), 28g pro. **Diabetic exchanges:** 4 lean meat, 1 vegetable, 1 fat, ½ starch, ½ fruit.

REFRESHING SHRIMP SALAD

Avocado, strawberries and shrimp are wonderful together in this filling yet light salad. Balsamic or raspberry vinaigrette dressings are a good match, as are Asian-inspired dressings.
—*Taste of Home* Test Kitchen

Takes: 15 min. • **Makes:** 4 servings

- 1 pkg. (5 oz.) spring mix salad greens
- 1 lb. cooked medium shrimp, peeled and deveined
- 1 large navel orange, peeled and sectioned
- 1 medium ripe avocado, peeled and chopped
- 1 cup fresh strawberries, quartered
- ½ cup thinly sliced green onions
  Salad dressing of your choice

On each of 4 serving plates, arrange the salad greens, shrimp, orange, avocado, strawberries and onions. Drizzle with your favorite salad dressing.
3 cups: 239 cal., 9g fat (1g sat. fat), 172mg chol., 181mg sod., 16g carb. (7g sugars, 6g fiber), 25g pro. **Diabetic exchanges:** 3 lean meat, 1½ fat, 1 vegetable, ½ fruit.

FETTUCCINE WITH BLACK BEAN SAUCE

When my husband needed to go on a heart-smart diet, I knew I had to get more vegetables into our daily menus. This meatless spaghetti sauce is a winner; it's delicious with spinach fettuccine.
—Marianne Neuman, East Troy, WI

Takes: 30 min. • **Makes:** 5 servings

- 6 oz. uncooked fettuccine
- 1 small green pepper, chopped
- 1 small onion, chopped
- 1 Tbsp. olive oil
- 2 cups garden-style pasta sauce
- 1 can (15 oz.) black beans, rinsed and drained
- 2 Tbsp. minced fresh basil or 2 tsp. dried basil
- 1 tsp. dried oregano
- ½ tsp. fennel seed
- ¼ tsp. garlic salt
- 1 cup shredded part-skim mozzarella cheese
  Additional chopped fresh basil, optional

1. Cook fettuccine according to package directions. In a large saucepan, saute green pepper and onion in oil until tender. Stir in pasta sauce, black beans and seasonings. Bring to a boil. Reduce heat; simmer, uncovered, for 5 minutes.

2. Drain the fettuccine. Top with sauce and sprinkle with cheese. If desired, top with chopped fresh basil.

Note: This recipe was tested with Ragu Super Vegetable Primavera pasta sauce.
¾ cup sauce with ¾ cup pasta: 350 cal., 10g fat (3g sat. fat), 17mg chol., 761mg sod., 51g carb. (12g sugars, 8g fiber), 16g pro.

HEALTH TIP As long as you're eating a healthy dinner, switch up your noodle game, too. Try this dish with whole wheat, buckwheat, quinoa, chickpea or multigrain pasta.

FETTUCCINE WITH BLACK BEAN SAUCE

Family-Friendly Fare

Pleasing picky eaters while making sure they're getting their needed vitamins can be a challenge. These recipes come to the rescue with meals that are quick, convenient and so delicious that even choosy children will happily clean their plates!

Quick Icebox Sandwiches (p. 174) **Chicken Parmesan Slider Bake** (p. 172) **Nutty Chicken Fingers** (p. 171)
Little Cheddar Meat Loaves (p. 173) **Monkey Bread** (p. 178)

SUGAR COOKIE S'MORES

Change up traditional s'mores by using sugar cookies and candy bars in place of the expected ingredients. This fun twist on the campfire classic will delight everyone!
—Taste of Home Test Kitchen

Takes: 15 min. • **Makes:** 4 servings

- 8 fun-size Milky Way candy bars
- 8 sugar cookies (3 in.)
- 4 large marshmallows

1. Place 2 candy bars on each of 4 cookies; place on grill rack. Grill, uncovered, over medium-hot heat for 1-1½ minutes or until the bottoms of the cookies are browned.
2. Meanwhile, using a long-handled fork, toast marshmallows 6 in. from the heat until golden brown, turning occasionally. Remove marshmallows from fork and place over candy bars; top with the remaining cookies. Serve immediately.

1 sandwich cookie: 271 cal., 10g fat (5g sat. fat), 13mg chol., 123mg sod., 43g carb. (31g sugars, 1g fiber), 3g pro.

ONE-PAN ROTINI WITH
TOMATO CREAM SAUCE

ONE-PAN ROTINI WITH TOMATO CREAM SAUCE

This one-pan recipe was proclaimed a winner by my family. Serve with crusty bread to dip into the sauce.
—Angela Lively, Conroe, TX

Prep: 15 min. • **Cook:** 30 min.
Makes: 6 servings

- 1 lb. lean ground beef (90% lean)
- 1 medium onion, chopped
- 2 garlic cloves, minced
- 1 tsp. Italian seasoning
- ½ tsp. pepper
- ¼ tsp. salt
- 2 cups beef stock
- 1 can (14½ oz.) fire-roasted diced tomatoes, undrained
- 2 cups uncooked spiral pasta
- 1 cup frozen peas
- 1 cup heavy whipping cream
- ½ cup grated Parmesan cheese

1. In a large skillet, cook beef and onion over medium heat until the beef is no longer pink and onion is tender, breaking up beef into crumbles, 5-10 minutes; drain. Add garlic and seasonings; cook 1 minute longer. Add stock and tomatoes; bring to a boil. Add pasta and peas; reduce heat. Simmer, covered, until the pasta is tender, 10-12 minutes.
2. Gradually stir in cream and cheese; heat through (do not allow to boil).

1 cup: 443 cal., 23g fat (13g sat. fat), 98mg chol., 646mg sod., 33g carb. (6g sugars, 3g fiber), 25g pro.

NUTTY CHICKEN FINGERS

Watch the room light up with smiles when you bring this fun dish to the table. Our children love the crunchy nut coating on these chicken strips. And with only a handful of ingredients, preparation is a snap.
—Beba Cates, Pearland, TX

Takes: 30 min. • **Makes:** 2 servings

- ½ cup finely chopped pecans
- ⅓ cup crushed cornflakes
- 1 Tbsp. dried parsley flakes
- ⅛ tsp. garlic powder
- ⅛ tsp. salt
- 2 Tbsp. 2% milk
- ¾ lb. boneless skinless chicken breasts, cut into 1-in. strips

1. Preheat oven to 400°. In a shallow bowl, combine the first 5 ingredients. Place milk in another shallow bowl. Dip chicken in milk, then roll in the pecan mixture.

2. Place chicken strips in a single layer in an ungreased 15x10x1-in. baking pan. Bake, uncovered, until juices run clear, 12-15 minutes.

5 oz. cooked chicken: 436 cal., 24g fat (3g sat. fat), 96mg chol., 346mg sod., 18g carb. (3g sugars, 3g fiber), 38g pro.

MARSHMALLOW BERRY PANCAKES

Growing on our little farm is a beautiful mulberry tree. I love developing new recipes using the berries to delight my friends and family. These pancakes are one of our favorites, served at breakfast or on a lazy weekend as a special treat. As a variation, replace the egg with ¼ cup of applesauce.
—Ruth Pople, Red Creek, NY

Prep: 15 min. • **Cook:** 15 min./batch
Makes: 6 servings

- 2 cups all-purpose flour
- 3 tsp. baking powder
- 1 tsp. salt
- 1 large egg, room temperature
- 1½ cups 2% milk
- ⅓ cup marshmallow creme
- 3 Tbsp. melted butter, divided
- 2 tsp. vanilla extract
- 2 cups fresh or frozen mulberries or blackberries
- Maple syrup, optional

1. In a large bowl, whisk flour, baking powder and salt. In another bowl, whisk egg, milk, marshmallow creme, 1 Tbsp. butter and the vanilla until blended. Add to the flour mixture; stir just until moistened. Fold in berries.

2. Preheat griddle over medium heat. Lightly grease griddle with the remaining remaining 2 Tbsp. butter. Pour batter by ¼ cupfuls onto the griddle; cook until bubbles on top begin to pop and the bottoms are golden brown, 5-6 minutes. Turn; cook until the second side is golden brown, 6-7 minutes longer. If desired, serve with maple syrup.

Freeze option: Freeze cooled pancakes between layers of waxed paper in a freezer container. To use, place pancakes on an ungreased baking sheet, cover with foil and reheat in a preheated 375° oven until heated through, 8-10 minutes. Or, place a stack of 3 pancakes on a microwave-safe plate and microwave on high until heated through, 45-90 seconds.

2 pancakes: 307 cal., 8g fat (5g sat. fat), 51mg chol., 725mg sod., 48g carb. (7g sugars, 1g fiber), 8g pro.

NUTTY CHICKEN FINGERS

HOMEMADE STRAWBERRY ICE CREAM

What could be better than a tubful of luscious homemade ice cream made with fresh strawberries?
—Esther Johnson, Merrill, WI

Prep: 20 min. + cooling
Process: 20 min./batch + freezing
Makes: 12 servings (about 1½ qt.)

- 6 large egg yolks
- 2 cups whole milk
- 1 cup sugar
- ¼ tsp. salt
- 1 tsp. vanilla extract
- 2 cups heavy whipping cream
- 2 cups crushed fresh strawberries, sweetened

1. Place egg yolks and milk in the top of a double boiler; beat. Add sugar and salt. Cook over simmering water, stirring until the mixture is thickened and coats a metal spoon. Cool.
2. Add vanilla, cream and strawberries. Pour into the cylinder of an ice cream freezer and freeze according to the manufacturer's directions. When the ice cream is frozen, transfer to freezer containers; freeze for another 2-4 hours before serving.

½ cup: 265 cal., 19g fat (11g sat. fat), 166mg chol., 88mg sod., 22g carb. (21g sugars, 1g fiber), 4g pro.

CHICKEN PARMESAN SLIDER BAKE

CHICKEN PARMESAN SLIDER BAKE

Sliders are the perfect finger food for any get-together, and this flavorful chicken Parmesan version won't disappoint.
—Nick Iverson, Denver, CO

Prep: 20 min. • **Bake:** 25 min.
Makes: 1 dozen

- 24 oz. frozen breaded chicken tenders
- 1 pkg. (12 oz.) Hawaiian sweet rolls
- 1 pkg. (7½ oz.) sliced provolone and mozzarella cheese blend
- 1 jar (24 oz.) marinara sauce

TOPPING
- ½ cup butter, cubed
- 1 tsp. garlic powder
- 1 tsp. crushed red pepper flakes
- ¼ cup grated Parmesan cheese
- 2 Tbsp. minced fresh basil

1. Preheat oven to 375°. Prepare chicken tenders according to package directions. Meanwhile, without separating rolls, cut horizontally in half; arrange roll bottoms in a greased 13x9-in. baking dish. Place half of cheese slices over roll bottoms. Bake until the cheese is melted, 3-5 minutes.
2. Layer rolls with half of sauce, chicken tenders, remaining sauce and remaining cheese slices. Replace top halves of rolls.
3. Microwave butter, garlic powder and red pepper flakes, covered, on high, stirring occasionally, until the butter is melted. Pour over rolls; sprinkle with Parmesan cheese. Bake, uncovered, until golden brown and heated through, 20-25 minutes. Sprinkle rolls with basil before serving.

1 slider: 402 cal., 23g fat (11g sat. fat), 62mg chol., 780mg sod., 34g carb. (10g sugars, 4g fiber), 17g pro.

TEST KITCHEN TIP
You can play with this recipe—try dinner rolls in place of the Hawaiian sweet rolls, or sneak a few slices of pepperoni or salami onto each roll.

LITTLE CHEDDAR MEAT LOAVES

These tiny loaves are great when you are craving meat loaf but don't want to wait for a full-sized loaf to bake. We love these served with au gratin or fried potatoes.
—Paula Petersen, Granite City, IL

Takes: 30 min. • **Makes:** 2 servings

- 1 large egg, lightly beaten
- ⅓ cup quick-cooking oats
- 2 Tbsp. ketchup
- 1 Tbsp. dried minced onion
- ½ lb. lean ground beef (90% lean)

TOPPING
- 4 tsp. ketchup
- 4 Tbsp. shredded cheddar cheese

1. Preheat oven to 400°. In a large bowl, combine egg, oats, ketchup and onion. Crumble beef over the mixture and mix well. Coat 4 muffin cups with cooking spray; fill three-fourths full with the meat mixture. Spread ketchup over loaves.

2. Bake for 15 minutes. Sprinkle with cheese. Bake until no pink remains and a thermometer reads 160°, about 5 minutes longer. Let stand for 5 minutes before removing from muffin cups.

2 mini meat loaves: 343 cal., 16g fat (7g sat. fat), 190mg chol., 463mg sod., 18g carb. (4g sugars, 2g fiber), 30g pro.

CHICKEN ALPHABET SOUP

I'm a teenager and love to make this fun chicken soup for my family. It makes me so happy when they tell me how much they like it!
—Sarah Mackey, New Smyrna Beach, FL

Takes: 25 min.
Makes: 10 servings (2½ qt.)

- 3 medium carrots, chopped
- 2 celery ribs, chopped
- ¾ cup chopped sweet onion
- 1 Tbsp. olive oil
- 2 qt. chicken broth
- 3 cups cubed cooked chicken breast
- ¼ tsp. dried thyme
- 1½ cups uncooked alphabet pasta
- 3 Tbsp. minced fresh parsley

In a Dutch oven, saute the carrots, celery and onion in oil until tender. Stir in the broth, chicken and thyme. Bring to a boil. Stir in the pasta. Reduce heat; simmer, uncovered, for 10 minutes or until the pasta is tender. Stir in parsley.

1 cup: 163 cal., 4g fat (1g sat. fat), 26mg chol., 828mg sod., 20g carb. (3g sugars, 2g fiber), 12g pro.

READER REVIEW

"I used spiral pasta instead of alphabet pasta and it turned out really well. Super easy to make and the kids and husband enjoyed it."

MKASKELA, TASTEOFHOME.COM

LITTLE CHEDDAR MEAT LOAVES

CHILI-GHETTI

I came up with this recipe when unexpected guests stopped by and I didn't have enough chili to go around. The spur-of-the-moment main dish is now a family favorite.
—Cindy Cuykendall, Skaneateles, NY

Takes: 30 min. • **Makes:** 6 servings

- 1 pkg. (7 oz.) spaghetti
- 1 lb. ground beef
- 1 small onion, chopped
- 1 can (16 oz.) kidney beans, rinsed and drained
- 1 can (14½ oz.) no-salt-added diced tomatoes, undrained
- 1 can (4 oz.) mushroom stems and pieces, drained
- ⅓ cup water
- 1 envelope chili seasoning
- 2 Tbsp. grated Parmesan cheese
- ¼ cup shredded part-skim mozzarella cheese

1. Cook spaghetti according to package directions. Meanwhile, in a large skillet, cook beef and onion over medium heat until the meat is no longer pink; drain.
2. Drain spaghetti; add to the beef mixture. Stir in the kidney beans, diced tomatoes, mushrooms, water, chili seasoning and Parmesan cheese. Cover and simmer for 10 minutes. Sprinkle with mozzarella cheese.

1¼ cups: 374 cal., 11g fat (4g sat. fat), 51mg chol., 706mg sod., 43g carb. (5g sugars, 6g fiber), 25g pro.

QUICK ICEBOX SANDWICHES

QUICK ICEBOX SANDWICHES

My mother liked making these cool, creamy treats when I was growing up in the States because she could make them so quickly. Now my three kids enjoy them!
—Sandy Armijo, Naples, Italy

Prep: 20 min. + freezing • **Makes:** 2 dozen

- 1 pkg. (3.4 oz.) instant vanilla pudding mix
- 2 cups cold whole milk
- 2 cups whipped topping
- 1 cup miniature semisweet chocolate chips
- 24 whole graham crackers, halved

1. Mix pudding and milk according to the package directions; refrigerate until set. Fold in the whipped topping and chocolate chips.
2. Place 24 graham cracker halves on a baking sheet; top each with about 3 Tbsp. filling. Place another graham cracker half on top. Wrap individual sandwiches in plastic; freeze until firm, about 1 hour. Serve frozen.

1 sandwich: 144 cal., 5g fat (3g sat. fat), 3mg chol., 162mg sod., 23g carb. (13g sugars, 1g fiber), 2g pro..

CHILI-GHETTI

QUICK SLOPPY JOES

QUICK SLOPPY JOES

You'll love this dish because it's quick, easy and inexpensive—and even the pickiest eaters love it! If you have any left over, it's also tasty served over biscuits, rice or baked potatoes.
—Laurie Hauser, Rochester, NY

Takes: 30 min. • **Makes:** 4 servings

- 1 lb. ground beef
- 1 cup ketchup
- ¼ cup water
- 2 Tbsp. brown sugar
- 2 tsp. Worcestershire sauce
- 2 tsp. prepared mustard
- ½ tsp. garlic powder
- ½ tsp. onion powder
- ½ tsp. salt
- 4 hamburger buns, split

In a large skillet, cook beef over medium heat until no longer pink; drain. Stir in the ketchup, water, brown sugar, Worcestershire sauce, mustard, garlic powder, onion powder and salt. Bring to a boil. Reduce heat; cover and simmer for 15-20 minutes. Serve on buns.
1 sandwich: 439 cal., 16g fat (6g sat. fat), 75mg chol., 1360mg sod., 46g carb. (17g sugars, 2g fiber), 27g pro.

TROPICAL PINEAPPLE COLESLAW

Pineapple adds pizzazz to traditional coleslaw, introducing both color and sweetness. A fast side dish, it's sure to be in demand at your next barbecue.
—Cheryl Dolan, Innerkip, ON

Takes: 15 min. • **Makes:** 4 servings

- 3 cups shredded cabbage
- ¾ cup shredded carrot
- 1 can (8 oz.) unsweetened crushed pineapple, drained
- ⅓ cup mayonnaise
- 4 tsp. sugar
- 4 tsp. white vinegar

In a small bowl, combine the cabbage, carrot and pineapple. In another small bowl, whisk the mayonnaise, sugar and vinegar; pour over pineapple mixture; toss to coat. Serve immediately.
¾ cup: 206 cal., 15g fat (2g sat. fat), 7mg chol., 126mg sod., 18g carb. (12g sugars, 2g fiber), 1g pro.

TEST KITCHEN TIP
If you're looking for other sweet but healthy additions that will make coleslaw more kid-friendly, try chopped apple and raisins.

MINIATURE PEANUT BUTTER TREATS

I have three children and eight grandchildren, and every one of them loves these "peanut butter thingies," as the grandchildren call them.
—Jodie McCoy, Tulsa, OK

Prep: 20 min. + chilling
Bake: 10 min./batch + cooling
Makes: 3½ dozen

COOKIE
- ½ cup butter, softened
- ½ cup sugar
- ½ cup packed brown sugar
- 1 large egg, room temperature
- ½ cup creamy peanut butter
- ½ tsp. vanilla extract
- 1¼ cups all-purpose flour
- ¾ tsp. baking soda
- ½ tsp. salt

FILLING
- 42 miniature peanut butter-chocolate cups

1. In a bowl, combine the butter, sugars, egg, peanut butter and vanilla; beat until smooth. Combine the flour, baking soda and salt; gradually add to the creamed mixture. Cover and chill for 1 hour or until easy to handle.
2. Preheat oven to 375°. Roll dough into 42 walnut-sized balls; place in greased miniature muffin cups. Bake for 8-9 minutes.
3. Remove from oven; gently press 1 peanut butter cup into each cookie, forming a depression. Cool 10 minutes before removing cookies to wire racks to cool completely.

1 treat: 108 cal., 6g fat (3g sat. fat), 11mg chol., 108mg sod., 12g carb. (9g sugars, 1g fiber), 2g pro.

MINIATURE PEANUT BUTTER TREATS

FAVORITE HAMBURGER NOODLE BAKE

This go-to recipe is ideal for busy cooks. You cook once and have two casseroles... one to bake now and the other to freeze and use later.
—Patricia Teller, Lewiston, ID

Prep: 20 min. • **Bake:** 35 min.
Makes: 2 casseroles (4 servings each)

- 5 cups uncooked egg noodles
- 2 lbs. ground beef
- 1 cup chopped onion
- ½ cup chopped green pepper
- 2 cans (10¾ oz. each) condensed tomato soup, undiluted
- 2 cups shredded cheddar cheese
- 1½ cups water
- ½ cup chili sauce
- 1½ cups soft bread crumbs
- 3 Tbsp. butter, melted

1. Preheat oven to 350°. Cook noodles according to the package directions until al dente; drain. In a large skillet, cook beef, onion and green pepper over medium-high heat for 10-12 minutes or until the meat is no longer pink; drain. Stir in the noodles, soup, cheese, water and chili sauce. Transfer to 2 greased 8-in. square baking dishes.
2. Toss bread crumbs and butter; sprinkle over casseroles. Bake, uncovered, 35-40 minutes or until bubbly and golden brown.
Freeze option: Cool unbaked casseroles; cover and freeze up to 3 months. To use, partially thaw in refrigerator overnight. Remove from refrigerator 30 minutes before baking. Cover casserole with foil; bake as directed, increasing covered time to 45-50 minutes or until heated through and a thermometer inserted in center reads 165°. Uncover; bake 10-15 minutes longer or until golden brown.

1 serving: 477 cal., 24g fat (13g sat. fat), 120mg chol., 794mg sod., 34g carb. (8g sugars, 2g fiber), 31g pro.

Finger Food at its Finest

Making this treat is almost as much fun as eating it. The kids will have a blast dipping and arranging the dough, and they'll love the hot, delicious result!

HOW TO
Make Monkey Bread

1. Prep
Preheat oven to 350°. In 1 bowl, combine all the dry ingredients. Pour butter into a second bowl. Cut the biscuits into quarters.

2. Dip
Working with several pieces at a time, use a spoon to dip them in the butter...

3. Coat
...and then place them in the mixture of dry ingredients. Toss to coat.

4. Place in pan
Arrange the pieces in a greased 10-in. fluted tube pan. Repeat steps 2-4 until all the biscuit pieces are coated and in the pan.

5. Bake!
Bake until bread is browned, 30-35 minutes. Cool for 5-10 minutes, then invert on a serving plate.

MONKEY BREAD

Both of my boys really enjoyed helping me make monkey bread when they were young. It seemed to taste twice as good when they helped fix it. It's still one of our favorites for breakfast or as a snack.
—Carol Allen, McLeansboro, IL

....

Prep: 15 min. • **Bake:** 30 min. + cooling
Makes: 12 servings

- 1   pkg. (3½ oz.) cook-and-serve butterscotch pudding mix
- ¾   cup sugar
- 3   tsp. ground cinnamon
- ½   cup finely chopped pecans, optional
- ½   cup butter, melted
- 3   tubes (10 oz. each) refrigerated biscuits

1 serving: 223 cal., 11g fat (5g sat. fat), 20mg chol., 343mg sod., 30g carb. (19g sugars, 1g fiber), 2g pro.

COLA BURGERS

The unusual combination of cola and French salad dressing gives these hamburgers fabulous flavor. The mix is also used as a basting sauce on the burgers, which are a family favorite.
—Melva Baumer, Millmont, PA

Takes: 30 min. • **Makes:** 6 servings

- 1 large egg
- ½ cup cola, divided
- ½ cup crushed saltines (about 15)
- 6 Tbsp. French salad dressing, divided
- 2 Tbsp. grated Parmesan cheese
- ¼ tsp. salt
- 1½ lbs. ground beef
- 6 hamburger buns, split
  Optional: Lettuce leaves, sliced tomato, sliced red onion, pickles and sliced cheese

1. In a large bowl, combine egg, ¼ cup cola, cracker crumbs, 2 Tbsp. salad dressing, Parmesan cheese and salt. Crumble beef over mixture and mix well. Shape into six ¾-in.-thick patties (mixture will be moist).

2. In a small bowl, combine remaining cola and salad dressing; set aside.

3. Grill burgers, covered, over medium heat for 3 minutes on each side. Brush with cola mixture. Continue grilling to desired doneness, 6-8 minutes, brushing and turning occasionally. For medium-rare, a thermometer should read 135°; medium, 140°; medium-well, 145°. Serve on buns. Serve burgers with optional toppings as desired.

1 burger: 461 cal., 24g fat (8g sat. fat), 112mg chol., 714mg sod., 30g carb. (8g sugars, 1g fiber), 29g pro.

OLD-FASHIONED APPLESAUCE

We had all kinds of apple trees in the yard when I was growing up, so I don't know for sure which ones Mother liked best for her applesauce. Today I use Cortlands. I do know that her applesauce was very pale. Her secret was to keep the apples in salt water while she peeled them so that they wouldn't darken.
—Doris Natvig, Jesup, IA

Takes: 30 min. • **Makes:** 6 cups

- 4 lbs. tart apples
- 1 cup water
- 1 cinnamon stick or ½ tsp. cinnamon extract
- ½ to 1 cup sugar

Peel, core and quarter the apples. In a Dutch oven, bring apples, water and cinnamon to a boil. Reduce heat; cover and simmer 10-15 minutes or until the apples are tender. Remove from the heat. Add sugar to taste and stir until dissolved. If you used a cinnamon stick, remove and discard. Mash apples with a potato masher until the desired texture is reached. Serve warm or chilled.

½ cup: 122 cal., 1g fat (0 sat. fat), 0 chol., 0 sod., 31g carb. (26g sugars, 4g fiber), 0 pro.

COLA BURGERS

Breakfast & Brunch Favorites

Rise and shine! Start your day off right with a picture-perfect breakfast, whether you're facing a busy work day or enjoying a relaxing weekend at home. Sweet or savory, prepped the night before or whipped up in just a few minutes, these recipes give you what you need.

German Potato Omelet (p. 188) **Bacon & Egg Bundles** (p. 193) **Raspberry-Coconut French Toast** (p. 184) **Breakfast in a Pan** (p. 186) **Slow-Cooker Cinnamon Roll** (p. 192)

ZIPPY PRALINE BACON

We live on a lake and have many overnight guests, so I'm always looking for ways to enhance the usual morning meal of eggs and bacon. My husband came home from a men's brunch raving about this one, and the hostess shared the recipe. Just be sure to make more than you think you need...everybody wants seconds!
—Myrt Pfannkuche, Pell City, AL

Takes: 20 min. • **Makes:** 20 pieces

- 1 lb. bacon strips
- 3 Tbsp. brown sugar
- 1½ tsp. chili powder
- ¼ cup finely chopped pecans

1. Preheat oven to 425°. Arrange bacon in a single layer in 2 foil-lined 15x10x1-in. pans. Bake for 10 minutes; carefully pour off the drippings.
2. Mix brown sugar and chili powder; sprinkle over the bacon. Sprinkle with pecans. Bake until the bacon is crisp, 5-10 minutes. Drain on paper towels.

1 slice: 58 cal., 4g fat (1g sat. fat), 8mg chol., 151mg sod., 2g carb. (2g sugars, 0 fiber), 3g pro.

POTATO OMELET

POTATO OMELET

Even folks who don't care for eggs will like this dish. The great taste of potatoes, onions and garlic come through.
—Edie DeSpain, Logan, UT

Takes: 30 min. • **Makes:** 4 servings

- 2 medium potatoes, peeled and diced
- 2 Tbsp. olive oil
- ½ cup sliced green onions
- ¼ cup minced fresh parsley
- 1 garlic clove, minced
- 6 large eggs
- ¼ cup water
- ½ tsp. salt
- ⅛ tsp. pepper
  Optional: Sour cream and crumbled cooked bacon

1. In a 10-in. skillet, cook potatoes in oil over medium-high heat for 10 minutes or until golden brown, stirring occasionally. Add the onions, parsley and garlic; cook until tender. Reduce heat to medium.
2. In a bowl, beat eggs, water, salt and pepper. Pour over the potato mixture; cover and cook for 8-10 minutes or until completely set. Cut into wedges. Serve with sour cream and bacon if desired.

1 piece: 236 cal., 14g fat (3g sat. fat), 279mg chol., 408mg sod., 16g carb. (2g sugars, 1g fiber), 11g pro. **Diabetic exchanges:** 1½ fat, 1 starch, 1 medium-fat meat.

ULTIMATE FRUITY GRANOLA

Honey, maple syrup and vanilla coat this wonderfully crunchy treat that's fantastic no matter how you serve it—on its own, with cold milk or in a yogurt parfait.
—Sarah Vasques, Milford, NH

Prep: 15 min. • **Bake:** 20 min. + cooling
Makes: 18 servings (9 cups)

- 5 cups old-fashioned oats
- 1 cup sliced almonds
- ½ cup sunflower kernels
- ½ cup ground flaxseed
- ½ cup packed brown sugar
- ¼ cup maple syrup
- ¼ cup honey
- 2 Tbsp. canola oil
- ½ tsp. salt
- ½ tsp. ground cinnamon
- 1 tsp. vanilla extract
- ½ cup dried cranberries
- ½ cup dried banana chips
- ½ cup dried apricots, halved

1. Preheat oven to 350°. In a large bowl, combine oats, almonds, sunflower kernels and flax. In a small saucepan, combine brown sugar, maple syrup, honey, oil, salt and cinnamon. Cook and stir over medium heat for 2-3 minutes or until brown sugar is dissolved and mixture is heated through. Remove from the heat; stir in vanilla. Pour over oat mixture and toss to coat.
2. Transfer to a 15x10x1-in. baking pan coated with cooking spray. Bake for 20-25 minutes or until golden brown, stirring every 8 minutes. Cool completely on a wire rack. Stir in dried fruits. Store in an airtight container.

½ cup: 253 cal., 10g fat (2g sat. fat), 0 chol., 86mg sod., 38g carb. (18g sugars, 5g fiber), 6g pro.
HEALTH TIP Granola typically has healthy whole grains and nuts, but added sugar and sweetened dried fruit, too. Eat this calorie-dense cereal in relatively small portion sizes.

CINNAMON APPLE COFFEE CAKE

Tender apples add nice flavor to my quick and easy cake. This nutty treat was a family favorite served warm after church on Sunday mornings.
—Gertrude Hart, Oak Creek, WI

Prep: 10 min. • **Bake:** 50 min.
Makes: 9 servings

- 1 pkg. (9 oz.) yellow cake mix
- 1 pkg. (3.4 oz.) instant vanilla pudding mix
- 2 large eggs, room temperature
- ½ cup sour cream
- ¼ cup butter, melted
- 2 medium tart apples, peeled and shredded
- ½ cup sugar
- ¼ cup chopped walnuts
- 1 tsp. ground cinnamon

1. Preheat oven to 350°. In a large bowl, beat the cake mix, pudding mix, eggs, sour cream and butter on low speed for 30 seconds. Beat on medium for 2 minutes.
2. Pour half of the batter into a greased 8-in. square baking dish. Top with apples. Combine the sugar, nuts and cinnamon; sprinkle half over the apples. Top with the remaining batter and sugar mixture.
3. Bake for 50-55 minutes or until a toothpick inserted in the center comes out clean. Cool on a wire rack.
1 slice: 326 cal., 13g fat (4g sat. fat), 56mg chol., 409mg sod., 48g carb. (35g sugars, 1g fiber), 4g pro.

ULTIMATE FRUITY GRANOLA

RASPBERRY-COCONUT FRENCH TOAST

I prep this the night before and start the slow cooker in the morning. It's ready by the time we're back from church! You can use regular milk or half-and-half, your favorite jam, and almond extract instead of vanilla.
—Teri Lee Rasey, Cadillac, MI

Prep: 20 min. + chilling • **Cook:** 2¾ hours
Makes: 12 servings

- 6 large eggs
- 1½ cups refrigerated sweetened coconut milk
- 1 tsp. vanilla extract
- 1 loaf (1 lb.) French bread, cubed
- 1 pkg. (8 oz.) cream cheese, cubed
- ⅔ cup seedless raspberry jam
- ½ cup sweetened shredded coconut
  Whipped cream, fresh raspberries and toasted sweetened shredded coconut

1. In a large bowl, whisk eggs, coconut milk and vanilla until blended. Place half of the bread in a greased 5- or 6-qt. slow cooker; layer with half each of the cream cheese, jam, coconut and egg mixture. Repeat layers. Refrigerate, covered, overnight.
2. Cook, covered, on low 2¾-3¼ hours or until a knife inserted in center comes out clean. Serve French toast warm with whipped cream, raspberries and toasted shredded coconut.

1 cup: 280 cal., 12g fat (7g sat. fat), 112mg chol., 338mg sod., 35g carb. (16g sugars, 1g fiber), 9g pro.

TEST KITCHEN TIP
If your slow cooker insert is ceramic, take it out of the fridge 30 minutes before turning on the heat to prevent thermal shock.

MINI HAM QUICHES

These quiches are delightful for brunch when you don't want to fuss. You can replace the ham with bacon, sausage, chicken or shrimp, and the olives with chopped onion, red pepper or zucchini.
—Marilou Robinson, Portland, OR

Prep: 15 min. • **Bake:** 20 min.
Makes: 1 dozen

MINI HAM QUICHES

- ¾ cup diced fully cooked ham
- ½ cup shredded sharp cheddar cheese
- ½ cup chopped ripe olives
- 3 large eggs, lightly beaten
- 1 cup half-and-half cream
- ¼ cup butter, melted
- 3 drops hot pepper sauce
- ½ cup biscuit/baking mix
- 2 Tbsp. grated Parmesan cheese
- ½ tsp. ground mustard

1. Preheat oven to 375°. In a large bowl, combine the ham, cheddar cheese and olives; divide among 12 greased muffin cups. In another bowl, combine the remaining ingredients just until blended.
2. Pour over ham mixture. Bake until a knife inserted in the center comes out clean, 20-25 minutes. Let stand for 5 minutes before serving.

1 quiche: 141 cal., 11g fat (6g sat. fat), 84mg chol., 332mg sod., 5g carb. (1g sugars, 0 fiber), 6g pro.

SLOW-COOKER HONEY NUT GRANOLA

I lightened up my friend's recipe and changed the add-ins to reflect our tastes. It's now a family favorite! You can vary this recipe to suit your family, too, by changing the nuts, seeds or dried fruits.

—Tari Ambler, Shorewood, IL

Prep: 20 min. • **Cook:** 1½ hours + cooling
Makes: 16 servings (8 cups)

- 4½ cups old-fashioned oats
- ½ cup sunflower kernels
- ⅓ cup toasted wheat germ
- ¼ cup unsweetened shredded coconut
- ¼ cup sliced almonds
- ¼ cup chopped pecans
- ¼ cup chopped walnuts
- ¼ cup ground flaxseed
- ½ cup honey
- ⅓ cup water
- 3 Tbsp. canola oil
- 1 tsp. ground cinnamon
- 1 tsp. vanilla extract
- ½ tsp. ground nutmeg
  Dash salt
- ¾ cup dried cranberries
- ¾ cup raisins
  Yogurt, optional

1. In a 3- or 4-qt. slow cooker, combine the first 8 ingredients. In a small bowl, whisk honey, water, oil, cinnamon, vanilla, nutmeg and salt until blended; stir into oat mixture. Cook, covered, on high until crisp, 1½-2 hours, stirring well every 20 minutes.

2. Stir in cranberries and raisins. Spread evenly onto waxed paper or baking sheets; cool completely. Store in airtight containers. If desired, serve with yogurt.

½ cup: 267 cal., 12g fat (2g sat. fat), 0 chol., 43mg sod., 39g carb. (19g sugars, 5g fiber), 6g pro.

TEST KITCHEN TIP
Be sure to stir the granola mixture thoroughly every 20 minutes to ensure even cooking.

SLOW-COOKER HONEY NUT GRANOLA

MAKEOVER
HASH & EGGS

MAKEOVER HASH & EGGS

A diner classic goes homestyle in this better-than-ever version that delivers fresh flavors with a healthy dose of fiber.
—*Taste of Home* Test Kitchen

Takes: 30 min. • **Makes:** 4 servings

- 1 large onion, chopped
- 1 Tbsp. canola oil, divided
- 6 medium red potatoes (about 1½ lbs.), cut into ½-in. cubes
- ¼ cup water
- 3 pkg. (2 oz. each) thinly sliced deli corned beef, coarsely chopped
- ¼ tsp. pepper
- 4 large eggs
   Additional pepper, optional

1. In a large nonstick skillet, saute onion in 2 tsp. oil until tender. Stir in the potatoes and water. Bring to a boil. Reduce heat; cover and simmer for 15-20 minutes or until the potatoes are tender. Stir in the corned beef and pepper; heat through.
2. Meanwhile, in a large nonstick skillet, fry eggs in the remaining oil as desired. (Sunny-side up or over easy works best.) Season with additional pepper if desired. Serve with corned beef hash.

1 egg with 1 cup hash: 301 cal., 12g fat (3g sat. fat), 239mg chol., 652mg sod., 31g carb. (4g sugars, 4g fiber), 18g pro.
Diabetic exchanges: 2 starch, 2 medium-fat meat, ½ fat.

BREAKFAST IN A PAN
PICTURED ON P. 181

Try this tasty one-pan dish for an easy, low-mess breakfast. This recipe also works well with bacon or sausage instead of ham. I sometimes saute chopped peppers and onions until tender and whisk them in with the eggs for added flavor and color.
—Andrea Bolden, Unionville, TN

Prep: 15 min. • **Bake:** 25 min.
Makes: 6 servings

- 1 tube (8 oz.) refrigerated crescent rolls
- 2 cups cubed fully cooked ham
- 2 cups frozen shredded hash brown potatoes, thawed
- 5 large eggs
- ½ cup 2% milk
- ½ tsp. pepper
- ⅛ tsp. salt
- 2 cups shredded cheddar cheese

1. Preheat oven to 350°. Unroll the crescent dough into a long rectangle; press perforations to seal. Press onto bottom of a greased 13x9-in. baking pan. Top with ham and potatoes.
2. In a large bowl, whisk eggs, milk, pepper and salt until blended; pour over the potatoes. Sprinkle with cheese. Bake until set and cheese is melted, 25-30 minutes.
1 piece: 434 cal., 26g fat (9g sat. fat), 222mg chol., 1216mg sod., 23g carb. (6g sugars, 0 fiber), 28g pro.

CHEDDAR & CHORIZO STRATA
Stratas are wonderful for using up bits and pieces of leftovers you have on hand. You can make them meatless, swap in different cheeses and meats—whatever appeals to you! This can be made a day before baking. If you like more heat, use pepper jack cheese.
—Kallee Krong-McCreery, Escondido, CA

Prep: 20 min. + chilling • **Bake:** 40 min.
Makes: 8 servings

- 7 cups day-old French bread cut into 1-in. cubes
- 2 cups shredded cheddar cheese, divided
- 1 pkg. (10 oz.) frozen chopped spinach, thawed and squeezed dry
- 6 oz. fresh chorizo, crumbled
- ⅓ cup chopped onion
- 6 large eggs
- 2¼ cups 2% milk
- 1 tsp. garlic salt
- 1 tsp. prepared mustard

1. Place 4 cups bread cubes in a single layer in a greased 13x9-in. baking dish. Sprinkle with 1 cup cheese and spinach. Layer with chorizo and onion; top with the remaining bread and cheese.
2. In a large bowl, whisk the eggs, milk, garlic salt and mustard. Pour over the bread. Refrigerate, covered, for several hours or overnight.
3. Preheat oven to 350°. Remove strata from refrigerator while the oven heats. Bake, uncovered, until golden brown and a knife inserted near the center comes out clean, 40-45 minutes. Let stand for 5-10 minutes before serving.
1 piece: 370 cal., 22g fat (10g sat. fat), 192mg chol., 946mg sod., 21g carb. (6g sugars, 2g fiber), 22g pro.

CHEDDAR &
CHORIZO STRATA

GERMAN POTATO OMELET

GERMAN POTATO OMELET

This is an old German dish that all of us kids enjoyed when we were growing up. With a side toast and jam, this flavorful omelet will make your family as happy as it made all of us.
—Katherine Stallwood, Richland, WA

Takes: 30 min. • **Makes:** 4 servings

- 2 large potatoes, thinly sliced
- ¼ cup butter, divided
- ½ cup sliced green onions
- 8 large eggs
- ¼ cup 2% milk
  Salt and pepper to taste

1. In a large skillet, cook potatoes in 2 Tbsp. butter for 15 minutes or until browned and tender. Sprinkle with onions; set aside and keep warm. In a large nonstick skillet, melt the remaining butter over medium-high heat. Whisk the eggs and milk. Add the egg mixture to the skillet (mixture should set immediately at edges).
2. As the eggs set, push the cooked edges toward the center, letting the uncooked portion flow underneath. When the eggs are set, spoon the potato mixture onto one side; fold the other side over filling. Invert omelet onto a plate to serve. Cut into wedges and season as desired.

1 piece: 400 cal., 22g fat (11g sat. fat), 404mg chol., 253mg sod., 35g carb. (3g sugars, 4g fiber), 17g pro.

APPLE BUTTER BISCUIT BREAKFAST BAKE

My grandmother created this recipe to use up the leftovers from Christmas Eve dinner. By combining the leftover ham and biscuits with her homemade apple butter, milk and eggs, she could serve us all a warm, delicious breakfast and still have time to spend with the grandchildren.
—Mary Leverette, Columbia, SC

Prep: 30 min. + chilling
Bake: 50 min. + standing
Makes: 12 servings

- 10 leftover biscuits (3-in. diameter)
- ¾ cup apple butter
- 2 cups shredded sharp cheddar cheese
- 1½ cups cubed fully cooked ham
- ¼ cup minced fresh parsley
- 6 large eggs
- 2½ cups 2% milk
- 1 tsp. salt
- ½ tsp. pepper
- ¼ tsp. ground mustard

1. Cut biscuits crosswise in half. Spread apple butter over cut sides of biscuits. Replace tops. Cut each biscuit into quarters; arrange in a single layer in a greased 13x9-in. baking dish. Top with cheese, ham and parsley.
2. In a large bowl, whisk eggs, milk, salt, pepper and mustard. Pour over the biscuits. Cover and refrigerate overnight.
3. Preheat oven to 325°. Remove strata from refrigerator while the oven heats. Bake, uncovered, until puffed and the edges are golden brown, 50-60 minutes. Let stand 10 minutes before cutting.

1 piece: 331 cal., 15g fat (7g sat. fat), 126mg chol., 976mg sod., 31g carb. (12g sugars, 1g fiber), 16g pro.

SCRAMBLED EGG MUFFINS

After enjoying scrambled egg muffins at a local restaurant, I came up with this savory version that my husband likes even better. Freeze the extras to reheat on busy mornings.
—Cathy Larkins, Marshfield, MO

Takes: 30 min. • **Makes:** 1 dozen

- ½ lb. bulk pork sausage
- 12 large eggs
- ½ cup chopped onion
- ¼ cup chopped green pepper
- ½ tsp. salt
- ¼ tsp. garlic powder
- ¼ tsp. pepper
- ½ cup shredded cheddar cheese

1. Preheat oven to 350°. In a large skillet, cook sausage over medium heat until no longer pink; drain.
2. In a large bowl, beat eggs. Add the onion, green pepper, salt, garlic powder and pepper. Stir in sausage and cheese.
3. Spoon by ⅓ cupfuls into muffin cups coated with cooking spray. Bake for 20-25 minutes or until a knife inserted in the center comes out clean.
Freeze option: Cool baked muffins. Cover and place on waxed paper-lined baking sheets; freeze until firm. Transfer muffins to freezer containers; return to freezer. To use, place in greased muffin pan, cover loosely with foil; reheat in a preheated 350° oven until heated through. Or, microwave each muffin until heated through, for 30-60 seconds.

1 muffin: 133 cal., 10g fat (4g sat. fat), 224mg chol., 268mg sod., 2g carb. (1g sugars, 0 fiber), 9g pro.

BACON BREAKFAST CASSEROLE

This easy breakfast dish allows me to make a comforting family favorite that doesn't take a lot of prep. It's also great for big brunch gatherings.
—Paula Lawson, Springfield, OH

Prep: 30 min. • **Cook:** 4 hours. + standing
Makes: 12 servings

- 1 lb. bacon strips, chopped
- 1 pkg. (28 oz.) frozen O'Brien potatoes, thawed
- 3 cups shredded Mexican cheese blend
- 12 large eggs
- 1 cup 2% milk
- ½ tsp. salt
- ½ tsp. pepper
  Minced fresh parsley, optional

1. In a large skillet, cook bacon in batches over medium heat until crisp. Remove to paper towels to drain.
2. In a greased 4- or 5-qt. slow cooker, layer a third of each of the following: potatoes, reserved bacon and cheese. Repeat layers twice. In a large bowl, whisk eggs, milk, salt and pepper; pour over top. Cook, covered, on low until the eggs are set, 4-5 hours. Turn off slow cooker. Remove crock insert to a wire rack; let stand, uncovered, 30 minutes before serving. If desired, sprinkle with parsley.

1 serving: 306 cal., 19g fat (8g sat. fat), 226mg chol., 606mg sod., 13g carb. (2g sugars, 2g fiber), 18g pro.

BACON BREAKFAST CASSEROLE

BAKED BANANA FRENCH TOAST

This easy overnight recipe makes a delightful brunch entree. The decadent flavor is reminiscent of banana pudding, so I sometimes serve it for dessert.
—Nancy Zimmerman, Cape May Court House, NJ

Prep: 20 min. + chilling
Bake: 55 min. + standing
Makes: 12 servings

- 2 cups sliced ripe bananas
- 2 Tbsp. lemon juice
- 9 cups cubed French bread
- 1 pkg. (8 oz.) cream cheese, cubed
- 9 large eggs
- 4 cups 2% milk
- ½ cup sugar
- ¼ cup butter, melted
- ¼ cup maple syrup
- ½ tsp. ground cinnamon

1. In a small bowl, toss bananas with lemon juice. Place half of the bread in a greased 13x9-in. baking dish; layer with cream cheese, bananas and the remaining bread.
2. In a large bowl, whisk eggs, milk, sugar, butter, syrup and cinnamon; pour over the bread. Cover and refrigerate for 8 hours or overnight.
3. Remove from refrigerator 30 minutes before baking. Bake, uncovered, at 350° for 55-65 minutes or until a knife inserted in the center comes out clean. Let stand 10 minutes before serving.

1 piece: 348 cal., 16g fat (9g sat. fat), 196mg chol., 361mg sod., 40g carb. (20g sugars, 1g fiber), 13g pro.

Easier than an Omelet!

A cross between an omelet and loaded scrambled eggs, a frittata is practically foolproof, so fill your skillet with your favorite breakfast ingredients!

POTATO SAUSAGE FRITTATA

With sausage, bacon, eggs and potatoes, this frittata is one hearty meal! Although I double the recipe for my large family, we never have any leftovers. As good as this dish is, you can experiment to customize it for your family. Try using ham, bell peppers, chorizo—the sky's the limit!
—Patricia Lee, Eatonton, GA

Takes: 30 min. • **Makes:** 4 servings

- ½ lb. bulk pork sausage
- 6 bacon strips, diced
- 1½ cups finely chopped red potatoes
- 1 medium onion, finely chopped
- 8 large eggs
- 2 tsp. dried parsley flakes
- ¾ tsp. salt
- ⅛ tsp. pepper

1 piece: 518 cal., 39g fat (13g sat. fat), 430mg chol., 1213mg sod., 16g carb. (3g sugars, 2g fiber), 25g pro.

1. Cook meat & veggies
In a large ovenproof skillet, cook sausage until no longer pink. Remove; cook bacon until crisp. Remove bacon to paper towels. Reserve 2 Tbsp. drippings in pan; saute potatoes and onion in drippings until tender.

2. Beat the eggs
Whisk eggs, dried parsley, salt and pepper.

3. Put it all together
Add sausage and bacon to skillet; top with egg mixture.

4. Cover & cook
Cover; cook over low heat until the eggs are almost set, 8-10 minutes.

5. Broil to finish
Uncover; broil 6 in. from the heat until eggs are set, about 2 minutes. Cut into wedges and serve.

COASTAL CAROLINA MUFFIN-TIN FRITTATAS

Incorporating the flavors of a low country South Carolina crab boil, these tasty frittatas are easy to make and fun to eat. If you have leftover cooked potatoes (roasted or boiled), try dicing them and substituting them for the refrigerated shredded potatoes in this recipe.
—Shannon Kohn, Summerville, SC

Prep: 30 min. • **Bake:** 30 min.
Makes: 12 servings

- ½ cup mayonnaise
- 1 Tbsp. lemon juice
- 2 tsp. sugar
- 1 tsp. seafood seasoning
- 2 cups refrigerated shredded hash brown potatoes
- 1½ cups chopped smoked sausage
- 1 can (8 oz.) jumbo lump crabmeat, drained
- ¼ cup chopped roasted sweet red peppers
- 7 large eggs, room temperature
- ¾ cup heavy whipping cream
- 1 Tbsp. Louisiana-style hot sauce
- ½ tsp. salt
- 12 bacon strips, cooked and crumbled
- ¼ cup thinly sliced green onions

1. Preheat oven to 350°. In a small bowl, combine mayonnaise, lemon juice, sugar and seafood seasoning. Refrigerate until ready to serve.
2. In a large bowl, combine potatoes, sausage, crab and red peppers. Divide among 12 greased jumbo muffin cups. In another large bowl, whisk eggs, cream, hot sauce and salt. Pour over the potato mixture. Top with bacon.
3. Bake until a knife inserted in center comes out clean, 30-35 minutes. Serve with sauce and green onions.

1 frittata: 292 cal., 23g fat (8g sat. fat), 164mg chol., 768mg sod., 7g carb. (2g sugars, 1g fiber), 13g pro.

TEST KITCHEN TIP
Lump crabmeat is worth the splurge in these frittatas because the flavor really shines through.

COASTAL CAROLINA MUFFIN-TIN FRITTATAS

COCONUT TROPICAL FRUIT SALAD

Add a serving of fruit to your breakfast with this delicious medley. Toasted coconut, mango and more bring the flavor of the tropics to winter menus.
—Katie Covington, Blacksburg, SC

Takes: 25 min. • **Makes:** 8 servings

- 1 medium mango, peeled and cubed
- 1 medium green apple, cubed
- 1 medium red apple, cubed
- 1 medium pear, cubed
- 1 medium navel orange, peeled and chopped
- 2 medium kiwifruit, peeled and chopped
- 10 seedless red grapes, halved
- 2 Tbsp. orange juice
- 1 firm medium banana, sliced
- ¼ cup sweetened shredded coconut, toasted

In a large bowl, combine first 7 ingredients. Drizzle with orange juice; toss gently to coat. Refrigerate until serving. Just before serving, fold in banana slices and sprinkle with coconut.

¾ cup: 101 cal., 1g fat (1g sat. fat), 0 chol., 10mg sod., 24g carb. (17g sugars, 3g fiber), 1g pro. **Diabetic exchanges:** 1½ fruit.

HEALTH TIP Looking for a flavorful fruit salad that isn't loaded with added sugar? Look no further. Use unsweetened coconut for a no-sugar-added version.

SLOW-COOKER CINNAMON ROLL

Come home to the heavenly aroma of fresh-baked cinnamon rolls! This better-for-you version tastes just as decadent as a regular cinnamon roll, but smartly sneaks in some whole grains.
—Nick Iverson, Denver, CO

Prep: 15 min. + rising • **Cook:** 3½ hours
Makes: 12 servings

- 1 pkg. (¼ oz.) active dry yeast
- ¾ cup warm water (110° to 115°)
- ½ cup quick-cooking oats
- ½ cup whole wheat flour
- ¼ cup packed brown sugar
- 2 Tbsp. butter, melted
- 1 large egg, room temperature
- 1 tsp. salt
- 1¾ to 2¼ cups all-purpose flour

FILLING
- 3 Tbsp. butter, softened
- ⅓ cup sugar
- 2 tsp. ground cinnamon

ICING
- 1 cup confectioners' sugar
- 2 Tbsp. half-and-half cream
- 4 tsp. butter, softened

1. Dissolve yeast in warm water. Add the next 6 ingredients plus 1 cup all-purpose flour. Beat on medium speed until smooth. Stir in enough of the remaining flour to form a soft dough (dough will be sticky).

2. Turn onto a lightly floured surface; knead until dough is smooth and elastic, 6-8 minutes. Roll into an 18x12-in. rectangle. For filling, spread dough with butter, then combine sugar and cinnamon; sprinkle over the dough to within ½ in. of the edges.

3. Roll up jelly-roll style, starting with a long side; pinch seam to seal. Cut crosswise in half to form 2 rolls. Place rolls side by side; pinch the top ends together to seal. Using a sharp knife, cut the rolls lengthwise in half; loosely twist strips around each other. Pinch bottom ends together to seal. Shape into a coil; place on parchment. Transfer the coil to a 6-qt. slow cooker. Let rise until doubled, about 1 hour.

4. Cook, covered, on low until bread is lightly browned, 3½-4 hours. Remove from slow cooker and cool slightly. Beat icing ingredients until smooth. Spread over warm rolls.

1 slice: 240 cal., 7g fat (4g sat. fat), 33mg chol., 254mg sod., 41g carb. (20g sugars, 2g fiber), 4g pro.

SAUSAGE BREAKFAST BURRITOS

SAUSAGE BREAKFAST BURRITOS

Breakfast routine in a rut? Shake things up with these speedy, savory wraps.
—Brenda Spann, Granger, IN

Takes: 20 min. • **Makes:** 8 servings

- 1 lb. bulk pork sausage
- 1 small onion, chopped
- ½ green pepper, chopped
- 1 can (4 oz.) mushroom stems and pieces, drained
- 1 Tbsp. butter
- 6 large eggs, beaten
- 8 flour tortillas (8 in.), warmed
- 1 cup shredded cheddar cheese
  Salsa, optional

1. In a large skillet, brown sausage. Drain, reserving 2 Tbsp. drippings. Saute the onion, green pepper and mushrooms in drippings until tender.

2. In a second skillet, melt butter over medium-high heat. Add the eggs; cook and stir until set.

3. Divide the sausage mixture among tortillas; top with eggs and cheese. Fold bottom of each tortilla over filling and roll up. Serve with salsa if desired.

1 burrito: 429 cal., 25g fat (9g sat. fat), 188mg chol., 778mg sod., 30g carb. (1g sugars, 2g fiber), 19g pro.

STRAWBERRY BLISS OMELET

Instead of the usual ham and cheese, try dressing up eggs with strawberries and cream cheese. I first tasted this dish while vacationing at the beach. We like it now as a change of pace. It can double as a delicate dessert in the evening, too.
—Selina Smith, Frostburg, MD

Takes: 15 min. • **Makes:** 3 servings

6 large eggs
2 Tbsp. water
½ tsp. salt
Dash pepper
2 Tbsp. butter
2 oz. cream cheese, cut into
½-in. cubes
3 Tbsp. brown sugar
1½ cups sliced fresh strawberries,
divided
Confectioners' sugar

1. In a large bowl, whisk the eggs, water, salt and pepper. Heat butter in a 10-in. nonstick skillet over medium heat; add the egg mixture. As the eggs set, lift the edges, letting the uncooked portion flow underneath.

2. When the eggs are almost set, sprinkle cream cheese, brown sugar and 1 cup strawberries over 1 side. Fold omelet in half. Cover and cook for 1-2 minutes or until the brown sugar begins to melt. Slide omelet onto a plate; top with the remaining strawberries and dust with confectioners' sugar.

⅓ omelet: 378 cal., 24g fat (12g sat. fat), 466mg chol., 659mg sod., 26g carb. (23g sugars, 2g fiber), 15g pro.

BACON & EGG BUNDLES
PICTURED ON P. 181

This is a fun way to serve bacon and eggs all in one bite! The recipe can easily be doubled for a larger group.
—Edith Landinger, Longview, TX

Prep: 20 min. • **Bake:** 15 min.
Makes: 6 servings

12 to 18 bacon strips
1 tsp. butter
6 large eggs
Freshly ground pepper, optional

1. Preheat oven to 325°. In a large skillet, cook the bacon over medium heat until partially cooked but not crisp. Drain on paper towels.

2. Lightly grease 6 muffin cups with 1 tsp. butter. Cut 6 bacon strips crosswise in half. Line the bottom of each muffin cup with 2 bacon halves. Line the sides of each muffin cup with 1 or 2 whole bacon strips. Break an egg into each cup.

3. Bake until the whites are completely set and yolks begin to thicken but are not yet hard, 12-18 minutes. If desired, sprinkle with pepper.

1 bundle: 311 cal., 28g fat (9g sat. fat), 225mg chol., 447mg sod., 1g carb. (1g sugars, 0 fiber), 13g pro.

STRAWBERRY BLISS OMELET

SLOW-COOKER OATMEAL

SLOW-COOKER OATMEAL

Waking up to this wonderful aroma and piping hot meal is a perfect way to start the day!
—Brandy Schaefer, Glen Carbon, IL

Prep: 10 min. • **Cook:** 3 hours
Makes: 4 servings

- 2 cups whole milk
- 1 cup old-fashioned oats
- 1 cup chopped peeled tart apple
- ½ cup raisins
- ¼ cup packed brown sugar
- ¼ cup chopped walnuts
- 1 Tbsp. butter, melted
- ½ tsp. ground cinnamon
- ¼ tsp. salt

In a 1½-qt. slow cooker coated with cooking spray, combine all ingredients. Cover and cook on low for 3-4 hours or until liquid is absorbed and oatmeal is tender. If desired, serve with additional milk, walnuts and cinnamon.
1 cup: 340 cal., 13g fat (5g sat. fat), 20mg chol., 225mg sod., 51g carb. (32g sugars, 3g fiber), 10g pro.
HEALTH TIP Using whole milk makes a rich breakfast treat. Switch to reduced-fat or fat-free to cut fat and calories.

ALL-IN-ONE BREAKFAST

Let your slow cooker do the work and don't worry about adding sides—this dish has everything that you need. Just sip your coffee, cut up some fresh fruit, and breakfast is served!
—Debbie Glasscock, Conway, AR

Prep: 20 min. • **Cook:** 3 hours
Makes: 6 servings

- 1 lb. bulk pork sausage
- 1 small onion, chopped
- 6 green onions, thinly sliced
- 1 pkg. (30 oz.) frozen shredded hash brown potatoes, thawed
- 2 cups shredded sharp cheddar cheese
- 1 can (10¾ oz.) condensed cream of mushroom soup, undiluted
- 1 cup sour cream
- 6 large eggs
- ¼ tsp. pepper

ALL-IN-ONE BREAKFAST

Chopped fresh parsley
Optional: Salsa and additional sour cream

1. In a large skillet, cook sausage, onion and green onions over medium heat until the sausage is no longer pink and the onions are tender, 6-8 minutes, breaking up sausage into crumbles; drain. Transfer to a greased 5- or 6-qt. slow cooker. Stir in hash browns, cheese, soup and sour cream until blended.
2. Cook, covered, on high for 2½ hours. With the back of a spoon, make 6 wells in the potato mixture. Break an egg into each well. Sprinkle the eggs with pepper. Cover and cook until egg whites are completely set and yolks begin to thicken but are not yet hard, 30-35 minutes longer. Sprinkle with parsley. If desired, serve with salsa and additional sour cream.
1 serving: 654 cal., 44g fat (19g sat. fat), 276mg chol., 1194mg sod., 36g carb. (5g sugars, 3g fiber), 29g pro.

TEST KITCHEN TIP
If you prefer your eggs scrambled, skip the last step and scramble them on the stovetop, then add them to the dish before serving.

BRUNCH CASSEROLE

A good friend shared the recipe for this egg casserole with me. Hash browns and ham make it flavorful and hearty. Squares of this dish are a wonderful addition to any Sunday brunch.
—Pat Clark, Richmond, IN

Prep: 10 min. • **Bake:** 45 min.
Makes: 8 servings

- 8 large eggs
- 1 cup whole milk
- ½ tsp. seasoned salt
- 2 cups frozen shredded hash brown potatoes
- 1 cup diced fully cooked ham
- 1 cup shredded cheddar cheese
- 1 Tbsp. dried minced onion

1. Preheat oven to 350°. In a large bowl, whisk together the eggs, milk and seasoned salt. Stir in the remaining ingredients. Pour into a greased 8-in. square baking dish.
2. Bake, uncovered, for 45-50 minutes or until a knife inserted in the center comes out clean.
1 piece: 188 cal., 11g fat (6g sat. fat), 241mg chol., 484mg sod., 7g carb. (2g sugars, 0 fiber), 14g pro.

Breads in a Jiffy

For breakfast, lunch or dinner, as a sweet treat or a savory side, there's nothing quite like home-baked bread. From quick breads to yeast breads, pull-aparts to beautiful braids, we've got you covered with these essential bread recipes.

Honey Cornbread (p. 204) **Rosemary Walnut Bread** (p. 199) **Banana Nut Bread** (p. 205)
Cinnamon Monkey Bread (p. 204) **Herb Buttermilk Dinner Rolls** (p. 200)

BEST EVER BREADSTICKS

Present these delicious breadsticks alongside an Italian favorite like lasagna or spaghetti. They're an attractive and edible addition to your table setting!
—Carol Wolfer, Lebanon, OR

Prep: 20 min. + rising
Bake: 10 min. + cooling • **Makes:** 2 dozen

- 3 to 3¼ cups all-purpose flour
- 1 pkg. (¼ oz.) quick-rise yeast
- 1 Tbsp. sugar
- 1 tsp. salt
- ¾ cup whole milk
- ¼ cup plus 1 Tbsp. water, divided
- 1 Tbsp. butter
- 1 large egg white
  Coarse salt

1. Combine 1½ cups flour, yeast, sugar and salt. In a small saucepan, heat milk, ¼ cup water and butter to 120°-130°. Add to dry ingredients; beat on medium speed just until moistened. Stir in enough remaining flour to form a stiff dough.
2. Turn dough onto a lightly floured surface; knead until smooth and elastic, 6-8 minutes. Place in a greased bowl, turning once to grease top. Cover and let rise in a warm place until doubled, about 30 minutes.
3. Punch down dough. Pinch off golf ball-sized pieces. On a lightly floured surface, shape piece each into a 6-in. rope. Place on greased baking sheets 1 in. apart. Cover and let rise for 15 minutes. Preheat oven to 400°.
4. Beat egg white and the remaining water; brush over breadsticks. Sprinkle with coarse salt. Bake until golden, about

10 minutes. Remove from pans to wire racks to cool.

1 breadstick: 69 cal., 1g fat (0 sat. fat), 2mg chol., 108mg sod., 13g carb. (1g sugars, 1g fiber), 2g pro. **Diabetic exchanges:** 1 starch.

QUICK & EASY PUMPKIN CRESCENTS

These are simple enough for my children to help with. Sprinkled with cinnamon sugar, the yummy crescents are perfect with hot cocoa on a chilly morning.
—Melinda Erickson, St George, UT

Takes: 25 min. • **Makes:** 16 rolls

- 1¾ cups all-purpose flour
- 2 tsp. baking powder
- ¼ tsp. baking soda
- ¼ tsp. ground nutmeg
- ⅛ tsp. salt
- ⅛ tsp. ground ginger
- 1½ tsp. ground cinnamon, divided
- ¾ cup canned pumpkin
- 3 Tbsp. canola oil
- 2 Tbsp. brown sugar
- 2 Tbsp. sugar
- 4 Tbsp. butter, melted, divided

1. Preheat oven to 400°. In a large bowl, whisk the first 6 ingredients; stir in ½ tsp. cinnamon. In another bowl, whisk the pumpkin, oil and brown sugar; stir into flour mixture just until moistened. In a small bowl, mix sugar and the remaining cinnamon; reserve 2 tsp. of the cinnamon sugar for topping.
2. Turn dough onto a lightly floured surface; knead gently 10 times. Divide in half; roll each portion into a 10-in. circle. Brush each circle with 1 Tbsp. melted butter; sprinkle with 2 tsp. cinnamon sugar. Cut each circle into 8 wedges. Roll up wedges from the wide ends.
3. Place 1 in. apart on a greased baking sheet, point side down; curve to form crescents. Brush with the remaining butter; sprinkle with the reserved cinnamon sugar. Bake 9-11 minutes or until golden brown. Remove from pan to a wire rack; serve warm.

1 roll: 116 cal., 6g fat (2g sat. fat), 8mg chol., 122mg sod., 15g carb. (4g sugars, 1g fiber), 2g pro.

QUICK & EASY
PUMPKIN CRESCENTS

FAVORITE IRISH SODA BREAD

My best friend, Rita, shared this irresistible recipe with me. It bakes up high, with a golden brown top and a combination of sweet and savory flavors.
—Jan Alfano, Prescott, AZ

Prep: 20 min. • **Bake:** 45 min. + cooling
Makes: 1 loaf (12 wedges)

- 3 cups all-purpose flour
- ⅔ cup sugar
- 3 tsp. baking powder
- 1 tsp. salt
- 1 tsp. baking soda
- 1 cup raisins
- 2 large eggs, room temperature, beaten
- 1½ cups buttermilk
- 1 Tbsp. canola oil

1. Preheat oven to 350°. In a large bowl, combine the first 5 ingredients. Stir in raisins. Set aside 1 Tbsp. beaten egg. In a bowl, combine buttermilk, oil and the remaining eggs; stir into the flour mixture just until moistened (dough will be sticky). Transfer to a greased 9-in. round baking pan; brush top with the reserved egg.

2. Bake for 45-50 minutes or until a toothpick inserted in the center comes out clean. Cool in pan for 10 minutes, then remove to a wire rack. Cool completely or serve warm. Cut into wedges.

1 wedge: 227 cal., 3g fat (1g sat. fat), 36mg chol., 447mg sod., 46g carb. (20g sugars, 1g fiber), 6g pro.

Caraway Irish Soda Bread: Add 2 Tbsp. caraway seeds to the dry ingredients.

ROSEMARY WALNUT BREAD
PICTURED ON P. 197

I received this recipe from a friend who was moving into a new apartment. To celebrate, she made this bread to share. Now we serve it at many of my own family functions.
—Robin Haas, Cranston, RI

Prep: 25 min. + rising • **Bake:** 20 min.
Makes: 1 loaf (9 slices)

- 1¼ tsp. active dry yeast
- ½ cup warm water (110° to 115°)
- ¼ cup whole wheat flour
- 1½ to 1¾ cups all-purpose flour
- 2 Tbsp. honey
- 1 Tbsp. olive oil
- 1½ tsp. dried rosemary, crushed
- ½ tsp. salt
- ⅓ cup finely chopped walnuts

1. In a small bowl, dissolve yeast in warm water. In a large bowl, mix whole wheat flour and ¼ cup all-purpose flour; stir in yeast mixture. Let stand, covered, 15 minutes. Add honey, oil, rosemary, salt and ¾ cup all-purpose flour; beat on medium speed until smooth. Stir in walnuts and enough of the remaining all-purpose flour to form a soft dough.

2. Turn dough onto a floured surface; knead dough until smooth and elastic, 6-8 minutes. Place in a greased bowl, turning once to grease the top. Cover and let rise in a warm place until doubled, about 45 minutes.

3. Punch down dough. Turn onto a lightly floured surface; divide into thirds. Roll each into a 12-in. rope. Place ropes on a greased baking sheet and braid. Pinch ends to seal; tuck under. Cover with a kitchen towel; let rise in a warm place until almost doubled, about 30 minutes.

4. Preheat oven to 375°. Bake for 20-25 minutes or until golden brown. Remove from pan to a wire rack to cool.

1 slice: 145 cal., 4g fat (0 sat. fat), 0 chol., 132mg sod., 23g carb. (4g sugars, 1g fiber), 4g pro. **Diabetic exchanges:** 1½ starch, ½ fat.

FAVORITE IRISH SODA BREAD

HERB BUTTERMILK DINNER ROLLS

When I couldn't find a recipe for dinner rolls, I created my own using a variety of herbs for extra flavor.
—Sue Friesen, Thorold, ON

Prep: 20 min. + rising • **Bake:** 25 min.
Makes: 2 dozen

- 1 pkg. (¼ oz.) active dry yeast
- ¼ cup warm water (110° to 115°)
- ¾ cup warm buttermilk (110° to 115°)
- 4 Tbsp. butter, melted, divided
- 2 Tbsp. sugar
- 1½ tsp. salt
- ½ tsp. dried basil
- ½ tsp. dried marjoram
- ½ tsp. dried thyme
- ¼ tsp. baking soda
- 1 large egg, room temperature
- 2¾ to 3¼ cups all-purpose flour

1. Dissolve yeast in warm water. Add buttermilk, 2 Tbsp. butter and the next 7 ingredients. Stir in 2 cups of flour. Beat until smooth. Stir in enough of the remaining flour to form a soft dough, which will be sticky.
2. Turn dough onto a heavily floured surface; knead until smooth and elastic, 6-8 minutes. Place in a greased bowl, turning once to grease top. Cover and let rise in a warm place until doubled, about 75 minutes.
3. Punch dough down. Turn onto a lightly floured surface; divide into 4 portions. Divide each portion into 6 pieces; shape each piece into a ball. Place in a greased 13x9-in. baking pan. Cover and let rise until doubled, about 50 minutes.

4. Preheat oven to 375°. Bake rolls until golden brown, 25-30 minutes. Cool 5 minutes before removing from pan to a wire rack. Brush with remaining butter. **Note:** Warmed buttermilk will appear curdled.
1 roll: 78 cal., 2g fat (1g sat. fat), 14mg chol., 186mg sod., 12g carb. (1g sugars, 0 fiber), 2g pro.

MOIST PUMPKIN SCONES

After trying a pumpkin scone at a coffeehouse, I was inspired to look for a recipe so I could make them at home. The sweet glaze nicely complements the pumpkin flavor.
—Amy McCavour, Gresham, OR

Prep: 15 min. • **Bake:** 15 min. + cooling
Makes: 16 scones

- 4½ cups all-purpose flour
- ½ cup packed brown sugar
- 4 tsp. baking powder
- 3 tsp. pumpkin pie spice
- 1 tsp. ground cinnamon
- ½ tsp. baking soda
- ½ tsp. salt

MOIST PUMPKIN SCONES

- 1 cup cold butter
- 2 large eggs, room temperature
- 1¼ cups canned pumpkin
- ¾ cup whole milk, divided
GLAZE
- 2 cups confectioners' sugar
- 3 Tbsp. whole milk
- ¼ tsp. pumpkin pie spice

1. Preheat oven to 400°. In a large bowl, combine the first 7 ingredients. Cut in butter until the mixture resembles coarse crumbs. In another bowl, whisk the eggs, pumpkin and ½ cup milk. Stir into the dry ingredients just until moistened.
2. Turn onto a floured surface; knead 10 times. Divide dough in half. Pat each portion into an 8-in. circle; cut each into 8 wedges. Separate wedges and place 1 in. apart on ungreased baking sheets. Brush with the remaining milk.
3. Bake 12-15 minutes or until golden brown. Remove to wire racks; cool for 10 minutes. Combine glaze ingredients; drizzle over scones. Serve warm.
1 scone: 338 cal., 13g fat (8g sat. fat), 59mg chol., 348mg sod., 51g carb. (23g sugars, 2g fiber), 5g pro.

DOUBLE CRANBERRY BANANA BREAD

We love quick breads, and they freeze nicely if properly wrapped. This is a scrumptious recipe to make before the holidays and freeze for last-minute guests or gifts.
—Joan Hallford, N. Richland Hills, TX

Prep: 25 min.
Bake: 50 min. + cooling
Makes: 1 loaf (12 slices)

⅓ cup shortening
⅔ cup sugar
2 large eggs, room temperature
1 cup mashed ripe banana
1 tsp. vanilla extract
1¾ cups all-purpose flour
2 tsp. baking powder
½ tsp. salt
¼ tsp. baking soda
1 cup whole-berry cranberry sauce
¾ cup chopped pecans, divided
½ cup dried cranberries

1. Preheat oven to 350°. In a large bowl, cream shortening and sugar until light and crumbly. Beat in eggs, banana and vanilla.
2. In a second bowl, whisk flour, baking powder, salt and baking soda; gradually beat into the creamed mixture. Stir in cranberry sauce, ½ cup pecans and the dried cranberries.
3. Transfer to a greased 8x4-in. loaf pan. Sprinkle with remaining pecans. Bake until a toothpick inserted in center comes out clean, 50-60 minutes. Cool in pan for 10 minutes before removing to a wire rack to cool completely.

Freeze option: Securely wrap cooled loaf in foil, then freeze. To use, thaw at room temperature.

1 slice: 289 cal., 11g fat (2g sat. fat), 31mg chol., 229mg sod., 45g carb. (24g sugars, 2g fiber), 4g pro.

DOUBLE CRANBERRY
BANANA BREAD

HAZELNUT CHOCOLATE CHIP SCONES

SWEET POTATO SPICE BREAD

It's a good thing this recipe makes two mini loaves because they'll go fast! For a small household, eat one loaf now and freeze the other for later.
—Ronnie Littles, VA Beach, VA

Prep: 15 min. • **Bake:** 25 min. + cooling
Makes: 2 mini loaves (6 slices each)

- 1 cup all-purpose flour
- 1½ tsp. baking powder
- ¼ tsp. each ground cinnamon, nutmeg and allspice
- ⅛ tsp. salt
- 1 large egg, room temperature
- ⅓ cup mashed sweet potato
- ⅓ cup honey
- 3 Tbsp. canola oil
- 2 Tbsp. molasses
- ⅓ cup chopped walnuts

1. Preheat oven to 325°. In a small bowl, combine the flour, baking powder, spices and salt. In another small bowl, whisk the egg, sweet potato, honey, canola oil and molasses. Stir into dry ingredients just until moistened. Fold in the walnuts.
2. Transfer batter to two 5¾x3x2-in. loaf pans coated with cooking spray. Bake for 25-30 minutes or until a toothpick inserted in the center comes out clean. Cool for 10 minutes before removing from pans to wire racks.

1 slice: 142 cal., 6g fat (1g sat. fat), 18mg chol., 85mg sod., 20g carb. (10g sugars, 1g fiber), 3g pro. **Diabetic exchanges:** 1½ starch, 1 fat.

READER REVIEW

"Great recipe. They were soft, moist and very flavorful. I will make them again, double the recipe for sure, and give them as gifts. Thanks for sharing!"
YUEHCHING, TASTEOFHOME.COM

HAZELNUT CHOCOLATE CHIP SCONES

With chocolate, hazelnuts and the tangy taste of buttermilk, these delicious scones are easy to make, come together fast and taste so good with your morning coffee.
—Trisha Kruse, Eagle, ID

Prep: 20 min. • **Bake:** 15 min.
Makes: 8 scones

- 2 cups all-purpose flour
- ¼ cup packed brown sugar
- 1½ tsp. baking powder
- ½ tsp. baking soda
- ½ tsp. salt
- ½ cup cold butter, cubed
- 1 large egg, room temperature
- ½ cup buttermilk
- 1½ tsp. vanilla extract
- 1 cup semisweet chocolate chips
- 1 cup hazelnuts, coarsely chopped

1. Preheat oven to 400°. Whisk together the first 5 ingredients; cut in butter until the mixture resembles coarse crumbs. In another bowl, whisk together egg, buttermilk and vanilla; stir into the crumb mixture just until moistened. Stir in the chocolate chips and hazelnuts.
2. Turn onto a lightly floured surface; knead gently 8 times. Pat dough into a 6-in. circle. Cut into 8 wedges; place on a greased baking sheet. Bake until golden brown, 15-20 minutes. Serve warm.

1 scone: 409 cal., 23g fat (10g sat. fat), 76mg chol., 327mg sod., 47g carb. (20g sugars, 3g fiber), 8g pro.

SWEET POTATO SPICE BREAD

CINNAMON MONKEY BREAD

CINNAMON MONKEY BREAD

Is it possible for four kids to cook together without creating total chaos? Yes, with the right recipe. This is a favorite with my bunch. They get to play with the dough as they roll it into balls—then they get to enjoy the results!
—Lisa Combs, Greenville, OH

Prep: 20 min. • **Bake:** 35 min.
Makes: 16 servings

- 4 tubes (7½ oz. each) refrigerated buttermilk biscuits
- ½ cup sugar
- 2 tsp. ground cinnamon
- ½ cup butter, melted
- ½ cup packed brown sugar

1. Preheat oven to 350° Cut each biscuit into 4 pieces; shape into balls. In a small bowl, combine sugar and cinnamon. Roll each ball in cinnamon sugar. Arrange evenly in a generously greased 9- or 10-in. fluted tube pan. Sprinkle with remaining cinnamon sugar.

2. Combine butter and brown sugar; pour over the top. Place tube pan on baking sheet; bake until dough is golden brown and cooked through, 35-45 minutes. Cool for 5 minutes before inverting bread onto a serving platter.

1 slice: 133 cal., 6g fat (4g sat. fat), 15mg chol., 174mg sod., 19g carb. (13g sugars, 0 fiber), 1g pro.

HONEY CORNBREAD
PICTURED ON P. 197

It's always a pleasure to serve this moist cornbread to family and guests. Honey gives it a slightly sweet taste. Most people find it's difficult to eat just one piece.
—Adeline Piscitelli, Sayreville, NJ

Takes: 30 min. • **Makes:** 9 servings

- 1 cup all-purpose flour
- 1 cup yellow cornmeal
- ¼ cup sugar
- 3 tsp. baking powder
- ½ tsp. salt
- 2 large eggs, room temperature
- 1 cup heavy whipping cream
- ¼ cup canola oil
- ¼ cup honey

1. Preheat oven to 400°. In a bowl, combine flour, cornmeal, sugar, baking powder and salt. In a small bowl, beat the eggs. Add cream, oil and honey; beat well. stir into the dry ingredients just until moistened. Pour into a greased 9-in. square baking pan.

2. Bake for 20-25 minutes or until a toothpick inserted in the center comes out clean. Serve warm.

1 piece: 318 cal., 17g fat (7g sat. fat), 83mg chol., 290mg sod., 37g carb. (14g sugars, 2g fiber), 5g pro.

GRANDMA'S SWEET POTATO BISCUITS

The recipe for these mild biscuits was my grandmother's. They're a family favorite that we always serve at holidays.
—Nancy Daugherty, Cortland, OH

Takes: 30 min. • **Makes:** 1½ dozen

2½ cups all-purpose flour
1 Tbsp. baking powder
1 tsp. salt
⅓ cup shortening
1 can (15¾ oz.) sweet potatoes, drained
¾ cup whole milk

1. Preheat oven to 425°. In a large bowl, combine the flour, baking powder and salt. Cut in shortening until the mixture resembles coarse crumbs. In another bowl, mash the sweet potatoes and milk. Add potato mixture to crumb mixture just until combined.
2. Turn onto a floured surface; knead 8-10 times. Roll to ½-in. thickness; cut with a 2½-in. biscuit cutter. Place on ungreased baking sheets.
3. Bake until golden brown, 8-10 minutes. Remove to wire racks. Serve warm.
1 biscuit: 124 cal., 4g fat (1g sat. fat), 1mg chol., 214mg sod., 19g carb. (4g sugars, 1g fiber), 2g pro.

BANANA NUT BREAD
PICTURED ON P. 197

This quick bread is a family favorite; I always try to have ripe bananas on hand for this recipe. I'm sure your family will love this tasty, nutty bread just as much as mine does.
—Susan Jones, La Grange Park, IL

Prep: 10 min. • **Bake:** 50 min. + cooling
Makes: 1 loaf (16 slices)

¼ cup butter, softened
¾ cup sugar
2 large eggs, room temperature
¾ cup mashed ripe banana (about 1 large)
½ cup sour cream
2¼ cups all-purpose flour
1 tsp. ground cinnamon
¾ tsp. baking soda
½ tsp. salt
½ cup chopped walnuts
   Additional walnuts, semisweet chocolate chips or coarse sugar, optional

1. Preheat oven to 350°. Beat butter and sugar until blended. Add 1 egg at a time, beating well after each addition. Stir in banana and sour cream. Whisk together flour, cinnamon, baking soda and salt. Add to the butter mixture, stirring just until moistened. Fold in ½ cup walnuts.
2. Transfer to a greased 9x5-in. loaf pan. If desired, sprinkle with additional walnuts.
3. Bake until a toothpick inserted in center comes out clean, 50-60 minutes. Cool in pan 10 minutes before removing to a wire rack to cool.
1 slice: 244 cal., 10g fat (4g sat. fat), 52mg chol., 220mg sod., 35g carb. (15g sugars, 1g fiber), 5g pro.
Banana Chip Bread: Fold in 1 cup semisweet chocolate chips or vanilla or white chips along with the walnuts. Bake as directed.

GRANDMA'S SWEET POTATO BISCUITS

Down-Home Delights

Nothing compares to homemade biscuits—topped with gravy for a hearty breakfast or with a pat of melting butter for dinner. Absolutely delicious!

1. Combine the dry...
Preheat oven to 400°. In a bowl, whisk together the first 4 ingredients. Cut in shortening until the mixture resembles coarse crumbs.

2. Add the wet...
Whisk together egg and milk. Add to the dry ingredients; stir just until moistened.

3. Knead and cut out...
On a well-floured surface, knead dough gently 8-10 times. Roll to ½-in. thickness; cut with a floured 2½-in. biscuit cutter.

4. ...and Bake!
Place on a lightly greased baking sheet. Bake until golden brown, 10-12 minutes. Serve warm.

FLUFFY BISCUITS

If you're looking for a flaky basic biscuit, this recipe is the best. These golden brown rolls bake up tall, light and tender. They taste even better served warm and spread with butter or jam.
—Nancy Horsburgh, Everett, ON

Takes: 30 min. • **Makes:** about 8 biscuits

- 2 cups all-purpose flour
- 4 tsp. baking powder
- 1 Tbsp. sugar
- ½ tsp. salt
- ½ cup shortening
- 1 large egg
- ⅔ cup 2% milk

1 biscuit: 249 cal., 13g fat (4g sat. fat), 25mg chol., 407mg sod., 26g carb. (3g sugars, 1g fiber), 5g pro.
Italian Biscuits: Add 1 tsp. Italian seasoning to the flour mixture.

HERBED BUBBLE BREAD

It takes just five ingredients to dress up a package of frozen rolls to make this buttery, crusty loaf.
—Anita Whorton, Powder Springs, GA

Prep: 10 min. + rising • **Bake:** 15 min.
Makes: 12 servings

- ¼ cup butter, melted
- 1 tsp. garlic powder
- 1 tsp. dried oregano
- ½ tsp. dried thyme
- 1 pkg. (16 oz.) frozen dinner-roll dough, thawed

1. In a bowl, combine the butter, garlic powder, oregano and thyme. Cut each roll in half; dip into the butter mixture.
2. Arrange in a greased 12-cup fluted tube pan. Pour the remaining herb mixture over top. Cover and let rise in a warm place for 1 hour or until doubled.
3. Bake at 350° for 15-20 minutes or until golden brown.

1 slice: 140 cal., 6g fat (2g sat. fat), 10mg chol., 249mg sod., 20g carb. (2g sugars, 1g fiber), 4g pro.

NUT-TOPPED STRAWBERRY RHUBARB MUFFINS

If the muffin top is your favorite part of the muffin, these tasty treats should get your attention! Pecans, cinnamon and brown sugar give a sweet crunch to every bite.
—Audrey Stallsmith, Hadley, PA

Prep: 25 min. • **Bake:** 20 min.
Makes: 1½ dozen

- 2¾ cups all-purpose flour
- 1⅓ cups packed brown sugar
- 2½ tsp. baking powder
- ½ tsp. baking soda
- ½ tsp. ground cinnamon
- ¼ tsp. salt
- 1 large egg, room temperature
- 1 cup buttermilk
- ½ cup canola oil
- 2 tsp. vanilla extract

- 1 cup chopped fresh strawberries
- ¾ cup diced fresh or frozen rhubarb

TOPPING
- ½ cup chopped pecans
- ⅓ cup packed brown sugar
- ½ tsp. ground cinnamon
- 1 Tbsp. cold butter

1. Preheat oven to 400°. In a large bowl, combine the first 6 ingredients. In a second bowl, whisk the egg, buttermilk, oil and vanilla. Stir into the dry ingredients just until moistened. Fold in strawberries and rhubarb. Fill greased or paper-lined muffin cups two-thirds full with batter.
2. In a small bowl, combine the pecans, brown sugar and cinnamon. Cut in butter until the mixture resembles coarse crumbs. Sprinkle over the batter.
3. Bake until a toothpick inserted in the center comes out clean, 20-25 minutes. Cool for 5 minutes before removing from pans to wire racks. Serve warm.
Note: If using frozen rhubarb, measure rhubarb while still frozen, then thaw completely. Drain in a colander, but do not press liquid out.
1 muffin: 243 cal., 10g fat (2g sat. fat), 14mg chol., 155mg sod., 37g carb. (21g sugars, 1g fiber), 3g pro.
HEALTH TIP Lighten up these muffins by swapping ¼ cup unsweetened applesauce for ¼ cup of the oil. This easy switch will save about 30 calories and 3 grams of fat per serving.

HERBED BUBBLE BREAD

Slow Cooker & Instant Pot®

Whether you prefer to cook it fast or simmer it for hours, these convenient modern kitchen gadgets make creating a home-cooked meal easier than ever. It's comfort food at its finest—on your schedule!

Pressure-Cooker Lemon Red Potatoes (p. 210) **Honey-Glazed Ham** (p. 210) **Pressure-Cooker Pumpkin Spice Oatmeal** (p. 220) **Shredded Chicken Tostadas** (p. 216) **Tomato Basil Tortellini Soup** (p. 217)

HONEY-GLAZED HAM

Here's an easy solution for feeding a large group. The simple ham is perfect for family dinners where time in the kitchen is as valuable as space in the oven. If you don't have ginger ale, you can use any other white soda.
—Jacquie Stolz, Little Sioux, IA

Prep: 10 min. • **Cook:** 4½ hours
Makes: 14 servings

- 1 boneless fully cooked ham (4 lbs.)
- 1½ cups ginger ale
- ¼ cup honey
- ½ tsp. ground mustard
- ½ tsp. ground cloves
- ¼ tsp. ground cinnamon

1. Cut ham in half; place in a 5-qt. slow cooker. Pour ginger ale over ham. Cover and cook on low until heated through, 4-5 hours.
2. Combine the honey, mustard, cloves and cinnamon; stir until smooth. Spread over ham; cook 30 minutes longer.

3 oz. cooked ham: 165 cal., 5g fat (2g sat. fat), 66mg chol., 1348mg sod., 8g carb. (7g sugars, 0 fiber), 24g pro.

PRESSURE-COOKER LEMON RED POTATOES

PRESSURE-COOKER LEMON RED POTATOES

Butter, lemon juice, parsley and chives enhance this simple side dish. I usually prepare these potatoes when I'm having company. They cook in the pressure cooker, so that leaves plenty of room on the stove for other dishes.
—Tara Branham, Austin, TX

Takes: 25 min. • **Makes:** 6 servings

- 1½ lbs. medium red potatoes
- ¼ cup butter, melted
- 3 Tbsp. minced fresh parsley
- 1 Tbsp. lemon juice
- 1 Tbsp. minced chives
  Salt and pepper to taste

1. Cut a strip of peel around the middle of each potato. Place the potatoes and ¼ cup water in a 6-qt. electric pressure cooker. Lock lid; close pressure-released valve. Adjust to pressure-cook on high for 12 minutes. Quick-release pressure. Drain any cooking liquid; return potatoes to pressure cooker.
2. In a small bowl, combine butter, parsley, lemon juice and chives. Pour over the potatoes; toss to coat. Sprinkle with salt and pepper.

1 serving: 150 cal., 8g fat (5g sat. fat), 20mg chol., 85mg sod., 18g carb. (1g sugars, 2g fiber), 2g pro.

CREAM OF POTATO & CHEDDAR SOUP

The Yukon Gold potatoes my daughter shares from her garden make this soup incredible. Add some cheddar cheese and crisp croutons, and it's just heavenly. Total comfort with the simplicity of good ingredients!

—Cindi Bauer, Marshfield, WI

Prep: 25 min. • **Cook:** 7½ hours
Makes: 11 servings (2¾ qt.)

- 8 medium Yukon Gold potatoes, peeled and cubed
- 1 large red onion, chopped
- 1 celery rib, chopped
- 2 cans (14½ oz. each) reduced-sodium chicken broth
- 1 can (10¾ oz.) condensed cream of celery soup, undiluted
- 1 tsp. garlic powder
- ½ tsp. white pepper
- 1½ cups shredded sharp cheddar cheese
- 1 cup half-and-half cream
  Optional: Salad croutons, crumbled cooked bacon, chives and additional shredded sharp cheddar cheese

1. Combine the first 7 ingredients in a 4- or 5-qt. slow cooker. Cover and cook on low for 7-9 hours or until the potatoes are tender.
2. Stir in cheese and cream. Cover and cook 30 minutes longer or until the cheese is melted. Garnish servings with toppings of your choice.

1 cup: 212 cal., 8g fat (5g sat. fat), 28mg chol., 475mg sod., 27g carb. (4g sugars, 3g fiber), 8g pro. **Diabetic exchanges:** 2 starch, 1½ fat.

CUBAN PULLED PORK SANDWICHES

I lived in Florida for a while and loved the Cuban-style pulled pork served there, so I went about making it for myself! You can use the flavorful meat in traditional pulled pork sandwiches and tacos, too.

—Lacie Griffin, Austin, TX

Prep: 20 min. • **Cook:** 25 min. + releasing
Makes: 16 servings

- 1 boneless pork shoulder butt roast (4 to 5 lbs.)
- 2 tsp. salt
- 2 tsp. pepper
- 1 Tbsp. olive oil
- 1 cup orange juice
- ½ cup lime juice
- 12 garlic cloves, minced
- 2 Tbsp. spiced rum, optional
- 2 Tbsp. ground coriander
- 2 tsp. white pepper
- 1 tsp. cayenne pepper

SANDWICHES
- 2 loaves (1 lb. each) French bread
  Yellow mustard, optional
- 16 dill pickle slices
- 1½ lbs. thinly sliced deli ham
- 1½ lbs. Swiss cheese, sliced

1. Cut pork roast into 2-in.-thick pieces; season with salt and pepper. Select saute or browning setting on a 6-qt. electric pressure cooker. Adjust for medium heat; add oil. When oil is hot, brown pork in batches. Remove from pressure cooker.
2. Add orange and lime juices, stirring to scrape browned bits from bottom of cooker. Add garlic, rum if desired, coriander, white pepper and cayenne pepper. Return pork and any collected juices to pressure cooker. Press cancel.
3. Lock lid in place; close pressure-release valve. Adjust to pressure-cook on high for 25 minutes. Let pressure release naturally for 10 minutes, then quick-release any remaining pressure. Remove roast; when cool enough to handle, shred with 2 forks. Remove 1 cup cooking liquid from cooker; add to pork and toss together.
4. Cut loaves of bread in half lengthwise. If desired, spread mustard over cut sides of bread. Layer bottom halves of bread with the pickles, pork, ham and cheese. Replace tops. Cut each loaf into 8 slices.

1 sandwich: 573 cal., 28g fat (12g sat. fat), 126mg chol., 1240mg sod., 35g carb. (5g sugars, 2g fiber), 45g pro.

TEST KITCHEN TIP
Make Cuban wraps by placing meat and toppings in a tortilla. Or use plain bread and create a pan-toasted sandwich similar to a grilled cheese.

CREAM OF POTATO & CHEDDAR SOUP

**GINGER CHICKEN
& QUINOA STEW**

PRESSURE-COOKER
SPICED SHORT RIBS

This is an ideal recipe when your family wants a big dinner, but you are short on time. The ribs are tender and the perfect amount of sweet and sour. You can use red wine instead of chicken stock. Instead of butter, add more olive oil or another oil of your choice.
—Shanon Tranchina, Massapequa Park, NY

Prep: 20 min. • **Cook:** 40 min. + releasing
Makes: 12 servings

- 1 Tbsp. olive oil
- 6 lbs. bone-in beef short ribs
- 2 Tbsp. butter
- 1 medium leek (white portion only), finely chopped
- 1 garlic clove, minced
- 1 cup chicken stock
- 1 can (6 oz.) tomato paste
- 2 Tbsp. ground mustard
- 2 Tbsp. red wine vinegar
- 2 Tbsp. Worcestershire sauce
- 2 tsp. paprika
- 2 tsp. celery salt
- 1 tsp. ground cinnamon
- ½ tsp. pepper

1. Select the saute setting on a 6-qt. electric pressure cooker. Adjust for medium heat; add oil. When oil is hot, brown ribs in batches; set aside.
2. Add butter to pressure cooker. When melted, add leeks. Cook and stir until the leeks are tender, 2-3 minutes. Add garlic; cook 1 minute longer. Add stock. Cook 1 minute, stirring to loosen browned bits from pan. Press cancel.
3. In a small bowl, combine remaining ingredients; spread over ribs. Return the ribs to pressure cooker. Lock lid and close pressure-release valve. Adjust to pressure-cook on high for 40 minutes. Let pressure release naturally.
1 serving: 232 cal., 14g fat (6g sat. fat), 60mg chol., 324mg sod., 5g carb. (2g sugars, 1g fiber), 20g pro.

GINGER CHICKEN
& QUINOA STEW

This Asian-inspired one-pot chicken dinner is healthy and tasty. You can serve it hot, cold or at room temperature.
—Doris Kwon, Newport Coast, CA

Prep: 25 min. • **Cook:** 3½ hours
Makes: 8 servings

- 2 lbs. boneless skinless chicken thighs, cut into 1-in. pieces
- 1 cup quinoa, rinsed
- 1 medium onion, cut into 1-in. pieces
- 1 medium sweet yellow pepper, cut into 1-in. pieces
- 1 medium sweet red pepper, cut into 1-in. pieces
- 2 cups chicken broth
- ½ cup honey
- ⅓ cup reduced-sodium soy sauce
- ¼ cup mirin (sweet rice wine) or sherry
- 1 Tbsp. minced fresh gingerroot
- 2 garlic cloves, minced
- ¼ to 1 tsp. crushed red pepper flakes
- 1 can (8 oz.) unsweetened pineapple chunks, drained
- 3 green onions, thinly sliced
- 2 tsp. sesame seeds

1. Place chicken thighs in a 4- or 5-qt. slow cooker. Top with quinoa, onion and peppers. In a small bowl, whisk the broth, honey, soy sauce, mirin, ginger, garlic and pepper flakes; pour into the slow cooker.
2. Cook, covered, on low until chicken is tender, 3½-4 hours. Serve with pineapple, green onions and sesame seeds.
1 cup: 373 cal., 10g fat (3g sat. fat), 77mg chol., 696mg sod., 43g carb. (26g sugars, 3g fiber), 26g pro.

GREEK-STYLE LENTIL SOUP

This healthy, warming soup is a satisfying vegetarian recipe, but you can use chicken broth or add cooked meat if you like.
—Mary E. Smith, Columbia, MO

Prep: 20 min. • **Cook:** 5 hours
Makes: 12 servings (3 qt.)

- 4 cups water
- 4 cups vegetable broth
- 2 cups dried lentils, rinsed
- 2 medium carrots, chopped
- 1 small onion, chopped
- 1 celery rib, chopped
- 1 tsp. dried oregano, divided
- 1 cup chopped fresh spinach
- ½ cup tomato sauce
- 1 can (2¼ oz.) sliced ripe olives, drained
- 3 Tbsp. red wine vinegar
- 2 garlic cloves, minced
- ½ tsp. salt
- ¼ tsp. pepper
  Optional: Chopped red onion, parsley and lemon wedges

1. Place the water, broth, lentils, carrots, onion, celery and ½ tsp. oregano in a 5- or 6-qt. slow cooker. Cook, covered, on low until the lentils are tender, 4-5 hours.
2. Stir in the spinach, tomato sauce, olives, vinegar, garlic, salt, pepper and remaining ½ tsp. oregano. Cook, covered, on low until the spinach is wilted, about 1 hour longer. If desired, serve with red onion, parsley and lemon wedges.

1 cup: 134 cal., 1g fat (0 sat. fat), 0 chol., 420mg sod., 24g carb. (2g sugars, 4g fiber), 9g pro. **Diabetic exchanges:** 1½ starch, 1 lean meat.
HEALTH TIP If lentils aren't in your regular meal rotation, they should be! They're easy on the budget and packed with fiber, protein, B vitamins and more.

TEST KITCHEN TIP
This soup thickens slightly as it stands. If you have leftovers, keep extra broth on hand in case you need it when reheating the soup.

GREEK-STYLE
LENTIL SOUP

PRESSURE-COOKER POTATO-CHEDDAR FRITTATA

PRESSURE-COOKER POTATO-CHEDDAR FRITTATA

I like to serve this pretty protein-packed frittata with toasted rustic bread. You can use leftover potatoes instead of the prepackaged potatoes with onions.
—Donna-Marie Ryan, Topsfield, MA

Prep: 15 min. + standing
Cook: 30 min. + releasing
Makes: 4 servings

- 1 Tbsp. canola oil
- 1½ cups refrigerated diced potatoes with onion
- 8 large egg whites
- 4 large eggs
- ½ cup fat-free milk
- 2 green onions, chopped
- 2 tsp. minced fresh parsley
- ¼ tsp. salt
- ¼ tsp. pepper
- ½ cup shredded cheddar cheese

1. In a large skillet, heat canola oil over medium-high heat. Add potatoes; cook and stir until lightly browned, 4-6 minutes. Transfer to a greased 1-½-qt. baking dish. Whisk next 7 ingredients; stir in shredded cheese. Pour egg mixture over potatoes. Loosely cover baking dish with foil.

2. Place trivet insert and 1 cup water in a 6-qt. electric pressure cooker. Fold an 18x12-in. piece of foil lengthwise into thirds, making a sling. Use the sling to lower dish onto trivet. Lock lid and close the pressure-release valve. Adjust to pressure-cook on high 30 minutes.

3. Let pressure release naturally for 10 minutes; quick-release any remaining pressure. Using foil sling, carefully remove baking dish. Let stand 10 minutes.

1 wedge: 241 cal., 13g fat (5g sat. fat), 201mg chol., 560mg sod., 11g carb. (2g sugars, 1g fiber), 18g pro. **Diabetic exchanges:** 2 medium-fat meat, 1 fat, ½ starch.

HEALTH TIP Replace some whole eggs with egg whites for a lighter version. If making with all whole eggs, use a total of 8.

GRANDMA EDNA'S CAJUN PORK

My grandma used to make this every year as part of our Christmas dinner. These days, I make it for my family at the holidays. We love to carry on the delicious tradition.
—Tonya Cline, Greenville, OH

Prep: 35 min. • **Cook:** 6 hours
Makes: 12 servings (2¼ cups sauce)

- 1 small onion
- 1 celery rib
- 1 small green pepper
- 3 Tbsp. butter
- 3 garlic cloves, minced
- 2 tsp. dried thyme
- 1 tsp. paprika
- ½ tsp. each salt, white pepper and black pepper
- ½ tsp. ground mustard
- ½ tsp. hot pepper sauce
- 1 boneless pork loin roast (4 lbs.)
- 2 Tbsp. cornstarch
- 2 Tbsp. cold water

1. Finely chop vegetables. In a large skillet, saute vegetables in butter until tender. Add garlic; cook 1 minute longer. Stir in seasonings and pepper sauce.

2. Cut several slits in the roast to within ½ in. of the bottom. Place in a 5-qt. slow cooker. Spoon the onion mixture into the slits and over the top of meat. Cover and cook on low for 6-8 hours or until the pork is tender.

3. Transfer roast to a serving platter; keep warm. Strain the cooking juices and pour into a small saucepan. Combine cornstarch and water until smooth; stir into the pan. Bring to a boil; cook and stir until thickened, about 2 minutes. Serve with roast.

4 oz. cooked pork with 3 Tbsp. sauce: 225 cal., 10g fat (4g sat. fat), 83mg chol., 167mg sod., 3g carb. (0 sugars, 1g fiber), 29g pro. **Diabetic exchanges:** 4 lean meat, ½ fat.

GRANDMA EDNA'S
CAJUN PORK

SHREDDED CHICKEN TOSTADAS

SHREDDED CHICKEN TOSTADAS

These flavorful tostadas are super easy and family-friendly. You won't believe how tender and juicy the chicken comes out! Load up the tostadas with your favorite fresh toppings, and you have one simple, sensational meal.

—Lisa Kenny, Houston, TX

Prep: 10 min. • **Cook:** 3 hours.
Makes: 8 servings

2½ lbs. boneless skinless chicken breasts
1 envelope reduced-sodium taco seasoning
1 can (10 oz.) diced tomatoes and green chiles, undrained
½ tsp. salt
16 tostada shell

2 cups shredded Mexican cheese blend
Optional: Shredded lettuce, chopped tomatoes, sliced avocado, sour cream, sliced jalapenos and fresh cilantro

1. Place chicken breasts in a 3- or 4-qt. slow cooker. Sprinkle with taco seasoning; top with the diced tomatoes and green chiles. Cover and cook on low until a thermometer inserted into chicken reads 165°, 3-4 hours.
2. Shred the meat with 2 forks. Return to slow cooker and add salt; heat through. Serve on tostada shells with cheese and if desired, optional ingredients.

Freeze option: Freeze the cooled meat mixture and juices in freezer containers. To use, partially thaw in refrigerator overnight. Heat in a saucepan, stirring occasionally; add a little water if necessary.

Pressure cooker option: Place ½ cup water in a 6-qt. electric pressure cooker. Add the chicken and sprinkle with taco seasoning. Top with diced tomatoes and green chiles. Lock lid and close pressure-release valve. Adjust to pressure-cook on high for 8 minutes. Let pressure release naturally for 10 minutes; quick-release any remaining pressure. A thermometer inserted into chicken should read at least 165° Shred meat with 2 forks. Return to pressure cooker and add salt; heat through. Serve on tostada shells with cheese and toppings as desired.

2 tostadas: 378 cal., 17g fat (7g sat. fat), 103mg chol., 858mg sod., 18g carb. (1g sugars, 1g fiber), 36g pro

TOMATO BASIL TORTELLINI SOUP

When my family first tried this soup they all had to have seconds. My husband is happy anytime I put it on the table. I'll sometimes include cooked, crumbled bacon and top it with mozzarella cheese.
—Christina Addison, Blanchester, OH

Prep: 25 min. • **Cook:** 6¼ hours
Makes: 18 servings (4½ qt.)

- 2 Tbsp. olive oil
- 1 medium onion, chopped
- 3 medium carrots, chopped
- 5 garlic cloves, minced
- 3 cans (28 oz. each) crushed tomatoes, undrained
- 1 carton (32 oz.) vegetable broth
- 1 Tbsp. sugar
- 1 tsp. dried basil
- 1 bay leaf
- 3 pkg. (9 oz. each) refrigerated cheese tortellini
- ¾ cup half-and-half cream
  Shredded Parmesan cheese and minced fresh basil

1. In a large skillet, heat olive oil over medium-high heat. Add chopped onion and carrot; cook and stir until crisp-tender, 5-6 minutes. Add garlic; cook 1 minute longer. Transfer to a 6- or 7-qt. slow cooker. Add tomatoes, broth, sugar, basil and bay leaf. Cook, covered, on low until the vegetables are tender, 6-7 hours.
2. Stir in tortellini. Cook, covered, on high 15 minutes. Reduce heat to low; stir in cream until heated through. Discard bay leaf. Serve with Parmesan cheese and basil.

Freeze option: Before stirring in the half & half, cool soup and freeze in freezer containers. To use, partially thaw in refrigerator overnight. Heat through in a saucepan, stirring occasionally, adding the half & half as directed.

1 cup: 214 cal., 7g fat (3g sat. fat), 23mg chol., 569mg sod., 32g carb. (9g sugars, 4g fiber), 9g pro. **Diabetic exchanges:** 2 starch, 1 fat.

> **TEST KITCHEN TIP**
> If you're cooking for a smaller group, make just one-third of the recipe in a small slow cooker and decrease the cooking time slightly.

SLOW-COOKER HONEY TERIYAKI CHICKEN

This recipe is a snap to whip up on a work day, and tastes just like Chinese takeout! My kids love it, and they don't even know it's healthy.
—Rachel Ruiz, Fort Walton Beach, FL

Prep: 20 min. • **Cook:** 3¾ hours
Makes: 8 servings

- 2 lbs. boneless skinless chicken thighs, cubed
- 1 medium onion, thinly sliced
- 4 garlic cloves, minced
- 1 Tbsp. minced fresh gingerroot
- 1 cup chicken broth
- ¼ cup soy sauce
- ¼ cup honey
- ½ to 1 tsp. crushed red pepper flakes
- ¼ tsp. pepper
- 3 Tbsp. cornstarch
- 3 Tbsp. cold water
  Hot cooked rice
  Minced fresh cilantro, optional

1. Place chicken in a 3- or 4-qt. slow cooker. Top with onion, garlic and ginger. Combine broth, soy sauce, honey, pepper flakes and pepper; pour over chicken. Cook, covered, on low until the chicken is no longer pink, 3½-4 hours.
2. In a small bowl, mix cornstarch and water until smooth; gradually stir into the slow cooker. Cook, covered, on high until sauce is thickened, 15-30 minutes. Serve with rice and cilantro, if desired.

⅔ cup: 223 cal., 8g fat (2g sat. fat), 76mg chol., 647mg sod., 14g carb. (9g sugars, 0 fiber), 22g pro. **Diabetic exchanges:** 3 lean meat, 1 starch.

TOMATO BASIL TORTELLINI SOUP

SLOW-COOKED BLACK BEAN SOUP

Life can get really crazy with young children, but I never want to compromise when it comes to cooking. This recipe is healthy and so easy thanks to the slow cooker!
—Angela Lemoine, Howell, NJ

Prep: 15 min. • **Cook:** 6 hours
Makes: 8 servings (1½ qt.)

- 2 cans (15 oz. each) black beans, rinsed and drained
- 1 medium onion, finely chopped
- 1 medium sweet red pepper, finely chopped
- 4 garlic cloves, minced
- 2 tsp. ground cumin
- 2 cans (14½ oz. each) vegetable broth
- 1 tsp. olive oil
- 1 cup fresh or frozen corn
  Dash pepper
  Minced fresh cilantro

1. In a 3-qt. slow cooker, combine the first 6 ingredients. Cook, covered, on low until the vegetables are softened, 6-8 hours.
2. Puree the soup using an immersion blender, or cool soup slightly and puree in batches in a blender. Return to the slow cooker and heat through.
3. In a small skillet, heat oil over medium heat. Add corn; cook and stir, until golden brown, 4-6 minutes. Sprinkle soup with pepper. Garnish with corn and cilantro.

¾ cup: 117 cal., 1g fat (0 sat. fat), 0 chol., 616mg sod., 21g carb. (3g sugars, 5g fiber), 6g pro. **Diabetic exchanges:** 1½ starch.

TEST KITCHEN TIP
This version of black bean soup is thinner than most. It's a great base recipe for different mix-ins like shredded chicken. Experiment with adding more toppings like salsa, sour cream, hot pepper sauce or lime.

SAUCY ITALIAN CHICKEN

This chicken certainly lives up to its name! Serve it with pasta, risotto or polenta to soak up all its saucy goodness. To make this recipe in the slow cooker, cook on low for 4-6 hours or high for 3-4 hours.
—Marisa Loper, Sammamish, WA

Prep: 20 min. • **Cook:** 10 min. + releasing
Makes: 4 servings

- 4 boneless skinless chicken breast halves (6 oz. each)

SAUCY ITALIAN CHICKEN

- 1 can (14½ oz.) diced tomatoes, undrained
- 1 jar (12 oz.) marinated quartered artichoke hearts, undrained
- 2 tsp. Italian seasoning
- ¾ tsp. garlic salt
- 1 cup shredded mozzarella cheese
- ¼ cup grated Parmesan cheese

Place chicken in a 6-qt. electric pressure cooker. Top with tomatoes, artichokes, Italian seasoning and garlic salt. Lock lid; close pressure-release valve. Adjust to pressure-cook on high for 10 minutes. Allow pressure to naturally release for 10 minutes and then quick-release any remaining pressure. Sprinkle with cheeses before serving.

1 chicken breast half with 1 cup tomato mixture: 414 cal., 22g fat (8g sat. fat), 120mg chol., 1303mg sod., 12g carb. (4g sugars, 7g fiber), 43g pro.

VEGETARIAN PEA SOUP

This recipe is my version of several online recipes—and a real favorite when I was a vegetarian for health reasons. Even my meat-loving husband asked for seconds!
—Corrie Gamache, Palmyra, VA

Prep: 15 min. • **Cook:** 7 hours
Makes: 8 servings (2 qt.)

- 1 pkg. (16 oz.) dried green split peas, rinsed
- 1 medium leek (white portion only), chopped
- 3 celery ribs, chopped
- 1 medium potato, peeled and chopped
- 2 medium carrots, chopped
- 1 garlic clove, minced
- ¼ cup minced fresh parsley
- 2 cartons (32 oz. each) reduced-sodium vegetable broth
- 1½ tsp. ground mustard
- ½ tsp. pepper
- ½ tsp. dried oregano
- 1 bay leaf

In a 5-qt. slow cooker, combine all the ingredients. Cover and cook on low for 7-8 hours or until peas are tender. Discard the bay leaf. Stir before serving.
1 cup: 248 cal., 1g fat (0 sat. fat), 0 chol., 702mg sod., 46g carb. (7g sugars, 16g fiber), 15g pro.

PRESSURE-COOKER FLAN IN A JAR

These delightful portable custards are a cute and fun take on the Mexican dessert classic. Tuck a jar into your lunch box for a sweet treat. You can use rum extract instead of rum if you prefer.
—Megumi Garcia, Milwaukee, WI

Prep: 25 min. + cooling
Cook: 6 min. + releasing
Makes: 6 servings

- ½ cup sugar
- 1 Tbsp. hot water
- 1 cup coconut milk or whole milk
- ⅓ cup whole milk
- ⅓ cup sweetened condensed milk
- 2 large eggs plus 1 large egg yolk, lightly beaten
  Dash salt
- 1 tsp. vanilla extract
- 1 tsp. dark rum, optional

1. Spread sugar over the bottom of a small heavy saucepan. Cook, without stirring, over medium-low heat until sugar begins to melt, then gently drag melted sugar to center of pan so it melts evenly. Cook, stirring constantly, until melted sugar turns a deep amber color, about 2 minutes. Immediately remove from heat and carefully stir in 1 Tbsp. hot water. Quickly pour into 6 hot 4-oz. jars.
2. In a small saucepan, heat coconut milk and whole milk until bubbles form around sides of pan; remove from heat. In a large bowl, whisk condensed milk, eggs, egg yolk and salt until blended but not foamy. Slowly stir in hot milk; stir in vanilla and, if desired, rum. Strain through a fine sieve. Pour egg mixture into prepared jars. Center lids on jars; screw on bands until fingertip tight.
3. Place trivet insert and 1 cup water in a 6-qt. electric pressure cooker. Place jars on trivet, offset-stacking as needed. Lock lid and close pressure-release valve. Adjust to pressure-cook on high for 6 minutes.
4. Allow pressure to naturally release for 10 minutes, then quick-release any remaining pressure. Cool jars 30 minutes at room temperature. Refrigerate until cold, about 1 hour. Run a knife around the sides of jars; invert the flans onto dessert plates.
⅓ cup: 223 cal., 10g fat (8g sat. fat), 100mg chol., 306mg sod., 28g carb. (27g sugars, 0 fiber), 5g pro.

VEGETARIAN PEA SOUP

SLOW-COOKER BUFFALO CHICKEN SALAD

My husband and boys love that these flavors are reminiscent of their favorite appetizer—chicken wings with blue cheese. You can make the chicken the day before in your slow cooker and re-heat it in the microwave when ready to serve.
—Shauna Havey, Roy, UT

Prep: 20 min. • **Cook:** 2½ hours
Makes: 6 servings

- 1½ lbs. boneless skinless chicken breast halves
- ¾ cup Buffalo wing sauce
- 3 Tbsp. butter
- 1 envelope ranch salad dressing mix
- 1 pkg. (10 oz.) hearts of romaine salad mix
- ½ cup blue cheese salad dressing
- 1 cup julienned carrot
- 1 medium ripe avocado, peeled and cubed
- ½ cup crumbled blue cheese

1. Place chicken in a 1½- or 3-qt. slow cooker. Top with wing sauce, butter and ranch dressing mix. Cook, covered, on low until a thermometer inserted in chicken reads 165°, 2½-3 hours.
2. Remove chicken; shred with 2 forks. Reserve ⅓ cup cooking juices; discard the remaining juices. Return shredded chicken and the reserved juices to slow cooker; heat through.
3. Divide romaine among 6 plates; drizzle with blue cheese dressing. Top with shredded chicken, carrots, avocado and blue cheese. Serve immediately.
1 salad: 385 cal., 26g fat (9g sat. fat), 93mg chol., 1693mg sod., 12g carb. (2g sugars, 4g fiber), 28g pro.

PRESSURE-COOKER PUMPKIN SPICE OATMEAL

PRESSURE-COOKER PUMPKIN SPICE OATMEAL

There's nothing like a bowl of warm oatmeal in the morning! As well as the suggested toppings, you can drizzle your dish with maple syrup, honey or agave nectar.
—Jordan Mason, Brookville, PA

Takes: 30 min. • **Makes:** 6 servings

- 1¼ cups steel-cut oats
- 3 Tbsp. brown sugar
- 1½ tsp. pumpkin pie spice
- 1 tsp. ground cinnamon
- ¾ tsp. salt
- 3 cups water
- 1½ cups 2% milk
- 1 can (15 oz.) pumpkin
  Optional: Toasted chopped pecans, ground cinnamon, additional brown sugar and 2% milk

1. Stir together the first 7 ingredients in a 6-qt. electric pressure cooker. Lock lid; close pressure-release valve. Adjust to pressure-cook on high for 10 minutes.
2. Allow pressure to naturally release for 10 minutes, then quick-release any remaining pressure. Stir in pumpkin; let stand 5-10 minutes to thicken. Serve with toppings as desired. Store leftovers in the refrigerator.
Note: Steel-cut oats are also known as Scotch oats or Irish oatmeal.
1 cup: 208 cal., 4g fat (1g sat. fat), 5mg chol., 329mg sod., 39g carb. (13g sugars, 6g fiber), 7g pro.

TEST KITCHEN TIP
To make gingerbread oatmeal, replace half the brown sugar with molasses and sprinkle with candied ginger pieces.

THAI BUTTERNUT SQUASH PEANUT SOUP

This seemingly exotic dish is simple, vegan, healthy and hearty. The peanut butter blends beautifully with the sweetness of the squash and Thai seasonings. You can also serve this soup without pureeing it first.
—Kayla Capper, Ojai, CA

Prep: 25 min. • **Cook:** 5 hours
Makes: 8 servings (1½ qt.)

3 cups cubed peeled butternut squash
1 can (13.66 oz.) light coconut milk
1 medium sweet red pepper, finely chopped
1 medium onion, finely chopped
1 cup vegetable stock
½ cup chunky peanut butter
3 Tbsp. lime juice
2 Tbsp. red curry paste
4 garlic cloves, minced
1 Tbsp. reduced-sodium soy sauce
1 tsp. minced fresh gingerroot
½ tsp. salt
¼ tsp. pepper
    Chopped fresh cilantro and chopped salted peanuts, optional

1. In a 4- or 5-qt. slow cooker, combine the first 13 ingredients. Cook, covered, on low until the squash is tender, 5-6 hours.

2. Puree the soup using an immersion blender, or cool slightly and puree soup in batches in a blender. Return to slow cooker and heat through. If desired, garnish with cilantro and peanuts.

¾ cup: 181 cal., 12g fat (4g sat. fat), 0 chol., 470mg sod., 16g carb. (5g sugars, 3g fiber), 5g pro. **Diabetic exchanges:** 1 starch, 1 high-fat meat, 1 fat.
HEALTH TIP This brightly colored soup provides you with a total daily dose of vitamin A, thanks to the butternut squash and red pepper.

THAI BUTTERNUT
SQUASH PEANUT SOUP

**SLOW-COOKED
VEGETABLE
WILD RICE SOUP**

SLOW-COOKED VEGETABLE WILD RICE SOUP

This thick and hearty soup is packed with colorful vegetables.
—Thomas Faglon, Somerset, NJ

Prep: 25 min. • **Cook:** 5 hours
Makes: 12 servings (3 qt.)

- 6 cups reduced-sodium vegetable broth
- 2 cans (14½ oz. each) fire-roasted diced tomatoes
- 2 celery ribs, sliced
- 2 medium carrots, chopped
- 1¾ cups sliced baby portobello mushrooms
- 1 medium onion, chopped
- 1 medium parsnip, peeled and chopped
- 1 medium sweet potato, peeled and cubed
- 1 medium green pepper, chopped
- 1 cup uncooked wild rice
- 2 garlic cloves, minced
- ¾ tsp. salt
- ¼ tsp. pepper
- 2 bay leaves
- 2 fresh thyme sprigs, plus more for topping

Combine all ingredients in a 6- or 7-qt. slow cooker. Cover and cook on high until the rice and vegetables are tender, 5-6 hours. Discard bay leaves and thyme sprigs before serving. If desired, remove leaves from additional thyme sprigs and sprinkle over soup when serving.
1 cup: 117 cal., 0 fat (0 sat. fat), 0 chol., 419mg sod., 25g carb. (7g sugars, 4g fiber), 4g pro. **Diabetic exchanges:** 2 vegetable, 1 starch.

> **TEST KITCHEN TIP**
> Chop the vegetables in advance and keep them in the refrigerator to reduce the time needed for last-minute prep.

OVERNIGHT PEACH OATMEAL

OVERNIGHT PEACH OATMEAL

Hearty oatmeal combined with bright, sweet peaches make this slow-cooker recipe a perfect breakfast or brunch. This is an excellent make-ahead meal for busy mornings.
—Rachel Lewis, Danville, VA

Prep: 10 min. • **Cook:** 7 hours
Makes: 6 servings

- 4 cups water
- 1 cup steel-cut oats
- 1 cup vanilla soy milk or vanilla almond milk
- 3 Tbsp. brown sugar
- ¼ tsp. salt
- ¼ tsp. vanilla or almond extract
- 2 medium peaches, sliced or 3 cups frozen unsweetened sliced peaches, thawed
  Optional: Sliced almonds, brown sugar, cinnamon and additional sliced peaches

In a well-greased 3-qt. slow cooker, combine the first 6 ingredients. Cook, covered, on low until steel-cut oats are tender, 7-8 hours. Stir in peaches just before serving.
Note: Steel-cut oats are also known as Scotch oats or Irish oatmeal.
Pressure cooker option: Decrease water to 3 cups. Add to a 6-qt. electric pressure cooker coated with cooking spray. Stir in the oats, soy milk, brown sugar, salt and vanilla. Lock lid; close pressure-release valve. Adjust to pressure-cook on high for 4 minutes. Let pressure release naturally. Stir in peaches just before serving. Oatmeal will thicken upon standing. If desired, top with optional toppings.
¾ cup: 163 cal., 2g fat (0 sat. fat), 0 chol., 116mg sod., 31g carb. (13g sugars, 4g fiber), 5g pro. **Diabetic exchanges:** 1½ starch, ½ fruit.
HEALTH TIP Steel-cut oats are 100% whole grain. They are slowly digested, giving you energy that will last.

PRESSURE-COOKER
CHICKEN CACCIATORE

PRESSURE-COOKER
CHICKEN CACCIATORE

My husband and I run a busy farm, and some days there's just no time left for cooking. It's really nice to be able to have dinner ready in just a few minutes.
—Aggie Arnold-Norman, Liberty, PA

Prep: 15 min. • **Cook:** 15 min. + releasing
Makes: 6 servings

- 2 **medium onions, thinly sliced**
- 1 **broiler/fryer chicken (3 to 4 lbs.), cut up and skin removed**
- 2 **garlic cloves, minced**
- 1 **to 2 tsp. dried oregano**
- 1 **tsp. salt**
- ½ **tsp. dried basil**
- ¼ **tsp. pepper**
- 1 **bay leaf**
- 1 **can (14½ oz.) diced tomatoes, undrained**
- 1 **can (8 oz.) tomato sauce**
- 1 **can (4 oz.) mushroom stems and pieces, drained**
- ¼ **cup white wine or water**
  Hot cooked pasta

Place onions in a 6-qt. electric pressure cooker. Add the next 11 ingredients. Lock lid; close pressure-release valve. Adjust to pressure-cook on high for 15 minutes. Allow pressure to naturally release for 10 minutes; quick-release any remaining pressure. Discard bay leaf. Serve chicken with sauce over pasta.

1 serving: 207 cal., 6g fat (2g sat. fat), 73mg chol., 787mg sod., 11g carb. (6g sugars, 3g fiber), 27g pro.

SPICED LIME &
CILANTRO CHICKEN

As a working mom, I strive to give my family fabulous and flavor-packed dinners. This slow-cooker recipe tastes like you've been in the kitchen all day!
—Mari Smith, Ashburn, VA

Prep: 15 min. • **Cook:** 3 hours
Makes: 6 servings

- 2 **tsp. chili powder**
- 1 **tsp. sea salt**
- 1 **tsp. ground cumin**
- 1 **tsp. pepper**
- ¼ **tsp. cayenne pepper**
- 6 **bone-in chicken thighs (about 2¼ lbs.)**
- ⅓ **cup lime juice (about 3 limes)**
- 1 **Tbsp. olive oil**
- ½ **cup fresh cilantro leaves**
- 5 **garlic cloves, halved**

Combine the first 5 ingredients; rub over chicken. Place in a 4 or 5-qt. slow cooker. Combine remaining ingredients in a blender; cover and process pureed. Pour over chicken. Cook, covered, on low until a thermometer inserted in chicken reads 170°-175°, 3-4 hours.

1 chicken thigh: 253 cal., 17g fat (4g sat. fat), 81mg chol., 390mg sod., 2g carb. (0 sugars, 0 fiber), 23g pro.

HAWAIIAN PULLED PORK LETTUCE WRAPS

We love this easy slow-cooker recipe on Sunday afternoons. It's equally comforting and light for lunch or dinner. We serve ours with sweet potato oven fries and roasted green beans.
—Arlene Rakoczy, Gilbert, AZ

Prep: 10 min. • **Cook:** 6 hours
Makes: 6 servings

- 1 boneless pork shoulder butt roast (3 to 4 lbs.)
- 1 tsp. rubbed sage
- 1 tsp. salt, divided
- ¼ tsp. pepper
- 1 can (20 oz.) unsweetened crushed pineapple, undrained
- 2 Tbsp. minced fresh gingerroot
- 18 Boston or Bibb lettuce leaves
  Thinly sliced green onions, optional

1. Rub roast with sage, ½ tsp. salt and pepper. Place in a 4- or 5-qt. slow cooker.

Top with pineapple and ginger. Cook, covered, on low until meat is tender, 6-8 hours.

2. Remove the roast; shred with 2 forks. Strain cooking juices. Reserve pineapple and 1 cup juices; discard remaining juices. Skim fat from reserved juices. Return pork and juices to slow cooker; stir in remaining ½ tsp. salt. Heat through. Serve in lettuce leaves with reserved pineapple and, if desired, green onions.

Freeze option: Freeze cooled meat mixture and juices in freezer containers. To use, partially thaw in refrigerator overnight. Heat through in a saucepan, stirring occasionally; add a little water if necessary.

3 wraps: 430 cal., 23g fat (8g sat. fat), 135mg chol., 535mg sod., 16g carb. (14g sugars, 1g fiber), 39g pro.

TEST KITCHEN TIP
Sage and ginger flavor this mildly sweet pork dish. If you'd like yours sweeter, add a drizzle of honey to the pork mixture.

ROSEMARY BEEF ROAST OVER CHEESY POLENTA

I love beef roast in the slow cooker, and it's fun to pair it with something a little different than potatoes! This is true comfort food.
—Elisabeth Larsen, Pleasant Grove, UT

Prep: 20 min. • **Cook:** 7 hours
Makes: 8 servings

- ¼ cup minced fresh rosemary
- 3 garlic cloves, minced
- 3 tsp. salt, divided
- 1 tsp. pepper
- 1 boneless beef chuck roast (3 lbs.)
- 1 Tbsp. canola oil
- 1 cup beef broth
- 2 cups water
- 2 cups 2% milk
- 1 cup cornmeal
- ½ cup shredded Parmesan cheese
- 3 Tbsp. butter, cubed

1. Mix rosemary, garlic, 2 tsp. salt and pepper; rub over meat. In a large skillet, heat oil over medium-high heat; brown meat. Transfer meat a 5- or 6-qt. slow cooker. Add broth to skillet; cook for 1 minute, stirring to loosen browned bits from pan. Pour over meat. Cook, covered, on low until the meat is tender, 7-9 hours.

2. For polenta, in a large heavy saucepan, bring water, milk and remaining 1 tsp. salt to a boil. Reduce heat to a gentle boil; slowly whisk in cornmeal. Cook and stir with a wooden spoon until the polenta is thickened and pulls away cleanly from sides of pan, 15-20 minutes. (The mixture will be very thick). Remove from heat; stir in Parmesan cheese and butter. Serve with roast.

1 serving: 471 cal., 25g fat (11g sat. fat), 130mg chol., 1216mg sod., 19g carb. (3g sugars, 1g fiber), 39g pro.

HAWAIIAN PULLED PORK LETTUCE WRAPS

CHEDDAR BACON BEER DIP

My tangy, smoky dip won the top prize at our office party recipe contest. Use whatever beer or ale you like, but steer clear of dark varieties.
—Ashley Lecker, Green Bay, WI

Takes: 25 min. • **Makes:** 4½ cups

- 18 oz. cream cheese, softened
- ¼ cup sour cream
- 1½ Tbsp. Dijon mustard
- 1 tsp. garlic powder
- 1 cup beer or nonalcoholic beer
- 1 lb. bacon strips, cooked and crumbled
- 2 cups shredded cheddar cheese
- ¼ cup heavy whipping cream
- 1 green onion, thinly sliced
  Soft pretzel bites

1. In a greased 6-qt. electric pressure cooker, combine cream cheese, sour cream, mustard and garlic powder until smooth. Stir in beer; add bacon, reserving 2 Tbsp. Lock lid; close pressure-release valve. Adjust to pressure-cook on high for 5 minutes. Quick-release pressure.
2. Select saute setting, and adjust for medium heat. Stir in cheese and heavy cream. Cook and stir until mixture has thickened, 3-4 minutes. Transfer to serving dish. Sprinkle with onion and reserved bacon. Serve with pretzel bun bites.
¼ cup: 213 cal., 19g fat (10g sat. fat), 60mg chol., 378mg sod., 2g carb. (1g sugars, 0 fiber), 8g pro.
HEALTH TIP To lighten this up, use reduced-fat cream cheese, light sour cream, half-and-half and reduced-fat shredded cheese. Serve with fresh celery and carrot sticks.

25-MINUTE TURKEY CHILI

25-MINUTE TURKEY CHILI

This is a nice change of pace from traditional beef chili, offering a whole different set of flavors to enjoy. It's also ready to serve fast, too. I like to serve cheddar cheese bread on the side, or try it over rice.
—Traci Wynne, Denver, PA

Takes: 25 min. + releasing
Makes: 8 servings (2 qt.)

- 1 can (16 oz.) kidney beans, rinsed and drained
- 1 can (15 oz.) black beans, rinsed and drained
- 1 can (14½ oz.) Mexican stewed tomatoes, undrained
- 1 can (8 oz.) tomato sauce
- 1 small sweet red pepper, finely chopped
- 1 small onion, chopped
- 1 cup beef broth
- 1 jalapeno pepper, seeded and minced
- 2 Tbsp. chili powder
- ½ tsp. salt
- ¼ tsp. pepper
- 1¼ lbs. ground turkey
  Optional: Sour cream and sliced jalapeno

1. Combine the first 11 ingredients in a 6-qt. electric pressure cooker. Crumble turkey over top; stir to combine. Lock lid; close pressure-release valve. Adjust to pressure-cook on high for 5 minutes.
2. Allow pressure to naturally release for 10 minutes, then quick-release any remaining pressure. Stir chili. If desired, serve with sour cream and additional sliced jalapenos.
Note: Wear disposable gloves when cutting hot peppers; the oils can burn exposed skin. Avoid touching your face.
1 cup: 231 cal., 6g fat (1g sat. fat), 47mg chol., 817mg sod., 24g carb. (4g sugars, 7g fiber), 21g pro.

BUFFALO SHRIMP MAC & CHEESE

Rich, creamy and slightly spicy, this shrimp and pasta dish does it all. It's a whole new twist on popular Buffalo chicken dishes.
—Robin Haas, Cranston, RI

Prep: 15 min. • **Cook:** 10 min.
Makes: 6 servings

- 2 cups 2% milk
- 1 cup half-and-half cream
- 1 Tbsp. unsalted butter
- 1 tsp. ground mustard
- ½ tsp. onion powder
- ¼ tsp. white pepper
- ¼ tsp. ground nutmeg
- 1½ cups uncooked elbow macaroni
- 2 cups shredded cheddar cheese
- 1 cup shredded Gouda or Swiss cheese
- ¾ lb. frozen cooked salad shrimp, thawed
- 1 cup crumbled blue cheese
- 2 Tbsp. Louisiana-style hot sauce
- 2 Tbsp. minced fresh chives

- 2 Tbsp. minced fresh parsley
  Additional Louisiana-style hot sauce, optional

1. In a 6-qt. electric pressure cooker, combine the first 7 ingredients; stir in macaroni. Lock lid; close pressure-release valve. Adjust to pressure-cook on high for 3 minutes. Allow pressure to naturally release for 4 minutes, then quick-release any remaining pressure.
2. Select saute setting and adjust for medium heat. Stir in shredded cheeses, shrimp, blue cheese and hot sauce. Cook until heated through, 5-6 minutes. Just before serving, stir in chives, parsley and, if desired, additional hot sauce.

1 serving: 551 cal., 34g fat (20g sat. fat), 228mg chol., 1269mg sod., 22g carb. (7g sugars, 1g fiber), 38g pro.

TEST KITCHEN TIP
Crumble your own blue cheese versus buying prepackaged crumbles. It will be creamier.

PRESSURE-COOKER SAUSAGE & WAFFLE BAKE

Here's an easy dish that's guaranteed to create excitement at the breakfast table! Absolutely nothing is missing from this indulgent sweet and savory combination.
—Courtney Lentz, Boston, MA

Prep: 20 min. • **Cook:** 20 min. + releasing
Makes: 6 servings

- 1 lb. bulk spicy breakfast pork sausage
- 1½ tsp. rubbed sage
- ¼ tsp. fennel seed
- 5 frozen waffles, cut into bite-sized pieces
- 4 large eggs
- ⅔ cup half-and-half cream
- 2 Tbsp. maple syrup
- ⅛ tsp. salt
- ⅛ tsp. pepper
- 1 cup shredded cheddar cheese
  Additional maple syrup

1. Select saute or browning setting on a 6-qt. electric pressure cooker; adjust for medium heat. Cook sausage until no longer pink, breaking into crumbles; drain. Add sage and fennel. Press cancel. Place waffles in a greased 1½-qt. baking dish; top with sausage. In a bowl, mix eggs, cream, syrup and seasonings. Pour over sausage and waffles; top with cheese. Cover baking dish with foil. Wipe pressure cooker clean.
2. Place trivet insert and 1 cup water in pressure cooker. Fold an 18x12-in. piece of foil lengthwise into thirds, making a sling. Use the sling to lower the dish onto the trivet. Lock lid; close pressure-release valve. Adjust to pressure-cook on high for 20 minutes. Let the pressure release naturally for 5 minutes; quick-release any remaining pressure.
3. Using foil sling, carefully remove baking dish. Serve with additional maple syrup.

1 serving: 445 cal., 31g fat (12g sat. fat), 201mg chol., 880mg sod., 20g carb. (7g sugars, 1g fiber), 19g pro.

PRESSURE-COOKER
BUFFALO SHRIMP
MAC & CHEESE

Hot off the Grill

In the summer months, grilling out in the backyard is the perfect way to enjoy the warm evenings. But you can make these recipes year-round—if the weather drives you indoors, just break out a grill pan and make magic happen in the kitchen.

Grilled Jerk Shrimp Orzo Salad (p. 243) **Grilled Cabbage** (p. 237) **Balsamic-Goat Cheese Grilled Plums** (p. 239)
Lime & Garlic Grilled Pork Chops (p. 233) **Skewered Ginger Shrimp with Plums** (p. 237)

GRILLED SPICY CORN ON THE COB

During a family picnic, we added jalapenos and hot pepper sauce to our homegrown corn. Now we spice up fresh ears every chance we get.
—Bernadette Walker, Waco, TX

Takes: 25 min. • **Makes:** 4 servings

- 4 **large ears sweet corn, husks removed**
- ¼ **cup butter, melted**
- 2 **tsp. dried thyme**
- 1 **Tbsp. hot pepper sauce**
- 1 **tsp. chicken bouillon granules**
- ¼ **cup chopped seeded jalapeno peppers**

1. Place each ear of corn on a double thickness of heavy-duty foil (about 18x12 in.). Combine butter, thyme, hot pepper sauce and bouillon granules. Brush over corn; sprinkle each with 1 Tbsp. jalapenos. Seal tightly.
2. Grill, covered, over medium heat until the corn is tender, 15-20 minutes. Open carefully to allow steam to escape.
Note: Wear disposable gloves when cutting hot peppers; the oils can burn exposed skin. Avoid touching your face.
1 ear of corn: 229 cal., 13g fat (7g sat. fat), 30mg chol., 335mg sod., 28g carb. (5g sugars, 4g fiber), 5g pro.

GRILLED POTATO FANS WITH ONIONS

GRILLED POTATO FANS WITH ONIONS

These seasoned potato fans are filled with tender onions, roasted garlic cloves and savory Parmesan cheese—they're my idea of the ultimate grilled potato.
—Sharon Crabtree, Graham, WA

Prep: 20 min. • **Grill:** 35 min.
Makes: 6 servings

- 6 **medium potatoes**
- 2 **small onions, halved and thinly sliced**
- 6 **Tbsp. butter, diced**
- 2 **garlic cloves, minced**
- 6 **Tbsp. grated Parmesan cheese**
- 1 **Tbsp. minced chives**
- ½ **tsp. crushed red pepper flakes**
  Dash salt

1. Prepare grill for indirect heat. With a sharp knife, cut each potato into ½-in. slices, leaving the slices attached at the bottom. Fan potatoes slightly. Place each on a 12-in. square of heavy-duty foil.
2. Insert onions, butter and garlic between the potato slices. Combine the cheese, chives, pepper flakes and salt; sprinkle between the slices. Fold the foil around the potatoes and seal tightly.
3. Grill, covered, over indirect medium heat for 35-45 minutes or until potatoes are tender. Open foil carefully to allow the steam to escape.
1 potato: 302 cal., 13g fat (8g sat. fat), 35mg chol., 195mg sod., 41g carb. (4g sugars, 4g fiber), 7g pro.

SAUCY GRILLED PORK CHOPS

My mamaw in Kentucky used this dip (as she called it) on many grilled meats, including chicken and steak.
—Misty Schneider, Bayport, MN

Prep: 5 min. • **Grill:** 10 min.
Makes: 8 servings

- ½ cup butter, cubed
- ½ cup packed light brown sugar
- ½ cup lemon juice
- 8 bone-in pork loin chops (¾ in. thick)
  Lemon wedges, optional

1. In a microwave-safe dish, microwave butter, covered, until melted; add brown sugar and lemon juice, stirring to dissolve sugar. Reserve ⅔ cup for drizzling.

2. Brush pork chops with the remaining sauce. Grill, covered, on an oiled rack over medium heat or broil 4 in. from the heat for 4-5 minutes on each side or until a thermometer reads 145°. Let stand for 5 minutes before serving.

3. Stir sauce to combine and gently reheat if necessary; drizzle over pork chops. Serve with lemon if desired.

1 pork chop: 476 cal., 30g fat (14g sat. fat), 141mg chol., 162mg sod., 15g carb. (14g sugars, 0 fiber), 36g pro.

READER REVIEW

"Tangy, sweet, buttery, succulent chops! Delicious!"

CYNANDTOM, TASTEOFHOME.COM

PESTO CROSTINI WITH GRILLED NECTARINES & BURRATA

This impressive-looking appetizer is simple to prepare and a worthy way to utilize beautiful produce. The pesto is complemented by the nectarines, which taste even sweeter once they are grilled. The creaminess of the burrata cheese brings the whole dish together to make it the perfect bite.
—Michele Kusma, Columbus, OH

Prep: 30 min. • **Grill:** 10 min.
Makes: 20 servings

- 2½ cups loosely packed fresh arugula
- 2 cups loosely packed basil leaves
- 2 Tbsp. pine nuts, toasted
- ½ tsp. salt
- 6 Tbsp. olive oil, divided
- ⅓ cup grated Parmesan cheese
- 20 slices French bread baguette (½ in. thick)
- 2 medium nectarines or peaches, halved
- 1 lb. fresh burrata or mozzarella cheese, cut into 20 pieces
- ¼ cup honey

1. Place the arugula, basil, pine nuts and salt in a food processor; pulse until chopped. Continue processing while gradually adding 3 Tbsp. oil in a steady stream, until pesto is smooth and creamy. Add Parmesan; pulse just until blended.

2. Brush baguette slices and nectarines with the remaining 3 Tbsp. oil. Grill bread, covered, over medium heat or broil 3 in. from heat until toasted, 1-2 minutes on each side.

3. Grill the nectarines, covered, over medium heat or broil 3 in. from heat until tender, 2-3 minutes on each side. When nectarines are cool enough to handle, cut each half into 5 pieces.

4. Spread pesto over the toasted bread; top with burrata cheese and nectarines. Drizzle with honey.

1 crostini: 151 cal., 10g fat (4g sat. fat), 19mg chol., 165mg sod., 10g carb. (5g sugars, 0 fiber), 6g pro.

SAUCY GRILLED PORK CHOPS

GRILLED VEGETABLE QUESADILLAS

I like having at least one or two meatless dinners every week. It forces me to get creative with vegetables. I recently made these quesadillas and they were a huge hit—even with my kids! They take just five ingredients and are so easy to make.
—Angela Lemoine, Howell, NJ

Takes: 30 min. • **Makes:** 4 servings

- 3 medium zucchini, cut lengthwise into 10 slices
- 2 medium ears sweet corn
- 2 Tbsp. olive oil
- ½ tsp. salt
- ¼ tsp. pepper
- 10 corn tortillas (6 in.)
- 1½ cups shredded white cheddar cheese
  Honey, optional

1. Brush zucchini and corn with olive oil; sprinkle with salt and pepper. Place the zucchini and corn on a grill rack over medium heat; close lid. Grill zucchini until tender, 2-3 minutes on each side. Grill corn until tender, 10-12 minutes, turning occasionally. Cut corn from cobs; cut zucchini slices in half.
2. Preheat griddle over medium heat. Sprinkle 5 corn tortillas with cheese, add zucchini and corn; top with the remaining tortillas. Place on the griddle; cook until golden brown and the cheese is melted, 1-2 minutes on each side. Cut quesadillas into 4 wedges each. If desired, drizzle with honey.

5 wedges: 431 cal., 24g fat (9g sat. fat), 42mg chol., 618mg sod., 42g carb. (7g sugars, 6g fiber), 17g pro.

GRILLED PINEAPPLE WITH LIME DIP

GRILLED PINEAPPLE WITH LIME DIP

Serve this fruity dish as an appetizer or dessert—the choice is yours! If desired, the pineapple wedges can be rolled in flaked coconut before grilling.
—*Taste of Home* Test Kitchen

Prep: 20 min. + marinating • **Grill:** 10 min.
Makes: 8 servings

- 1 fresh pineapple
- ¼ cup packed brown sugar
- 3 Tbsp. honey
- 2 Tbsp. lime juice

LIME DIP
- 3 oz. cream cheese, softened
- ¼ cup plain yogurt
- 2 Tbsp. honey
- 1 Tbsp. brown sugar
- 1 Tbsp. lime juice
- 1 tsp. grated lime zest

1. Peel and core the pineapple; cut vertically into 8 wedges. Cut each wedge horizontally into 2 spears. In a bowl or shallow dish, combine the brown sugar, honey and lime juice; add the pineapple and turn to coat. Cover and refrigerate for 1 hour.
2. In a small bowl, beat the cream cheese until smooth. Beat in the yogurt, honey, brown sugar, lime juice and zest. Cover and refrigerate until serving.
3. Coat grill rack with cooking spray before starting the grill. Drain pineapple, discarding the marinade. Grill pineapple spears, covered, over medium heat for 3-4 minutes on each side or until golden brown. Serve with lime dip.

2 spears with 2 Tbsp. dip: 160 cal., 4g fat (2g sat. fat), 12mg chol., 41mg sod., 32g carb. (28g sugars, 2g fiber), 2g pro.

LIME & GARLIC GRILLED PORK CHOPS

These juicy chops are a sizzling good reason for the summer grill. The pork is so tender and the zing it gets from lime, garlic, cilantro and ginger is amazing.
—Deborah Yasbah, North Middletown, NJ

Prep: 15 min. + marinating
Grill: 10 min. • **Makes:** 6 servings

- 1 can (12 oz.) frozen limeade concentrate, thawed
- ¼ cup white vinegar
- 2 Tbsp. minced fresh cilantro
- 5 garlic cloves, minced
- 1 Tbsp. minced fresh gingerroot
- 1 tsp. salt
- 1 tsp. pepper
- 4 drops jalapeno pepper sauce
- 6 bone-in pork loin chops (8 oz. each)
  Chopped fresh cilantro, optional

1. In a small bowl, combine the first 8 ingredients. Pour 1¼ cups marinade into a large shallow dish. Add the pork; turn to coat. Cover and refrigerate for at least 4 hours. Cover the remaining marinade for basting; refrigerate.
2. Drain pork, discarding the marinade in the dish. On a lightly oiled rack, grill chops, covered, over medium heat or broil 4 in. from heat for 4-6 minutes on each side or until a thermometer reads 160°; baste occasionally with the reserved marinade. If desired, top with chopped cilantro.

1 pork chop: 386 cal., 19g fat (7g sat. fat), 111mg chol., 303mg sod., 17g carb. (14g sugars, 0 fiber), 36g pro.

TEST KITCHEN TIP
For even more flavor, serve these chops with mango salsa on the side.

LIME & GARLIC GRILLED PORK CHOPS

FLAT IRON STEAK SALAD

GRILLED TILAPIA WITH MANGO

This is a different twist on tilapia that I created for my wife. She enjoyed the combination of mango with Parmesan. Somehow it tastes even better outside on the deck with a cold glass of iced tea.
—Gregg May, Columbus, OH

Takes: 20 min. • **Makes:** 4 servings

- 4 tilapia fillets (6 oz. each)
- 1 Tbsp. olive oil
- ½ tsp. salt
- ½ tsp. dill weed
- ¼ tsp. pepper
- 1 Tbsp. grated Parmesan cheese
- 1 medium lemon, sliced
- 1 medium mango, peeled and thinly sliced

1. Brush tilapia fillets with oil; sprinkle with salt, dill and pepper.
2. Grill fillets, covered, on a lightly oiled rack over medium heat for 5 minutes. Turn tilapia; top with cheese, lemon and mango. Grill 4-6 minutes longer or until fish flakes easily with a fork.

1 fillet: 213 cal., 5g fat (1g sat. fat), 84mg chol., 377mg sod., 10g carb. (8g sugars, 1g fiber), 32g pro. **Diabetic exchanges:** 5 lean meat, ½ fruit, ½ fat.

HEALTH TIP Making mango a regular fruit choice helps boosts your intake of important nutrients like vitamins C and A, and potassium.

DID YOU KNOW?
Mangoes were first grown in India more than 5,000 years ago. The traditional Indian paisley pattern is based on the shape of the fruit.

FLAT IRON STEAK SALAD

My steak salad with avocado and radishes is a big plate of summer deliciousness. I sometimes add dried cranberries and cherry tomatoes—you can customize it to suit your tastes.
—Marla Clark, Albuquerque, NM

Takes: 30 min. • **Makes:** 4 servings

- ¾ lb. beef flat iron steak or top sirloin steak
- ¾ tsp. salt, divided
- ½ tsp. pepper, divided
- ¼ cup olive oil
- 2 Tbsp. balsamic vinegar
- 2 tsp. lemon juice
- 5 oz. fresh baby spinach (about 6 cups)
- 1 medium beefsteak tomato, sliced
- ½ medium ripe avocado, peeled and sliced
- 4 radishes, thinly sliced
- ¼ cup crumbled blue cheese, optional

1. Sprinkle steak with ½ tsp. salt and ¼ tsp. pepper. Grill, covered, over medium heat or broil 4 in. from heat 6-8 minutes on each side or until the meat reaches desired doneness (for medium-rare, a thermometer should read 135°; medium, 140°; medium-well, 145°). Let stand for 5 minutes.
2. Meanwhile, in a small bowl, whisk olive oil, vinegar, lemon juice and the remaining salt and pepper. Divide the fresh spinach among 4 plates. Add the tomato, avocado and radishes.
3. Cut steak into slices; place over salad. Drizzle with dressing; if desired, sprinkle with cheese.

1 salad: 321 cal., 25g fat (6g sat. fat), 55mg chol., 529mg sod., 7g carb. (3g sugars, 3g fiber), 18g pro.

HEALTH TIP Include vitamin C-rich fruits or vegetables in spinach salads, like the beefsteak tomato in this recipe, to increase the absorption of iron from the spinach.

GRILLED TILAPIA
WITH MANGO

MAPLE-GLAZED SALMON

MAPLE-GLAZED SALMON

When it comes to family-favorite, heart-healthy salmon recipes, this one is always a hit. I serve it this way at least once a week!
—David Krisko, Becker, MN

....

Takes: 20 min. • **Makes:** 4 servings

- ¼ cup ruby red grapefruit juice
- 2 Tbsp. balsamic vinegar
- 2 Tbsp. maple syrup
- 2 garlic cloves, minced
- 2 tsp. olive oil
- 4 salmon fillets (4 oz. each)
- ¼ tsp. salt
- ¼ tsp. pepper
  Fresh thyme sprigs, optional

1. In a small saucepan, bring grapefruit juice, vinegar, syrup and garlic to a boil. Reduce heat; simmer, uncovered, for 5 minutes. Transfer 2 Tbsp. glaze to a small bowl; add oil. Set the remaining glaze aside.

2. Sprinkle salmon with salt and pepper; place skin side down on lightly oiled grill rack. Grill, covered, over medium heat or broil 4-6 in. from the heat until fish flakes easily with a fork, 10-12 minutes, basting occasionally with maple-oil mixture.

3. Before serving, drizzle salmon with the reserved 2 Tbsp. glaze. If desired, garnish with fresh thyme sprigs.

1 fillet: 266 cal., 15g fat (3g sat. fat), 67mg chol., 218mg sod., 10g carb. (9g sugars, 0 fiber), 23g pro. **Diabetic exchanges:** 3 lean meat, ½ starch, ½ fat.

GRILLED CHICKEN WITH PEACH SAUCE

I've been cooking since I was a young girl growing up on a farm in Indiana. This delicious chicken recipe was adapted from a peach pie filling. I've served it many times to family and friends, and folks always seem to like it.
—Beverly Minton, Milan, MI

....

Takes: 30 min. • **Makes:** 4 servings

- 1 cup sugar
- 2 Tbsp. cornstarch
- 1 cup water
- 2 Tbsp. peach or orange gelatin
- 1 medium peach, peeled and finely chopped
- 4 boneless skinless chicken breast halves (4 oz. each)

1. In a small saucepan, combine sugar, cornstarch and water until smooth. Bring to a boil over medium heat; cook and stir for 2 minutes. Remove from heat. Stir in gelatin powder and peach; mix well until the gelatin powder is dissolved. Set aside 1 cup for serving.

2. Grill chicken, uncovered, over medium heat for 3 minutes on each side. Baste with some of the peach sauce. Continue grilling, basting and turning several times, for 6-8 minutes or until a thermometer reads 170°. Serve with the reserved sauce.

1 serving: 275 cal., 1g fat (0 sat. fat), 16mg chol., 31mg sod., 62g carb. (57g sugars, 1g fiber), 7g pro.

SKEWERED GINGER SHRIMP WITH PLUMS

Sweet, simple and sensational, these shrimp skewers pack in loads of flavor with just four ingredients. Throw them on the grill for a quick dinner or a tasty potluck dish.

—Taste of Home Test Kitchen

Takes: 25 min. • **Makes:** 4 servings

- 1 lb. uncooked large shrimp, peeled and deveined
- 2 medium plums or peaches, cut into wedges
- ½ cup sesame ginger marinade, divided
- 1 green onion, thinly sliced
  Optional: Sesame seeds and lime wedges

1. In a large bowl, combine shrimp and plums. Drizzle with ¼ cup marinade and toss to coat. Alternately thread shrimp and plum wedges on 4 metal or soaked wooden skewers.

2. On a lightly oiled rack, grill skewers, covered, over medium heat or broil 4 in. from heat until the shrimp turn pink, 6-8 minutes, turning occasionally and basting frequently with remaining marinade during the last 3 minutes of cooking. Serve with green onion and, if desired, sesame seeds and lime wedges.

1 skewer: 173 cal., 2g fat (0 sat. fat), 138mg chol., 1295mg sod., 19g carb. (15g sugars, 1g fiber), 19g pro.

GRILLED CABBAGE

PICTURED ON P. 229

The first time I made this, I couldn't believe how good it was! We served it with grilled burgers and our dinner was complete. I never thought I'd skip dessert because I was full from too much cabbage!

—Elizabeth Wheeler, Thornville, OH

Takes: 30 min. • **Makes:** 8 servings

- 1 medium head cabbage (about 1½ lbs.)
- ⅓ cup butter, softened
- ¼ cup chopped onion
- ½ tsp. garlic salt
- ¼ tsp. pepper

1. Cut cabbage into 8 wedges; place on a double thickness of heavy-duty foil (about 24 in. x 12 in.). Spread cut sides with butter. Sprinkle with onion, garlic salt and pepper.

2. Fold foil around the cabbage and seal tightly. Grill, covered, over medium heat for 20 minutes or until tender. Open foil carefully to allow steam to escape.

1 wedge: 98 cal., 8g fat (5g sat. fat), 20mg chol., 188mg sod., 7g carb. (4g sugars, 3g fiber), 2g pro. **Diabetic exchanges:** 1½ fat, 1 vegetable.

READER REVIEW

"The butter, onion and spices went perfectly with the cabbage. That combination and grilling it gave the cabbage a caramelized taste. Very tasty!"

CARRIEBERRY4CHAD, TASTEOFHOME.COM

SKEWERED GINGER SHRIMP WITH PLUMS

BARBECUE SEASONING

SAVORY STEAK RUB

GARLIC- PEPPER RUB

Extraordinary Spices!

A great spice rub makes a simple grilled dish into something special. With these mixtures in your pantry, you'll always be ready for a cookout!

BARBECUE SEASONING

I use this rub on country-style ribs, pork chops and chicken. You'll likely have all of the seasonings on hand to make a batch, and if you don't use it all, it will keep for the next time.

—Rose Rainier, Sheridan, WY

Takes: 10 min. • **Makes:** 1 cup

- ¼ cup beef bouillon granules
- ¼ cup chili powder
- ¼ cup paprika
- 1 Tbsp. sugar
- 1 Tbsp. garlic salt
- 1 Tbsp. onion salt
- 1 tsp. celery salt
- 1 tsp. cayenne pepper
- 1 tsp. pepper
- ½ tsp. curry powder
- ½ tsp. dried oregano

Combine all the ingredients. Store in an airtight container in a cool, dry place up to 6 months.

1 tsp.: 6 cal., 0 fat (0 sat. fat), 0 chol., 476mg sod., 1g carb. (0 sugars, 0 fiber), 0 pro.

GARLIC-PEPPER RUB

This rub adds a tasty mix of garlic, pepper and lemon to any burger. Spice up your grilling experience!

—Ann Marie Moch, Kintyre, ND

Takes: 5 min. • **Makes:** ⅔ cup

- 6 Tbsp. lemon-pepper seasoning
- 2 Tbsp. dried thyme
- 2 Tbsp. paprika
- 2 tsp. garlic powder
- 1 tsp. sugar
- ½ tsp. salt
- ¼ tsp. ground coriander
- ⅛ tsp. ground cumin
- ⅛ tsp. cayenne pepper

Combine all ingredients; store in a covered container. Rub over meat or poultry; let stand at least 30 minutes before grilling or broiling.

1 tsp.: 5 cal., 0 fat (0 sat. fat), 0 chol., 296mg sod., 1g carb. (0 sugars, 0 fiber), 0 pro.

BALSAMIC-GOAT CHEESE GRILL PLUMS

SAVORY STEAK RUB

Marjoram stars in this recipe. I use the rub on a variety of beef cuts—it locks in the natural juices of the meat for mouthwatering results. A batch will make enough to season four or five steaks.

—Donna Brockett, Kingfisher, OK

Takes: 5 min. • **Makes:** ¼ cup

- 1 Tbsp. dried majoram
- 1 Tbsp. dried basil
- 2 tsp. garlic powder
- 2 tsp. dried thyme
- 1 tsp. dried rosemary, crushed
- ¾ tsp. dried oregano

Combine all the ingredients; store in an airtight container. Rub over steaks before grilling or broiling.

1 Tbsp.: 12 cal., 0 fat (0 sat. fat), 0 chol., 2mg sod., 3g carb. (0 sugars, 1g fiber), 1g pro.

BALSAMIC-GOAT CHEESE GRILLED PLUMS

Make a real statement at your summer dinner party with this simple and elegant treat. Ripe plums are grilled, then dressed up with a balsamic reduction and tangy goat cheese.

—Ariana Abelow, Holliston, MA

Takes: 25 min. • **Makes:** 8 servings

- 1 cup balsamic vinegar
- 2 tsp. grated lemon zest
- 4 medium firm plums, halved and pitted
- ½ cup crumbled goat cheese

1. For the glaze, in a small saucepan, combine vinegar and lemon zest; bring to a boil. Cook 10-12 minutes or until mixture is thickened and reduced to about ⅓ cup (do not overcook).

2. Grill plums, covered, over medium heat 2-3 minutes on each side or until tender. Drizzle with glaze; top with cheese.

1 plum half with 1 Tbsp. cheese and 2 tsp. glaze: 58 cal., 2g fat (1g sat. fat), 9mg chol., 41mg sod., 9g carb. (8g sugars, 1g fiber), 2g pro. **Diabetic exchanges:** ½ starch, ½ fat.

SPICY FLANK STEAK

The cool and creamy sour cream sauce in this recipe is a wonderful companion to the spicy steak. You can grill or broil the steak, whichever you prefer.
—*Taste of Home* Test Kitchen

Takes: 25 min. • **Makes:** 6 servings

- ⅓ cup sour cream
- 2 Tbsp. mayonnaise
- ½ tsp. garlic powder
- ¼ tsp. celery salt
- 2 Tbsp. chili sauce
- 1 Tbsp. lime juice
- ½ to 1 tsp. crushed red pepper flakes
- ¼ tsp. salt
- 1 beef flank steak (1½ lbs.)

1. In a small bowl, combine sour cream, mayonnaise, garlic powder and celery salt; cover and refrigerate until serving. Combine the chili sauce, lime juice, pepper flakes and salt; brush on each side of steak.
2. Place on a lightly oiled grill rack over medium heat or broil 2-3 in. from the heat for 4-6 minutes on each side or until meat reaches desired doneness (for medium-rare, a thermometer should read 135°; medium, 140°; medium-well, 145°). Let stand for 5 minutes. To serve, thinly slice across the grain. Serve with sour cream sauce.

3 oz. cooked beef with about 1 Tbsp. sauce: 230 cal., 14g fat (6g sat. fat), 57mg chol., 318mg sod., 2g carb. (2g sugars, 0 fiber), 22g pro.
HEALTH TIP Flank steak is one of many cuts of lean beef. It packs in 10 essential nutrients, including more than 20 grams of protein per serving. Other lean cuts include top sirloin steak, strip steak and tenderloin.

GRILLED CRANBERRY PEAR CRUMBLE

GRILLED CRANBERRY PEAR CRUMBLE

My husband loves it when I make dessert. Fruit crisps are quick to prepare, so I make them often! I created this fall-flavored grilled version with fresh pears and items I had on hand. We loved it.
—Ronna Farley, Rockville, MD

Takes: 30 min. • **Makes:** 6 servings

- 3 medium ripe pears, sliced
- ½ cup dried cranberries
- ¼ cup sugar
- 2 Tbsp. all-purpose flour
- ¼ tsp. ground cinnamon
- 1 Tbsp. butter

TOPPING
- 2 Tbsp. butter, melted
- ¼ tsp. ground cinnamon
- 1 cup granola without raisins

1. Toss pears and cranberries with sugar, flour and cinnamon. Place 1 Tbsp. butter in a 9-in. cast-iron skillet. Place on grill rack over medium heat until the butter is melted. Stir in fruit; grill, covered, until pears are tender, 15-20 minutes, stirring occasionally.
2. For topping, mix melted butter and cinnamon; toss with granola. Sprinkle over pears. Grill, covered, 5 minutes. Serve warm.

1 serving: 258 cal., 9g fat (4g sat. fat), 15mg chol., 54mg sod., 47g carb. (29g sugars, 7g fiber), 4g pro.

GRILLED PORK & POBLANO PEPPERS

My husband and I entertain a lot in summer, and this has quickly become the most-requested dish. I usually serve it with Mexican rice and a tossed salad.
—Donna Gay Harris, Springdale, AR

Prep: 10 min. • **Grill:** 20 min.
Makes: 6 servings

- 3 large poblano peppers
- 1½ cups shredded Monterey Jack cheese
- 4½ tsp. chili powder
- 1½ tsp. onion powder
- 1½ tsp. ground cumin
- ½ tsp. garlic powder
- ¼ tsp. salt
- ⅛ tsp. aniseed, ground
- ⅛ tsp. cayenne pepper
- 2 pork tenderloins (about 1 lb. each)

1. Cut peppers in half and remove seeds. Stuff peppers with cheese; set aside.

2. Combine the seasonings; rub over pork. Grill, covered, over medium-hot heat until a thermometer reads 145°, about 15 minutes. Place the poblano peppers over indirect heat; cook until peppers are tender and cheese is melted, 8-10 minutes.
Note: Wear disposable gloves to cut hot peppers; the oils can burn exposed skin. Avoid touching your face.
3 oz. cooked pork with ½ pepper: 304 cal., 14g fat (7g sat. fat), 110mg chol., 389mg sod., 5g carb. (2g sugars, 2g fiber), 38g pro.

HERBED POTATO PACKS

Fingerlings are small, waxy and tender, and are often sold in bags of assorted colors (red, purple and gold). These little potatoes feel festive in convenient single-serve foil packs.
—*Taste of Home* Test Kitchen

Takes: 25 min. • **Makes:** 4 servings

- 2 lbs. fingerling potatoes
- 2 Tbsp. olive oil
- 2 garlic cloves, minced
- 1 tsp. salt
- 2 tsp. minced fresh thyme
- ½ tsp. coarsely ground pepper

1. Pierce potatoes with a fork. Place in a large microwave-safe dish; cover and microwave for 4-7 minutes or until crisp-tender, stirring halfway. Add the remaining ingredients; toss to coat.
2. Place one-fourth of the potatoes on a double thickness of heavy-duty foil (about 14x12 in.). Fold the foil around potatoes and seal tightly. Repeat with the remaining potatoes.
3. Grill, covered, over medium-high heat for 6-9 minutes on each side or until the potatoes are tender. Open foil carefully to allow steam to escape.
1 packet: 178 cal., 4g fat (0 sat. fat), 0 chol., 597mg sod., 30g carb. (1g sugars, 4g fiber), 5g pro. **Diabetic exchanges:** 2 starch, ½ fat.

GRILLED PORK & POBLANO PEPPERS

**GRILLED JERK
SHRIMP ORZO SALAD**

GRILLED JERK SHRIMP ORZO SALAD

It doesn't matter what the temperature outside is—you'll feel as if you're in the Caribbean when you take your first bite of this salad.
—Eileen Budnyk, Palm Beach Gardens, FL

Prep: 25 min. • **Grill:** 10 min.
Makes: 2 servings

- ⅓ cup uncooked whole wheat orzo pasta
- ½ lb. uncooked shrimp (31-40 per lb.), peeled and deveined
- 1 Tbsp. Caribbean jerk seasoning
- 1 medium ear sweet corn
- 1 tsp. olive oil
- 6 fresh asparagus spears, trimmed
- 1 small sweet red pepper, chopped

DRESSING
- 3 Tbsp. lime juice
- 1 Tbsp. water
- 1 Tbsp. olive oil
- ⅛ tsp. salt
- ⅛ tsp. pepper

1. Cook orzo according to the package directions. Drain and rinse with cold water; drain well.
2. Meanwhile, toss shrimp with jerk seasoning; thread onto metal or soaked wooden skewers. Brush corn with oil.
3. On a covered grill over medium heat, cook the ear of corn until tender and lightly browned, 10-12 minutes, turning occasionally; cook asparagus until crisp-tender, 5-7 minutes, turning occasionally. Grill shrimp until they turn pink, 1-2 minutes per side.
4. Cut corn from cob; cut asparagus into 1-in. pieces. Remove shrimp from skewers. In a large bowl, combine orzo, grilled vegetables, shrimp and red pepper. Whisk together the dressing ingredients; toss with salad.

2 cups: 340 cal., 12g fat (2g sat. fat), 138mg chol., 716mg sod., 35g carb. (6g sugars, 7g fiber), 25g pro. **Diabetic exchanges:** 2 starch, 3 lean meat, 1 vegetable, 1 fat.

LEMONY GRILLED SALMON FILLETS WITH DILL SAUCE

LEMONY GRILLED SALMON FILLETS WITH DILL SAUCE

Grilled lemons add smoky tartness to a butter sauce made to enjoy with grilled salmon. A touch of dill adds a fresh, clean finish.
—April Lane, Greeneville, TN

Takes: 30 min.
Makes: 4 servings (¾ cup sauce)

- 2 medium lemons
- 4 salmon fillets (6 oz. each)

LEMON-DILL SAUCE
- 2½ tsp. cornstarch
- ½ cup water
- ⅓ cup lemon juice
- 4 tsp. butter
- 3 lemon slices, quartered
- 1 Tbsp. snipped fresh dill
- ¼ tsp. salt
- ⅛ tsp. dried chervil
  Dash cayenne pepper

1. Trim both ends from each lemon; cut lemons into thick slices. Grill salmon and lemon slices, covered, over high heat on an oiled grill rack or broil 3-4 in. from the heat for 3-5 minutes on each side or until the fish flakes easily with a fork and the lemons are lightly browned.
2. For the sauce, in a small saucepan, combine cornstarch, water and lemon juice; add butter. Cook and stir over medium heat until thickened and bubbly. Remove from heat; stir in the quartered lemon slices and seasonings. Serve with salmon and grilled lemon slices.

1 fillet with 3 Tbsp. sauce: 320 cal., 20g fat (6g sat. fat), 97mg chol., 266mg sod., 6g carb. (1g sugars, 1g fiber), 29g pro. **Diabetic exchanges:** 3 lean meat, 1 fat.

**GINGER-GLAZED
GRILLED HONEYDEW**

GINGER-GLAZED
GRILLED HONEYDEW

*If you've never grilled fruit like this before,
you're in for a real treat! I love the idea of
cooking everything from appetizers to
desserts on the grill. This makes a sweet,
light treat for summer.*
—Jacqueline Correa, Landing, NJ

Takes: 25 min.
Makes: 6 servings

- ¼ cup peach preserves
- 1 Tbsp. lemon juice
- 1 Tbsp. finely chopped
  crystallized ginger
- 2 tsp. grated lemon zest
- ⅛ tsp. ground cloves
- 1 medium honeydew melon,
  cut into 2-in. cubes

1. In a small bowl, combine the first
5 ingredients. Thread honeydew onto
6 metal or soaked wooden skewers;
brush with half the glaze.

2. On a lightly oiled rack, grill honeydew,
covered, over medium-high heat or broil
4 in. from the heat just until the melon
begins to soften and brown, 4-6 minutes,
turning and basting frequently with the
remaining glaze.
1 skewer: 101 cal., 0 fat (0 sat. fat),
0 chol., 18mg sod., 26g carb. (23g sugars,
1g fiber), 1g pro. **Diabetic exchanges:**
1 fruit, ½ starch.
HEALTH TIP These honeydew skewers
are a sweet (and delicious) way to get a
healthy dose of vitamin C and potassium.

GRILLED PEPPERED STEAKS

*I once wanted a peppered steak for
supper, so I tossed some spices together
and came up with this recipe. My family
thoroughly enjoyed it.*
—Stephanie Moon, Boise, ID

Takes: 25 min. • **Makes:** 4 servings

- 1½ to 2 tsp. coarsely ground pepper
- 1 tsp. onion salt

- 1 tsp. garlic salt
- ¼ tsp. paprika
- 4 boneless beef top loin steaks
  (8 oz. each)

1. In a small bowl, combine the pepper,
onion salt, garlic salt and, if desired,
paprika. Rub onto both sides of steaks.
2. Grill, covered, over medium heat until
meat reaches desired doneness (for
medium-rare, a thermometer should
read 135°; medium, 140°; medium-well,
145°), 8-10 minutes on each side.
Note: Top loin steak may be labeled as strip
steak, Kansas City steak, New York strip
steak, ambassador steak or boneless club
steak in your region.
1 steak: 301 cal., 10g fat (4g sat. fat),
100mg chol., 1039mg sod., 1g carb.
(0 sugars, 0 fiber), 48g pro.

STEAK SANDWICH KABOBS

Seasoned steak, grilled with bread and veggies and topped with cheese, makes a fantastic meal. Deli coleslaw, spruced up with chopped walnuts, is a great pairing.
—*Taste of Home* Test Kitchen

Takes: 25 min. • **Makes:** 4 servings

- 1 lb. beef top sirloin steak, cut into 1-in. cubes
- 1 tsp. steak seasoning
- 1 medium sweet red pepper, cut into 1-in. chunks
- 6 oz. focaccia bread, cut into 1-in. cubes
- 1 medium onion, cut into 1-in. chunks
- 1 Tbsp. olive oil
- 3 slices provolone cheese, cut into strips
- 2 cups deli coleslaw
- ½ cup chopped walnuts

1. Sprinkle beef with steak seasoning. Alternately thread the beef, red pepper, bread cubes and onion onto 4 metal or soaked wooden skewers; brush with oil.
2. Grill, covered, over medium heat for 8-10 minutes or until the meat reaches desired doneness, turning occasionally. For medium-rare, a thermometer should read 135°; medium, 140°; medium-well, 145°. Top with cheese; grill 1-2 minutes longer or until cheese is melted.
3. Combine coleslaw and walnuts. Serve with kabobs.
1 kabob with ½ cup coleslaw: 597 cal., 33g fat (6g sat. fat), 83mg chol., 729mg sod., 45g carb. (17g sugars, 5g fiber), 32g pro.

GRILLED STEAK BRUSCHETTA SALAD FOR 2

Fire up the grill for this tasty salad. The meat will be done in a snap, leaving you more time to enjoy the summer evening.
—Devon Delaney, Westport, CT

Takes: 25 min. • **Makes:** 2 servings

- ½ lb. beef tenderloin steaks (1 in. thick)
- ¼ tsp. salt
- ⅛ tsp. pepper
- 2 slices Italian bread (½ in. thick)
- 1 cup fresh arugula or fresh baby spinach
- ⅓ cup bruschetta topping
- ⅓ cup blue cheese salad dressing

1. Sprinkle steaks with salt and pepper. Grill, covered, over medium heat for 6-8 minutes on each side or until the meat reaches desired doneness (for medium-rare, a thermometer should read 135°; medium, 140°; medium-well, 145°). Let stand for 5 minutes.
2. Grill bread, covered, for 1-2 minutes on each side or until toasted; place on salad plates.
3. Thinly slice steak; arrange over the toast. Top with arugula and bruschetta topping; sprinkle with cheese if desired. Drizzle with dressing.
Note: Look for bruschetta topping in the pasta aisle or your grocer's deli case.
1 serving: 460 cal., 31g fat (7g sat. fat), 57mg chol., 1183mg sod., 17g carb. (3g sugars, 1g fiber), 28g pro.

STEAK SANDWICH KABOBS

Potlucks & Parties

When you're stumped for what to take to your next potluck, look no further than this chapter. All year round, your contribution will be the talk of the town!

Luscious Almond Cheesecake (p. 249) **Mini Sausage Quiches** (p. 258) **Aunt Frances' Lemonade** (p. 250)
Garden Bounty Panzanella Salad (p. 256) **Reese's Chocolate Snack Cake** (p. 261)

CITRUS CIDER PUNCH

I share this refreshing punch recipe with people who visit our apple cider mill. It's the perfect beverage for crisp autumn gatherings.
—Carolyn Beck, St Johns, MI

Takes: 5 min.
Makes: 19 servings (4¾ qt.)

- 1 gallon apple cider, chilled
- 1 can (12 oz.) frozen lemonade concentrate, thawed
- 1 medium lemon, sliced
- 4 spiced apple rings

In a large punch bowl, combine cider and lemonade. Add lemon slices and apple rings. If desired, serve with additional lemon slices and apple rings.

1 cup: 138 cal., 0 fat (0 sat. fat), 0 chol., 22mg sod., 35g carb. (30g sugars, 0 fiber), 0 pro.

GRILLED GLAZED DRUMMIES

GRILLED GLAZED DRUMMIES

My family prefers these mild, slightly sweet chicken wings to the traditional hot wings. They've a favorite at so many of our get-togethers.
—Laura Mahaffey, Annapolis, MD

Prep: 10 min. + marinating • **Grill:** 15 min.
Makes: about 2 dozen

- 1 cup ketchup
- ⅓ cup reduced-sodium soy sauce
- 4 tsp. honey
- ¾ tsp. ground ginger
- ½ tsp. garlic powder
- 3 lbs. fresh or frozen chicken drumettes, thawed
  Optional: Sliced green onions and ranch dressing

1. In a small bowl, combine the first 5 ingredients. Pour 1 cup marinade into a large shallow dish. Add the chicken; turn to coat. Cover and refrigerate for at least 4 hours or overnight. Cover and refrigerate the remaining marinade for basting.

2. Drain chicken, discarding marinade. Grill, covered, over medium heat for 15-20 minutes or until the juices run clear, turning and basting occasionally with the reserved marinade. If desired, top with sliced green onions and serve with ranch dressing on the side.

1 piece: 141 cal., 9g fat (2g sat. fat), 43mg chol., 311mg sod., 3g carb. (3g sugars, 0 fiber), 11g pro.

MINI PIZZA CUPS

Served hot or cold, these little pizzas are wonderful. Their small size makes them ideal for an after-school snack or kid-friendly party. Plus, they're so easy to make, your little ones can help you in the kitchen!
—Jane Jones, Cedar, MN

Prep: 25 min. • **Bake:** 15 min.
Makes: 32 appetizers

- 2 tubes (8 oz. each) refrigerated round crescent rolls
- 1 can (8 oz.) pizza sauce
- ¼ cup finely chopped onion
- ⅓ cup finely chopped green pepper
- 2 oz. sliced turkey pepperoni, chopped
- 1 cup shredded part-skim mozzarella cheese

1. Preheat oven to 375°. Separate tubes of dough into 8 rolls each; halve the rolls. Press dough onto the bottom and up the sides of miniature muffin cups coated with cooking spray.
2. Spoon pizza sauce into each cup. Sprinkle with onion, green pepper, pepperoni and cheese. Bake until the crusts are browned and the cheese is melted, 15-18 minutes.

1 pizza cup: 75 cal., 4g fat (2g sat. fat), 4mg chol., 193mg sod., 7g carb. (1g sugars, trace fiber), 3g pro.

MINI PIZZA CUPS

LUSCIOUS ALMOND CHEESECAKE

PICTURED ON P. 247
Almonds and almond extract give a traditional sour cream-topped cheesecake a tasty twist.
—Brenda Clifford, Overland Park, KS

Prep: 15 min. • **Bake:** 55 min. + chilling
Makes: 16 servings

- 1¼ cups crushed vanilla wafers (about 40 wafers)
- ¾ cup finely chopped almonds
- ¼ cup sugar
- ⅓ cup butter, melted

FILLING
- 4 pkg. (8 oz. each) cream cheese, softened
- 1¼ cups sugar
- 4 large eggs, room temperature, lightly beaten
- 1½ tsp. almond extract
- 1 tsp. vanilla extract

TOPPING
- 2 cups sour cream
- ¼ cup sugar
- 1 tsp. vanilla extract
- ⅛ cup toasted sliced almonds

1. Preheat oven to 350°. In a bowl, combine the wafer crumbs, almonds and sugar; stir in butter and mix well. Press into the bottom of a greased 10-in. springform pan; set aside.
2. In a large bowl, beat cream cheese and sugar until smooth. Add eggs; beat on low speed just until combined. Stir in extracts. Pour into crust. Place on a baking sheet.
3. Bake for 50-55 minutes or until the center is almost set. Remove from oven; let stand for 5 minutes (leave oven on). Combine the sour cream, sugar and vanilla. Spoon around the edge of the cheesecake; carefully spread over the filling. Return cheesecake to oven and bake 5 minutes longer. Cool on a wire rack for 10 minutes. Carefully run a knife around the edge of the pan to loosen; cool 1 hour longer. Refrigerate overnight.
4. Just before serving, sprinkle with almonds and remove the sides of the pan. Refrigerate any leftovers.

1 slice: 329 cal., 20g fat (10g sat. fat), 100mg chol., 140mg sod., 32g carb. (26g sugars, 1g fiber), 5g pro.

AUNT FRANCES' LEMONADE

When I was growing up, my sister and I spent a week each summer with our Aunt Frances, who kept a stoneware crock filled with this thirst-quenching lemonade in the refrigerator. It makes a refreshing drink after a hot day of running around.
—Debbie Reinhart, New Cumberland, PA

Takes: 15 min.
Makes: 16 servings (1 gallon)

5 lemons
5 limes
5 oranges
3 qt. water
1½ to 2 cups sugar

1. Squeeze the juice from 4 each of the lemons, limes and oranges; pour into a gallon container.
2. Add water and sugar to the juices; mix well. Store in the refrigerator.
3. Thinly slice the remaining fruit and set aside for garnish. Serve lemonade over ice with fruit slices.

1 cup: 92 cal., 0 fat (0 sat. fat), 0 chol., 1mg sod., 24g carb. (21g sugars, 1g fiber), 0 pro.

POTLUCK ENCHILADA MEATBALLS

POTLUCK ENCHILADA MEATBALLS

This is a twist on the ordinary potluck meatballs. If you like, try serving them with tortilla chip scoops—they taste like mini tacos! Set them out on the buffet with traditional taco toppings.
—Terina Lewis, Decatur, IL

Prep: 1 hour + cooling • **Cook:** 3 hours
Makes: 6 dozen

2 pkg. (8½ oz. each) cornbread/muffin mix
2 envelopes reduced-sodium taco seasoning, divided
2 large eggs, lightly beaten
3 cans (10 oz. each) enchilada sauce, divided
2 lbs. lean ground beef (90% lean)
1 jar (16 oz.) salsa
1 can (4 oz.) chopped green chiles
1 cup shredded Mexican cheese blend, divided

1. Preheat oven to 400°. Prepare and bake muffin mix according to package directions. Cool completely and crumble; transfer to a large bowl. Add 1 envelope taco seasoning, eggs, 1½ cups enchilada sauce and meat; mix lightly but thoroughly. Shape meat mixture into 1½-in. balls; bake on greased racks in 15x10x1-in. baking pans lined with foil until lightly browned, 10-12 minutes.
2. Place meatballs in a 5- or 6-qt. slow cooker. Combine remaining enchilada sauce, salsa, chiles, ½ cup cheese and remaining envelope taco seasoning; pour over the meatballs. Sprinkle with remaining cheese. Cook, covered, on low until meatballs are cooked through, about 3 hours.

1 meatball: 68 cal., 3g fat (1g sat. fat), 20mg chol., 227mg sod., 7g carb. (2g sugars, 0 fiber), 4g pro.

PULL-APART GARLIC BREAD

People go wild over this golden, garlicky loaf whenever I serve it. There's intense flavor in every bite.
—Carol Shields, Summerville, PA

Prep: 10 min. + rising • **Bake:** 30 min.
Makes: 16 servings

- ¼ cup butter, melted
- 1 Tbsp. dried parsley flakes
- 1 tsp. garlic powder
- ¼ tsp. garlic salt
- 1 loaf (1 lb.) frozen white bread dough, thawed

1. In a small bowl, combine the butter, parsley, garlic powder and garlic salt. Cut dough into 1-in. pieces; dip into butter mixture. Layer in a greased 9x5-in. loaf pan. Cover and let rise until doubled, about 1 hour.
2. Bake at 350° for 30 minutes or until golden brown.

1 serving: 104 cal., 4g fat (2g sat. fat), 8mg chol., 215mg sod., 15g carb. (1g sugars, 1g fiber), 3g pro.

PARTY PITAS

Whenever the ladies of our church host a gathering, these pita sandwiches are sure to be on the menu. Not only are they easy and delicious, they add color to the table.
—Janette Root, Ellensburg, WA

Takes: 15 min. • **Makes:** 16 pieces

- 1 pkg. (8 oz.) cream cheese, softened
- ½ cup mayonnaise
- ½ tsp. dill weed
- ¼ tsp. garlic salt
- 4 whole pita breads
- 1½ cups fresh baby spinach
- 1 lb. shaved fully cooked ham
- ½ lb. thinly sliced Monterey Jack cheese

1. Mix cream cheese, mayonnaise, dill week and garlic salt. Carefully cut each pita horizontally in half; spread 2 Tbsp. filling mixture onto each cut surface.
2. On 4 pita halves, layer spinach, ham and cheese. Top with the remaining pita halves. Cut each sandwich into 4 wedges; secure with toothpicks.

1 piece: 225 cal., 15g fat (6g sat. fat), 45mg chol., 557mg sod., 10g carb. (1g sugars, 0 fiber), 12g pro.

PULL-APART GARLIC BREAD

MACARONI COLESLAW

1 cup soy sauce
6 green onions, divided
1 Tbsp. sesame seeds

Using a sharp knife, cut through the 2 wing joints; discard wing tips. Place remaining wing pieces in a 4 or 5-qt. slow cooker. Stir in barbecue sauce, soy sauce and 4 green onions. Cook, covered, on high until tender, 3-4 hours. Sprinkle with the sesame seeds and remaining green onions.
1 piece: 68 cal., 4g fat (1g sat. fat), 14mg chol., 452mg sod., 3g carb. (2g sugars, 0 fiber), 6g pro.

5i BACON-WRAPPED STUFFED JALAPENOS

Sunday is grill-out day for my husband, and these zesty peppers are one of his specialties. We usually feature them at our annual Daytona 500 party—they disappear from the appetizer tray in no time.
—Therese Pollard, Hurst, TX

Prep: 1 hour • **Grill:** 35 min.
Makes: 2 dozen

24 medium jalapeno peppers
1 lb. uncooked chorizo or bulk spicy pork sausage
2 cups shredded cheddar cheese
12 bacon strips, cut in half

1. Make a lengthwise cut in each jalapeno, about 1/8 in. deep; remove seeds. Combine sausage and cheese; stuff into jalapenos. Wrap each in a piece of bacon and secure with a toothpick.
2. Grill, covered, over indirect medium heat for 36-40 minutes, turning once. (A thermometer should read 160°.)
3. Grill, covered, over direct heat until bacon is crisp, 1-2 minutes.
Note: Wear disposable gloves when cutting hot peppers; the oils can burn exposed skin. Avoid touching your face.
1 stuffed jalapeno: 132 cal., 10g fat (4g sat. fat), 30mg chol., 365mg sod., 1g carb. (1g sugars, 0 fiber), 8g pro.

MACARONI COLESLAW

My friend Peggy brought this coleslaw to one of our picnics, and everyone liked it so much, we all had to have the recipe!
—Sandra Matteson, Westhope, ND

Prep: 25 min. + chilling
Makes: 16 servings

1 pkg. (7 oz.) ring macaroni or ditalini
1 pkg. (14 oz.) coleslaw mix
2 medium onions, finely chopped
2 celery ribs, finely chopped
1 medium cucumber, finely chopped
1 medium green pepper, finely chopped
1 can (8 oz.) whole water chestnuts, drained and chopped

DRESSING
1½ cups Miracle Whip Light
⅓ cup sugar
¼ cup cider vinegar
½ tsp. salt
¼ tsp. pepper

1. Cook macaroni according to package directions; drain and rinse in cold water. Transfer to a large bowl; add the coleslaw mix, onions, celery, cucumber, green pepper and water chestnuts.

2. In a small bowl, whisk the dressing ingredients. Pour over salad; toss to coat. Cover and refrigerate for at least 1 hour.
¾ cup: 150 cal., 5g fat (1g sat. fat), 6mg chol., 286mg sod., 24g carb. (12g sugars, 2g fiber), 3g pro. **Diabetic exchanges:** 1 starch, 1 vegetable, 1 fat.

> **DID YOU KNOW?**
> The term coleslaw is derived from the Dutch word *koolsla* translated as "cabbage salad." The term has evolved to refer to many types of crunchy, shredded-vegetable salads.

5i SO-EASY STICKY CHICKEN WINGS

These tangy wings have been a family favorite ever since my neighbor shared them at a potluck. The Asian flavors of soy and sesame take them beyond the expected barbecue wings!
—Jo Vanderwolf, Lillooet, BC

Prep: 10 min. • **Cook:** 3 hours
Makes: 40 servings

4 lbs. chicken wings
1 cup barbecue sauce

BACON-WRAPPED STUFFED JALAPENOS

ITALIAN HERB &
CHEESE BREADSTICKS

ITALIAN HERB & CHEESE BREADSTICKS

Thanks to frozen bread dough, these delectable breadsticks couldn't be easier to make. The cheesy bites are perfect dipped in warm marinara sauce.
—Rebekah Beyer, Sabetha, KS

Prep: 20 min. • **Bake:** 20 min.
Makes: 2 dozen

- 1   loaf (1 lb.) frozen bread dough, thawed
- ⅓   cup butter, softened
- 1   Tbsp. Italian seasoning
- 1   garlic clove, minced
- ¾   cup shredded part-skim mozzarella cheese
- ½   cup grated Parmesan cheese, divided
      Marinara sauce, warmed, optional

1. On a lightly floured surface, roll dough into a 12-in. square. Mix butter, seasoning and garlic; spread over dough. Sprinkle mozzarella cheese and ¼ cup Parmesan cheese over butter mixture. Fold dough in thirds over filling; pinch seams to seal.
2. Cut the filled dough crosswise into twenty-four ½-in.-wide strips. Twist each strip 2 or 3 times. Place 2 in. apart on greased baking sheets. Cover and let rise until almost doubled, about 30 minutes.
3. Preheat oven to 375°. Sprinkle with the remaining Parmesan cheese. Bake until golden brown, 20-22 minutes. If desired, serve with marinara sauce.

1 breadstick: 93 cal., 4g fat (2g sat. fat), 10mg chol., 180mg sod., 10g carb. (1g sugars, 1g fiber), 3g pro.

TEST KITCHEN TIP
Italian seasoning blends might contain any number of herbs, including marjoram, thyme, rosemary, savory, sage, oregano and basil. You can mix up your own—try substituting ¼ tsp. each of basil, thyme, rosemary and oregano for each teaspoon of Italian seasoning.

NANA'S ROCKY ROAD FUDGE

We make rocky road-style fudge every Christmas, but why wait until the holidays for a recipe this good? There's nothing that says you can't have this delightful treat any time of year.
—Ashley Berry, Montgomery Village, MD

Prep: 15 min. • **Cook:** 5 min. + chilling
Makes: about 2½ lbs.

- 1½ tsp. plus 1 Tbsp. butter, divided
- 2 cups semisweet chocolate chips
- 1 can (14 oz.) sweetened condensed milk
- 2 cups salted peanuts, plus additional for topping
- 1 pkg. (10½ oz.) miniature marshmallows, plus additional for topping

1. Line a 13x9-in. baking pan with foil, letting the ends of the foil extend over the sides of the pan by 1 in. Grease the foil with 1½ tsp. butter; set aside.
2. In a large saucepan, combine the chocolate chips, milk and the remaining butter. Cook and stir over medium heat until the mixture is smooth. Remove from the heat; stir in peanuts.
3. Place marshmallows in a large bowl; add the chocolate mixture and stir well. Spread into prepared pan. Sprinkle with additional peanuts and marshmallows. Refrigerate until firm.
4. Using foil, lift fudge out of pan. Cut into 1½-in. squares.

1 piece: 153 cal., 8g fat (4g sat. fat), 4mg chol., 39mg sod., 20g carb. (16g sugars, 1g fiber), 3g pro.

CHEESE & SAUSAGE APPETIZERS

I got this recipe from a home economics instructor when I was living and teaching in Oklahoma. I think it represents the Southwest because of its spicy flavor. It can be used as an appetizer before a Mexican meal or served as a snack.
—Debbie Hogan, Tsaile, AZ

Prep: 20 min. • **Bake:** 15 min.
Makes: about 5½ dozen appetizers

- 4 cups shredded cheddar cheese
- 1 cup butter, softened
- 2 cups all-purpose flour
- ½ tsp. salt
- ½ tsp. black or cayenne pepper
- 8 oz. pork sausage, cooked and drained

1. Preheat oven to 400°. In large bowl, beat the cheese, butter, flour, salt and pepper on medium-low speed. Stir in cooked sausage. Form dough into 1-in. balls; place on ungreased baking sheet.
2. Bake for 15-20 minutes or until light golden brown. Serve warm or cold. Store in refrigerator or freezer.

3 appetizers: 208 cal., 16g fat (10g sat. fat), 48mg chol., 304mg sod., 10g carb. (0 sugars, 0 fiber), 6g pro.

READER REVIEW

"This is one of my staples for the the holidays—they always disappear from the plate by evening's end."
RITASISTOS, TASTEOFHOME.COM

NANA'S ROCKY ROAD FUDGE

GARDEN BOUNTY PANZANELLA SALAD

When my sister gave me fresh tomatoes and basil from her garden, I made this traditional salad. The longer it sits, the more the bread soaks up the seasonings.
—Jannine Fisk, Malden, MA

Prep: 15 min. • **Cook:** 20 min.
Makes: 16 servings

- ¼ cup olive oil
- 12 oz. French or ciabatta bread, cut into 1-in. cubes (about 12 cups)
- 4 large tomatoes, coarsely chopped
- 1 English cucumber, coarsely chopped
- 1 medium green pepper, cut into 1-in. pieces
- 1 medium sweet yellow pepper, cut into 1-in. pieces
- 1 small red onion, halved and thinly sliced
- ½ cup coarsely chopped fresh basil
- ¼ cup grated Parmesan cheese
- ¾ tsp. kosher salt
- ¼ tsp. coarsely ground pepper
- ½ cup Italian salad dressing

Heat 2 Tbsp. oil in a skillet over medium heat. Add half the bread cubes; cook and stir until toasted, about 8 minutes. Remove from pan. Repeat with remaining oil and bread. Combine bread, tomatoes, cucumber, peppers, onion, basil, cheese, salt and pepper. Toss with dressing.

1 cup: 131 cal., 6g fat (1g sat. fat), 1mg chol., 310mg sod., 18g carb. (3g sugars, 2g fiber), 3g pro.

RHUBARB TORTE

RHUBARB TORTE

Each year when Grandmother asked what kind of birthday cake I wanted, I always said I wanted her rhubarb torte!
—Lois Heintz, Holmen, WI

Prep: 20 min. • **Bake:** 1 hour
Makes: 16 servings

- 1¾ cups all-purpose flour
- 1 tsp. baking powder
- 2 large egg yolks, room temperature
- ½ cup shortening
- 2 Tbsp. sugar
- ½ cup chopped walnuts

FILLING
- 4 cups chopped fresh or frozen rhubarb
- 2 cups sugar
- 2 large egg yolks, room temperature
- ¼ cup all-purpose flour

MERINGUE
- 4 large egg whites, room temperature
- ½ cup sugar
- 1 tsp. vanilla extract

1. Preheat oven to 350°. Mix the first 6 ingredients with a fork until crumbly. Press into a greased 13x9-in. baking dish.
2. Combine the filling ingredients; mix well. Pour over the crust. Bake for 50-60 minutes.
3. For the meringue topping, beat egg whites until stiff. Gradually add sugar and vanilla, beating well. Spread over the hot filling. Return to the oven until lightly browned, 10-15 minutes longer.

1 piece: 289 cal., 10g fat (2g sat. fat), 53mg chol., 42mg sod., 47g carb. (33g sugars, 1g fiber), 4g pro.

GARLIC HERBED BEEF TENDERLOIN

You don't need much seasoning to add flavor to a good-quality beef roast. The mild blend of rosemary, basil and garlic does the trick with this tenderloin.
—Ruth Andrewson, Leavenworth, WA

Prep: 5 min. • **Bake:** 40 min. + standing
Makes: 12 servings

- 1 beef tenderloin roast (3 lbs.)
- 2 tsp. olive oil
- 2 garlic cloves, minced
- 1½ tsp. dried basil
- 1½ tsp. dried rosemary, crushed
- 1 tsp. salt
- 1 tsp. pepper

1. Preheat oven to 425°. Tie tenderloin at 2-in. intervals with kitchen string. Combine oil and garlic; brush over meat. Combine basil, rosemary, salt and pepper; sprinkle evenly over meat. Place on a rack in a shallow roasting pan.

2. Bake, uncovered, until meat reaches desired doneness (for medium-rare, a thermometer should read 135°; medium, 140°; medium-well, 145°), 40-50 minutes. Let stand for 10 minutes before slicing.

3 oz. cooked beef: 198 cal., 10g fat (4g sat. fat), 78mg chol., 249mg sod., 1g carb. (0 sugars, 0 fiber), 25g pro.
Diabetic exchanges: 3 lean meat.

APPLE WONTON BUNDLES

When preparing the food for a fondue party, don't forget to have a fondue dessert as well! These deliciously different treats taste just like caramel apples.
—Darlene Brenden, Salem, OR

Prep: 20 min. • **Cook:** 20 min.
Makes: 64 bundles

- 4 medium tart apples, peeled
- 64 wonton wrappers
- 2 to 3 cups canola oil
- 1 jar (12 oz.) caramel ice cream topping, warmed

1. Cut each apple into 4 wedges; cut each wedges into 4 pieces. Place a piece of apple in the center of each wonton wrapper. Brush edges of wrapper with water and bring up around apple; pinch to seal. Cover until ready to cook.

2. Heat oil in a fondue pot to 375°. Use fondue forks to cook wonton bundles until golden brown, about 1 minute. Cool slightly. Serve with caramel topping.

4 wontons: 403 cal., 28g fat (4g sat. fat), 3mg chol., 257mg sod., 37g carb. (17g sugars, 1g fiber), 3g pro.

READER REVIEW

"These are so easy, and so good! My husband loves them and declared the recipe a winner! I'll be making these frequently, and it's so easy in my deep fryer."

ALBERTAGIRL40, TASTEOFHOME.COM

GARLIC HERBED BEEF TENDERLOIN

5i

SUMMERTIME WATERMELON PUNCH FOR A CROWD

I attended a patio party years ago where the hostess had a clever watermelon bowl with a scalloped edge and filled with this punch. It was the hit of the party, and she was kind enough to share the delicious punch recipe with me.
—Joan Hallford, North Richland Hills, TX

Prep: 30 min. + chilling
Makes: 32 servings

- 30 **cups cubed seedless watermelon (about 10 lbs.)**
- 1 **can (12 oz.) frozen orange juice concentrate, thawed**
- ½ **cup lemon juice**
- 1 **bottle (750 ml) sweet white wine, chilled**
- 3 **cups chilled ginger ale**

1. Process the watermelon in batches in a food processor until smooth. Press through a fine-mesh strainer into a bowl; discard pulp. Pour juice into a large pitcher or punch bowl. Stir in juice concentrate and lemon juice. Refrigerate until chilled.
2. Stir in wine and ginger ale before serving. Serve over ice with additional watermelon.
¾ cup: 81 cal., 0 fat (0 sat. fat), 0 chol., 8mg sod., 19g carb. (17g sugars, 1g fiber), 1g pro.

MINI SAUSAGE QUICHES

MINI SAUSAGE QUICHES

These bite-sized quiches are loaded with sausage and cheese—and all nestled into easy crescent roll dough. Serve the cute muffinettes at any brunch or potluck gathering.
—Jan Mead, Milford, CT

Prep: 25 min. • **Bake:** 20 min.
Makes: 4 dozen

- ½ **lb. bulk hot Italian sausage**
- 2 **Tbsp. dried minced onion**
- 2 **Tbsp. minced chives**
- 1 **tube (8 oz.) refrigerated crescent rolls**
- 4 **large eggs, lightly beaten**
- 2 **cups shredded Swiss cheese**
- 1 **cup 4% cottage cheese**
- ⅓ **cup grated Parmesan cheese Paprika**

1. Preheat oven to 375°. In a large skillet, brown the Italian sausage and onion over medium heat until the meat is no longer pink, 4-5 minutes; drain. Stir in chives.
2. On a lightly floured surface, unroll crescent dough into a long rectangle; seal seams and perforations. Cut into 48 pieces. Press dough onto the bottom and up the sides of greased miniature muffin cups.
3. Fill each cup with about 2 tsp. sausage mixture. In a large bowl, combine the eggs and cheeses. Spoon 2 teaspoonfuls over sausage mixture. Sprinkle with paprika.
4. Bake until a knife inserted in the center comes out clean, 20-25 minutes. Cool 5 minutes before removing from pans to wire racks. If desired, sprinkle with additional minced chives. Serve warm.
1 mini quiche: 66 cal., 5g fat (2g sat. fat), 27mg chol., 116mg sod., 2g carb. (1g sugars, 0 fiber), 4g pro.

BUTTERMILK POUND CAKE

Now that I've retired from teaching, I have more time to bake, and this cake is the one I make most often. It is a truly southern recipe, and one that can't be topped— once people taste it, they won't go back to their other pound cake recipes!
—Gracie Hanchey, DeRidder, LA

Prep: 10 min. • **Bake:** 70 min. + cooling
Makes: 20 servings

- 1 cup butter, softened
- 2½ cups sugar
- 4 large eggs, room temperature
- 1 tsp. vanilla extract
- 3 cups all-purpose flour
- ¼ tsp. baking soda
- 1 cup buttermilk
  Confectioners' sugar, optional

1. Preheat oven to 325°. In a large bowl, cream butter and sugar until light and fluffy. Add 1 egg at a time, beating well after each addition. Beat in the vanilla. Combine flour and baking soda; add alternately with buttermilk and beat well.
2. Pour into a greased and floured 10-in. fluted tube pan. Bake until a toothpick inserted in the center comes out clean, about 70 minutes. Cool in pan for 15 minutes before removing to a wire rack to cool completely. When cool, dust with confectioners' sugar if desired.

1 slice: 285 cal., 10g fat (6g sat. fat), 68mg chol., 134mg sod., 45g carb. (30g sugars, 1g fiber), 4g pro.

BUTTERMILK POUND CAKE

BAKED ASPARAGUS DIP

FRUIT DIP

BUTTERMILK
VEGETABLE DIP

Three by Three
These three dips each call for only three
ingredients—which means it's always party time!

BAKED ASPARAGUS DIP

Since I'm from Wisconsin, I thought it was only logical to put together vegetables and a cheese—two foods my state produces in abundance!
—Sandra Baratka, Phillips, WI

Takes: 30 min. • **Makes:** about 2 cups

- 1 lb. diced cooked fresh asparagus, drained
- 1 cup grated Parmesan cheese
- 1 cup mayonnaise
  Baked pita chips

In a large bowl, combine asparagus, cheese and mayonnaise. Place in a 6-in. cast-iron skillet or 2-cup ovenproof bowl. Bake at 375° until heated through, about 20 minutes. Serve warm with pita chips.
2 Tbsp. dip: 120 cal., 11g fat (2g sat. fat), 5mg chol., 162mg sod., 2g carb. (1g sugars, 0 fiber), 2g pro.

BUTTERMILK VEGETABLE DIP

This homemade ranch is versatile and tangy—use as a dip for vegetables or a dressing for salad.
—Julissa Coblentz, Westminster, SC

Takes: 5 min. • **Makes:** 1 cup

- ¾ cup mayonnaise
- ¼ cup buttermilk
- 2½ tsp. Italian salad dressing mix
  Assorted fresh vegetables

Combine the mayonnaise, buttermilk and dressing mix. Cover and refrigerate until serving. Serve with vegetables.
2 Tbsp. dip: 140 cal., 15g fat (2g sat. fat), 2mg chol., 221mg sod., 1g carb. (1g sugars, 0 fiber), 0 pro.

FRUIT DIP

This is a perfect recipe to take to any potluck or get-together. It is delightful and refreshing.
—*Taste of Home* Test Kitchen

Takes: 30 min. • **Makes:** 1½ cups

- 1 pkg. (8 oz.) cream cheese, softened
- 1 jar (7 oz.) marshmallow creme
- 4½ tsp. maraschino cherry juice

REESE'S CHOCOLATE SNACK CAKE

In a small bowl, beat the cream cheese. Stir in the marshmallow creme and cherry juice. Refrigerate until serving.
2 Tbsp. dip: 124 cal., 7g fat (4g sat. fat), 19mg chol., 72mg sod., 11g carb. (11g sugars, 0 fiber), 1g pro.

REESE'S CHOCOLATE SNACK CAKE

This cake is constantly requested by my family. Its yellow and orange toppings make it the perfect dessert for a Halloween party.
—Eileen Travis, Ukiah, CA

Prep: 15 min. • **Bake:** 30 min. + cooling
Makes: 20 servings

- 3⅓ cups all-purpose flour
- ⅔ cup sugar
- ⅔ cup packed brown sugar
- ½ cup baking cocoa
- 2 tsp. baking soda
- 1 tsp. salt
- 2 cups water
- ⅓ cup canola oil
- ⅓ cup unsweetened applesauce
- 2 tsp. white vinegar
- 1 tsp. vanilla extract
- 1 cup Reese's Pieces
- ½ cup coarsely chopped salted peanuts

1. Preheat oven to 350°. Coat a 13x9-in. pan with cooking spray.
2. Whisk together the first 6 ingredients. In another bowl, whisk together water, oil, applesauce, vinegar and vanilla. Add to the flour mixture, stirring just until blended. Transfer to the prepared pan. Sprinkle with the Reese's Pieces and chopped peanuts.
3. Bake until a toothpick inserted in center comes out clean, 30-35 minutes. Cool on a wire rack.
1 piece: 240 cal., 8g fat (2g sat. fat), 0 chol., 280mg sod., 38g carb. (19g sugars, 2g fiber), 5g pro.

Holiday & Seasonal Pleasers

The most wonderful time of the year is...whenever you gather together with your loved ones! Good food is an essential part of any celebration— and here are some suggestions just right for parties the year-round, from Cinco de Mayo to Christmas!

Sopaipillas (p. 267) **Herbed Roast Turkey Breast** (p. 277) **Chipotle Berry Fruit Salsa** (p. 266)
Gingerbread Meringue Bars (p. 287) **Warm Cabbage, Fennel & Pear Salad** (p. 279)

Cinco de Mayo Celebration

This May 5, celebrate Mexico's most delicious contributions to our melting pot with your friends! Fresh fruit and vegetables, spicy meats and fish, sweet and light sopaipillas...this spring celebration of Mexican American heritage bursts with flavor!

PORK TENDERLOIN FAJITAS

PORK TENDERLOIN FAJITAS

This easy recipe offers loads of taste appeal. Sizzling pork tenderloin and veggies are coated with a zippy cilantro mixture and tucked into tortillas.
—Rachel Hozey, Pensacola, FL

Takes: 25 min. • **Makes:** 4 servings

- ¼ cup minced fresh cilantro
- ½ tsp. garlic powder
- ½ tsp. chili powder
- ½ tsp. ground cumin
- 1 pork tenderloin (1 lb.), thinly sliced
- 1 Tbsp. canola oil
- 1 small onion, sliced and separated into rings
- 1 medium green pepper, julienned
- 4 flour tortillas (8 in.), warmed
  Optional: Shredded cheddar cheese and sour cream

1. In a small bowl, combine cilantro, garlic powder, chili powder and cumin; set aside. In a large skillet, saute pork in oil until no longer pink. Add onion and green pepper; cook until crisp-tender.
2. Sprinkle with seasoning mixture; toss to coat. Spoon onto tortillas; serve with cheese and sour cream if desired.

1 fajita: 327 cal., 11g fat (2g sat. fat), 63mg chol., 299mg sod., 29g carb. (2g sugars, 1g fiber), 28g pro. **Diabetic exchanges:** 3 lean meat, 1½ starch, 1 vegetable, ½ fat.

10-MINUTE ZESTY SALSA

We have a great view of Pikes Peak from our mountain home, so we frequently eat on our porch in good weather. During family get-togethers, we savor this salsa with chips while enjoying the natural beauty around us.
—Kim Morin, Lake George, CO

Takes: 10 min. • **Makes:** 1½ cups

- 1 can (10 oz.) diced tomatoes and green chiles, undrained
- 1 Tbsp. seeded chopped jalapeno pepper
- 1 Tbsp. chopped red onion
- 1 Tbsp. minced fresh cilantro
- 1 garlic clove, minced
- 1 Tbsp. olive oil
  Dash salt
  Dash pepper
  Tortilla chips

In a small bowl, combine the tomatoes, jalapeno, onion, cilantro, garlic, oil, salt and pepper. Refrigerate until serving. Serve with tortilla chips.
Note: Wear disposable gloves when cutting hot peppers; the oils can burn exposed skin. Avoid touching your face.
¼ cup: 29 cal., 2g fat (0 sat. fat), 0 chol., 214mg sod., 2g carb. (0 sugars, 1g fiber), 0 pro. **Diabetic exchanges:** ½ fat.

DID YOU KNOW?
Cinco de Mayo isn't actually Mexico's Independence Day—that's Sept. 16. Instead, it's an observation of the Mexican victory over France at the Battle of Puebla.

Margarita Sangria

Is it sangria? Or is it a margarita? With a drink this refreshing, it doesn't really matter what you call it!

Combine 1 bottle white wine, one 12-oz. can lemon-lime soda, 1 sliced lemon, 1 cup tequila, ½ cup halved seedless red grapes, ½ cup fresh berries, ¼ cup honey (or agave nectar) and 3 Tbsp. lemon juice. Refrigerate at least 2 hours. Serve over ice.

SPICY REFRIED BEANS

Jazz up a can of plain refried beans with jalapeno pepper, seasonings and cheese. Serve with tortilla chips on the side for tasty scooping.
—*Taste of Home* Test Kitchen

Takes: 15 min. • **Makes:** 2 cups

- 1 small onion, chopped
- 1 jalapeno pepper, seeded and chopped
- 1 garlic clove, minced
- 2 tsp. vegetable oil
- 1 can (16 oz.) refried beans
- 2 Tbsp. water
- 1 tsp. hot pepper sauce
- ¼ tsp. ground cumin
- ¼ tsp. chili powder
- ⅛ tsp. cayenne pepper
- ½ cup shredded Monterey Jack cheese

In a large skillet, saute onion, jalapeno and garlic in oil for 2-3 minutes or until tender. Stir in beans, water, hot pepper sauce, cumin, chili powder and cayenne. Cook and stir over medium-low heat until heated through. Transfer to a serving bowl; sprinkle with cheese.

Note: Wear disposable gloves when cutting hot peppers; the oils can burn exposed skin. Avoid touching your face.

¼ cup: 95 cal., 4g fat (2g sat. fat), 11mg chol., 212mg sod., 10g carb. (2g sugars, 3g fiber), 5g pro. **Diabetic exchanges:** 1 fat, ½ starch.

THE ULTIMATE FISH TACOS

This recipe is my favorite meal to prepare. Adding my own personal touch to the marinade makes the fish pop with flavor. I warm corn tortillas on the grill and add salsa, cilantro, purple cabbage and fresh-squeezed lime.

—Yvonne Molina, Moreno Valley, CA

Prep: 20 min. + marinating • **Grill:** 10 min.
Makes: 6 servings

- ¼ cup olive oil
- 1 tsp. ground cardamom
- 1 tsp. paprika
- 1 tsp. salt
- 1 tsp. pepper
- 6 mahi mahi fillets (6 oz. each)
- 12 corn tortillas (6 in.)
- 2 cups chopped red cabbage
- 1 cup chopped fresh cilantro
  Salsa verde, optional
- 2 medium limes, cut into wedges
  Hot pepper sauce
  (Tapatío preferred)

1. In a 13x9-in. baking dish, whisk first 5 ingredients. Add fillets; turn to coat. Refrigerate, covered, for 30 minutes.

2. Drain fish and discard the marinade. On an oiled grill rack, grill fillets, covered, over medium-high heat (or broil 4 in. from heat) until fish flakes easily with a fork, 4-5 minutes per side. Remove fish. Place tortillas on grill rack and heat for 30-45 seconds. Keep warm.

3. To assemble, divide fish among the tortillas; layer with red cabbage, cilantro and, if desired, salsa verde. Sprinkle a little lime juice and hot pepper sauce over the fish mixture; fold sides of tortilla over filling. Serve with lime wedges and additional pepper sauce.
2 tacos: 284 cal., 5g fat (1g sat. fat), 124mg chol., 278mg sod., 26g carb. (2g sugars, 4g fiber), 35g pro. **Diabetic exchanges:** 5 lean meat, 1½ starch, ½ fat.

CHIPOTLE BERRY FRUIT SALSA

CHIPOTLE BERRY FRUIT SALSA

Not too hot, but with a bit of a kick, this salsa is a perfect topping for grilled fish or chicken. It's also a delectable chip dip—just double the recipe and watch it disappear! The spice is quite mild, but cut down on (or increase!) the chipotle peppers to suit your taste. If you like, add lime zest for an added twist!

—Trisha Kruse, Eagle, ID

Prep: 20 min. + chilling • **Makes:** 4 cups

- 2 cups chopped fresh strawberries
- 2 cups fresh blackberries, halved
- 2 medium kiwifruit, peeled and chopped
- 2 Tbsp. orange marmalade spreadable fruit
- 2 Tbsp. lime juice
- 1 Tbsp. minced chipotle pepper in adobo sauce
- ⅛ tsp. salt
- ⅛ tsp. cayenne pepper
  Cinnamon sugar pita chips

In a large bowl, combine the first 8 ingredients. Cover and refrigerate until serving. Serve with pita chips.
¼ cup: 26 cal., 0 fat (0 sat. fat), 0 chol., 25mg sod., 6g carb. (4g sugars, 2g fiber), 1g pro.

SOPAIPILLAS

PICTURED ON P. 263

Light, crispy pastry puffs, sopaipillas are a sweet way to round out a spicy meal. We love to serve them warm and top them off with honey or sugar.

—Mary Anne McWhirter, Pearland, TX

Prep: 15 min. + standing • **Cook:** 25 min.
Makes: 12 servings

- 1 cup all-purpose flour
- 1½ tsp. baking powder
- ¼ tsp. salt
- 1 Tbsp. shortening
- ⅓ cup warm water
  Oil for deep-fat frying
  Optional: Honey and
  confectioners' sugar

1. In a large bowl, combine the flour, baking powder and salt. Cut in shortening until the mixture resembles fine crumbs. Gradually add water, tossing with a fork until a loose ball forms (the dough will be crumbly).
2. On a lightly floured surface, knead dough for 3 minutes or until smooth. Cover and let rest for 10 minutes. Roll out into a 12x10-in. rectangle. Cut into 12 squares with a knife or 12 circles using a round biscuit cutter.
3. In a deep-fat fryer, heat 2 in. oil to 375°. Fry sopaipillas for 1-2 minutes on each side. Drain on paper towels; keep warm. Serve with honey and/or dust with confectioners' sugar if desired.
1 sopaipilla: 57 cal., 2g fat (0 sat. fat), 0 chol., 109mg sod., 8g carb. (0 sugars, 0 fiber), 1g pro.

CHIPOTLE MEXICAN STREET CORN DIP WITH GOAT CHEESE

I was craving the Mexican street corn that I had tried during a recent trip to Puerto Vallarta, so I came up with this recipe. It blends the traditional profile of the popular street food with updated flavors for a delightful dip.

—Joseph A. Sciascia, San Mateo, CA

Prep: 30 min. + cooling • **Bake:** 35 min.
Makes: 3 cups

- 3 medium ears sweet corn
- 1 Tbsp. olive oil

- 1 cup crumbled goat cheese
- ¾ cup mayonnaise
- 1 can (4 oz.) chopped green chiles
- 1 jar (4 oz.) diced pimientos, drained
- 2 green onions, chopped
- 2 Tbsp. finely chopped chipotle peppers in adobo sauce
- 1 Tbsp. minced fresh cilantro
- 1 to 2 Tbsp. lime juice
- 1½ tsp. grated lime zest
- 1 tsp. ground cumin
- 1 tsp. chili powder
  Tortilla chips

1. Brush corn with oil. Grill corn, covered, over medium heat until lightly browned and tender, 10-12 minutes, turning occasionally. Cool slightly.
2. Preheat oven to 350°. Cut corn from cobs; transfer to a large bowl. Stir in goat cheese, mayonnaise, green chiles, pimientos, green onions, chipotle pepper, cilantro, lime juice and zest, cumin and chili powder.
3. Transfer to a greased 1½-qt. baking dish. Bake until bubbly and golden brown, 35-40 minutes. Serve with tortilla chips.
¼ cup: 157 cal., 14g fat (3g sat. fat), 13mg chol., 182mg sod., 7g carb. (2g sugars, 1g fiber), 3g pro.

TEST KITCHEN TIP
Three medium ears of corn will yield about 2 cups kernels.

CHIPOTLE MEXICAN
STREET CORN DIP
WITH GOAT CHEESE

Mother's Day Luncheon

For a perfectly lovely Mother's Day, why not celebrate with a cool, sophisticated lunch? Salads, entrees and of course, sweet desserts all with a grown-up, elegant edge that let Mom know how much she means to you.

PESTO SHRIMP PASTA

PESTO SHRIMP PASTA

A dash of red pepper puts zip in this lively main dish. You can serve this dish hot or cold—it's equally good as a main-course pasta and a pasta salad. Just the thing for an elegant luncheon!
—Gloria Jones Grenga, Newnan, GA

Takes: 30 min. • **Makes:** 4 servings

- 8 oz. uncooked spaghetti
- 3 Tbsp. olive oil, divided
- 1 cup loosely packed fresh basil leaves
- ¼ cup lemon juice
- 2 garlic cloves, peeled
- ½ tsp. salt
- 1 lb. fresh asparagus, trimmed and cut into 2-in. pieces
- ¾ lb. uncooked medium shrimp, peeled and deveined
- ⅛ tsp. crushed red pepper flakes

1. Cook spaghetti according to package directions. Meanwhile, in a blender, combine 1 Tbsp. olive oil, basil, lemon juice, garlic and salt; cover and process until smooth.
2. In a large skillet, saute asparagus in remaining oil until crisp-tender. Add shrimp and pepper flakes. Cook and stir until the shrimp turn pink.
3. Drain spaghetti; place in a large bowl. Add the basil mixture; toss to coat. Add shrimp mixture and mix well.

1 cup: 385 cal., 12g fat (2g sat. fat), 126mg chol., 451mg sod., 47g carb. (3g sugars, 3g fiber), 23g pro.

ORANGE BLOSSOM MINT TEA

Not a fan of regular iced tea, I came up with this recipe instead. It has the perfect combination of freshness and sweetness, and the orange blossom water gives it a distinctive flavor. People always ask me for the recipe!
—Juliana Gauss, Centennial, CO

Prep: 10 min. + chilling • **Cook:** 6 hours
Makes: 20 servings

- 20 cups water
- 1 bunch fresh mint (about 1 cup)
- 1 cup sugar
- 1 large navel orange
- 1 to 2 Tbsp. orange blossom water or 1½ to 2½ tsp. orange extract
- Optional: Orange slices and additional fresh mint

1. Place water and mint in a 6-qt. slow cooker. Cover and cook on high until heated through, about 6 hours. Strain tea; discard mint.
2. Whisk in sugar until dissolved. Cut orange crosswise in half; squeeze juice from orange. Stir in juice and orange blossom water. Transfer to a pitcher. Refrigerate until cold, 4-6 hours. Serve over ice with orange slices and additional mint, if desired.

1 cup: 43 cal., 0 fat (0 sat. fat), 0 chol., 0 sod., 11g carb. (11g sugars, 0 fiber), 0 pro.

TEST KITCHEN TIP
Orange blossom water, also called orange flower water, can be found at most specialty grocery stores or spice shops. Using orange extract instead will add a hint of orange flavor; the blossom water adds a unique floral note.

1⅔ cups: 362 cal., 11g fat (3g sat. fat), 15mg chol., 657mg sod., 52g carb. (7g sugars, 9g fiber), 15g pro.
HEALTH TIP Make this refreshing main-dish salad a gluten-free recipe by replacing the couscous with about 1½ cups cooked quinoa.

CHOCOLATE BREAD PUDDING
This is a fun recipe because the chocolate makes it different from traditional bread pudding. It's a rich, comforting dessert.
—Mildred Sherrer, Fort Worth, TX

Prep: 15 min. + standing • **Bake:** 30 min.
Makes: 2 servings

- 2 oz. semisweet chocolate
- ½ cup half-and-half cream
- ⅔ cup sugar
- ½ cup 2% milk
- 1 large egg, room temperature
- 1 tsp. vanilla extract
- ¼ tsp. salt
- 4 slices day-old bread, crusts removed and cut into cubes (about 3 cups)
  Optional: Confectioners' sugar and whipped cream

1. Preheat oven to 350°. In a small microwave-safe bowl, melt chocolate; stir until smooth. Stir in cream; set aside.
2. In a large bowl, whisk the sugar, milk, egg, vanilla and salt. Stir in chocolate mixture. Add bread cubes and toss to coat. Let stand for 15 minutes.
3. Spoon into 2 greased 2-cup souffle dishes. Bake until a knife inserted in the center comes out clean, 30-35 minutes.
4. If desired, sprinkle with confectioners' sugar and top with whipped cream.
1 serving: 622 cal., 17g fat (9g sat. fat), 145mg chol., 656mg sod., 105g carb. (79g sugars, 2g fiber), 12g pro.

COUSCOUS TABBOULEH WITH FRESH MINT & FETA

COUSCOUS TABBOULEH WITH FRESH MINT & FETA
Using couscous instead of bulgur for tabbouleh really speeds up the process of making this colorful salad. Other quick-cooking grains such as barley or quinoa work well, too.
—Elodie Rosinovsky, Brighton, MA

Takes: 20 min. • **Makes:** 3 servings

- ¾ cup water
- ½ cup uncooked couscous
- 1 can (15 oz.) garbanzo beans or chickpeas, rinsed and drained
- 1 large tomato, chopped
- ½ English cucumber, halved and thinly sliced
- 3 Tbsp. lemon juice
- 2 tsp. grated lemon zest
- 2 tsp. olive oil
- 2 tsp. minced fresh mint
- 2 tsp. minced fresh parsley
- ¼ tsp. salt
- ⅛ tsp. pepper
- ¾ cup crumbled feta cheese
  Lemon wedges, optional

1. In a small saucepan, bring water to a boil. Stir in couscous. Remove from the heat; cover and let stand for 5-8 minutes or until water is absorbed. Fluff couscous with a fork.
2. In a large bowl, combine the beans, tomato and cucumber. In a small bowl, whisk the lemon juice, lemon zest, oil and seasonings. Drizzle over the bean mixture. Add couscous; toss to combine. Serve immediately or refrigerate until chilled. Sprinkle with cheese. If desired, serve with lemon wedges.

CHICKEN PICCATA POCKETS

CHICKEN PICCATA POCKETS

For a spin on traditional chicken piccata, I wrapped it in puff pastry with a bit of cream cheese—it tasted sensational! My husband took one for lunch at work, everyone asked what he was eating because it smelled so good.

—Arlene Erlbach, Morton Grove, IL

Prep: 15 min. • **Cook:** 20 min.
Makes: 4 servings

- 1 pkg. (8 oz.) cream cheese, softened
- 2 Tbsp. lemon juice
- ¼ tsp. salt
- ¼ tsp. pepper
- 2 Tbsp. capers, drained
- 1 large shallot, finely chopped
- 1 sheet frozen puff pastry, thawed
- 4 chicken tenderloins, cubed
- 1 large egg, well beaten
- 1 Tbsp. water
- 4 thin lemon slices
- 2 Tbsp. chopped fresh parsley

1. Preheat oven to 425°. Beat cream cheese, lemon juice, salt and pepper on medium speed until well combined. Fold in capers and shallot.

2. Unfold the puff pastry; roll into a 12-in. square. Cut into 4 smaller squares. Spread the cream cheese mixture over squares to within ¼ in. of edges and top with chicken.

3. Fold a corner of each pastry square over the chicken, forming a triangle. Pinch triangle edges to seal; flatten with a fork for a tighter seal. Whisk egg and water; brush over the pastry pockets, including edges. Discard leftover egg mixture. Pierce each pocket twice with a fork to vent.

4. Bake on a parchment-lined baking sheet until golden brown, 18-25 minutes. Remove from oven; cool for 5 minutes. Serve pockets with lemon slices and chopped parsley.

Freeze option: Cover and freeze unbaked pockets on a waxed paper-lined baking sheet until firm. Transfer to an airtight container; return to freezer. To use, bake pockets as directed, increasing time about 5 minutes.

1 chicken pocket: 559 cal., 38g fat (15g sat. fat), 126mg chol., 698mg sod., 40g carb. (3g sugars, 5g fiber), 18g pro.

🥄🕐

CRAB-STUFFED AVOCADOS

We enjoy this creamy and crunchy salad out on our deck on summer evenings. And it goes together in minutes flat!
—Gail VanGundy, Parker, CO

Takes: 20 min. • **Makes:** 2 servings

- 1 can (6 oz.) crabmeat, drained, flaked and cartilage removed
- ½ cup sliced celery
- ½ cup shredded lettuce
- 3 Tbsp. mayonnaise
- 1 tsp. finely chopped onion
- ½ tsp. lemon juice
- ⅛ to ¼ tsp. seafood seasoning
- ⅛ tsp. paprika
- 1 medium ripe avocado, halved and pitted

In a bowl, combine the first 8 ingredients. Spoon onto avocado halves. Serve immediately.

½ stuffed avocado: 326 cal., 26g fat (4g sat. fat), 84mg chol., 654mg sod., 7g carb. (1g sugars, 5g fiber), 17g pro. **HEALTH TIP** These stuffed avocados are low in carbs and gluten free. Double or triple the recipe when you have guests who follow a special diet.

CARAMEL CREME BRULEE

This crowd-pleasing recipe comes out perfect every time. A torch works best to get the sugar caramelized while keeping the rest of the custard cool. You may want to use even more sugar to create a thicker, more even crust on top.
—Jenna Fleming, Lowville, NY

Prep: 20 min. • **Bake:** 40 min. + chilling
Makes: 14 servings

- 4½ cups heavy whipping cream
- 1½ cups half-and-half cream
- 15 large egg yolks, room temperature
- 1⅓ cups sugar, divided
- 3 tsp. caramel extract
- ¼ tsp. salt
- ⅓ cup packed brown sugar

1. Preheat oven to 325°. In a large saucepan, heat whipping cream and cream until bubbles form around the sides of the pan; remove from heat. In a bowl, whisk egg yolks, 1 cup sugar, extract and salt until blended but not foamy. Slowly stir in hot cream mixture.

2. Place an ungreased broiler-safe 13x9-in. baking dish in a baking pan large enough to hold it without touching the sides. Pour egg mixture into dish. Place pan on oven rack; add very hot water to pan to within 1 in. of top of dish. Bake until the center is just set and top appears dull, 40-50 minutes. Immediately remove dish from water bath to a wire rack; cool for 1 hour. Refrigerate until cold.

3. Mix brown sugar and remaining sugar. Sprinkle custard evenly with sugar mixture. Caramelize topping with a kitchen torch by holding the torch flame about 2 in. above custard surface and rotating it slowly until the sugar is evenly caramelized. Serve immediately or refrigerate up to 1 hour. **Note:** This recipe was tested with Watkin's caramel extract.

½ cup: 452 cal., 35g fat (21g sat. fat), 298mg chol., 86mg sod., 28g carb. (27g sugars, 0 fiber), 6g pro.

TEST KITCHEN TIP
To caramelize the topping in a broiler, let custard stand at room temperature for 30 minutes before sprinkling it with the sugar mixture. Broil 3-4 in. from heat until sugar is caramelized, 2-3 minutes.

CARAMEL CREME BRULEE

July 4th Backyard Blast

Independence Day is the time to get friends and family together for a cookout—grilled burgers, summer salads, crowd-pleasing appetizers and desserts all welcome the nation's birthday in style!

ALL-AMERICAN HAMBURGERS

SWEET ONION PIMIENTO CHEESE DEVILED EGGS

For my mother's 92nd birthday, we had deviled eggs topped with pimientos as part of the spread. They're timeless and always in good taste.
—Linda Foreman, Locust Grove, OK

Takes: 15 min. • **Makes:** 1 dozen

- 6 hard-boiled large eggs
- ¼ cup finely shredded sharp cheddar cheese
- 2 Tbsp. mayonnaise
- 4 tsp. diced pimientos, drained
- 2 tsp. finely chopped sweet onion
- 1 tsp. Dijon mustard
- 1 small garlic clove, minced
- ¼ tsp. salt
- ⅛ tsp. pepper
    Additional diced pimientos and finely shredded sharp cheddar cheese

Cut eggs lengthwise in half. Remove yolks, reserving whites. In a bowl, mash yolks. Stir in cheese, mayonnaise, pimientos, onion, mustard, garlic, salt and pepper. Spoon or pipe into egg whites. Sprinkle with additional pimientos and cheese. Refrigerate, covered, until serving.
1 stuffed egg half: 67 cal., 5g fat (2g sat. fat), 96mg chol., 128mg sod., 1g carb. (0 sugars, 0 fiber), 4g pro.

ALL-AMERICAN HAMBURGERS

We do a lot of camping and outdoor cooking—and hamburgers are on our menu more than any other food! Of all the burgers we make, this is our favorite.
—Diane Hixon, Niceville, FL

Takes: 20 min. • **Makes:** 4 servings

- 1 lb. ground beef
- 2 Tbsp. finely chopped onion
- 2 Tbsp. chili sauce
- 2 tsp. Worcestershire sauce
- 2 tsp. prepared mustard
- 4 slices process American cheese or cheddar cheese, halved diagonally
- 2 slices Swiss cheese, halved diagonally
- 4 hamburger buns, split and toasted
    Optional: Lettuce leaves, sliced tomato and onion, cooked bacon strips, ketchup and mustard

1. Combine first 5 ingredients, mixing lightly but thoroughly. Shape into mixture into 4 patties. Grill burgers, covered, on a greased rack over medium direct heat until a thermometer reads 160° and juices run clear, about 6 minutes on each side.
2. During the last minute of cooking, top each patty with 2 triangles American cheese and 1 triangle Swiss cheese. Serve on toasted buns. As desired, top with lettuce, tomato, onion, bacon, ketchup or mustard .
1 serving: 421 cal., 21g fat (11g sat. fat), 82mg chol., 760mg sod., 27g carb. (6g sugars, 1g fiber), 30g pro.

RED, WHITE & BLUE SUMMER SALAD

ROOT BEER FLOAT PIE

This is the kind of recipe your kids will look back on and always remember. And the only appliance you need is the refrigerator!

—Cindy Reams, Philipsburg, PA

Prep: 15 min. + chilling
Makes: 8 servings

- 1 carton (8 oz.) frozen reduced-fat whipped topping, thawed, divided
- ¾ cup cold diet root beer
- ½ cup fat-free milk
- 1 pkg. (1 oz.) sugar-free instant vanilla pudding mix
- 1 9-in. graham cracker crust (about 6 oz.)
  Maraschino cherries, optional

1. Set aside and refrigerate ½ cup whipped topping for garnish. In a large bowl, whisk the root beer, milk and pudding mix for 2 minutes. Fold in half the remaining whipped topping. Spread into graham cracker crust.
2. Spread remaining whipped topping over the pie. Freeze at least 8 hours or overnight.
3. Dollop the reserved whipped topping over each serving; top with a maraschino cherry if desired.

1 piece: 185 cal., 8g fat (4g sat. fat), 0 chol., 275mg sod., 27g carb. (14g sugars, 0 fiber), 1g pro. **Diabetic exchanges:** 2 starch, 1 fat.

READER REVIEW

"I have made this at least eight times and it's always a hit. If you use an electric beater to mix it, it firms up better. I've also made this with orange soda—it tastes like a creamsicle! Really a family favorite."

KK6576, TASTEOFHOME.COM

RED, WHITE & BLUE SUMMER SALAD

Caprese and fresh fruit always remind me of summer. This salad combines traditional Caprese flavors with summer fruit and added prosciutto for saltiness, creating a balanced and flavor-packed popular side dish.

—Emily Falke, Santa Barbara, CA

Takes: 25 min. • **Makes:** 12 servings

- ⅔ cup extra virgin olive oil
- ½ cup julienned fresh basil
- ⅓ cup white balsamic vinegar
- ¼ cup julienned fresh mint leaves
- 2 garlic cloves, minced
- 2 tsp. Dijon mustard
- 1 tsp. sea salt
- 1 tsp. sugar
- 1 tsp. pepper
- 2 cups cherry tomatoes
- 8 cups fresh arugula
- 1 carton (8 oz.) fresh mozzarella cheese pearls, drained
- 2 medium peaches, sliced
- 2 cups fresh blueberries
- 6 oz. thinly sliced prosciutto, julienned

1. In a small bowl, whisk together the first 9 ingredients. Add tomatoes; let stand while preparing salad.
2. In a large bowl, combine the arugula, mozzarella, peach slices, blueberries and prosciutto. Pour the tomato mixture over top; toss to coat. Garnish with additional mint leaves. Serve immediately.

1 cup: 233 cal., 18g fat (5g sat. fat), 27mg chol., 486mg sod., 10g carb. (8g sugars, 2g fiber), 8g pro.

TEST KITCHEN TIP
White balsamic vinegar is an excellent alternative to keep bright colors in your salads.

HOT DOG SLIDERS WITH MANGO-PINEAPPLE SALSA

For parties, we shrink down lots of foods to slider size, including these quick hot dogs. Pile on the easy but irresistible fruit salsa for a burst of fresh flavor.
—Carole Resnick, Cleveland, OH

Takes: 30 min.
Makes: 2 dozen (2 cups salsa)

- 3 Tbsp. lime juice
- 2 Tbsp. honey
- ¼ tsp. salt
- 1 cup cubed fresh pineapple (½ in.)
- 1 cup cubed peeled mango (½ in.)
- ¼ cup finely chopped red onion
- 2 Tbsp. finely chopped sweet red pepper
- 12 hot dogs
- 12 hot dog buns, split

1. In a small bowl, whisk lime juice, honey and salt until blended. Add pineapple, mango, onion and pepper; toss to coat.
2. Grill hot dogs, covered, over medium heat or broil 4 in. from heat until heated through, 7-9 minutes, turning occasionally.
3. Place hot dogs in buns; cut each crosswise in half. Serve with fruit salsa.

1 slider with 1 Tbsp. salsa: 146 cal., 8g fat (3g sat. fat), 13mg chol., 361mg sod., 15g carb. (5g sugars, 1g fiber), 5g pro.

FRIED POTATO SALAD

This recipe began with some leftover fried potatoes I had on hand. We liked it so much that now I fry potatoes just to make this unique potato salad! Sometimes I add grated sharp cheddar for a cheesy twist.
—Leann Stallard, Dryden, VA

Prep: 30 min.
Cook: 15 min./batch + cooling
Makes: 10 servings

- 8 medium potatoes, peeled and cut into ¼-in. pieces (about 8 cups)
- 3 Tbsp. applewood seasoning rub
- ½ cup canola oil
- 1 small onion, finely chopped
- 1 small green pepper, finely chopped
- 2 cups Miracle Whip
- 4 hard-boiled large eggs, chopped
- 1 tsp. salt
- ½ tsp. pepper

1. Sprinkle potatoes with applewood seasoning. In a large skillet, heat oil over medium heat. Add potatoes in batches; cook, stirring frequently, until potatoes are tender, 15-20 minutes. Cool completely. Transfer to a large bowl.
2. Add remaining ingredients; gently toss to coat. Refrigerate until serving.

¾ cup: 362 cal., 25g fat (3g sat. fat), 78mg chol., 585mg sod., 28g carb. (6g sugars, 2g fiber), 5g pro.

GRILLED ZUCCHINI WITH ONIONS

Wondering what to do with all of your garden-grown zucchini in the summer? Give it sizzle and a little heat with this healthy side. It's also an easy recipe to double or triple for summer cookouts.
—Alia Shuttleworth, Auburn, CA

Takes: 20 min.
Makes: 4 servings

- 6 small zucchini, halved lengthwise
- 4 tsp. olive oil, divided
- 2 green onions, thinly sliced
- 2 Tbsp. lemon juice
- ½ tsp. salt
- ⅛ tsp. crushed red pepper flakes

1. Drizzle zucchini with 2 tsp. oil. Grill, covered, over medium heat 8-10 minutes or until tender, turning once.

2. Place zucchini in a large bowl with green onions, lemon juice, salt, pepper flakes and remaining oil; toss to coat.
3 zucchini halves: 73 cal., 5g fat (1g sat. fat), 0 chol., 314mg sod., 7g carb. (3g sugars, 2g fiber), 2g pro. **Diabetic exchanges:** 1 vegetable, 1 fat.

TRIPLE BEAN BAKE WITH BACON

Ordinary baked beans become extraordinary when you mix bean varieties and add the zing of horseradish.
—Sherri Melotik, Oak Creek, WI

Prep: 15 min. • **Bake:** 30 min.
Makes: 8 servings

- ½ lb. bacon strips, cut into ½-in. pieces
- ⅔ cup chopped onion (about 1 medium)
- 1 can (15½ oz.) great northern beans, undrained
- 1 can (16 oz.) butter beans, rinsed and drained
- 1 can (16 oz.) kidney beans, rinsed and drained
- ¾ cup packed brown sugar
- 1 Tbsp. prepared horseradish
- 1 Tbsp. yellow mustard

1. Preheat oven to 325°. In a Dutch oven, cook bacon over medium heat until crisp. Remove to paper towels with a slotted spoon; drain, reserving 1 Tbsp. drippings. Add onion to the reserved drippings; cook and stir over medium heat until tender.
2. Stir in remaining ingredients; return bacon to pan. Transfer to a greased 2-qt. baking dish. Cover and bake until heated through, 30-35 minutes. Uncover and continue to bake until beans are the desired consistency.
¾ cup: 278 cal., 6g fat (2g sat. fat), 12mg chol., 588mg sod., 47g carb. (23g sugars, 8g fiber), 13g pro.

Cheesecake Berry Parfaits

End your Fourth of July party with a finale of luscious red, white and blue layers.

Beat 4 oz. softened cream cheese with 3 Tbsp. sugar. Fold in 1⅓ cups sweetened whipped cream or whipped topping. Layer with fresh berries in 4 dessert dishes.

Thanksgiving Dinner

All the Thanksgiving classic flavors are here—turkey, mashed potatoes, cranberries and more—and with a modern twist that makes everything just a little bit different! Create a pull-out-the-stops feast with this collection of quick and easy recipes, giving you more time to be with your friends and family.

OLIVE OIL MASHED POTATOES WITH PANCETTA

OLIVE OIL MASHED POTATOES WITH PANCETTA

Classic American mashed potatoes take a trip to Italy with the flavors of olive oil, garlic and pancetta.
—Bryan Kennedy, Kaneohe, HI

Prep: 20 min. • **Cook:** 20 min.
Makes: 8 servings

- 3 lbs. Yukon Gold potatoes, peeled and cubed
- 3 slices pancetta or bacon, chopped
- 1 Tbsp. plus ¼ cup olive oil, divided
- 4 garlic cloves, minced
- ⅓ cup minced fresh parsley
- ½ tsp. salt
- ½ tsp. pepper

1. Place potatoes in a large saucepan and cover with water. Bring to a boil. Reduce heat; cover and simmer until tender, 15-20 minutes.
2. Meanwhile, in a large skillet, cook pancetta in 1 Tbsp. oil over medium heat until crisp. Add garlic; cook for 1 minute longer. Remove from the heat.
3. Drain potatoes and transfer to a large bowl. Mash potatoes with the remaining ¼ cup oil. Stir in the parsley, pancetta mixture, salt and pepper.
⅔ cup: 206 cal., 11g fat (2g sat. fat), 7mg chol., 313mg sod., 23g carb. (2g sugars, 2g fiber), 4g pro. **Diabetic exchanges:** 2 fat, 1½ starch.

TLC (THANKSGIVING LEFTOVER CASSEROLE)

Turkey, stuffing and veggies come together into a fabulous casserole that you can make out of leftovers. There's comfort in every bite.
—Barbara Lento, Houston, PA

Prep: 20 min. + standing • **Bake:** 65 min.
Makes: 8 servings

- 4 cups seasoned stuffing cubes
- 4 cups cubed cooked turkey
- 2 celery ribs, finely chopped
- 1 cup frozen peas
- 1 cup fresh or frozen cranberries
- ½ cup chopped sweet onion
- ¼ cup all-purpose flour
- 4 large eggs
- 3 cups 2% milk
- 1 can (8¼ oz.) cream-style corn
- ½ tsp. salt
- ½ tsp. pepper
- 2 Tbsp. butter
- ⅓ cup coarsely chopped pecans

1. Preheat oven to 350°. Layer first 6 ingredients in a greased 13x9-in. baking dish. Whisk flour, eggs and milk until smooth. Add corn, salt and pepper; mix well. Pour over top; let stand 15 minutes. Dot with butter and sprinkle with pecans.
2. Cover and bake 35 minutes. Uncover and bake 30-35 minutes or until a knife inserted in the center comes out clean.
1½ cups: 415 cal., 15g fat (5g sat. fat), 173mg chol., 768mg sod., 38g carb. (9g sugars, 4g fiber), 32g pro. **Diabetic exchanges:** 3 lean meat, 2½ starch, 1½ fat.

HERBED ROAST TURKEY BREAST

EASY CHEESY BISCUITS

I'm a big fan of homemade biscuits...but not of all the rolling and cutting that goes into making them. This easy drop biscuit method solves everything!
—Christina Addison, Blanchester, OH

Takes: 30 min. • **Makes:** 1 dozen

- 3 cups all-purpose flour
- 3 tsp. baking powder
- 1 Tbsp. sugar
- 1 tsp. salt
- ¾ tsp. cream of tartar
- ½ cup cold butter
- 1 cup shredded sharp cheddar cheese
- 1 garlic clove, minced
- ¼ to ½ tsp. crushed red pepper flakes
- 1¼ cups 2% milk

1. Preheat oven to 450°. In a large bowl, whisk flour, baking powder, sugar, salt and cream of tartar. Cut in butter until mixture resembles coarse crumbs. Stir in cheese, garlic and pepper flakes. Add milk; stir just until moistened.
2. Drop dough by heaping ¼ cupfuls 2 in. apart onto a greased baking sheet. Bake 18-20 minutes or until golden brown. Serve warm.

1 biscuit: 237 cal., 12g fat (7g sat. fat), 32mg chol., 429mg sod., 26g carb. (2g sugars, 1g fiber), 7g pro.

HERBED ROAST TURKEY BREAST

If your Thanksgiving crowd fights over the white meat, consider this main course. I made this turkey breast for my first dinner party as a newlywed. It was such a success that it's become a standby on all of my entertaining menus.
—Lisa Mahon Fluegeman, Cincinnati, OH

Prep: 10 min. • **Bake:** 2 hours + standing
Makes: 12 servings

- 1 bone-in turkey breast (5 to 6 lbs.)
- 5 tsp. lemon juice
- 1 Tbsp. olive oil
- 1 to 2 tsp. pepper
- 1 tsp. dried rosemary, crushed
- 1 tsp. dried thyme
- 1 tsp. garlic salt
- 1 medium onion, cut into wedges
- 1 celery rib, cut into 2-in. pieces
- ½ cup white wine or chicken broth

1. Preheat oven to 325°. With fingers, carefully loosen the skin from both sides of turkey breast. Combine lemon juice and oil; brush under the skin. Combine pepper, rosemary, thyme and garlic salt; rub over turkey.
2. Place onion and celery in a 3-qt. baking dish. Top with turkey breast, skin side up. Pour wine into the dish. Bake, uncovered, 2-2½ hours or until a thermometer reads 170°. (Cover loosely with foil if turkey browns too quickly.) Cover and let stand 15 minutes before carving.

5 oz. cooked turkey: 285 cal., 11g fat (3g sat. fat), 102mg chol., 241mg sod., 2g carb. (1g sugars, 0 fiber), 40g pro.
Diabetic exchanges: 5 medium-fat meat.
Savory Turkey Breast: Omit the lemon juice, oil, pepper, rosemary, thyme and salt. Combine ¼ cup softened butter, 2 tsp. rubbed sage, 3 minced garlic cloves, 1 tsp. each dried minced onion and thyme, ½ tsp. salt and ¼ tsp. pepper. Loosen the skin on the turkey breast as directed. Spread 2 Tbsp. butter mixture under turkey skin; spread the remaining mixture over skin. Proceed as directed.

NANTUCKET
CRANBERRY TART

NANTUCKET CRANBERRY TART

While everyone is enjoying a bountiful meal, this eye-catching tart can be baking to perfection in the oven. I love it because it calls for just a few ingredients, and is a snap to assemble.
—Jackie Zack, Riverside, CT

....

Prep: 15 min. • **Bake:** 40 min. + cooling
Makes: 12 servings

- 1   pkg. (12 oz.) fresh or frozen cranberries, thawed
- 1   cup sugar, divided
- ½   cup sliced almonds
- 2   large eggs, room temperature
- ¾   cup butter, melted
- 1   tsp. almond extract
- 1   cup all-purpose flour
- 1   Tbsp. confectioners' sugar

1. Preheat oven to 325°. In a small bowl, combine cranberries, ½ cup sugar and the almonds. Transfer to a greased 11-in. fluted tart pan with a removable bottom. Place pan on a baking sheet.

2. In a small bowl, beat the eggs, butter, extract and the remaining sugar. Beat in flour just until moistened (batter will be thick). Spread evenly over berries.

3. Bake for 40-45 minutes or until a toothpick inserted in the center comes out clean. Cool in pan on a wire rack. Dust with confectioners' sugar. Refrigerate any leftovers.

1 piece: 255 cal., 14g fat (8g sat. fat), 65mg chol., 93mg sod., 30g carb. (19g sugars, 2g fiber), 3g pro.

CORNBREAD PUDDING CASSEROLE

My niece shared her recipe for a holiday side dish—and I tinkered to make it healthier! (The original used regular sour cream and ½ cup butter.) I also added turkey bacon, bell pepper, and green onions for added flavor and presentation.
—Mary Shivers, Ada, OK

....

Prep: 15 min. • **Bake:** 50 min.
Makes: 8 servings

- 1   cup fat-free sour cream
- ¼   cup vegetable broth
- 1   large egg, lightly beaten
- ¼   tsp. salt
- ¼   tsp. pepper
- 3   turkey bacon strips, diced and cooked
- 1¾ cups frozen corn, thawed
- 1   can (14¾ oz.) cream-style corn
- 1   pkg. (8½ oz.) cornbread/muffin mix
- 3   Tbsp. finely chopped sweet red pepper
- 2   green onions, thinly sliced

1. Preheat oven to 350°. In a large bowl, combine sour cream, broth, egg, salt and pepper. Stir in the remaining ingredients and transfer to a 8-in. square baking dish coated with cooking spray.

2. Bake, uncovered, for 50-60 minutes or until golden brown.

⅔ cup: 246 cal., 5g fat (1g sat. fat), 44mg chol., 609mg sod., 44g carb., 2g fiber, 8g pro.

 5i ⏱

OLD-FASHIONED GREEN BEANS

Mom prepared home-grown green beans using this recipe, and boy did they ever taste good! Bacon provides rich flavor and brown sugar a touch of sweetness. This is one irresistible side dish.
—Willa Govoro, St. Clair, MO

Takes: 30 min. • **Makes:** 8 servings

- 6 bacon strips, cut into ½-in. pieces
- 2 lbs. fresh green beans
- 3 Tbsp. brown sugar
- ½ cup water

In a large skillet, cook bacon over medium heat until crisp, about 5 minutes. Add the beans, brown sugar and water. Stir gently; bring to a boil. Reduce heat; cover and simmer for 15 minutes or until beans are crisp-tender. Remove to a serving bowl with a slotted spoon.

¾ cup: 145 cal., 10g fat (4g sat. fat), 11mg chol., 132mg sod., 12g carb. (8g sugars, 3g fiber), 3g pro.

⏱

WARM CABBAGE, FENNEL & PEAR SALAD

This crunchy salad makes an elegant first course or side, but it's hearty enough to be an entree when paired with a crusty artisan bread. We love it served warm.
—Grace Voltolina, Westport, CT

Takes: 25 min. • **Makes:** 4 servings

- 2 firm medium pears
- ¼ cup brandy or Cognac, optional
- 3 Tbsp. olive oil

- 1 large fennel bulb, halved, cored and thinly sliced
- 4 cups shredded or thinly sliced cabbage
- ¼ cup water
- 3 Tbsp. lemon juice
- 2 tsp. honey or agave nectar
- 1 tsp. kosher salt
- ½ tsp. pepper
- ¾ cup crumbled or sliced Gorgonzola cheese
- ½ cup chopped walnuts, toasted

1. Peel and core pears; cut into ½-in. slices. If desired, toss with brandy. Set the pears aside.
2. In a large skillet, heat olive oil over medium-high heat. Add fennel; saute until crisp-tender, 2-3 minutes. Add cabbage and toss with the fennel. Cook until both are tender, 2-3 minutes longer. Add the pears, water, lemon juice, honey, salt and pepper to the skillet, gently combining the ingredients. Cook until the liquid is evaporated, 6-8 minutes.
3. Transfer to a serving bowl. Top with Gorgonzola cheese and toasted walnuts. Serve warm or at room temperature.

Note: To toast nuts, bake in a shallow pan in a 350° oven for 5-10 minutes or cook in a skillet over low heat until lightly browned, stirring occasionally.

1 cup: 391 cal., 26g fat (7g sat. fat), 19mg chol., 810mg sod., 28g carb. (14g sugars, 8g fiber), 9g pro.

TEST KITCHEN TIP
If you choose not to use brandy or Cognac, toss the pears in 1 Tbsp. lemon juice to preserve their color and freshness.

WARM CABBAGE, FENNEL & PEAR SALAD

Yuletide Cheer

Deck the halls and set the table—Christmas is the season of good food and good cheer. Whether you're sitting down with your family or hosting a holiday party for friends, these dishes are just what you need to make spirits bright.

MAPLE & BACON GLAZED BRUSSELS SPROUTS

CALIFORNIA ROAST LAMB

This recipe is easy to make and requires little attention. It goes especially well with any rice dish—and most any occasion.
—Ann Eastman, Santa Monica, CA

Prep: 10 min. • **Bake:** 2½ hours
Makes: 12 servings

- 1 leg of lamb (4 to 5 lbs.)
- 2 to 3 garlic cloves, halved
- 1 tsp. seasoned salt
- 1 tsp. pepper
- 1 tsp. dried oregano
- 2 cans (8 oz. each) tomato sauce
- 1 cup water
  Juice of 1 lemon
- 3 to 5 large fresh artichokes, quartered
  Roasted lemon wedges, fresh oregano and fresh thyme sprigs

1. Preheat oven to 400°. Cut slits in lamb; insert garlic. Rub meat with salt, pepper and oregano. Roast for 30 minutes. Reduce heat to 350°; roast 1 hour more.
2. Skim off any fat in pan; pour tomato sauce, water and lemon juice over lamb. Place artichokes around meat. Roast 1 hour longer or until the meat reaches desired doneness (for medium-rare, a thermometer should read 135°; medium, 140°; medium-well, 145°). Garnish with lemons and fresh herbs.
3 oz. cooked lamb: 152 cal., 5g fat (2g sat. fat), 68mg chol., 365mg sod., 6g carb. (1g sugars, 3g fiber), 21g pro.

MAPLE & BACON GLAZED BRUSSELS SPROUTS

Here's a fantastic side dish that even children will love. Count on sweet maple syrup and smoky bacon to complement the Brussels sprouts.
—Jan Valdez, Chicago, IL

Prep: 15 min. • **Cook:** 20 min.
Makes: 4 servings

- 5 bacon strips, chopped
- 1 lb. fresh Brussels sprouts, trimmed
- 3 Tbsp. butter
- ½ cup chicken broth
- ¼ cup chopped pecans
- ¼ cup maple syrup
- ¼ tsp. salt
- ¼ tsp. pepper

1. In a small skillet, cook bacon over medium heat until crisp. Remove to paper towels with a slotted spoon; drain.
2. Cut an X in the core of each Brussels sprout. In a large skillet, saute sprouts in butter until lightly browned, 4-5 minutes.
3. Stir in the broth, pecans, maple syrup, salt and pepper. Bring to a boil. Reduce heat; cover and simmer for 5 minutes. Uncover; cook and stir until Brussels sprouts are tender, 8-10 minutes longer. Sprinkle with bacon.
¾ cup: 273 cal., 18g fat (7g sat. fat), 32mg chol., 544mg sod., 25g carb. (15g sugars, 5g fiber), 8g pro.

BABY SWISS CHRISTMAS CHEESECAKE

STANDING RIB ROAST

Treat your family to tender slices of standing rib roast or use the seasoning blend on a different cut of beef for a hearty and delicious main dish. I love to prepare this recipe for special occasions.
—Lucy Meyring, Walden, CO

Prep: 5 min. • **Bake:** 2¼ hours + standing
Makes: 10 servings

- 3 tsp. lemon-pepper seasoning
- 3 tsp. paprika
- 1½ tsp. garlic salt
- 1 tsp. dried rosemary, crushed
- ½ tsp. cayenne pepper
- 1 bone-in beef rib roast (6 to 7 lbs.)
- 2 cups beef stock

1. Preheat oven to 325°. In a small bowl, mix the first 5 ingredients. Place roast in a roasting pan, fat side up; rub with the seasoning mixture.
2. Roast for 2¼-2¾ hours or until the meat reaches desired doneness (for medium-rare, a thermometer should read 135°; medium, 140°; medium-well, 145°). Remove roast from oven; tent with foil. Let stand 15 minutes before carving.
3. Meanwhile, pour the drippings and loosened browned bits from the roasting pan into a small saucepan. Skim fat. Add beef stock to drippings; bring to a boil. Serve jus with roast.

4 oz. cooked beef with about 3 Tbsp. jus: 322 cal., 18g fat (7g sat. fat), 0 chol., 438mg sod., 1g carb. (1g sugars, 0 fiber), 37g pro.

BABY SWISS CHRISTMAS CHEESECAKE

This beautiful cheesecake appetizer can be refrigerated up to 24 hours before serving, so it's the perfect make-ahead recipe for holiday gatherings.
—Marilyn Edelman, Sabetha, KS

Prep: 35 min. + cooling
Bake: 35 min. + chilling
Makes: 24 servings

- 1½ cups crushed Ritz crackers (about 36 crackers)
- 3 Tbsp. butter, melted
- 3 pkg. (8 oz. each) cream cheese, softened
- ¼ cup heavy whipping cream
- 1 Tbsp. oil from sun-dried tomatoes
- 3 large eggs, room temperature, lightly beaten
- 6 oz. baby Swiss cheese, shredded
- ½ cup oil-packed sun-dried tomatoes, patted dry and thinly sliced
- 4 green onions, chopped
  Crackers

1. Preheat oven to 375°. In a small bowl, mix cracker crumbs and butter. Press onto bottom of a greased 9-in. springform pan.

Place pan on a baking sheet. Bake until golden brown, about 10 minutes. Cool on a wire rack. Reduce oven setting to 325°.
2. In a large bowl, beat the cream cheese until smooth. Beat in cream and oil. Add eggs; beat on low speed just until blended. Fold in cheese, tomatoes and green onions. Pour over the crust. Return pan to baking sheet in oven.
3. Continue to bake until the center is almost set, 35-40 minutes. Cool on a wire rack for 10 minutes. Loosen sides from pan with a knife. Cool for 1 hour longer. Refrigerate overnight, covering when completely cooled.
4. Remove rim from pan. Serve the cheesecake with your choice of crackers.
Freeze option: Wrap the baked and cooled cheesecake in plastic wrap and freeze up to 3 weeks. To use, thaw overnight in the refrigerator.
1 slice: 197 cal., 17g fat (9g sat. fat), 65mg chol., 176mg sod., 6g carb. (2g sugars, 0 fiber), 5g pro.

TEST KITCHEN TIP
This has a mild Swiss cheese flavor, so if you want a more intense cheesy flavor, substitute aged Swiss or Gruyere cheese.

5i

SUPER SIMPLE SCALLOPED POTATOES

I've made many types of scalloped potatoes but I always come back to this rich, creamy, foolproof recipe. The dish gets scraped clean every time I make it.
—Kallee Krong-McCreery, Escondido, CA

Prep: 20 min. • **Bake:** 45 min. + standing
Makes: 10 servings

- 3 cups heavy whipping cream
- 1½ tsp. salt
- ½ tsp. pepper
- 1 tsp. minced fresh thyme, optional
- 3 lbs. russet potatoes, thinly sliced (about 10 cups)

1. Preheat oven to 350°. In a large bowl, combine cream, salt, pepper and, if desired, thyme. Arrange potatoes in a greased 13x9-in. baking dish. Pour cream mixture over top.

2. Bake, uncovered, until the potatoes are tender and the top is lightly browned, 45-55 minutes. Let stand for 10 minutes before serving.

¾ cup: 353 cal., 27g fat (17g sat. fat), 99mg chol., 390mg sod., 26g carb. (3g sugars, 3g fiber), 4g pro.

PERFECT WINTER SALAD

PERFECT WINTER SALAD

This is my most-requested salad recipe. It is delicious as a main dish with grilled chicken breast or as a side salad. It's so good, I sometimes eat it at the end of the meal, instead of dessert!
—DeNae Shewmake, Burnsville, MN

Takes: 20 min. • **Makes:** 12 servings

- ¼ cup reduced-fat mayonnaise
- ¼ cup maple syrup
- 3 Tbsp. white wine vinegar
- 2 Tbsp. minced shallot
- 2 tsp. sugar
- ½ cup canola oil
- 2 pkg. (5 oz. each) spring mix salad greens
- 2 medium tart apples, thinly sliced
- 1 cup dried cherries
- 1 cup pecan halves
- ¼ cup thinly sliced red onion

In a small bowl, mix the first 5 ingredients; gradually whisk in oil until blended. Refrigerate, covered, until ready to serve. To serve, place the remaining ingredients in a large bowl; toss with dressing.

1 cup: 235 cal., 18g fat (1g sat. fat), 2mg chol., 47mg sod., 20g carb. (15g sugars, 2g fiber), 2g pro.

READER REVIEW

"When asked to bring a salad to a family gathering, I wanted to do something homemade and tasty. This salad was easy to prepare and received rave reviews from everyone!"

KELLY, TASTEOFHOME.COM

FINNISH MULLED WINE

I found this recipe tucked in the pages of my Finnish grandmother's Bible. It takes 24 hours to make. Store tightly bottled in the fridge up to two weeks.
—Judy Batson, Tampa, FL

Prep: 15 min. + chilling • **Cook:** 30 min.
Makes: 6 servings

- ⅔ cup vodka
- ⅔ cup port wine
- 15 whole cloves
- 3 cinnamon sticks (3 in.)
- 2 orange zest strips (1 to 3 in.)
- 1 orange slice
- 1 lemon zest strip (1 to 3 in.)
- 1 lemon slice
- 1 piece fresh gingerroot (about 2 in.), peeled and thinly sliced
- 1 tsp. cardamom pods
- 3 cups dry red wine
- 1 cup packed brown sugar
  Optional: Raisins and blanched almonds

1. In a large bowl, combine the first 10 ingredients. Refrigerate, covered, overnight.

2. Transfer to a large saucepan; stir in red wine and brown sugar. Bring just to a simmer (do not boil). Reduce heat; simmer gently, uncovered, until flavors are blended, about 30 minutes, stirring to dissolve the sugar. Strain.

3. Serve warm over raisins and blanched almonds, if desired.

⅔ cup: 339 cal., 0 fat (0 sat. fat), 0 chol., 18mg sod., 43g carb. (38g sugars, 0 fiber), 0 pro.

GRANDMA'S CHRISTMAS CAKE

One bite of this old-fashioned spice cake will bring back memories. Loaded with raisins and nuts, it tastes extra special drizzled with the rich buttery sauce.
—Linda Stemen, Monroeville, IN

Prep: 25 min. • **Bake:** 45 min. + cooling
Makes: 16 servings (2⅔ cups sauce)

- 2 cups sugar
- 2 cups raisins
- 2 cups water
- 1 cup butter, cubed
- 3½ cups all-purpose flour
- 1 tsp. baking soda
- 1 tsp. ground cinnamon
- ½ tsp. each ground nutmeg and cloves
- 1 cup chopped pecans

BRANDY BUTTER SAUCE
- 1 cup heavy whipping cream
- 1 cup butter, cubed
- 1 cup sugar
- 4 large egg yolks, lightly beaten
- ¼ cup brandy

1. Preheat oven to 350°. In a large saucepan, combine sugar, raisins, water and butter. Bring to a boil. Reduce heat to medium; cook, uncovered, until sugar is dissolved, about 5 minutes. Remove from heat; cool.

2. Combine flour, baking soda, cinnamon, nutmeg and cloves. Add the raisin mixture; beat until blended. Fold in pecans.

3. Pour into a greased and floured 10-in. fluted tube pan. Bake until cake springs back when lightly touched, 45-55 minutes. Cool for 10 minutes before removing from pan to a wire rack to cool completely.

4. For sauce, in a large saucepan, bring cream to a boil; stir in butter and sugar until smooth. Reduce heat; stir a small amount of the hot liquid into egg yolks. Return all to the pan, stirring constantly. Cook until the sauce is slightly thickened and coats the back of a spoon (do not boil). Remove from heat; stir in brandy. Serve warm with cake.

1 slice with about 3 Tbsp. sauce: 624 cal., 35g fat (19g sat. fat), 124mg chol., 271mg sod., 75g carb. (49g sugars, 2g fiber), 5g pro.

GRANDMA'S CHRISTMAS CAKE

HERB FOCACCIA ROLLS

HERB FOCACCIA ROLLS

These yeast rolls speckled with fresh herbs are a breeze—no kneading or long wait times. Break out the good butter!
—Linda Schend, Kenosha, WI

Prep: 15 min. + rising • **Bake:** 20 min.
Makes: 1½ dozen

- 3 cups all-purpose flour
- 1 pkg. (¼ oz.) quick-rise yeast
- 2 Tbsp. minced fresh thyme, divided
- 2 Tbsp. minced fresh rosemary, divided
- 1 Tbsp. sugar
- 1½ tsp. kosher salt, divided
- 1½ cups warm water (120° to 130°)
- 6 Tbsp. extra-virgin olive oil, divided

1. Combine flour, yeast, 1 Tbsp. thyme, 1 Tbsp. rosemary, sugar and 1 tsp. salt. Add water and 2 Tbsp. oil; beat 1 minute (dough will be very sticky).

2. Divide the dough among 18 greased muffin cups. Let rise in a warm place until doubled, about 30 minutes.

3. In a small saucepan over medium-low heat, stir together the remaining herbs, salt and olive oil just until the herbs are fragrant and oil is hot, about 1½ minutes. Remove from heat; cool.

4. Gently spoon cooled herb mixture over each roll. Bake until golden brown, 20-25 minutes.

Note: To make standard focaccia, spread dough in a greased 13x9-in. pan, then let rise in a warm place until doubled, about 30 minutes. Top with herb mixture; bake at 375° until golden brown, 25-30 minutes.

1 roll: 120 cal., 5g fat (1g sat. fat), 0 chol., 161mg sod., 17g carb. (1g sugars, 1g fiber), 2g pro.

MASHED CAULIFLOWER

This side dish is lower in carbs than mashed potatoes, but just as flavorful and satisfying. It makes an enticing addition to a holiday table. Chopped green onions can add a festive garnish.
—Tina Martini, Sparks, NV

Takes: 25 min. • **Makes:** 2½ cups

- 1 medium head cauliflower, broken into florets
- ½ cup shredded Swiss cheese
- 1 Tbsp. butter
- ¾ tsp. salt
- ¼ tsp. pepper
- ⅛ tsp. garlic powder
- 2 to 3 Tbsp. 2% milk

1. In a large saucepan, bring 1 in. water to a boil. Add cauliflower; cook, covered, 8-12 minutes or until very tender. Drain.

2. Mash the cauliflower, adding cheese, butter, seasonings and enough milk to reach desired consistency.

¾ cup: 160 cal., 10g fat (6g sat. fat), 28mg chol., 718mg sod., 11g carb. (4g sugars, 4g fiber), 9g pro.

MAPLE PECAN PIE

Our Vermont maple syrup can't be beat, and this is one of my favorite pies. It's also quick and easy to make.
—Mildred Wescom, Belvidere, VT

Prep: 10 min. • **Bake:** 40 min. + cooling
Makes: 8 servings

  Pastry for single-crust pie
3 large eggs, room temperature
½ cup sugar
1 cup maple syrup
3 Tbsp. butter, melted
½ tsp. vanilla extract
¼ tsp. salt
2 cups pecan halves
  Whipped cream, optional

1. Preheat oven to 375°. Roll out dough to fit a 9-in. pie plate. Transfer to pie plate. Trim crust to 1-in. beyond edge of plate; flute the edges.
2. In a bowl, whisk eggs and sugar until smooth. Add maple syrup, butter, vanilla, salt and pecans. Pour into prepared crust.
3. Bake until a knife inserted in the center comes out clean, 30-40 minutes. Cool on a wire rack for 1 hour. If desired, top with whipped cream to serve. Store leftovers in the refrigerator.
1 piece: 561 cal., 35g fat (12g sat. fat), 111mg chol., 294mg sod., 58g carb. (38g sugars, 3g fiber), 7g pro.
Pastry for single-crust pie (9 in.): Combine 1¼ cups all-purpose flour and ¼ tsp. salt; cut in ½ cup cold butter until crumbly. Gradually add 3-5 Tbsp. ice water, tossing with a fork until the dough holds together when pressed. Wrap dough and refrigerate 1 hour.

TUSCAN-STYLE ROASTED ASPARAGUS

The bright red and green of this side dish make it perfect for a Christmas table. It is convenient for celebrations because you can serve it hot or cold.
—Jannine Fisk, Malden, MA

Prep: 20 min. • **Bake:** 15 min.
Makes: 8 servings

1½ lbs. fresh asparagus, trimmed
1½ cups grape tomatoes, halved
3 Tbsp. pine nuts
3 Tbsp. olive oil, divided
2 garlic cloves, minced
1 tsp. kosher salt
½ tsp. pepper
1 Tbsp. lemon juice
⅓ cup grated Parmesan cheese
1 tsp. grated lemon zest

1. Preheat oven to 400°. Place asparagus, tomatoes and pine nuts on a foil-lined 15x10x1-in. baking pan. Mix 2 Tbsp. oil, garlic, salt and pepper; add to asparagus and toss to coat.
2. Bake for 15-20 minutes or just until the asparagus is tender. Drizzle with remaining oil and the lemon juice; sprinkle with cheese and lemon zest. Toss to combine.
1 serving: 95 cal., 8g fat (2g sat. fat), 3mg chol., 294mg sod., 4g carb. (2g sugars, 1g fiber), 3g pro. **Diabetic exchanges:** 1½ fat, 1 vegetable.

TEST KITCHEN TIP
Common olive oil works better for cooking at high heat than virgin or extra-virgin oil. The higher grades have ideal flavor for cold foods, but smoke at lower temperatures.

TUSCAN-STYLE ROASTED ASPARAGUS

Christmas Gingerbread Treats

Gingerbread is one of the most classic and enduring flavors of Christmas. Cookies, bars, pie, candy and even ice cream...with this collection of recipes, you can have a different gingerbread treat every day from Christmas Eve to New Year's!

FROSTED GINGERBREAD NUT COOKIES

enough cream to achieve the desired consistency. Frost cooled cookies. Top each with a walnut half if desired.

1 cookie: 74 cal., 3g fat (1g sat. fat), 8mg chol., 62mg sod., 12g carb. (7g sugars, 0 fiber), 1g pro.

NO-CHURN GINGERBREAD ICE CREAM

Christmas is gingerbread time! And this ice cream says it all. I've found that dark brown sugar works better than light.
—Jacqueline McComas, Paoli, PA

Prep: 15 min. + freezing
Makes: 8 servings (1 qt.)

- 2 cups heavy whipping cream
- 1 jar (7 oz.) marshmallow creme
- 3 Tbsp. molasses
- 2 Tbsp. dark brown sugar
- ½ tsp. ground allspice
- ½ tsp. ground cloves

1. Place heavy cream and marshmallow creme in a food processor; process for 10 seconds. Add remaining ingredients; process until thickened, about 30 seconds.
2. Transfer to freezer containers, allowing headspace for expansion. Freeze until firm, 8 hours or overnight.

½ cup: 325 cal., 22g fat (14g sat. fat), 68mg chol., 39mg sod., 26g carb. (26g sugars, 0 fiber), 2g pro.

FROSTED GINGERBREAD NUT COOKIES

I received the recipe for these soft ginger cookies from a dear friend, who has since passed away. A comforting classic like this always satisfies my sweet tooth.
—Karyn Rogers, Hemet, CA

Prep: 15 min
Bake: 10 min./batch + cooling
Makes: 5 dozen

- ½ cup butter, softened
- ⅔ cup sugar
- 1 large egg, room temperature
- ½ cup molasses
- 2¾ cups all-purpose flour
- 1 tsp. baking soda
- 1 tsp. ground cinnamon
- 1 tsp. ground ginger
- ½ tsp. salt
- ¼ tsp. ground cloves
- ½ cup buttermilk
- ½ cup chopped walnuts

FROSTING
- 1½ cups confectioners' sugar
- 4½ tsp. butter, softened
- ½ tsp. vanilla extract
- 2 to 3 Tbsp. half-and-half cream
  Walnut halves, optional

1. Preheat oven to 350°. In a large bowl, cream butter and sugar until light and fluffy. Beat in egg and molasses. Combine flour, baking soda, cinnamon, ginger, salt and cloves; add to the creamed mixture alternately with buttermilk; beat well after each addition. Stir in chopped walnuts.
2. Drop by tablespoonfuls 2 in. apart onto greased baking sheets. Bake for 10-12 minutes or until the edges are firm. Remove to wire racks to cool.
3. For frosting, in a small bowl, combine confectioners' sugar, butter, vanilla and

CRANBERRY GINGERBREAD SCONES

GINGERBREAD MERINGUE BARS

PICTURED ON P. 263

For the best of both worlds, I combined my grandmother's gingerbread recipe with my aunt's special brown sugar meringue.

—Eden Dranger, Los Angeles, CA

Prep: 20 min. • **Bake:** 30 min. + cooling
Makes: 2 dozen

- ¼ cup butter, softened
- 1 cup molasses
- 2 large egg yolks, room temperature
- 1 large egg, room temperature
- ¼ cup canned pumpkin
- 1 tsp. vanilla extract
- 1½ cups whole wheat flour
- 2½ tsp. ground cinnamon
- 2 tsp. ground ginger
- 1 tsp. baking powder
- 1 tsp. baking soda
- ¾ tsp. ground allspice
- ¼ tsp. salt
- 1 cup miniature marshmallows
- ½ cup chopped pecans
- ½ cup semisweet chocolate chips

MERINGUE

- 4 large egg whites, room temperature
- ½ cup packed brown sugar

1. Preheat oven to 350°. Beat butter and molasses until blended. Add egg yolks and egg, 1 at a time, beating well after each addition. Beat in pumpkin and vanilla.
2. Combine the flour, cinnamon, ginger, baking powder, baking soda, allspice and salt. Gradually add to molasses mixture. Pour into a greased 13x9-in. baking pan. Sprinkle with marshmallows, pecans and chocolate chips. Bake for 20 minutes.
3. Meanwhile, in a small bowl, beat egg whites on medium speed until soft peaks form. Gradually beat in brown sugar, 1 Tbsp. at a time, on high until stiff glossy peaks form and the sugar is dissolved.
4. Remove gingerbread from oven; spread with meringue. Bake until meringue is lightly browned, 9-11 minutes longer. Cool completely. Cut into bars.
1 bar: 135 cal., 4g fat (2g sat. fat), 31mg chol., 129mg sod., 24g carb. (15g sugars, 1g fiber), 2g pro. **Diabetic exchanges:** 1½ starch, 1 fat.

CRANBERRY GINGERBREAD SCONES

Cranberry-studded scones are perfect for a holiday brunch. The aroma is inviting, so I bake these scones as guests arrive.

—Lisa Varner, El Paso, TX

Prep: 20 min. • **Bake:** 15 min.
Makes: 8 servings

- 2 cups all-purpose flour
- 2 tsp. baking powder
- 1 tsp. ground ginger
- 1 tsp. ground cinnamon
- ¼ tsp. salt
- ¼ tsp. baking soda
- ¼ tsp. ground nutmeg
- ½ cup cold butter, cubed
- ⅓ cup heavy whipping cream
- ⅓ cup molasses
- ½ cup dried cranberries

TOPPING

- 1 Tbsp. sugar
- ¼ tsp. ground cinnamon
- 1 Tbsp. finely chopped pecans

1. Preheat oven to 400°. In a large bowl, whisk together the first 7 ingredients. Cut in butter until the mixture resembles coarse crumbs. In another bowl, whisk together cream and molasses; stir into the crumb mixture just until moistened. Stir in cranberries.
2. Turn onto a lightly floured surface; knead gently 5 times. Pat dough into an 8-in. circle; cut into 8 wedges. Place on an ungreased baking sheet.
3. Mix sugar and cinnamon; sprinkle over the scones. Top with pecans. Bake until light brown, 12-14 minutes. Serve warm.
1 scone: 326 cal., 16g fat (10g sat. fat), 44mg chol., 314mg sod., 43g carb. (17g sugars, 2g fiber), 4g pro.

GINGERBREAD CUTOUT COOKIES

GINGERBREAD CUTOUT COOKIES

The smell of these cookies makes me remember going to Grandma's house when I was young. My boys always linger around the kitchen when I make them— the aroma is irresistible!
—Christy Thelen, Kellogg, IA

Prep: 30 min. + chilling
Bake: 10 min./batch + cooling
Makes: 5 dozen

- ¾ cup butter, softened
- 1 cup packed brown sugar
- 1 large egg, room temperature
- ¾ cup molasses
- 4 cups all-purpose flour
- 2 tsp. ground ginger
- 1½ tsp. baking soda
- 1½ tsp. ground cinnamon
- ¾ tsp. ground cloves
- ¼ tsp. salt
  Vanilla frosting of your choice
  Red and green paste food coloring

1. In a large bowl, cream butter and brown sugar until light and fluffy. Add egg and molasses. Combine flour, ginger, baking soda, cinnamon, cloves and salt; gradually add to creamed mixture and mix well. Cover and refrigerate until easy to handle, about 4 hours or overnight.
2. Preheat oven to 350°. On a lightly floured surface, roll the dough to ⅛-in. thickness. Cut with floured 2½-in. cookie cutters. Place 1 in. apart on ungreased baking sheets.
3. Bake until edges are firm, 8-10 minutes. Remove to wire racks to cool completely. Tint some of the frosting red and some green; leave the remaining frosting plain. Decorate cookies as desired.
1 cookie: 77 cal., 2g fat (1g sat. fat), 10mg chol., 69mg sod., 13g carb. (6g sugars, 0 fiber), 1g pro.

GINGERBREAD WAFFLES

Our family enjoys all types of waffles, but these are our favorite. They're softer than traditional waffles, and the mix of spices provides a distinctive flavor. This recipe doubles easily to feed a crowd. Top with your favorites like fruit, butter and syrup.
—Ann Nace, Perkasie, PA

Prep: 15 min. • **Bake:** 20 min.
Makes: 6 waffles (about 4 in.)

- 1 cup all-purpose flour
- 1½ tsp. baking powder
- 1 tsp. ground ginger
- ¾ tsp. ground cinnamon
- ½ tsp. ground allspice
- ½ tsp. baking soda
- ¼ tsp. ground mustard
- ¼ tsp. salt
- ⅓ cup packed brown sugar
- 1 large egg, separated, room temperature
- ¾ cup buttermilk
- ¼ cup molasses
- 3 Tbsp. butter, melted
- ⅓ cup chopped raisins
- ⅛ tsp. cream of tartar
  Optional: Assorted fresh fruit, butter and maple syrup

1. In a bowl, combine the flour, baking powder, ginger, cinnamon, allspice, baking soda, mustard and salt; set aside.
2. Beat brown sugar and egg yolk until fluffy. Add buttermilk, molasses and butter; stir into dry ingredients just until combined. Add raisins. In a small bowl, beat egg white and cream of tartar until soft peaks form. Gently fold into batter.
3. Bake in a preheated waffle iron according to manufacturer's directions until golden brown. Top as desired.
2 waffles: 521 cal., 14g fat (8g sat. fat), 104mg chol., 830mg sod., 92g carb. (54g sugars, 2g fiber), 9g pro.

GINGERBREAD TRUFFLES

I never received compliments on my baking until I brought these cinnamon-ginger truffles to a party. Every Christmas, family, friends and even co-workers ask me to make these.

—Angela Randjelovic, Independence, OH

Prep: 50 min. • **Cook:** 10 min. + chilling
Makes: 3 dozen

- 14 oz. white baking chocolate, chopped
- ½ cup heavy whipping cream
- 1 tsp. ground cinnamon
- ½ tsp. ground ginger
- ¼ tsp. ground cloves
- 1 pkg. (10 oz.) dark chocolate chips
- 5 tsp. shortening
- 3 Tbsp. crystallized ginger

1. Place white chocolate in a small bowl. In a small saucepan, bring whipping cream just to a boil. Pour over white chocolate; whisk until smooth. Stir in cinnamon, ginger and cloves. Cool to room temperature, stirring occasionally. Cover and refrigerate until firm, about 3 hours.
2. Shape mixture into ¾-in. balls. Place on waxed paper-lined baking sheets. Refrigerate for at least 1 hour.
3. In a microwave, melt dark chocolate chips and shortening; stir until smooth. Dip truffles in chocolate; allow excess to drip off. Place on waxed paper. Sprinkle with crystallized ginger. Store in an airtight container in the refrigerator.

1 truffle: 113 cal., 7g fat (5g sat. fat), 4mg chol., 12mg sod., 13g carb. (12g sugars, 1g fiber), 1g pro.

GINGERBREAD-SPICED PUMPKIN PIE

Ever since I was a kid, pumpkin pie has been my favorite. The first time I made this pie was for Christmas a few years ago. The following Christmas, I received a gift with all the ingredients in it and a note asking me to make it again as soon as time permitted!

—Rod Dombek, Mazeppa, MN

Prep: 20 min. • **Bake:** 45 min.
Makes: 8 servings

Pastry for single-crust pie
FILLING
- 2 large eggs, lightly beaten
- 1½ cups canned pumpkin

- 1 cup evaporated milk
- ⅔ cup sugar
- ⅓ cup water
- ¼ cup dark molasses
- 1 tsp. ground cinnamon
- ½ tsp. salt
- ½ tsp. ground ginger
- ¼ tsp. ground nutmeg
- ¼ tsp. ground cloves
- Additional pastry for single-crust pie, optional
- Whipped cream, optional

1. Preheat the oven to 425°. On a lightly floured surface, roll dough to a ⅛-in.-thick circle; transfer to a 9-in. pie plate. Trim crust to ½ in. beyond rim of plate; flute edge. Refrigerate while preparing filling.
2. In a large bowl, whisk filling ingredients. Pour into crust. Bake on a lower oven rack for 15 minutes.
3. Reduce oven setting to 350°; bake until a knife inserted in the center comes out clean, 30-35 minutes longer. Cool on a wire rack; serve within 2 hours. Garnish with whipped cream if desired. Refrigerate any leftovers.

1 piece: 341 cal., 15g fat (9g sat. fat), 87mg chol., 356mg sod., 46g carb. (29g sugars, 2g fiber), 6g pro.
Pastry for single-crust pie (9 in.): Combine 1¼ cups all-purpose flour and ¼ tsp. salt; cut in ½ cup cold butter until crumbly. Gradually add 3-5 Tbsp. ice water, tossing with a fork until the dough holds together when pressed. Wrap and refrigerate for 1 hour.

TEST KITCHEN TIP
To add decorative cutouts, as in the photo below, make a second batch of pastry dough. Roll ⅛-in.-thick; cut out with leaf-shaped cookie cutters. With a sharp knife, score veins on leaves. Bake leaves on an ungreased baking sheet at 400° until golden brown, 6-8 minutes. Remove to a wire rack to cool. Arrange around edge of pie.

GINGERBREAD-SPICED PUMPKIN PIE

Delectable Desserts

When dinner is over, it's time for the best part of the day—dessert!
These scrumptious, tempting desserts come together with little fuss,
making them the perfect end to a weeknight dinner or
just what you need for a special weekend treat.

Key Lime Cream Pie (p. 298) **Chocolate Eclair Delight** (p. 301) **Spiced Rum Fruitcake** (p. 294)
Butter Pecan Syrup (p. 302) **Makeover Pineapple Upside-Down Cake** (p. 294)

SQUASH CUSTARD PIE

Acorn squash has been a favorite of mine since I was little. I made up the recipe for this pie when I had a surplus of garden squash one year. Serve it as a different dessert at Thanksgiving or Christmas.
—Mary Kelly, Hopland, CA

Prep: 10 min. + chilling
Bake: 55 min. + cooling
Makes: 8 servings

- 1 cup sugar
- 1 cup mashed cooked winter squash
- 1 cup heavy whipping cream
- 3 large eggs, lightly beaten
- 1 tsp. ground ginger
- 1 tsp. ground cinnamon
- ½ tsp. ground nutmeg
  Dash salt
- 1 unbaked pastry shell
  Whipped cream or topping
    or garnish

1. Preheat oven to 375°. In a bowl, combine the first 8 ingredients.
2. Pour into the pastry shell; bake for 10 minutes. Reduce heat to 350°; bake for 45 minutes or until set. Cool on a wire rack. Chill. Garnish with whipped cream.
1 slice: 361 cal., 20g fat (10g sat. fat), 125mg chol., 154mg sod., 43g carb. (27g sugars, 1g fiber), 4g pro.

PEACH COBBLER COOKIES

PEACH COBBLER COOKIES

When my sister brought fresh peaches, we decided to make these fruity cookies. Or try making ice cream sandwiches—just spread some vanilla ice cream between two cookies for a delicious summer treat!
—Anna Miller, Churdan, IA

Prep: 30 min. • **Bake:** 15 min./batch
Makes: about 4½ dozen

- 1 cup butter, softened
- 1 cup sugar
- ⅓ cup packed brown sugar
- 1 large egg, room temperature
- 1 tsp. vanilla extract
- ¼ tsp. almond extract
- 3 cups all-purpose flour
- 1½ tsp. ground cinnamon
- 1 tsp. cream of tartar
- 1 tsp. baking soda
- ½ tsp. salt
- ¼ tsp. ground nutmeg
- 1 cup chopped peeled fresh peaches

1. Preheat oven to 350°. In a large bowl, cream butter and sugar until light and fluffy. Beat in egg and extracts. In another bowl, whisk flour, cinnamon, cream of tartar, baking soda, salt and nutmeg; gradually beat into the creamed mixture. Stir in peaches.
2. Drop dough by tablespoonfuls 2 in. apart onto parchment-lined baking sheets. Bake until set, 14-16 minutes. Cool on pans for 2 minutes. Remove to wire racks to cool. Store in an airtight container.
1 cookie: 78 cal., 4g fat (2g sat. fat), 12mg chol., 74mg sod., 11g carb. (5g sugars, 0 fiber), 1g pro.

EASY STRAWBERRY LEMONADE FREEZER PIE

Three simple ingredients mixed together and spread into a graham crust make magic while your freezer does the all the work. Make this pie ahead and freeze it overnight or even longer. Feel free to vary the fruit if you'd like!
—Debbie Glasscock, Conway, AR

Prep: 15 min. + freezing
Makes: 8 servings

- 1 container (23.2 oz.) frozen sweetened sliced strawberries, thawed (2½ cups thawed)
- 1 pkg. (3.4 oz.) instant lemon pudding mix
- 1 carton (8 oz.) frozen whipped topping, thawed
- 1 9-in. graham cracker crust (about 6 oz.)
  Optional: Additional whipped topping and fresh strawberries

1. In a large bowl, combine strawberries (with juices) and pudding mix; let stand until slightly thickened, about 5 minutes. Fold in whipped topping. Spread into the graham cracker crust.
2. Freeze at least 8 hours or overnight. Let stand 5-10 minutes before serving. If desired, serve with additional whipped topping and strawberries.
1 piece: 306 cal., 10g fat (6g sat. fat), 0 chol., 273mg sod., 51g carb. (45g sugars, 2g fiber), 1g pro.

EASY STRAWBERRY LEMONADE FREEZER PIE

ORCHARD PEAR PIE

At a recent family dinner, I served this pie made with Barlett pears fresh from the orchard. In the winter, you can use canned pears instead.
—Mary Anne Thygesen, Portland, OR

Prep: 30 min. + chilling
Bake: 30 min. + cooling
Makes: 8 servings

    Pastry for single-crust pie
- 1 large egg, room temperature
- ¾ cup sour cream
- ½ cup sugar
- ¼ cup all-purpose flour
- ¼ cup plain Greek yogurt
- 1 tsp. vanilla extract
- ¼ tsp. salt
- 4 large ripe pears, peeled and chopped (about 4 cups)

TOPPING
- ¾ cup all-purpose flour
- ¾ cup old-fashioned oats
- ½ cup packed brown sugar
- 2 Tbsp. chopped pecans
- ½ tsp. ground cardamom
- ½ cup cold butter

1. On a lightly floured surface, roll dough to a ⅛-in.-thick circle; transfer to a 9-in. pie plate. Trim to ½ in. beyond rim of plate; flute edge. Refrigerate 30 minutes. Preheat oven to 400°.
2. In a small bowl, whisk egg, sour cream, sugar, flour, yogurt, vanilla and salt. Gently stir in pears. Pour into the crust. Bake for 15 minutes.
3. In a small bowl, combine flour, oats, brown sugar, pecans and cardamom. Cut in butter until crumbly; sprinkle over pie.
4. Bake until a knife inserted in the center comes out clean and topping is golden brown, 15-20 minutes. Cover edge with foil during the last 10 minutes to prevent overbrowning if necessary. Cool pie completely on a wire rack. Store in the refrigerator.
1 piece: 599 cal., 31g fat (18g sat. fat), 91mg chol., 346mg sod., 77g carb. (39g sugars, 5g fiber), 7g pro.
Pastry for single-crust pie (9 inches): Combine 1¼ cups all-purpose flour and ¼ tsp. salt; cut in ½ cup cold butter until crumbly. Gradually add 3-5 Tbsp. ice water, tossing with a fork until the dough holds together when pressed. Wrap dough and refrigerate 1 hour.

SPICED RUM FRUITCAKE

This fruitcake not only can be made weeks ahead, it tastes better that way! You can substitute Brazil nuts, pecans and hazelnuts for the walnuts—or use a combination of nuts.
—Jason Boor, Manchester, NY

....

Prep: 25 min. • **Bake:** 1¼ hours + cooling
Makes: 1 loaf (16 slices)

- ¾ cup all-purpose flour
- ½ tsp. baking powder
- ¼ tsp. salt
- 2 cups chopped walnuts
- 1 pkg. (8 oz.) pitted dates, chopped
- 1 cup maraschino cherries, halved
- ½ cup dried mangoes, chopped
- 3 large eggs, room temperature
- ¾ cup packed brown sugar
- 1 cup spiced rum, divided

1. Preheat oven to 300°. Line a 9x5-in. loaf pan with parchment, letting the ends extend up the sides of the pan; grease and set aside.

2. In a large bowl, mix the flour, baking powder and salt. Add the walnuts, dates, cherries and mangoes; toss to coat. In a small bowl, whisk eggs, brown sugar and ½ cup rum until blended; stir into the fruit mixture. Transfer to prepared pan.

3. Bake until a toothpick inserted in the center comes out clean, 1¼-1½ hours. Cool in pan on a wire rack for 20 minutes.

Slowly pour the remaining rum over cake. Cool completely. Wrap tightly and store in a cool, dry place overnight. Cut with a serrated knife.

1 slice: 256 cal., 11g fat (1g sat. fat), 35mg chol., 96mg sod., 35g carb. (25g sugars, 3g fiber), 4g pro

> **TEST KITCHEN TIP**
> Try leftover slices toasted and spread with spiced cream cheese. Fruitcake can be stored in the refrigerator up to 2-3 months.

MAKEOVER PINEAPPLE UPSIDE-DOWN CAKE

Both my boys love this lighter take on a family favorite. Even my husband, who is a bit picky, asks for a piece the next day!
—Mary Lou Moeller, Wooster, OH

....

Prep: 15 min. • **Bake:** 35 min.
Makes: 9 servings

- 3 Tbsp. butter, melted
- ⅓ cup packed brown sugar

MAKEOVER PINEAPPLE UPSIDE-DOWN CAKE

- 9 canned unsweetened pineapple slices
- 9 maraschino cherries halves
- ⅔ cup sugar
- ⅔ cup fat-free milk
- 3 Tbsp. canola oil
- 1 large egg, room temperature
- 1 tsp. lemon extract
- ½ tsp. vanilla extract
- 1⅓ cups cake flour
- 1¼ tsp. baking powder
- ¼ tsp. salt

1. Preheat oven to 350°. Pour butter into a 9-in. square baking pan; sprinkle with brown sugar. Arrange pineapple slices in a single layer in pan; place cherry halves in center of pineapple slices; set aside.

2. In a large bowl, beat sugar, milk, oil, egg and extracts until well blended. Combine the flour, baking powder and salt; gradually beat into the sugar mixture until blended. Pour into prepared pan.

3. Bake for 35-40 minutes or until a toothpick comes out clean. Immediately invert onto a serving plate. Serve warm.

1 piece: 288 cal., 9g fat (3g sat. fat), 34mg chol., 172mg sod., 49g carb. (32g sugars, 1g fiber), 3g pro.

MAKEOVER TRADITIONAL CHEESECAKE

Though softer than a full-fat cheesecake, this lightened-up dessert has all of the original's delectable flavor. Omit the candy toppings and enjoy it plain with coffee if you prefer.

—Anne Addesso, Sheboygan, WI

Prep: 40 min. • **Bake:** 1½ hours + chilling
Makes: 16 servings

- 1¾ cups graham cracker crumbs
- 2 Tbsp. confectioners' sugar
- ¼ cup butter, melted

FILLING
- 1 Tbsp. lemon juice
- 1 Tbsp. vanilla extract
- 2 cups 1% cottage cheese
- 2 cups reduced-fat sour cream, divided
- 2 pkg. (8 oz. each) reduced-fat cream cheese
- 1¼ cups sugar
- 2 Tbsp. all-purpose flour
- 4 large eggs, lightly beaten
- 1 Tbsp. fat-free caramel ice cream topping
- 2 Heath candy bars (1.4 oz. each), chopped

1. Preheat oven to 325°. Place a 9-in. springform pan coated with cooking spray on a double thickness of heavy-duty foil (about 18 in. square). Securely wrap foil around pan.

2. In a small bowl, combine the graham cracker crumbs and confectioners' sugar; stir in butter. Press onto the bottom and 1 in. up the sides of prepared pan. Place on a baking sheet. Bake for 18-22 minutes or until lightly browned. Set on a wire rack to cool.

3. Place the lemon juice, vanilla, cottage cheese and 1 cup sour cream in a blender; cover and process for 2 minutes or until smooth.

4. In a large bowl, beat the cream cheese and sugar until smooth. Beat in remaining sour cream. Add flour and pureed cottage cheese mixture; mix well. Add eggs; beat on low speed just until combined. Pour into crust.

5. Place the springform pan in a larger baking pan; add ¾ in. hot water to the larger pan. Bake at 325° for 1½ hours or until the center is just set and the top appears dull. Remove springform pan from water bath. Cool on a wire rack for 10 minutes.

6. Carefully run a knife around edge of the pan to loosen; cool 1 hour longer. Refrigerate overnight. Remove sides of pan. Garnish with caramel topping and chopped candy.

1 slice: 311 cal., 15g fat (9g sat. fat), 93mg chol., 369mg sod., 32g carb. (25g sugars, 0 fiber), 11g pro.

HEALTH TIP Even reduced-fat cream cheese is quite rich. Use more 1% cottage cheese in place of some of the cream cheese to help save further on calories, fat and total fat in this cheesecake.

MAKEOVER
TRADITIONAL CHEESECAKE

**CHOCOLATE
CHEESECAKE BARS**

CHOCOLATE
CHEESECAKE BARS

*When you don't have time to bake a
real cheesecake, reach for this easy
recipe. An almond-flavored dough
serves as both crust and topping for
the soft chocolaty filling.*
—Louise Good, Flemington, NJ

Prep: 15 min. • **Bake:** 35 min. + cooling
Makes: 4 dozen

- 1 cup butter, softened
- 1½ cups sugar
- 2 large eggs, room temperature
- ½ tsp. almond extract
- 3 cups all-purpose flour
- 1 tsp. baking powder
- ½ tsp. salt

FILLING

- 2 cups (12 oz.) semisweet
  chocolate chips
- 1 pkg. (8 oz.) cream cheese
- 1 can (5 oz.) evaporated milk
- 1 cup chopped walnuts
- ½ tsp. almond extract

1. Preheat oven to 375°. In a large
bowl, cream butter and sugar until light
and fluffy. Add 1 egg at a time, beating
well after each addition. Beat in extract.
Combine the flour, baking powder and
salt; gradually add to creamed mixture
and mix well. Press half the dough onto
the bottom of a greased 13x9-in. baking
pan. Set aside the remaining dough for
the topping.
2. In a large saucepan, combine the
chocolate chips, cream cheese and milk;
cook and stir over low heat until smooth.
Remove from heat; stir in walnuts and
extract. Spread over the dough in pan.
3. Break off small pieces of the remaining
dough; drop over filling. Bake until the
topping is golden brown, 35-40 minutes.
Cool completely on a wire rack. Cut into
bars. Refrigerate any leftovers.
1 bar: 160 cal., 9g fat (5g sat. fat), 25mg
chol., 92mg sod., 17g carb. (11g sugars,
1g fiber), 3g pro.

FRIED ICE CREAM
DESSERT BARS

*Fried ice cream is a delicious treat, but
it can be a hassle to make the individual
servings. This recipe gives you the same
fabulous flavor in an easy and convenient
bar form.*
—Andrea Price, Grafton, WI

Prep: 25 min. + freezing
Cook: 5 min. + cooling
Makes: 16 servings

- ½ cup butter, cubed
- 2 cups crushed cornflakes
- 1½ tsp. ground cinnamon
- 3 Tbsp. sugar
- 1¾ cups heavy whipping cream
- ¼ cup evaporated milk
- ⅛ tsp. salt
- 1 can (14 oz.) sweetened
  condensed milk
- 2 tsp. vanilla extract
  Optional: Honey, whipped cream
  and maraschino cherries

1. In a large skillet, melt butter over
medium heat. Add the cornflakes and
cinnamon; cook and stir until golden
brown, about 5 minutes. Remove from
heat; stir in sugar. Cool completely.
2. In a large bowl, beat whipping cream,
evaporated milk and salt until the mixture
begins to thicken. Gradually beat in the
condensed milk and vanilla until thickened.
3. Sprinkle half the cornflakes onto the
bottom of a greased 9-in. square baking
pan. Pour the filling over the cornflakes;
sprinkle with the remaining cornflakes.
Cover and freeze overnight. Cut into bars.
If desired, serve with honey, whipped
cream and cherries.
1 bar: 276 cal., 18g fat (11g sat. fat), 55mg
chol., 187mg sod., 27g carb. (18g sugars,
0 fiber), 4g pro.

FRIED ICE CREAM DESSERT BARS

KEY LIME CREAM PIE

KEY LIME CREAM PIE

I am very proud of this luscious no-bake beauty. It's so cool and refreshing—and always ideal for any summer potluck or get-together. Wherever I take this pie, it quickly disappears, with everyone asking for the recipe.
—Shirley Rickis, The Villages, FL

Prep: 40 min. + chilling
Makes: 12 servings

- 1 pkg. (11.3 oz.) pecan shortbread cookies, crushed (about 2 cups)
- ⅓ cup butter, melted
- 4 cups heavy whipping cream
- ¼ cup confectioners' sugar
- 1 tsp. coconut extract
- 1 pkg. (8 oz.) cream cheese, softened
- 1 can (14 oz.) sweetened condensed milk
- ½ cup Key lime juice
- ¼ cup sweetened shredded coconut, toasted
    Optional: Key limes, sliced, and maraschino cherries with stems

1. In a small bowl, mix crushed cookies and butter. Press onto bottom and up the sides of a greased 9-in. deep-dish pie plate.

2. In a large bowl, beat cream until it begins to thicken. Add confectioners' sugar and extract; beat until stiff peaks form. In another large bowl, beat cream cheese, condensed milk and lime juice until blended. Fold in 2 cups whipped cream. Spoon into the prepared crust.

3. Top with the remaining whipped cream; sprinkle with coconut. Refrigerate until serving, at least 4 hours. If desired, garnish with cherries and limes.

1 piece: 646 cal., 52g fat (30g sat. fat), 143mg chol., 252mg sod., 41g carb. (29g sugars, 0 fiber), 8g pro.

CARAMELIZED PEAR & WALNUT BREAD PUDDING

This rich dessert is perfect for fall! You can replace the pears with apples or use different nuts. For a personal touch, bake individual servings in ramekins.
—April Harris, Sugar Mountain, NC

Prep: 25 min. • **Bake:** 45 min.
Makes: 9 servings

- 1 Tbsp. butter
- 2 medium pears, peeled and chopped
- 3 large eggs
- 1¾ cups heavy whipping cream
- 1 cup sugar
- 1½ tsp. vanilla extract
- 7 cups cubed bread or egg bread
- ½ cup chopped walnuts, toasted and divided

1. Preheat oven to 350°. In a large skillet, heat butter over medium-high heat. Add pears; cook and stir 4-6 minutes or until pears are tender. Cool slightly.

2. In a large bowl, whisk eggs, cream, sugar and vanilla until blended. Stir in the pears and ¼ cup walnuts. Stir in bread.

3. Transfer the mixture to a greased 8-in. square baking dish. Sprinkle with the remaining ¼ cup walnuts. Bake until puffed, golden and a knife inserted in center comes out clean, 45-50 minutes. Serve warm.

Note: To toast nuts, bake in a shallow pan in a 350° oven for 5-10 minutes or cook in a skillet over low heat until lightly browned, stirring occasionally.

1 serving: 420 cal., 25g fat (13g sat. fat), 118mg chol., 181mg sod., 44g carb. (29g sugars, 2g fiber), 7g pro.

DANISH RHUBARB PUDDING

My grandmother used to make this fruity pudding. It's one of my favorite traditional Danish desserts.

—Kay Sundheim, Nashua, MT

Prep: 20 min. + chilling • **Cook:** 10 min.
Makes: 8 servings

    6   cups chopped fresh or frozen
        rhubarb, thawed
    6   cups water
    2   cups sugar
    ¼   cup cornstarch
    3   Tbsp. cold water
        Half-and-half cream

1. In a saucepan, bring rhubarb and water to a boil. Reduce heat; simmer, uncovered, until the rhubarb is tender, 10-15 minutes. Drain, reserving liquid; discard pulp. Measure 4 cups liquid; return to the pan.
2. Add sugar; bring to a boil. Combine cornstarch and cold water until smooth; stir into the rhubarb liquid. Cook and stir until slightly thickened, 1-2 minutes. Pour into individual dishes. Refrigerate for at least 4 hours before serving. If desired, serve with cream.

½ cup: 228 cal., 0 fat (0 sat. fat), 0 chol., 5mg sod., 58g carb. (51g sugars, 2g fiber), 1g pro.

IRRESISTIBLE APPLE BLACKBERRY CRUMBLE

When I visited Ireland with my mom and sister, one of the desserts we enjoyed was an apple-blackberry crumble at a tiny cafe on the Dingle Peninsula. When I got home I recreated the dessert for my husband and kids. The tart apples and sweet blackberries are wonderful together under the crumble topping. And with every bite I get to reminisce about our unforgettable trip! If fresh blackberries aren't available, use frozen instead.

—Nancy Mock, Colchester, VT

Prep: 30 min. • **Bake:** 30 min.
Makes: 6 servings

    6   medium tart apples (about 2½ lbs.),
        peeled and cut into 1-in. pieces
    ½   cup sugar, divided
    1   Tbsp. lemon juice
    ⅛   tsp. ground cloves
        Dash salt
  1¼   cups fresh blackberries
    1   cup all-purpose flour
    ½   cup cold butter
        Whipped cream, optional

1. Preheat oven to 400°. Grease an 2-qt. baking dish. In a large bowl, toss apples, 2 Tbsp. sugar, lemon juice, cloves and salt. Gently stir in blackberries. Transfer to the prepared dish.
2. In a small bowl, combine flour and the remaining 6 Tbsp. sugar. Cut in butter until crumbly. Sprinkle over the apple mixture. Bake until lightly browned and apples are tender, 30-35 minutes. Serve warm with whipped cream, if desired.

1 serving: 353 cal., 16g fat (10g sat. fat), 41mg chol., 147mg sod., 52g carb. (32g sugars, 4g fiber), 3g pro.

DANISH RHUBARB PUDDING

Palmiers

These exquisite little treats are no longer the exclusive province of bakeries—prepared puff pastry makes it easy to create them at home!

PALMIERS

It takes just two ingredients to make these impressive but easy-to-do French pastries, which are often called palm leaves. Once these light, crispy treats have cooled, store them in airtight containers; they'll keep for a few days. You can freeze palmiers, but before serving, heat them in a 325° oven for 5-10 minutes to restore their crispness.
—*Taste of Home* Test Kitchen

Prep: 20 min. + freezing • **Bake:** 10 min.
Makes: 2 dozen

- 1 cup sugar, divided
- 1 sheet frozen puff pastry, thawed

1 pastry: 83 cal., 3g fat (1g sat. fat), 0mg chol., 34mg sod., 14g carb. (8g sugars, 1g fiber), 1g pro.

HOW TO MAKE
Palmiers

1. Roll it out...
Sprinkle surface with ¼ cup sugar; unfold pastry sheet. Sprinkle with 2 Tbsp. sugar. Roll into a 14x10-in. rectangle. Sprinkle ½ cup sugar to within ½ in. of edges. Lightly press into pastry. Lightly score a line across the middle.

2. ...Then roll it up!
Starting at a short side, roll up jelly-roll style; stop at the score mark. Roll up the other side to score mark. Freeze 20-30 minutes.

3. Slice...
Cut into ⅜-in. slices.

4. ...Then bake!
Place cut side up 2 in. apart on parchment-lined baking sheets; sprinkle with sugar. Bake at 425° for 8 minutes. Turn over; sprinkle with sugar. Bake until golden brown and glazed, 3 minutes longer. Cool on wire racks.

EASY FRESH STRAWBERRY PIE

For my mother's birthday, I made this pie instead of a cake. It was mid-May in Oklahoma, so the berries were just perfect. It was a memorable occasion for the whole family.
—Josh Carter, Birmingham, AL

Prep: 20 min. + cooling
Bake: 15 min. + chilling
Makes: 8 servings

- 1 sheet refrigerated pie crust
- ¾ cup sugar
- 2 Tbsp. cornstarch
- 1 cup water
- 1 pkg. (3 oz.) strawberry gelatin
- 4 cups sliced fresh strawberries
  Whipped cream, optional

1. Preheat the oven to 450°. Line the unpricked crust with a double thickness of heavy-duty foil or parchment. Bake for 8 minutes. Remove foil and bake 5 minutes longer. Cool on a wire rack.
2. In a small saucepan, combine the sugar, cornstarch and water until smooth. Bring to a boil; cook and stir until thickened, about 2 minutes. Remove from heat; stir in gelatin until dissolved. Refrigerate until slightly cooled, 15-20 minutes.
3. Meanwhile, arrange strawberries in the crust. Pour the gelatin mixture over berries. Refrigerate until set. Serve with whipped cream if desired.
1 slice: 264 cal., 7g fat (3g sat. fat), 5mg chol., 125mg sod., 49g carb. (32g sugars, 2g fiber), 2g pro.

TEST KITCHEN TIP
For a different presentation, use whole fresh strawberries and arrange them pointed end up in the pastry shell. This also is a timesaver because you won't have to slice the berries.

CHOCOLATE ECLAIR DELIGHT
PICTURED ON P.291

It's amazing how the layers of this eclair torte soften overnight into a cakelike texture. Before serving, I dust it with cocoa.
—Agnes Ward, Stratford, ON

Prep: 15 min. • **Cook:** 15 min. + chilling
Makes: 9 servings

- ½ cup sugar
- ⅓ cup baking cocoa
- 2 Tbsp. plus 1 tsp. cornstarch
- ⅛ tsp. salt
- ⅛ tsp. ground cinnamon
- 1 can (12 oz.) fat-free evaporated milk
- 1 cup fat-free milk
- ½ cup egg substitute
- 1 tsp. vanilla extract

TOPPING
- 2 cups reduced-fat whipped topping
- 1 Tbsp. plus ½ tsp. baking cocoa, divided
- 9 whole graham crackers, halved

1. In a large heavy saucepan, combine the first 5 ingredients. Gradually whisk in evaporated milk and milk until smooth. Cook and stir over medium heat until mixture comes to a boil. Reduce heat; cook and stir 2 minutes longer or until thickened.
2. Remove from heat. Stir a small amount of the hot filling into egg substitute; return all to pan, stirring constantly. Bring to a gentle boil; cook and stir 2 minutes longer. Remove from the heat. Gently stir in vanilla. Press plastic wrap onto surface of filling; cover and refrigerate until cooled.
3. In a small bowl, combine whipped topping and 1 Tbsp. cocoa; set aside. Arrange half the crackers in a 9-in. square pan coated with cooking spray. Layer half each of the filling and topping over the crackers. Repeat the layers. Cover and refrigerate overnight. Just before serving, sprinkle with remaining cocoa.
1 piece: 209 cal., 4g fat (2g sat. fat), 2mg chol., 213mg sod., 37g carb. (22g sugars, 1g fiber), 7g pro.

TEST KITCHEN TIP
Feel free to use 2 large eggs instead of the egg substitute.

EASY FRESH STRAWBERRY PIE

SLOW-COOKER STRAWBERRY PUDDING CAKE

I created this recipe because of my love of strawberry cheesecake. I had these ingredients in my pantry and thought I'd give it a whirl. The flavors are like a warm, comforting cake version of my beloved strawberry cheesecake. It's a whole lot easier than making traditional cheesecake, too!
—Lisa Renshaw, Kansas City, MO

Prep: 20 min. • **Cook:** 4 hours + standing
Makes: 10 servings

- 3 cups cold 2% milk
- 1 pkg. (3.4 oz.) instant cheesecake or vanilla pudding mix
- 1 pkg. strawberry cake mix (regular size)
- 1 cup water
- 3 large eggs, room temperature
- ⅓ cup canola oil
- 2 cups toasted coconut marshmallows, quartered
  Optional: Strawberry ice cream topping and sliced fresh strawberries

1. In a large bowl, whisk milk and pudding mix 2 minutes. Transfer to a greased 4- or 5-qt. slow cooker. Prepare cake mix batter according to the package directions; pour over the pudding layer.

2. Cook, covered, on low until the edges of the cake are golden brown (center will be moist), about 4 hours.

3. Remove slow-cooker insert; sprinkle cake with marshmallows. Let cake stand, uncovered, 10 minutes before serving. If desired, serve with ice cream topping and fresh strawberries.

1 serving: 377 cal., 13g fat (4g sat. fat), 62mg chol., 540mg sod., 56g carb. (37g sugars, 1g fiber), 6g pro.

BUTTER PECAN SYRUP

My family loves butter pecan anything, and this recipe is perfect over vanilla ice cream, cake or waffles. It's a special treat they really enjoy.
—Angela Lively, Conroe, TX

Prep: 10 min. • **Cook:** 3 hours
Makes: 2 cups

BUTTER PECAN SYRUP

- 1 cup packed brown sugar
- 5 tsp. cornstarch
  Dash salt
- 1 cup water
- ⅓ cup butter, cubed
- ¾ cup chopped pecans, toasted
- 1 tsp. vanilla extract
  Vanilla ice cream

In a 1½-qt. slow cooker, mix the brown sugar, cornstarch and salt. Whisk in water. Cover and cook on high until thickened and bubbly, 3-3½ hours, stirring every 30 minutes. Whisk in butter until melted. Stir in pecans and vanilla. Serve with ice cream.

¼ cup: 251 cal., 15g fat (5g sat. fat), 20mg chol., 87mg sod., 30g carb. (27g sugars, 1g fiber), 1g pro.

TEST KITCHEN TIP
Make this syrup with dark brown sugar for a deeper flavor.

GRANNY'S RHUBARB PIE

This recipe came from my grandmother, who baked many different rhubarb desserts. This was always a favorite of mine.

—Blanche Baninski, Minto, ND

Prep: 20 min. • **Bake:** 1¼ hours
Makes: 8 servings

- 3 cups all-purpose flour
- 1½ tsp. salt
- 1 cup shortening
- 1 large egg, room temperature
- 5 Tbsp. cold water
- 1 tsp. white vinegar

FILLING

- 3 cups sliced fresh or frozen rhubarb (½-in. pieces)
- 2 cups sliced peeled tart apples
- 1 can (8 oz.) crushed pineapple, drained
- ¼ cup honey
- 1 Tbsp. lemon juice
- 1 cup sugar
- 3 Tbsp. all-purpose flour
- 1 Tbsp. butter

1. In a large bowl, combine flour and salt. Cut in shortening until mixture resembles coarse crumbs. Combine the egg, water and vinegar; stir into the flour mixture until a ball forms. Divide dough in half. Shape each half into a disk; wrap and refrigerate 1 hour or overnight.

2. Preheat oven to 350°. In a large bowl, combine the rhubarb, apples, pineapple, honey and lemon juice. Combine sugar and flour; add to the rhubarb mixture.

3. On a lightly floured surface, roll 1 disk of dough into a ⅛-in.-thick circle; transfer to a 9-in. pie plate. Trim crust even with the rim of the plate. Add filling; dot with butter. Roll out the remaining dough to a ⅛-in.-thick circle. Place over the filling. Trim, seal and flute edge. Cut slits in top.

4. Bake until crust is golden brown and the apples are tender, about 1¼ hours.

Note: If using frozen rhubarb, measure rhubarb while still frozen and then thaw completely. Drain in a colander, but do not press liquid out.

1 slice: 595 cal., 27g fat (7g sat. fat), 30mg chol., 469mg sod., 83g carb. (42g sugars, 3g fiber), 7g pro.

HEALTH TIP Granny's Rhubarb Pie is well worth the calories on special occasions, but double-crust pies are almost always super rich. For a lighter version, skip the top crust and add just a little bit of your favorite streusel topping instead.

GRANNY'S RHUBARB PIE

CHERRY RHUBARB CRUNCH

CHERRY RHUBARB CRUNCH

My husband's grandmother gave me this recipe, along with a bundle of rhubarb, when we were first married. I had never cared for rhubarb, but after trying this dessert, I changed my mind. Now my children dig in, too!
—Sharon Wasikowski, Middleville, MI

....

Prep: 20 min. • **Bake:** 45 min.
Makes: 15 servings

  1 **cup rolled oats**
  1 **cup packed brown sugar**
  1 **cup all-purpose flour**
  ¼ **tsp. salt**
  ½ **cup cold butter, cubed**
  4 **cups diced rhubarb**
  1 **cup sugar**
  2 **Tbsp. cornstarch**
  1 **cup water**
  1 **tsp. almond extract**
  1 **can (21 oz.) cherry pie filling**
  ½ **cup finely chopped walnuts**
      Vanilla ice cream

1. Preheat oven to 350°. In a large bowl, combine oats, brown sugar, flour and salt; stir well. Cut in butter until crumbly. Pat 2 cups of mixture into a greased 13x9-in. baking dish; cover with rhubarb.

2. In a saucepan, combine sugar and cornstarch. Stir in water; cook until mixture is thickened and clear. Stir in extract and cherry filling; spoon over rhubarb. Combine nuts with reserved crumb mixture; sprinkle over cherries. Bake until filling is bubbly and topping is lightly browned, 40-45 minutes. If desired, serve with ice cream.

1 piece: 294 cal., 9g fat (4g sat. fat), 16mg chol., 116mg sod., 52g carb. (38g sugars, 2g fiber), 3g pro.

ORANGE CORNMEAL CAKE

This cake bakes up tender and light with a subtle orange taste. It tastes rich but is comparatively low in saturated fat. Serve the cake as is, or dress it up with a dollop of whipped cream and strawberries or raspberries. The cake is wonderful warm, but the flavor improves as it sits, so make it a day or two before you plan to serve it. Store the cake at room temperature.
—Leigh Rys, Herndon, VA

....

Prep: 25 min. • **Bake:** 40 min. + cooling
Makes: 12 servings

ORANGE CORNMEAL CAKE

  1 **cup sugar**
  ½ **cup canola oil**
  3 **large eggs, room temperature**
  1 **cup fat-free plain yogurt**
  ¼ **cup orange juice**
  4 **tsp. grated orange zest**
1¼ **cups all-purpose flour**
  ½ **cup yellow cornmeal**
  1 **tsp. baking powder**
  ½ **tsp. salt**
  ¼ **tsp. baking soda**
    GLAZE
  ½ **cup sugar**
  ½ **cup orange juice**
  1 **Tbsp. butter**
      Sweetened whipped cream
      Grated orange zest, optional

1. Preheat oven to 350°. In a large bowl, beat sugar and oil until blended. Beat in eggs, yogurt, orange juice and zest. In another bowl, whisk the flour, cornmeal, baking powder, salt and baking soda; gradually beat into the sugar mixture. Pour batter into a greased 9-in. springform pan. Place pan on a baking sheet.

2. Bake until golden brown and a toothpick inserted in the center comes out with moist crumbs, 40-45 minutes. Place cake in pan on a wire rack.

3. For the glaze, in a microwave-safe bowl, combine sugar, orange juice and butter; microwave on high 2-3 minutes, stirring every 30 seconds. Slowly drizzle ½ cup glaze over warm cake; let stand 5 minutes. Slowly drizzle the remaining glaze over cake; loosen sides from pan with a knife, but do not remove the rim. Cool completely in pan. Cover and let stand overnight. Remove rim from pan. Serve with whipped cream and, if desired, orange zest.

1 piece: 294 cal., 12g fat (2g sat. fat), 49mg chol., 202mg sod., 44g carb. (28g sugars, 1g fiber), 4g pro.

**MAMA'S
BLACKBERRY COBBLER**

MAMA'S
BLACKBERRY COBBLER

*Alabama has some tasty
fresh blackberries. Fifty
years ago my mama was
going to pick blackberries
to make a cobbler, but she
went to the hospital to have me instead!
This is her mama's recipe.*
—Lisa Allen, Joppa, AL

....

Prep: 15 min. • **Bake:** 45 min.
Makes: 6 servings

  ½ **cup plus 2 Tbsp. melted
      butter, divided**
  1 **cup self-rising flour**
1½ **cups sugar, divided**
  1 **cup 2% milk**
  ½ **tsp. vanilla extract**
  3 **cups fresh blackberries or frozen
      unsweetened blackberries**

1. Preheat oven to 350°. Pour ½ cup
melted butter into an 8-in. square baking
dish. In a small bowl, combine flour, 1 cup
sugar, milk and vanilla until blended; pour
into prepared dish. In another bowl,
combine blackberries, the remaining
½ cup sugar and the remaining 2 Tbsp.
melted butter; toss until combined.
Spoon over batter.

2. Bake until topping is golden brown and
fruit is tender, 45-50 minutes. Serve warm.
¾ cup: 491 cal., 21g fat (13g sat. fat),
54mg chol., 421mg sod., 75g carb.
(56g sugars, 4g fiber), 5g pro.

> **TEST KITCHEN TIP**
> Be sure to disperse the berry
> mixture evenly and all the way
> to the edges of the dish.

🟢 **5i**

CHOCOLATE-DIPPED
CARAMEL APPLE SLICES

*This nifty treat is the perfect blend of
tart, juicy apples and sweet, decadent
chocolate and caramel. The candy coating
holds in the fresh apple, resulting in an
explosion of flavor when you bite down!*
—*Taste of Home* Test Kitchen

....

Prep: 20 min. + chilling
Makes: 8 servings

  2 **large tart apples**
  8 **wooden pops or lollipop sticks**
  4 **oz. semisweet chocolate, melted**
  ½ **cup Kraft caramel bits**
  2 **tsp. 2% milk**
  1 **oz. white baking chocolate, melted
      Optional toppings: Chopped salted
      peanuts, miniature pretzels,
      sprinkles and candies**

1. Line a baking sheet with parchment;
set aside. Wash and thoroughly dry
apples; core. Slice across the apple
perpendicular to the hollow of the core
into ½-in.-thick slices. Insert pop sticks
into slices; pat dry.

2. Dip each apple slice in chocolate; allow
excess to drip off. Place on the prepared
baking sheet. Refrigerate until set.

3. In a microwave, melt the caramel and
milk; stir until smooth. Drizzle over pops.
Drizzle with white chocolate. Immediately
decorate with any toppings as desired,
pressing lightly to adhere; refrigerate until
set. Store in the refrigerator up to 1 day.
1 pop: 173 cal., 8g fat (5g sat. fat), 0 chol.,
39mg sod., 22g carb. (19g sugars, 2g
fiber), 1g pro.

GRANDMA'S ENGLISH TRIFLE

I remember Mother telling me stories from her girlhood—especially how her mother would make an enormous dish of this dessert for Saturday night dinners. If there were leftovers, they'd have that trifle for dessert every night that week until it was gone! On our dairy farm, this recipe goes over big with my husband and our six children.
—Ruth Verratti, Gasport, NY

Prep: 30 min. + chilling
Makes: 10 servings

- 1 prepared loaf pound cake or 1 pkg. (10¾ oz.) frozen pound cake, thawed
- ¼ to ½ cup raspberry jam
- 1 pkg. (3 to 3½ oz.) regular or instant vanilla pudding mix
- 2½ cups 2% milk
- 1 cup chilled heavy whipping cream
- 3 Tbsp. confectioners' sugar
  Slivered almonds
  Maraschino cherries, halved

1. Slice pound cake in half horizontally. Spread with jam and replace top of cake. Slice cake into 9 pieces. Line the sides and fill the center of a 2-qt. glass serving bowl with cake pieces.
2. Prepare pudding with milk according to package directions. Pour over cake. Chill.
3. Beat cream and sugar until soft peaks form; spread over cake and pudding. Chill at least 4 hours. Garnish with almonds and cherries before serving.
1 serving: 292 cal., 16g fat (10g sat. fat), 76mg chol., 176mg sod., 31g carb. (24g sugars, 0 fiber), 4g pro.

CHOCOLATE TOMATO SPICE CAKE

With tons of tomatoes in my garden, I'm always trying to find new ways to enjoy them. In this unusual recipe, the natural sweetness and acidity of tomatoes make them an unexpectedly perfect ingredient for this light and fluffy chocolate cake.
—Lisa Brockwell, Necedah, WI

Prep: 45 min. • **Bake:** 20 min. + cooling
Makes: 15 servings

- 3 large tomatoes (about 1½ lbs.)
- ½ cup sugar
- ½ cup 2% milk
- ½ cup canola oil
- ⅓ cup packed brown sugar
- 2 large eggs, room temperature
- 1 tsp. vanilla extract
- 1½ cups all-purpose flour
- ½ cup baking cocoa
- 3 tsp. baking soda
- 2 tsp. ground cinnamon
- ¾ tsp. ground nutmeg
- ¼ tsp. salt

1. Preheat oven to 350°. Halve tomatoes and place in an ungreased 15x10x1-in. baking pan, cut side down. Bake until skins begin to loosen, 25-30 minutes. Peel off and discard skins. Place tomatoes in a food processor; process until pureed. Press through a fine-mesh strainer into a small bowl; discard seeds and pulp. Reserve 1½ cups juice (save the remaining juice for another use).
2. Grease a 13x9-in. baking pan. In a large bowl, beat sugar, milk, oil, brown sugar, eggs, vanilla and the reserved tomato juice until well blended. In another bowl, whisk the flour, cocoa, baking soda, cinnamon, nutmeg and salt; gradually beat into the tomato mixture.
3. Transfer batter to prepared pan. Bake until a toothpick inserted in center comes out clean, 20-25 minutes. Cool completely in pan on a wire rack.
1 piece: 187 cal., 9g fat (1g sat. fat), 25mg chol., 308mg sod., 25g carb. (13g sugars, 2g fiber), 3g pro. **Diabetic exchanges:** 2 fat, 1½ starch.

GRANDMA'S ENGLISH TRIFLE

Easy Odds & Ends

Sheet-pan suppers deliver a full-course meal in one dish (and clean up is a snap). Homemade sauces and relishes add a perfect finishing touch. Dump-and-go desserts couldn't be easier. These delicious recipes make it simple to handle even the most hectic weeknights.

Pumpkin Pecan Custard (p. 319) **Cherry Pudding Cake** (p. 318) **Old-Fashioned Corn Relish** (p. 311)
Sheet-Pan Lemon Garlic Chicken (p. 317) **Chunky Fruit & Nut Relish** (p. 313)

Finishing Touches

Elevate your cooking with the perfect sauce or relish—they're easy to make (and make ahead). Take a simply cooked steak or chicken breast to another level!

EASY RHUBARB RELISH

FAMILY-FAVORITE CARAMELIZED ONIONS

This recipe was given to me by my mother-in-law. After a few tweaks, these onions are better than ever and, to my husband's disappointment, there are rarely any leftovers. The good news is that they can easily be made ahead and reheated.
—Sharon Gibson, Hendersonville, NC

Prep: 10 min. • **Cook:** 45 min.
Makes: 8 servings

- 3 Tbsp. butter
- ⅓ cup packed brown sugar
- 1 Tbsp. lemon juice
- ¼ tsp. pepper
- 4 jars (15 oz. each) whole onions, drained

In a large skillet over medium heat, melt butter; stir in brown sugar, lemon juice and pepper. Cook and stir until the sugar is dissolved, 1-2 minutes. Add onions. Reduce heat to medium-low; cook until light brown, 30-40 minutes, stirring occasionally. Stir in the remaining onions. Cook until deep golden brown, about 15 minutes longer.

¼ cup: 135 cal., 4g fat (3g sat. fat), 11mg chol., 769mg sod., 23g carb. (18g sugars, 4g fiber), 1g pro.

EASY RHUBARB RELISH

I remember eating this relish at my grandmother's over 50 years ago. My mother made it and now my daughters make it, too—it's truly a family treasure. The relish complements any meat, but I find it a must with meat loaf.
—Helen Brooks, Lacombe, AB

Prep: 10 min. • **Cook:** 2 hours + chilling
Makes: 4 pints

- 12 cups finely chopped fresh or frozen rhubarb
- 1 medium onion, chopped
- 2 cups sugar
- 1 cup cider vinegar
- 1 tsp. salt
- 1 tsp. ground cloves
- 1 tsp. ground allspice
- ¼ tsp. paprika
- 1 tsp. ground cinnamon

1. Rinse four 2-cup freezer containers and lids with boiling water. Dry thoroughly.
2. Combine all ingredients in a saucepan. Bring to a boil. Reduce heat and simmer until mixture thickens, about 2 hours, stirring occasionally. Fill all containers to within ½ in. of tops. Wipe off top edges of containers; cover with lids. Refrigerate up to 3 weeks.
Freeze option: Freeze up to 12 months. Thaw in refrigerator before serving.
2 Tbsp.: 31 cal., 0 fat (0 sat. fat), 0 chol., 38mg sod., 8g carb. (7g sugars, 0 fiber), 0 pro.

DR PEPPER
BBQ SAUCE

Dr Pepper
BBQ
Sauce

DR PEPPER BBQ SAUCE

My family is stationed in Italy with my husband. He grew up in Memphis, and I'm from Texas, so the dish that spells home for us more than any other is a good ol' barbecue. I have my own recipe for barbecue sauce that we like to pour all over sliced brisket. It reminds us of weekend barbecues with our families.
—Tina Blackman, Naples, AE

Prep: 5 min. • **Cook:** 35 min.
Makes: 1 cup

 1 can (12 oz.) Dr Pepper
 1 cup crushed tomatoes
 ¼ cup packed brown sugar
 2 Tbsp. spicy brown mustard
 1 Tbsp. orange juice
 1 Tbsp. Worcestershire sauce
 1 garlic clove, minced
 ¼ tsp. salt
 ⅛ tsp. pepper

In a small saucepan, combine all the ingredients; bring to a boil. Reduce heat; simmer, uncovered, 30-35 minutes or until slightly thickened, stirring occasionally. Refrigerate leftovers.
2 Tbsp.: 60 cal., 0 fat (0 sat. fat), 0 chol., 193mg sod., 15g carb. (12g sugars, 1g fiber), 1g pro.

OLD-FASHIONED CORN RELISH

PICTURED ON P. 309

This was the first "country" recipe I received after moving away from the city—a new neighbor shared it. It's wonderful made with garden-fresh ingredients and tasty served with your favorite meat.
—Jean Peterson, Mulliken, MI

Takes: 30 min. • **Makes:** 6½ cups

 2 cups fresh or frozen corn
 2 cups chopped onions
 2 cups chopped seeded cucumbers
 2 cups chopped tomatoes
 1 large green pepper, chopped
 1 cup sugar
 1 cup cider vinegar
 1½ tsp. celery seed
 1½ tsp. mustard seed
 1 tsp. salt
 ½ tsp. ground turmeric

In a large saucepan, combine all of the ingredients. Bring to a boil. Reduce heat; simmer, uncovered, for 20-30 minutes or until thickened. Store in the refrigerator.
2 Tbsp.: 27 cal., 0 fat (0 sat. fat), 0 chol., 47mg sod., 6g carb. (5g sugars, 0 fiber), 0 pro. **Diabetic exchanges:** 1 starch.

ZUCCHINI HONEY RELISH

Being able to harvest many zucchinis and onions from my garden, I made this relish using honey. Delicious! For more seasonings, add ginger, nutmeg or ground mustard; if you like a little more bite, add garlic or horseradish to the mixture.
—Raymonde Bourgeois, Swastika, ON

Prep: 1 hour + chilling
Process: 15 min. **Makes:** 6 pints

 3½ lbs. medium zucchini
 4 large onions
 2 large green peppers
 1 large sweet yellow pepper
 1 large sweet red pepper
 ⅓ cup canning salt
 2 garlic cloves, minced
 2½ cups honey
 2½ cups cider vinegar
 4 tsp. cornstarch
 1 tsp. ground turmeric
 1 tsp. curry powder
 1 tsp. celery seed

1. Cut the zucchini, onions and peppers into 1-in. pieces. Pulse in batches in a food processor until finely chopped. Transfer to a large bowl. Add salt and garlic; toss to combine. Cover and refrigerate overnight. Drain; rinse and drain thoroughly.
2. In a Dutch oven, combine the remaining ingredients. Bring to a boil, stirring to dissolve sugar. Reduce heat; simmer 5 minutes to allow flavors to blend. Add the zucchini mixture; return to a boil, stirring occasionally. Reduce heat; simmer, uncovered, 4-5 minutes or until heated through.
3. Carefully ladle the hot mixture into 6 hot 1-pint jars, leaving ½-in. headspace. Remove air bubbles and, if necessary, adjust headspace by adding hot pickling liquid. Wipe rims. Center lids on jars; screw on bands until fingertip tight.
4. Place jars into canner with simmering water, ensuring they are completely covered with water. Bring to a boil; process for 15 minutes. Remove jars and cool.
¼ cup: 66 cal., 0 fat (0 sat. fat), 0 chol., 222mg sod., 16g carb. (15g sugars, 1g fiber), 1g pro.

TOMATO APPLE CHUTNEY

TOMATO APPLE CHUTNEY

I love to make different kinds of chutney during the holidays and give jars to family and friends for gifts. Cook the chutney in a slow cooker, and you don't have to fuss with it until you are ready to serve.
—Nancy Heishman, Las Vegas, NV

Prep: 15 min. • **Cook:** 5 hours
Makes: 30 servings

3 cans (14½ oz. each) fire-roasted diced tomatoes with garlic, undrained
2 medium red onions, chopped
1 large apple, peeled and chopped
1 cup golden raisins
¾ cup cider vinegar
½ cup packed brown sugar
1 Tbsp. chopped seeded jalapeno pepper
1 Tbsp. minced fresh cilantro
2 tsp. curry powder
½ tsp. salt
¼ tsp. ground allspice
Baked pita chips

Combine the first 11 ingredients in a greased 3-qt. slow cooker. Cook, uncovered, on high, until thickened, 5-6 hours. Serve warm with pita chips.
¼ cup: 48 cal., 0 fat (0 sat. fat), 0 chol., 152mg sod., 11g carb. (8g sugars, 1g fiber), 1g pro.

TEST KITCHEN TIP
It's unusual to cook something uncovered in the slow cooker, but it's essential for this chutney. Keeping the cover off allows the liquid to evaporate during cooking.

PEACHY KEEN PEPPER SAUCE

Every year I have an overabundance of hot peppers from my garden. This has become one of my favorite hot pepper sauce recipes. You can use jalapenos or any other similar-sized, mild-heat pepper in place of the Sugar Rush Peach variety.
—Adam Meth, Buchanan, NY

Takes: 25 min. • **Makes:** 4 cups

20 ripe Sugar Rush Peach chile peppers or habanero peppers
2 small ripe peaches, sliced
1½ cups cider vinegar
¼ cup ketchup
2 Tbsp. lemon juice
3 garlic cloves, halved
1 tsp. minced fresh cilantro
½ tsp. salt
¼ tsp. pepper

Cut peppers in half; discard stems and seeds. In batches, place all ingredients in a blender; cover and process until smooth. Transfer to covered containers. (If freezing, use freezer-safe containers and fill to within ½ in. of tops.) Refrigerate up to 1 week or freeze up to 12 months.
Note: Wear disposable gloves when cutting hot peppers; the oils can burn exposed skin. Avoid touching your face.
1 tsp.: 3 cal., 0 fat (0 sat. fat), 0 chol., 11mg sod., 1g carb. (0 sugars, 0 fiber), 0 pro. **Diabetic exchanges:** Free food.

CHUNKY KETCHUP

I came up with this chunky homemade ketchup to jazz up chopped steak sandwiches and hot sausage sandwiches for my family. I gave some to our friends, too, and they enjoyed it on hamburgers and stuffed peppers. It's fresh-tasting and delicious.
—Susan Stahr, Driftwood, PA

Prep: 20 min. • **Cook:** 1½ hours
Makes: 3½ cups

- 4 cups peeled, seeded and chopped tomatoes
- 1 medium onion, chopped
- 1 medium green pepper, chopped
- 1 cup sugar
- 1 can (6 oz.) tomato paste
- 1 Tbsp. salt
- ¼ cup white vinegar

1. In a large saucepan, combine the tomatoes, onion, green pepper, sugar, tomato paste and salt; bring to a boil. Reduce heat; simmer, uncovered, until slightly thickened, about 1½ hours.
2. Stir in vinegar; heat through. Cool to room temperature; store up to 2 weeks in the refrigerator.
2 Tbsp.: 40 cal., 0 fat (0 sat. fat), 0 chol., 258mg sod., 10g carb. (9g sugars, 1g fiber), 0 pro.

5i **L**

CRANBERRY PESTO

I updated a classic Italian pesto to include cranberries and walnuts. It's so good slathered on pork loin, pasta or turkey sandwiches!
—Aysha Schurman, Ammon, ID

Takes: 10 min. • **Makes:** 1¼ cups

- ⅔ cup loosely packed basil leaves
- ½ cup dried cranberries
- ¼ cup chopped walnuts
- 1 green onion, chopped
- 3 garlic cloves, coarsely chopped
- ½ tsp. pepper
- ¼ tsp. salt
- ⅔ cup olive oil

Place the first 7 ingredients in a food processor; pulse until coarsely chopped. Continue processing while gradually adding oil in a steady stream. Store in an airtight container in the refrigerator for up to 1 week.
2 Tbsp.: 168 cal., 16g fat (2g sat. fat), 0 chol., 60mg sod., 6g carb. (4g sugars, 1g fiber), 1g pro.

CHUNKY FRUIT & NUT RELISH
PICTURED ON P. 309

I tuck a jar of this colorful condiment alongside the fudge and cookies in my holiday baskets. Packed with pecans, the fruit relish pairs well with ham or poultry.
—Donna Brockett, Kingfisher, OK

Prep: 5 min. • **Cook:** 10 min. + chilling
Makes: 6 cups

- 2 pkg. (12 oz. each) fresh or frozen cranberries
- 1½ cups sugar
- 1 cup orange juice
- 1 can (15¼ oz.) sliced peaches, drained and cut up
- 1 cup chopped pecans
- ¾ cup pineapple tidbits
- ½ cup golden raisins

1. In a large saucepan, bring cranberries, sugar and orange juice to a boil, stirring occasionally. Reduce heat; simmer, uncovered, until the cranberries pop, 8-10 minutes.
2. Remove from heat; stir in peaches, pecans, pineapple and raisins. Cool. Cover and refrigerate at least 3 hours.
¼ cup: 114 cal., 4g fat (0 sat. fat), 0 chol., 3mg sod., 21g carb. (19g sugars, 1g fiber), 1g pro.

CRANBERRY PESTO

Amazing All-in-Ones

A sheet-pan supper might just be the ideal weeknight meal. With quick prep times and minimal cleanup, the only thing easier than making dinner is doing the dishes!

SLICED HAM WITH ROASTED VEGETABLES

SLICED HAM WITH ROASTED VEGETABLES

To prepare this colorful, zesty oven meal, I "shop" in my backyard for the garden vegetables and oranges (we have our own tree!) that spark the ham's hearty flavor. It's my family's favorite main dish.
—Margaret Pache, Mesa, AZ

Prep: 10 min. • **Bake:** 35 min.
Makes: 6 servings

-     Cooking spray
- 6 medium potatoes, peeled and cubed
- 5 medium carrots, sliced
- 1 medium turnip, peeled and cubed
- 1 large onion, cut into thin wedges
- 6 slices (4 to 6 oz. each) fully cooked ham, halved
- ¼ cup thawed orange juice concentrate
- 2 Tbsp. brown sugar
- 1 tsp. prepared horseradish
- 1 tsp. grated orange zest
-     Coarsely ground pepper

1. Preheat oven to 425°. Grease two 15x10x1-in. baking pans with cooking spray. Add the potatoes, carrots, turnip and onion; generously coat with cooking spray. Bake, uncovered, until tender, 25-30 minutes.
2. Arrange ham slices over the vegetables. In a bowl, combine the juice concentrate, brown sugar, horseradish and orange zest. Spoon over the ham and vegetables. Bake until the ham is heated through, about 10 minutes longer. Sprinkle with pepper.
1 serving: 375 cal., 5g fat (1g sat. fat), 71mg chol., 1179mg sod., 55g carb. (15g sugars, 7g fiber), 31g pro.

CHICKEN VEGGIE FAJITAS

Our family loves the spicy flavor of these fajitas. I also love the fact that they're so fast to fix.
—Eleanor Martens, Rosenort, MB

Takes: 20 min. • **Makes:** 4 servings

- 3 Tbsp. lemon juice
- 1 Tbsp. soy sauce
- 1 Tbsp. Worcestershire sauce
- 2 tsp. canola oil
- 1 garlic clove, minced
- ½ tsp. ground cumin
- ½ tsp. dried oregano
- ¾ lb. boneless skinless chicken breasts, cut into ½-in. strips
- 1 small onion, sliced and separated into rings
- ½ each medium green, sweet red and yellow pepper, julienned
- 4 flour tortillas (6 in.), warmed
-     Shredded cheddar cheese, optional

1. Preheat the broiler. In a small bowl, combine the first 7 ingredients. Place chicken strips and vegetables in a single layer in a greased 15x10x1-in. baking pan; drizzle with ¼ cup lemon juice mixture. Broil 4-6 in. from the heat for 4 minutes.
2. Turn chicken and vegetables; drizzle with the remaining lemon juice mixture. Broil 4 minutes longer or until the chicken juices run clear. Serve on tortillas with cheese if desired.
1 fajita: 231 cal., 7g fat (1g sat. fat), 47mg chol., 460mg sod., 20g carb. (3g sugars, 1g fiber), 21g pro. **Diabetic exchanges:** 2½ lean meat, 1 starch, 1 vegetable.

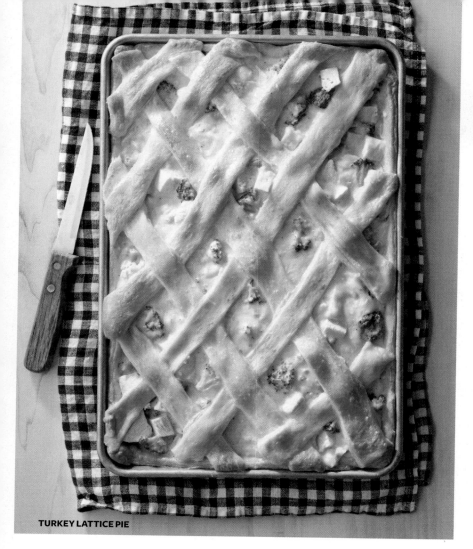
TURKEY LATTICE PIE

TURKEY LATTICE PIE

With its pretty lattice crust, this cheesy baked dish is as appealing as it is tasty. It's easy to make, too, since it uses ready-to-go crescent roll dough.
—Lorraine Naig, Emmetsburg, IA

Prep: 20 min. • **Bake:** 20 min.
Makes: 12 servings

- 3 tubes (8 oz. each) refrigerated crescent rolls
- 4 cups cubed cooked turkey
- 1½ cups shredded cheddar or Swiss cheese
- 3 cups frozen chopped broccoli, thawed and drained
- 1 can (10¾ oz.) condensed cream of chicken soup, undiluted
- 1⅓ cups 2% milk
- 2 Tbsp. Dijon mustard
- 1 Tbsp. dried minced onion
- ½ tsp. salt
  Dash pepper
- 1 large egg, lightly beaten

1. Preheat oven to 375°. Unroll 2 tubes of crescent roll dough and separate into rectangles. Place the rectangles in an ungreased 15x10x1-in. baking pan. Press onto the bottom and ¼ in. up the sides of pan to form a crust, sealing seams and perforations. Bake for 5-7 minutes or until light golden brown.

2. Meanwhile, in a large bowl, combine turkey, cheese, broccoli, soup, milk, mustard, onion, salt and pepper. Spoon over crust.

3. Unroll the remaining dough; divide into rectangles. Seal perforations. Cut each rectangle into four 1-in. strips. Using strips, make a lattice design on top of the turkey mixture. Brush with egg. Bake 17-22 minutes longer or until the top crust is golden brown and filling is bubbly.

1 piece: 396 cal., 20g fat (4g sat. fat), 81mg chol., 934mg sod., 30g carb. (8g sugars, 2g fiber), 24g pro.

ROASTED KIELBASA & VEGETABLES

The first reason I like this dish featuring kielbasa and veggies is it's so hearty. Second, it's both easy to make and to clean up. That's a win-win dinner! To feed smaller households, cut the recipe in half and use only one pan.
—Marietta Slater, Justin, TX

Prep: 20 min. • **Bake:** 40 min.
Makes: 6 servings

- 3 medium sweet potatoes, peeled and cut into 1-in. pieces
- 1 large sweet onion, cut into 1-in. pieces
- 4 medium carrots, cut into 1-in. pieces
- 2 Tbsp. olive oil
- 1 lb. smoked kielbasa or Polish sausage, halved and cut into 1-in. pieces
- 1 medium yellow summer squash, cut into 1-in. pieces
- 1 medium zucchini, cut into 1-in. pieces
- ¼ tsp. salt
- ¼ tsp. pepper
  Dijon mustard, optional

1. Preheat oven to 400°. Divide sweet potatoes, onion and carrots between 2 greased 15x10x1-in. baking pans. Drizzle with olive oil and toss to coat. Roast 25 minutes, stirring occasionally.

2. Add half the kielbasa, squash and zucchini to each pan; sprinkle with salt and pepper. Roast until vegetables are tender, 15-20 minutes longer. Transfer to a serving bowl and toss to combine. Serve with mustard, if desired.

1⅔ cups: 378 cal., 25g fat (8g sat. fat), 51mg chol., 954mg sod., 26g carb. (12g sugars, 4g fiber), 13g pro.

TARA'S SPANISH CHICKEN

This recipe has simple flavors that take me back to Grandma's house. She knew a million ways to cook a chicken, but this was my favorite.
—Tara Imig, Fort Worth, TX

Prep: 25 min. • **Bake:** 55 min.
Makes: 6 servings

- 1 broiler/fryer chicken (3 to 4 lbs.), cut up
- 1 large sweet red pepper, sliced
- 1 medium lemon, sliced
- ¼ cup sliced pimiento-stuffed olives
- 2 Tbsp. capers, drained
- ¼ cup olive oil
- 2 Tbsp. dried oregano
- 1 Tbsp. smoked paprika
- 1 tsp. salt
- ½ tsp. pepper

Preheat oven to 350°. Place the first 5 ingredients in a large bowl. Combine the remaining ingredients; drizzle over the chicken mixture. Toss to coat. Transfer to a 15x10x1-in. baking pan. Bake, uncovered, until chicken juices run clear, 55-60 minutes.

4 oz. cooked chicken: 402 cal., 27g fat (6g sat. fat), 104mg chol., 673mg sod., 5g carb. (2g sugars, 2g fiber), 34g pro.

MINI MEAT LOAF SHEET-PAN MEAL

I grew up with this meat loaf recipe, but I adapted it to mini meatloaves so that it would bake quicker. The sauce topping is always a hit. I added the potatoes and asparagus to make the meal easier.
—Deanne Johnson, Reading, PA

Prep: 35 min. • **Bake:** 40 min. + standing
Makes: 6 servings

- 2 large eggs, lightly beaten
- 1 cup tomato juice
- ¾ cup quick-cooking oats
- ¼ cup finely chopped onion
- ½ tsp. salt
- 1½ lbs. lean ground beef (90% lean)
- ¼ cup ketchup
- 3 Tbsp. brown sugar
- 1 tsp. prepared mustard
- ¼ tsp. ground nutmeg
- 3 large potatoes, peeled and cut into ½-in. pieces
- 3 Tbsp. olive oil, divided
- ½ tsp. garlic salt, divided
- ¼ tsp. pepper, divided
- 1 lb. fresh asparagus, trimmed and halved

1. Preheat oven to 425°. In a large bowl, combine eggs, tomato juice, oats, onion and salt. Add beef; mix lightly but thoroughly. Shape into six 4x2½-in. loaves; place on a sheet pan or in a large shallow roasting pan. Combine ketchup, brown sugar, mustard and nutmeg; brush over meat loaves.
2. Combine potatoes with 2 Tbsp. oil, ¼ tsp. garlic salt and ⅛ tsp. pepper; toss to coat. Add to pan in a single layer. Bake for 25 minutes.
3. Combine asparagus with remaining 1 Tbsp. oil, ¼ tsp. garlic salt and ⅛ tsp. pepper; toss to coat. Add to pan. Bake until a thermometer inserted into the meat loaves reads 160° and vegetables are tender, 15-20 minutes. Let stand for 5-10 minutes before serving.

1 meat loaf with 1¼ cups vegetables: 460 cal., 19g fat (5g sat. fat), 133mg chol., 690mg sod., 45g carb. (13g sugars, 3g fiber), 29g pro.

SHEET-PAN LEMON GARLIC CHICKEN

PICTURED ON P. 309

Everyone needs an easy meal. Try this sheet-pan chicken with roasted potatoes for a simple and tasty meal guaranteed to please the whole family. If you use fresh lemon juice, garnish each serving with a little lemon zest for bright flavor.
—Andrea Potischman, Menlo Park, CA

Prep: 20 min. + marinating • **Bake:** 40 min.
Makes: 6 servings

- ¼ cup olive oil
- 2 Tbsp. lemon juice
- 3 garlic cloves, minced
- 1½ tsp. minced fresh thyme or ¾ tsp. dried thyme
- 1 tsp. salt
- ½ tsp. minced fresh rosemary or ¼ tsp. dried rosemary, crushed
- ¼ tsp. pepper
- 6 bone-in chicken thighs
- 6 chicken drumsticks
- 1 lb. baby red potatoes, halved
- 1 medium lemon, sliced
- 2 Tbsp. minced fresh parsley

1. In a small bowl, whisk first 7 ingredients until blended. Pour ¼ cup marinade into a large bowl or shallow dish. Add chicken and turn to coat. Refrigerate 30 minutes. Cover and refrigerate the remaining marinade mixture.

2. Preheat oven to 425°. Drain chicken, discarding any marinade remaining in the bowl. Place the chicken in a 15x10x1-in. baking pan; add the potatoes in a single layer. Drizzle reserved marinade over the potatoes; top with lemon slices. Bake until a thermometer inserted in chicken reads 170°-175° and the potatoes are tender, 40-45 minutes. If desired, broil the chicken 3-4 in. from heat until deep golden brown, 3-4 minutes. Sprinkle with minced parsley before serving.

1 chicken thigh and 1 chicken leg with ½ cups potatoes: 483 cal., 29g fat (7g sat. fat), 128mg chol., 507mg sod., 15g carb. (1g sugars, 1g fiber), 39g pro.

POTATO & PEPPER SAUSAGE BAKE

When my family smells this dish baking in the oven, they know they're in for a treat! If you like spice, add a pinch of red pepper flakes or switch the mild Italian sausage to hot Italian sausage.
—Ashli Claytor, Chesapeake, VA

Prep: 25 min. • **Bake:** 30 min.
Makes: 5 servings

- 5 large Yukon Gold potatoes, peeled and cut into 1-in. cubes
- 1 large sweet orange pepper, sliced
- 1 large sweet red pepper, sliced
- 1 shallot, chopped
- 4 garlic cloves, minced
- 1 Tbsp. olive oil
- 2 tsp. paprika
- ¾ tsp. salt
- ½ tsp. dried thyme
- ½ tsp. pepper
- 1 pkg. (19 oz.) Italian sausage links
  Minced fresh thyme, optional

1. Preheat oven to 400°. Place potatoes, sweet peppers, shallot and garlic in a greased 15x10x1-in. baking pan. Drizzle with oil. Sprinkle with seasonings; toss to coat. Spread evenly over the pan, leaving room for the sausage. Add sausage to pan.

2. Bake, uncovered, until a thermometer inserted in the sausage reads 160° and vegetables are tender, 30-35 minutes. If desired, sprinkle with minced fresh thyme before serving.

1 sausage link with ¾ cup vegetables: 446 cal., 26g fat (8g sat. fat), 58mg chol., 1021mg sod., 38g carb. (5g sugars, 4g fiber), 16g pro.

> **TEST KITCHEN TIP**
> To allow the potatoes to cook evenly, arrange the sausages directly onto the pan instead of on the potatoes.

POTATO & PEPPER SAUSAGE BAKE

Sweet & Easy Dessert

Want to satisfy your sweet tooth with a minimum of fuss? Try one of these delicious—and deliciously simple—dessert recipes.

NEW ENGLAND INDIAN PUDDING

CHERRY PUDDING CAKE

A cross between a cake and a cobbler, this cherry dessert is awesome. Add it to your list of trusty potluck recipes, because this one is sure to go fast.
—Brenda Parker, Kalamazoo, MI

Prep: 10 min. • **Bake:** 40 min.
Makes: 12 servings

- 2 cups all-purpose flour
- 2½ cups sugar, divided
- 4 tsp. baking powder
- 1 cup 2% milk
- 2 Tbsp. canola oil
- 2 cans (14½ oz. each) water-packed pitted tart red cherries, well drained
- 2 to 3 drops red food coloring, optional
- ⅛ tsp. almond extract
  Optional: Whipped cream or ice cream

1. Preheat oven to 375°. Combine flour, 1 cup sugar, baking powder, milk and oil; pour into a greased shallow 3-qt. baking dish. Combine cherries, food coloring if desired, extract and the remaining sugar; spoon over batter.
2. Bake 40-45 minutes or until a toothpick inserted in the cake portion comes out clean. Serve warm, with whipped cream or ice cream if desired.
1 serving: 296 cal., 3g fat (1g sat. fat), 3mg chol., 147mg sod., 65g carb. (48g sugars, 1g fiber), 3g pro.

NEW ENGLAND INDIAN PUDDING

This recipe was inspired by traditional New England Indian pudding, but made in the slow cooker. Use real molasses; if it's too strong, cut the amount to ⅓ cup.
—Susan Bickta, Kutztown, PA

Prep: 15 min. • **Cook:** 3½ hours
Makes: 8 servings

- 1 pkg. (8½ oz.) cornbread/muffin mix
- 1 pkg. (3.4 oz.) instant butterscotch pudding mix
- 4 cups whole milk
- 3 large eggs, lightly beaten
- ½ cup molasses
- 1 tsp. ground cinnamon
- ¼ tsp. ground cloves
- ¼ tsp. ground ginger
  Vanilla ice cream or sweetened whipped cream, optional

1. In a large bowl, whisk cornbread mix, pudding mix and milk until blended. Add eggs, molasses and spices; whisk until combined. Transfer to a greased 4- or 5-qt. slow cooker. Cover and cook on high for 1 hour.
2. Reduce heat to low; stir, making sure to scrape the sides well. Cover and cook 1 hour longer. Stir; cover and cook 1 hour longer. Stir; cover and cook until very thick, 30-60 minutes longer. Serve warm, with ice cream or whipped cream if desired.
⅔ cup: 330 cal., 9g fat (4g sat. fat), 83mg chol., 526mg sod., 51g carb. (36g sugars, 2g fiber), 8g pro

**BLUEBERRY, APPLE &
PINEAPPLE DUMP CAKE**

BLUEBERRY, APPLE &
PINEAPPLE DUMP CAKE

*I call this B.A.P. dump cake. I usually take it
to our church potlucks and it is always the
first dessert to go! Sometimes I sprinkle
a little extra sugar over the nuts.*
—Mitzi Erthal, Godfrey, IL

Prep: 10 min. • **Bake:** 45 min.
Makes: 15 servings

- 1 **can (21 oz.) apple pie filling**
- ¾ **cup unsweetened crushed
     pineapple, drained**
- 1 **pkg. (12 oz.) frozen unsweetened
     blueberries**
- ½ **cup sugar**
- 1 **pkg. white cake mix (regular size)**
- ⅔ **cup butter, melted**
- 1 **cup chopped walnuts**
- ½ **cup sliced almonds**
     **Optional: Vanilla ice cream, heavy
     cream or half & half cream**

1. Preheat oven to 350°. Mix pie filling
and pineapple in a greased 13x9-in.
baking dish until combined. Toss the
blueberries with sugar; spoon over pie
filling mixture. Sprinkle with cake mix;
drizzle with butter. Top with walnuts and
almonds (do not stir).

2. Bake until golden brown and bubbly,
45-55 minutes. Serve warm with ice
cream, heavy cream or half & half.
⅔ cup: 332 cal., 16g fat (6g sat. fat), 22mg
chol., 285mg sod., 47g carb. (28g sugars,
3g fiber), 3g pro.

BLACK FOREST DUMP CAKE

*I make a Black Forest cake the easy way:
Dump everything into a dish and let the
magic happen! To give it a cherry topping,
stir two tablespoons of the juice from the
canned cherries into whipped cream.*
—Meghan McDermott, Springfield, MO

Prep: 10 min. • **Bake:** 40 min.
Makes: 12 servings

- 1 **can (21 oz.) cherry pie filling**
- 1 **can (15 oz.) pitted dark sweet
     cherries, undrained**
- 1 **chocolate cake mix (regular size)**
- ½ **cup sliced almonds**
- ¾ **cup butter, cubed**

1. Preheat oven to 375°. Spread the pie
filling into a greased 13x9-in. baking dish;
top with undrained cherries. Sprinkle
with cake mix and almonds. Top with
cubed butter.

2. Bake 40-50 minutes or until topping is
set. Serve warm or at room temperature.
1 serving: 347 cal., 16g fat (8g sat. fat),
31mg chol., 346mg sod., 49g carb.
(21g sugars, 2g fiber), 3g pro.

PUMPKIN PECAN CUSTARD
PICTURED ON P. 309
*My family loves pumpkin pie, but it's not
something we can eat all the time! This is
a delicious, creamy, healthier alternative,
and we don't miss the crust at all.*
—Abby Booth, Coweta, OK

Prep: 20 min. • **Bake:** 35 min. + chilling
Makes: 8 servings

- 1 **can (15 oz.) pumpkin**
- 1 **can (12 oz.) reduced-fat
     evaporated milk**
- ¾ **cup egg substitute**
- ⅓ **cup packed brown sugar**
- 1½ **tsp. vanilla extract**
- 1 **tsp. ground cinnamon**
- ½ **tsp. ground ginger**
- ¼ **tsp. ground cloves**
- ⅛ **tsp. salt**
  TOPPING
- 3 **Tbsp. all-purpose flour**
- 3 **Tbsp. brown sugar**
- ½ **tsp. ground cinnamon**
- 2 **Tbsp. cold butter**
- ½ **cup chopped pecans**

1. In a large bowl, combine the first
9 ingredients. Transfer to eight 6-oz.
ramekins or custard cups. Place in a
baking pan; add 1 in. boiling water to
pan. Bake, uncovered, at 325° for
20 minutes.
2. Meanwhile, for topping, in a small
bowl, combine flour, brown sugar and
cinnamon. Cut in butter until crumbly.
Stir in the pecans. Sprinkle over custards.
Bake 15-20 minutes longer or until a knife
inserted in the center comes out clean.
3. Remove ramekins from water bath;
cool for 10 minutes. Cover and refrigerate
at least 4 hours.
½ cup: 213 cal., 9g fat (3g sat. fat), 11mg
chol., 160mg sod., 27g carb. (21g sugars,
3g fiber), 7g pro. **Diabetic exchanges:**
2 starch, 1½ fat.

CARDAMOM PUMPKIN PUDDING CAKE

CARDAMOM PUMPKIN PUDDING CAKE

This no-egg cake is quick, easy and bursting with flavor. I like to serve it with ice cream or whipped cream.
—J. Fleming, Almonte, ON

Prep: 20 min. • **Bake:** 25 min. + cooling
Makes: 9 servings

- 1¼ cups all-purpose flour
- ¾ cup sugar
- 2 tsp. baking soda
- 1¼ tsp. ground cinnamon
- 1 tsp. ground cardamom
- ¼ tsp. salt
- ½ cup evaporated milk
- ½ cup canned pumpkin
- ¼ cup butter, melted
- 1 tsp. vanilla extract
- ½ cup chopped pecans

TOPPING
- 1 cup packed brown sugar
- ½ tsp. ground cinnamon
- 1½ cups boiling water
  Optional: Vanilla ice cream or sweetened whipped cream

1. Preheat oven to 350°. In a large bowl, combine the first 6 ingredients. Add milk, pumpkin, butter and vanilla; mix until blended. Stir in pecans. Transfer to a greased 9-in. square baking pan.
2. For topping, combine brown sugar and cinnamon; sprinkle over batter. Pour water over top (do not stir).
3. Bake until a toothpick inserted in the center comes out clean and liquid is bubbling around the edges, 25-30 minutes. Cool completely in pan on a wire rack. Serve with ice cream or whipped cream if desired.
1 piece: 334 cal., 11g fat (4g sat. fat), 18mg chol., 407mg sod., 58g carb. (43g sugars, 2g fiber), 4g pro.

CHERRY & SPICE RICE PUDDING

Traverse City is the Cherry Capital of the world, and what better way to celebrate our wonderful orchards than by using plump, tart dried cherries in my favorite desserts? This slow-cooked rice pudding always turns out perfect.
—Deb Perry, Traverse City, MI

Prep: 10 min. • **Cook:** 2 hours
Makes: 12 servings

- 4 cups cooked long grain rice
- 1 can (12 oz.) evaporated milk
- 1 cup 2% milk
- ⅓ cup sugar
- ¼ cup water
- ¾ cup dried cherries
- 3 Tbsp. butter, softened
- 2 tsp. vanilla extract
- ½ tsp. ground cinnamon
- ¼ tsp. ground nutmeg

1. In a large bowl, combine the rice, evaporated milk, milk, sugar and water. Stir in the remaining ingredients. Transfer mixture to a 3-qt. slow cooker coated with cooking spray.
2. Cover and cook on low for 2-3 hours or until thickened. Stir lightly before serving. Serve warm or cold. Refrigerate leftovers.
½ cup: 193 cal., 5g fat (4g sat. fat), 19mg chol., 61mg sod., 31g carb. (15g sugars, 0 fiber), 4g pro. **Diabetic exchanges:** 2 starch, 1 fat.

TEST KITCHEN TIP
To make this into a fun adults-only dessert, soak the cherries in alcohol before using.

APPLE-SWEET POTATO PECAN DUMP CAKE

This quick cake has lots of delicious apples, sweet potatoes, spices, pecans and caramel. My surprise of white cheddar cheese enhances the wonderful filling.
—Kathy Specht, Clinton, MT

Prep: 15 min. • **Bake:** 45 min. + standing
Makes: 15 servings

- 1 can (21 oz.) apple pie filling
- 1 can (16 oz.) cut sweet potatoes in syrup, drained and cut into ½-in. pieces
- 1 tsp. ground cinnamon
- ½ tsp. pumpkin pie spice
- 1 pkg. butter pecan cake mix (regular size)
- ¾ cup shredded white cheddar cheese
- ¾ cup butter, cubed
- ½ cup caramel ice cream topping
- 1 cup chopped pecans
  Vanilla ice cream or sweetened whipped cream, optional

Preheat oven to 350°. Combine pie filling, sweet potatoes, cinnamon and pie spice in a greased 13x9-in. baking dish. Sprinkle with cake mix and cheese; dot with butter. Drizzle with caramel and sprinkle with pecans. Bake until golden brown, 45-50 minutes. Let stand 10 minutes. Serve warm, with ice cream or whipped cream if desired.

½ cup: 347 cal., 17g fat (8g sat. fat), 29mg chol., 373mg sod., 48g carb. (29g sugars, 3g fiber), 3g pro.

CHOCOLATE-PEANUT BUTTER DUMP CAKE

I am a huge fan of the chocolate-peanut butter combination. I'm also a fan of easy recipes, including dump cakes! On occasion, I'll omit the peanut butter chips and use 1½ cups semisweet chocolate chips with tasty results.
—Lisa Varner, El Paso, TX

Prep: 15 min. • **Bake:** 20 min. + cooling
Makes: 15 servings

- 1 pkg. (3.9 oz.) instant chocolate pudding mix
- 1¾ cups 2% milk
- 1 pkg. chocolate cake mix or devil's food cake mix (regular size)
- 6 pkg. (1½ oz. each) peanut butter cups, chopped
- ¾ cup peanut butter chips
- ¾ cup semisweet chocolate chips
- ½ cup chopped unsalted peanuts
  Vanilla ice cream or sweetened whipped cream, optional

1. Preheat oven to 350°. Grease a 13x9-in. baking pan. In a large bowl, combine the pudding mix and milk until blended. Stir in cake mix (the batter will be thick). Fold in peanut butter cups, peanut butter chips and chocolate chips. Spread into the prepared pan. Sprinkle with peanuts.

2. Bake until a toothpick inserted in the center comes out with moist crumbs, 20-25 minutes. Cool completely in pan on a wire rack. Serve with ice cream or whipped cream if desired.

1 piece: 349 cal., 14g fat (6g sat. fat), 3mg chol., 373mg sod., 51g carb. (33g sugars, 3g fiber), 7g pro.

CHOCOLATE-PEANUT BUTTER DUMP CAKE

General Recipe Index

This handy index lists every recipe by food category, major ingredient and cooking method, so you can easily locate the recipes that suit your needs.

||||||||||||||||||||||||||||||||||||||||||||||||||||||||||||||||||||||||||||||||||||||||

APPETIZERS & SNACKS
Cold Appetizers
Black Bean Tortilla Pinwheels, 19
Cold Chicken-Cheese Kabobs, 14
Easy Roast Beef Roll-Ups, 15
Fruit on a Stick, 25
Greek Shrimp Canapes, 14
Party Pitas, 251
Sweet Onion Pimiento
  Cheese Deviled Eggs, 272
Dips & spreads
10-Minute Zesty Salsa, 264
Appetizer Blue Cheese Logs, 27
Artichoke Spread with Garlic Bread, 12
Baby Swiss Christmas Cheesecake, 281
Baked Asparagus Dip, 261
Buttermilk Vegetable Dip, 261

Cheddar Bacon Beer Dip, 226
Cheesy Bruschetta Spread, 16
Chipotle Berry Fruit Salsa, 266
Chipotle Mexican Street Corn Dip with
  Goat Cheese, 267
Fast Fruit Salsa, 18
Fruit Dip, 261
Marinara-Mozzarella Dip, 21
Hot Appetizers
Apple Wonton Bundles, 257
Bacon-Wrapped Stuffed Jalapenos, 252
Balsamic-Goat Cheese Grilled Plums, 239
Banh Mi Skewers, 13
California Turkey Sliders, 19
Cheddar Bacon Toasts, 18
Cheese & Sausage Appetizers, 255
Chicken & Broccoli Cups, 21

Grilled Glazed Drummies, 248
Grilled Pineapple with Lime Dip, 232
Hot Dog Sliders with Mango-Pineapple
  Salsa, 274
Italian Herb & Cheese Breadsticks, 254
Italian-Style Pizzas, 19
Mini Pizza Cups, 249
Mini Sausage Quiches, 258
Pepperoni Pinwheels, 13
Pesto Crostini with Grilled Nectarines &
  Burrata, 231
Potluck Enchilada Meatballs, 250
Pull-Apart Garlic Bread, 251
Quinoa Arancini, 23
Skewered Ravioli with Creamy Tomato
  Dipping Sauce, 16
So-Easy Sticky Chicken Wings, 252
Spanakopita Spring Rolls, 20
Zippy Shrimp Skewers, 22

APPLES
Apple-Sweet Potato Pecan
  Dump Cake, 321
Apple Wonton Bundles, 257
Apples & Onion Topped Chops, 162

APPLES & ONION TOPPED CHOPS, 162

Blueberry, Apple & Pineapple
   Dump Cake, 319
Chocolate-Dipped Caramel
   Apple Slices, 306
Cinnamon Apple Coffee Cake, 183
Irresistible Apple Blackberry
   Crumble, 299
Old-Fashioned Applesauce, 179
Tarragon Chicken with
   Apples for Two, 113
Tomato Apple Chutney, 312

APRICOTS
Apricot Fluff, 51
Apricots with Herbed Goat Cheese, 45

ARTICHOKES
Artichoke Chicken Pesto Pizza, 86
Artichoke Spread with Garlic Bread, 12
Tuna Artichoke Melts, 65

ASPARAGUS
Asparagus Beef Teriyaki, 120
Baked Asparagus Dip, 261
Mini Meat Loaf Sheet-Pan Meal, 316
Roasted Asparagus & Tomatoes, 42
Tuscan-Style Roasted Asparagus, 285

AVOCADO
Avocado Egg Salad Toast, 85
Crab-Stuffed Avocados, 271

BACON & PANCETTA
Bacon & Egg Bundles, 193
Bacon Breakfast Casserole, 188
Bacon-Wrapped Stuffed Jalapenos, 252
Cheddar Bacon Beer Dip, 226
Cheddar Bacon Toasts, 18
Grilled Bacon-Tomato Sandwiches, 72
Maple & Bacon Glazed
   Brussels Sprouts, 280
Olive Oil Mashed Potatoes with
   Pancetta, 276
Orzo with Caramelized Butternut Squash
   & Bacon, 45
Triple Bean Bake with Bacon, 275
Zippy Praline Bacon, 182

BANANAS
Baked Banana French Toast, 188
Banana Nut Bread, 205
Double Cranberry Banana Bread, 201

BEANS, LENTILS & LEGUMES
(also see Green Beans)
Bean Counter Chowder, 56
Black Bean Tortilla Pinwheels, 19
Black-Eyed Peas with Collard Greens, 32

Chickpea Tortilla Soup, 73
Chorizo & Chickpea Soup, 65
Fettuccine with Black Bean Sauce, 167
Greek-Style Lentil Soup, 213
Lentil Taco Cups, 152
Nacho Pie, 114
Penne with Veggies & Black Beans, 115
Slow-Cooked Black Bean Soup, 218
Spicy Refried Beans, 265
Triple Bean Bake with Bacon, 275

BEEF & CORNED BEEF
(also see Ground Beef)
Appetizers
Easy Roast Beef Roll-Ups, 15
Sandwiches
Champion Roast Beef Sandwiches, 69
Cheddar French Dip Sandwiches, 63
Gourmet Barbecue Beef Sandwiches, 74
Salads
Flat Iron Steak Salad, 234
Grilled Steak Bruschetta
   Salad for Two, 245
Zesty Steak Salad, 140
Main Dishes
Asparagus Beef Teriyaki, 120
Beef Steaks with Blue Cheese, 88
Blue Cheese-Stuffed Steaks for Two, 92
Easy Beef Stroganoff, 151
Easy Salisbury Steak, 121
Garlic Herbed Beef Tenderloin, 257
Grilled Peppered Steaks, 244
Mushroom-Blue Cheese Tenderloin, 130
Pressure-Cooker Spiced Short Ribs, 212
Rosemary Beef Roast over
   Cheesy Polenta, 225
Saturday Afternoon Oven Pot Roast, 129
Southwestern Beef Barley Stew, 142
Spicy Flank Steak, 240
Standing Rib Roast, 281
Steak Frites Salad, 155
Steak Sandwich Kabobs, 245
Steakhouse Pizza, 135
Triple-Citrus Steaks with Jicama &
   Mango, 147

BEETS
Borscht with Garden Vegetables, 56
Cranberry & Roasted Beet Salad, 36
Simple Orange-Glazed Beets, 41

BERRIES
Blackberry Balsamic Spinach Salad, 46
Blueberry, Apple & Pineapple
   Dump Cake, 319
Blueberry-Dijon Chicken, 118
Cheesecake Berry Parfaits, 275
Chipotle Berry Fruit Salsa, 266

Irresistible Apple Blackberry
   Crumble, 299
Mama's Blackberry Cobbler, 306
Marshmallow Berry Pancakes, 171
Raspberry-Coconut French Toast, 184
Raspberry Coleslaw, 52
Turkey Sandwich with Raspberry-
   Mustard Spread, 57

BEVERAGES
Aunt Frances' Lemonade, 250
Black Russian, 15
Chocolate-Caramel Rum Coffee, 22
Citrus Cider Punch, 248
Dill Bloody Marys, 25
Finnish Mulled Wine, 283
Margarita Sangria, 265
Orange Blossom Mint Tea, 268
Orange Razzletini, 12
Rosemary & Thyme Lemon Cocktail, 25
Summertime Watermelon Punch
   for a Crowd, 258
Vanilla Bean Fizz, 20

BISCUITS
Easy Cheesy Biscuits, 277
Fluffy Biscuits, 206
Grandma's Sweet Potato Biscuits, 205

BREADS & ROLLS
(also see Biscuits; Coffee Cakes;
   Corn Bread, Cornmeal & Grits;
   Muffins & Quick Breads; Scones;
   Yeast Breads)
Artichoke Spread with Garlic Bread, 12
Herb Buttermilk Dinner Rolls, 200
Herb Focaccia Rolls, 284
Monkey Bread, 178
Pull-Apart Garlic Bread, 251
Slow-Cooker Cinnamon Roll, 192

BREAKFAST & BRUNCH
(also see Coffee Cakes)
All-In-One Breakfast, 195
Apple Butter Biscuit Breakfast Bake, 187
Bacon & Egg Bundles, 193
Baked Banana French Toast, 188
Breakfast in a Pan, 186
Brunch Casserole, 195
Butter Pecan Syrup, 302
Coastal Carolina Muffin-Tin
   Frittatas, 191
German Potato Omelet, 187
Gingerbread Waffles, 288
Makeover Hash & Eggs, 186
Marshmallow Berry Pancakes, 171
Overnight Peach Oatmeal, 223
Potato Omelet, 182

Pressure-Cooker Potato-Cheddar
   Frittata, 214
Pressure-Cooker Pumpkin
   Spice Oatmeal, 220
Pressure-Cooker Sausage & Waffle
   Bake, 227
Raspberry-Coconut French Toast, 184
Sausage Breakfast Burritos, 192
Scrambled Egg Muffins, 187
Slow-Cooker Cinnamon Roll, 192
Slow-Cooker Honey Nut Granola, 185
Slow-Cooker Oatmeal, 195
Strawberry Bliss Omelet, 193
Ultimate Fruity Granola, 183
Zippy Praline Bacon, 182

BROCCOLI
Broccoli Chowder, 58
Broccoli Rice Casserole, 47
Cheddar Broccoli Quinoa, 115
Chicken & Broccoli Cups, 21

BURGERS
All-American Hamburgers, 272
Cheese-Stuffed Burgers for Two, 62
Cola Burgers, 179
Sweet & Sour Burgers, 69
Szechuan Burgers with Bok Choy
   Slaw, 63
Taco Burgers, 59

CABBAGE, SLAW & SAUERKRAUT
Cabbage & Rutabaga Slaw, 47
Cabbage Barley Soup, 79
Caribbean Island Coleslaw, 33
Fried Cabbage, 39
Grilled Cabbage, 237
Macaroni Coleslaw, 252
Raspberry Coleslaw, 52
Sausage & Sauerkraut, 86
Thai Salad with Cilantro Lime
   Dressing, 44
Tropical Pineapple Coleslaw, 176
Warm Cabbage, Fennel & Pear
   Salad, 279
Szechuan Burgers with Bok Choy
   Slaw, 63

CAKES & CHEESECAKES
(also see Coffee Cakes)
Apple-Sweet Potato Pecan
   Dump Cake, 321
Black Forest Dump Cake, 319
Blueberry, Apple &
   Pineapple Dump Cake, 319
Buttermilk Pound Cake, 259
Cardamom Pumpkin Pudding Cake, 320
Cherry Pudding Cake, 318

Chocolate-Peanut Butter
   Dump Cake, 321
Chocolate Tomato Spice Cake, 307
Grandma's Christmas Cake, 283
Luscious Almond Cheesecake, 249
Makeover Pineapple Upside-Down
   Cake, 294
Makeover Traditional Cheesecake, 295
Orange Cornmeal Cake, 305
Reese's Chocolate Snack Cake, 261
Rhubarb Torte, 256
Slow-Cooker Strawberry Pudding
   Cake, 302
Spiced Rum Fruitcake, 294

CANDY & FUDGE
Gingerbread Truffles, 289
Nana's Rocky Road Fudge, 255

CARAMEL
Caramel Creme Brulee, 271
Chocolate-Dipped Caramel Apple
   Slices, 306

CARROTS
Citrus Peach Carrots, 39
Fresh Ginger Carrot Salad, 53

CASSEROLES
Breakfast Dishes
All-In-One Breakfast, 195
Apple Butter Biscuit Breakfast Bake, 187
Bacon Breakfast Casserole, 188
Brunch Casserole, 195
Cheddar & Chorizo Strata, 186
Coastal Carolina Muffin-Tin Frittatas, 191
Mini Ham Quiches, 184
Potato Sausage Frittata, 190
Pressure-Cooker Potato-Cheddar
   Frittata, 214
Pressure-Cooker Sausage & Waffle
   Bake, 227
Main Dishes
Angel Hair Shrimp Bake, 130
Cheesy Hamburger Supper, 116
Dinner in a Bag, 102
Favorite Hamburger Noodle Bake, 177
Makeover Tater-Topped Casserole, 126
Makeover Traditional Lasagna, 159
Pork & Green Chile Casserole, 135
Tater-Topped Italian Casserole, 137
TLC (Thanksgiving Leftover
   Casserole), 276
Tomato Potpie, 127
Tuna Noodle Casserole, 128
Turkey Squash Casserole, 133
Weeknight Ravioli Lasagna, 95
Zucchini-Parmesan Bake, 93

Side Dishes
Broccoli Rice Casserole, 47
Cornbread Pudding Casserole, 278
Special Scalloped Corn, 32
Triple Bean Bake with Bacon, 275

CAULIFLOWER
Mashed Cauliflower, 284
Roasted Peppers & Cauliflower, 52

CHEESE
Appetizers
Cold Chicken-Cheese Kabobs, 14
Sweet Onion Pimiento
   Cheese Deviled Eggs, 272
Appetizer Blue Cheese Logs, 27
Baby Swiss Christmas Cheesecake, 281
Cheddar Bacon Beer Dip, 226
Cheesy Bruschetta Spread, 16
Chipotle Mexican Street Corn Dip with
   Goat Cheese, 267
Marinara-Mozzarella Dip, 21
Balsamic-Goat Cheese Grilled Plums, 239
Cheddar Bacon Toasts, 18
Cheese & Sausage Appetizers, 255
Pesto Crostini with Grilled Nectarines
   & Burrata, 231
Quinoa Arancini, 23
Sweet Onion Pimiento
   Cheese Deviled Eggs, 272
Breads
Easy Cheesy Biscuits, 277
Italian Herb & Cheese Breadsticks, 254
Main Dishes
Beef Steaks with Blue Cheese, 88
Blue Cheese-Stuffed Steaks for Two, 92
Cheddar & Chorizo Strata, 186
Cheddar French Dip Sandwiches, 63
Cheese-Stuffed Burgers for Two, 62
Cheesy Hamburger Supper, 116
Couscous Tabbouleh with Fresh
   Mint & Feta, 269
Enchilada Chicken, 85
Feta Tomato-Basil Fish, 156
Ham & Cheese Pockets, 71
Ham & Swiss with a Twist, 79
Lemon Feta Chicken, 84
Little Cheddar Meat Loaves, 173
Makeover Deluxe Grilled Cheese, 60
Mushroom-Blue Cheese Tenderloin, 130
Nutty Cheese Tortellini, 90
Parmesan Chicken Breasts, 91
Parmesan Pork Medallions, 84
Pork Chops with Parmesan Sauce, 160
Swiss Mushroom Chicken, 108
Salad & Side Dishes
Apricots with Herbed Goat Cheese, 45
Cottage Cheese Cantaloupe Salad, 39

Orzo with Feta & Arugula, 40
Red, White & Blue Summer Salad, 273
Soups
Cream of Potato & Cheddar Soup, 211

CHERRIES
Black Forest Dump Cake, 319
Cherry & Spice Rice Pudding, 320
Cherry Chicken Croissants, 64
Cherry Pudding Cake, 318
Cherry Rhubarb Crunch, 305
Rosemary Pork with Cherry
   Topping, 133

CHICKEN
Appetizers
Chicken & Broccoli Cups, 21
Cold Chicken-Cheese Kabobs, 14
Grilled Glazed Drummies, 248
So-Easy Sticky Chicken Wings, 252
Main Dishes
Artichoke Chicken Pesto Pizza, 86
Asian Chicken Dinner, 164
Blueberry-Dijon Chicken, 118
Cacciatore Chicken Breasts, 152
Chicken Cordon Bleu in Pastry, 89
Chicken Cordon Bleu Puffs, 127
Chicken Orzo Skillet, 154
Chicken Piccata Pockets, 270
Chicken Skillet Supper, 122
Chicken Thighs with Shallots
   & Spinach, 143
Chicken Veggie Fajitas, 314
Chicken with Couscous, 166
Cornmeal Oven-Fried Chicken, 128
Cranberry Chipotle Chicken
   Enchiladas, 165
Cranberry Maple Chicken, 91
Creamy Chicken & Thyme, 152
Creamy Chicken Enchilada Pizza, 27
Creamy Curried Chicken, 116
Deviled Chicken Thighs, 137
Enchilada Chicken, 85
Ginger Chicken & Quinoa Stew, 212
Grilled Chicken with Peach Sauce, 236
Honey-Glazed Chicken, 95
Lemon Feta Chicken, 84
Lemon Mushroom Chicken, 156
Maple-Roasted Chicken
   & Acorn Squash, 83
Nutty Chicken Fingers, 171
Old-Fashioned Chicken Potpie, 134
One-Pot Salsa Chicken, 149
Parmesan Chicken Breasts, 91
Pressure-Cooker Chicken
   Cacciatore, 224
Quick Cilantro Chicken, 114
Sassy Chicken & Peppers, 148

Saucy Italian Chicken, 218
Sheet-Pan Lemon Garlic Chicken, 317
Shredded Chicken Tostadas, 216
Slow-Cooker Honey
   Teriyaki Chicken, 217
Spiced Lime & Cilantro Chicken, 224
Spicy Chicken Stew, 144
Swiss Mushroom Chicken, 108
Tara's Spanish Chicken, 316
Tarragon Chicken with
   Apples for Two, 113
Teriyaki Glazed Chicken, 98
Salads & Sandwiches
Cajun Chicken Club, 70
Cherry Chicken Croissants, 64
Chicken Caesar Wraps, 66
Chicken Parmesan Slider Bake, 172
Cobb Salad Wraps, 70
Dilly Chicken Sandwiches, 78
Moroccan Chicken Tagine
   Pockets, 25
Nectarine Chicken Salad, 147
Slow-Cooker Buffalo Chicken
   Salad, 220
Spicy Buffalo Chicken Wraps, 76
Soups
Chicken Alphabet Soup, 173
Chicken Tomatillo Soup, 64
Creamy Chicken Rice Soup, 69
Curried Chicken Soup, 72

CHILI
25-Minute Turkey Chili, 226
Chili-ghetti, 174
Easy Chili Verde, 88

CHOCOLATE
Cakes
Black Forest Dump Cake, 319
Chocolate-Peanut Butter
   Dump Cake, 321
Chocolate Tomato Spice Cake, 307
Candy
Gingerbread Truffles, 289
Nana's Rocky Road Fudge, 255
Cookies & Bars
Chocolate Cheesecake Bars, 296
Miniature Peanut Butter Treats, 177
Desserts
Chocolate Bread Pudding, 269
Chocolate-Dipped Caramel
   Apple Slices, 306
Chocolate Eclair Delight, 301
Reese's Chocolate Snack Cake, 261
Other
Chocolate-Caramel Rum Coffee, 22
Hazelnut Chocolate Chip Scones, 202
Sugar Cooke S'mores, 170

CINNAMON
Cinnamon Apple Coffee Cake, 183
Cinnamon Monkey Bread, 204

COBBLERS, CRISPS & CRUMBLES
Cherry Rhubarb Crunch, 305
Grilled Cranberry Pear Crumble, 240
Irresistible Apple Blackberry
   Crumble, 299
Mama's Blackberry Cobbler, 306

COCONUT
Coconut Tropical Fruit Salad, 191
Raspberry-Coconut French Toast, 184
Sausage-Tomato Coconut Curry, 104

COFFEE CAKES
Cinnamon Apple Coffee Cake, 183
Cinnamon Monkey Bread, 204
Monkey Bread, 178

CONDIMENTS
Barbecue Seasoning, 239
Butter Pecan Syrup, 302
Chunky Fruit & Nut Relish, 313
Chunky Ketchup, 313
Cranberry Pesto, 313
Dr Pepper BBQ Sauce, 311
Easy Rhubarb Relish, 310
Family-Favorite Caramelized Onions, 310
Garlic-Pepper Rub, 239
Old-Fashioned Applesauce, 179
Old-Fashioned Corn Relish, 311
Peachy Keen Pepper Sauce, 312
Savory Steak Rub, 239
Tilapia with Cucumber Relish, 142
Tomato Apple Chutney, 312
Tomatoes with Parsley Pesto, 37
Zucchini Honey Relish, 311

COOKIES & BARS
Chocolate Cheesecake Bars, 296
Fried Ice Cream Dessert Bars, 296
Frosted Gingerbread Nut Cookies, 286
Gingerbread Cutout Cookies, 288
Gingerbread Meringue Bars, 287
Miniature Peanut Butter Treats, 177
Palmiers, 300
Peach Cobbler Cookies, 292
Sugar Cookie S'mores, 170

CORN
Chipotle Mexican Street Corn Dip with
   Goat Cheese, 267
Grilled Spicy Corn on the Cob, 230
Makeover Creamed Corn, 42
Old-Fashioned Corn Relish, 311
Special Scalloped Corn, 32

CORNBREAD, CORNMEAL & GRITS

Cornbread Pudding Casserole, 278
Cornmeal Oven-Fried Chicken, 128
Honey Cornbread, 204
Orange Cornmeal Cake, 305
Rosemary Beef Roast over Cheesy
 Polenta, 225
Southern Shrimp & Grits, 123

CRANBERRIES

Cranberry & Roasted Beet Salad, 36
Cranberry Chipotle Chicken
 Enchiladas, 165
Cranberry Gingerbread Scones, 287
Cranberry Maple Chicken, 91
Cranberry Pesto, 313
Double Cranberry Banana Bread, 201
Grilled Cranberry Pear Crumble, 240
Nantucket Cranberry Tart, 278

DESSERTS

*(also see Cookies & Bars; Cakes
 & Cheesecakes; Candy & Fudge;
 Cobblers, Crisps & Crumbles;
 Pies & Tarts; Frozen Desserts)*
Caramel Creme Brulee, 271
Caramelized Pear & Walnut Bread
 Pudding, 298
Cheesecake Berry Parfaits, 275
Cherry & Spice Rice Pudding, 320
Chocolate Bread Pudding, 269
Chocolate-Dipped Caramel
 Apple Slices, 306
Chocolate Eclair Delight, 301
Danish Rhubarb Pudding, 299
Ginger-Glazed Grilled Honeydew, 244
Grandma's English Trifle, 307
New England Indian Pudding, 318
Pressure-Cooker Flan in a Jar, 219
Pumpkin Pecan Custard, 319
Sopaipillas, 267

EGGS

Avocado Egg Salad Toast, 85
Bacon & Egg Bundles, 193
Breakfast in a Pan, 186
Coastal Carolina Muffin-Tin
 Frittatas, 191
German Potato Omelet, 187
Greek Veggies Egg Wraps, 117
Makeover Hash & Eggs, 186
Potato Omelet, 182
Potato Sausage Frittata, 190
Scrambled Egg Muffins, 187
Strawberry Bliss Omelet, 193
Sweet Onion Pimiento Cheese
 Deviled Eggs, 272

FISH, SEAFOOD & SHELLFISH

Almond-Topped Fish, 144
Angel Hair Shrimp Bake, 130
Baked Breaded Cod, 91
Balsamic-Salmon Spinach
 Salad, 164
Buffalo Shrimp Mac & Cheese, 227
Cajun Shrimp, 146
Cod with Sweet Peppers, 158
Crab-Stuffed Avocados, 271
Crab-Stuffed Portobellos, 105
Crab-Topped Fish Fillets, 102
Crabmeat Boats, 74
Crumb-Topped Sole, 132
Easy Clam Chowder, 71
Feta Tomato-Basil Fish, 156
Fish Tacos, 150
Flounder Zucchini Bundles, 120
Garlic Shrimp Spaghetti, 157
Glazed Salmon, 86
Greek Shrimp Canapes, 14
Grilled Jerk Shrimp Orzo Salad, 243
Grilled Tilapia with Mango, 234
Honey Walleye, 100
Honeydew Shrimp Salad, 31
Lemony Grilled Salmon
 Fillets with Dill Sauce, 243*
Maple-Glazed Salmon, 236
Orange-Pecan Salmon, 89
Orange Tilapia in Parchment, 136
Pan-Fried Scallops with White Wine
 Reduction, 141
Pesto Shrimp Pasta, 268
Refreshing Shrimp Salad, 162
Rich Seafood Chowder, 75
Scallops in Sage Cream, 82
Sensational Spiced Salmon, 127
Shrimp & Noodle Bowls, 144
Skewered Ginger Shrimp
 with Plums, 237
Southern Shrimp & Grits, 123
Spinach & Shrimp Fra Diavolo, 160
Stir-Fried Shrimp & Mushrooms, 140
Tarragon Tuna Salad, 154
Tilapia with Cucumber Relish, 142
Tuna Artichoke Melts, 65
Tuna Noodle Casserole, 128
Tuna Potato Supper, 98
The Ultimate Fish Tacos, 266
Zippy Shrimp Skewers, 22

FROZEN DESSERTS

Fried Ice Cream Dessert Bars, 296
Homemade Strawberry
 Ice Cream, 172
No-Churn Gingerbread
 Ice Cream, 286
Quick Icebox Sandwiches, 174

FRUIT

(also see individual kinds)
Balsamic-Goat Cheese Grilled Plums, 239
Chunky Fruit & Nut Relish, 313
Cottage Cheese Cantaloupe Salad, 39
Fast Fruit Salsa, 18
Fruit Dip, 261
Fruit on a Stick, 25
Ginger-Glazed Grilled Honeydew, 244
Grilled Tilapia with Mango, 234
Honeydew Shrimp Salad, 31
Hot Dog Sliders with
 Mango-Pineapple Salsa, 274
Nectarine Chicken Salad, 147
Pesto Crostini with Grilled
 Nectarines & Burrata, 231
Red, White & Blue Summer Salad, 273
Ribs with Plum Sauce, 82
 with Plums, 237
Spiced Rum Fruitcake, 294
Tangerine Tossed Salad, 48
Triple-Citrus Steaks with Jicama
 & Mango, 147
Ultimate Fruity Granola, 183

GARLIC

Garlic Herbed Beef Tenderloin, 257
Garlic Oregano Zucchini, 41
Garlic-Pepper Rub, 239
Garlic Shrimp Spaghetti, 157
Lime & Garlic Grilled Pork Chops, 233
Pull-Apart Garlic Bread, 251
Sauteed Garlic Mushrooms, 33
Sheet-Pan Lemon Garlic Chicken, 317
Warm Garlicky Grape Tomatoes, 51

GINGER

Cranberry Gingerbread Scones, 287
Fresh Ginger Carrot Salad, 53
Frosted Gingerbread Nut Cookies, 286
Ginger Chicken & Quinoa Stew, 212
Ginger-Glazed Grilled Honeydew, 244
Gingerbread Cutout Cookies, 288
Gingerbread Meringue Bars, 287
Gingerbread-Spiced Pumpkin Pie, 289
Gingerbread Truffles, 289
Gingerbread Waffles, 288
Gingered Pork Tenderloin, 111
No-Churn Gingerbread Ice Cream, 286
Skewered Ginger Shrimp with
 Plums, 23

GREEN BEANS

Green Beans Amandine, 35
Old-Fashioned Green Beans, 279
Oregano Green Beans with
 Toasted Pine Nuts, 46
Red Potatoes with Beans, 51

GROUND BEEF
(also see Meatballs & Meatloaf, Burgers)
Cheesy Hamburger Supper, 116
Cheesy Stuffed Peppers, 126
Chili-ghetti, 174
Curried Beef Pita Pockets, 66
Dinner in a Bag, 102
Favorite Hamburger Noodle Bake, 177
Ground Beef Spaghetti Skillet, 101
Indian-Spiced Beefy Lettuce Wraps, 78
Nacho Pie, 114
Pizza Sloppy Joes, 76
Quick Sloppy Joes, 176
Roadside Diner Cheeseburger
   Quiche, 136
Southwestern Beef & Rice Skillet, 112

HAM & PROSCIUTTO
(also see Bacon & Pancetta)
Ham & Cheese Pockets, 71
Ham & Scalloped Potatoes, 99
Ham & Swiss with a Twist, 79
Honey-Glazed Ham, 210
Hurry-Up Ham & Noodles, 122
Mini Ham Quiches, 184
Party Pitas, 251
Prosciutto-Pepper Pork Chops, 93
Sliced Ham with Roasted
   Vegetables, 314
Springtime Penne, 113
Sugar-Glazed Ham, 90

HERBS
Creamy Chicken & Thyme, 152
Dilly Chicken Sandwiches, 78
Feta Tomato-Basil Fish, 156
Garlic Oregano Zucchini, 41
Herb Buttermilk Dinner Rolls, 200
Herb Focaccia Rolls, 284
Herb-Glazed Turkey Slices, 158
Herbed Pork Medallions, 122
Herbed Pork with Mushroom Sauce, 95
Herbed Potato Packs, 241
Herbed Roast Turkey Breast, 277
Herbed Bubble Bread, 207
Lemony Grilled Salmon Fillets
   with Dill Sauce, 243
Oregano Green Beans with
   Toasted Pine Nuts, 46
Quick Cilantro Chicken, 114
Rosemary Beef Roast over Cheesy
   Polenta, 225
Rosemary Pork with Cherry Topping, 133
Rosemary-Thyme Lamb Chops, 92
Rosemary Walnut Bread, 199
Scallops in Sage Cream, 82
Spiced Lime & Cilantro Chicken, 224

Tarragon Chicken with Apples, 113
Tarragon Tuna Salad, 154
Tomatoes with Parsley Pesto, 37

HONEY
Honey Cornbread, 204
Honey-Glazed Chicken, 95
Honey-Glazed Ham, 210
Honey Mustard Pork, 123
Honey Walleye, 100
Slow-Cooker Honey Teriyaki
   Chicken, 217
Zucchini Honey Relish, 311

LAMB
California Roast Lamb, 280
Rosemary-Thyme Lamb Chops, 92

LEMON & LIME
Easy Strawberry Lemonade
   Freezer Pie, 293
Grilled Pineapple with Lime Dip, 232
Key Lime Cream Pie, 298
Lemon Feta Chicken, 84
Lemon Mushroom Chicken, 156
Lemony Grilled Salmon Fillets with
   Dill Sauce, 243
Lime & Garlic Grilled Pork Chops, 233
Sheet-Pan Lemon Garlic Chicken, 317
Spiced Lime & Cilantro Chicken, 224
Triple-Citrus Steaks with Jicama &
   Mango, 147

MAPLE
Cranberry Maple Chicken, 91
Maple & Bacon Glazed Brussels
Sprouts, 280
Maple-Glazed Salmon, 236
Maple Pecan Pie, 285
Maple-Roasted Chicken &
   Acorn Squash, 83

MEATBALLS & MEAT LOAF
Little Cheddar Meat Loaves, 173
Mini Meat Loaf Sheet-Pan Meal, 316
Potluck Enchilada Meatballs, 250
Tangy Sweet & Sour Meatballs, 117

MEATLESS ENTREES
Cheddar Broccoli Quinoa, 115
Couscous Tabbouleh with Fresh Mint &
   Feta, 269
Creamy Pasta Primavera, 146
Creamy Tomato Fettuccine with
   Zucchini, 99
Cumin Quinoa Patties, 149
Easy Lazy Lasagna, 92
Fettuccine with Black Bean Sauce, 167

Greek Veggies Egg Wraps, 117
Grilled Vegetable Quesadillas, 232
Hearty Asian Lettuce Salad, 163
Lentil Taco Cups, 152
Meatless Taco Salad, 107
Nutty Cheese Tortellini, 90
Penne with Veggies & Black Beans, 115
Tuscan Portobello Stew, 150
Vegetarian Pea Soup, 219

MUFFINS & QUICK BREADS
Banana Nut Bread, 205
Double Cranberry Banana Bread, 201
Favorite Irish Soda Bread, 199
Nut-Topped Strawberry Rhubarb
   Muffins, 207
Quick & Easy Pumpkin Crescents, 198
Sweet Potato Spice Bread, 202
Turkey Dinner Muffins, 111

MUSHROOMS
Crab-Stuffed Portobellos, 105
Easy Salisbury Steak, 121
Gnocchi with Mushrooms & Onion, 49
Herbed Pork with Mushroom Sauce, 95
Lemon Mushroom Chicken, 156
Mushroom-Blue Cheese Tenderloin, 130
Sauteed Garlic Mushrooms, 33
Stir-Fried Shrimp & Mushrooms, 140
Swiss Mushroom Chicken, 108
Tuscan Portobello Stew, 150

MUSTARD
Blueberry-Dijon Chicken, 118
Honey Mustard Pork, 123
Pork with Mustard Sauce, 106
Turkey Sandwich with Raspberry-
   Mustard Spread, 57

NUTS
(also see Peanuts & Peanut Butter)
Almond-Topped Fish, 144
Apple-Sweet Potato Pecan
   Dump Cake, 321
Caramelized Pear & Walnut Bread
   Pudding, 298
Chunky Fruit & Nut Relish, 313
Frosted Gingerbread Nut Cookies, 286
Hazelnut Chocolate Chip Scones, 202
Luscious Almond Cheesecake, 249
Maple Pecan Pie, 285
Nutty Chicken Fingers, 171
Orange-Pecan Salmon, 89
Oregano Green Beans with
   Toasted Pine Nuts, 46
Pecan Pork Chops, 155
Pumpkin Pecan Custard, 319
Rosemary Walnut Bread, 199

OATS & GRANOLA

Overnight Peach Oatmeal, 223
Pressure-Cooker Pumpkin Spice
   Oatmeal, 220
Slow-Cooker Honey Nut Granola, 185
Slow-Cooker Oatmeal, 195
Ultimate Fruity Granola, 183

ONIONS

Apples & Onion Topped Chops, 162
Baked Vidalia Onions, 30
Chicken Thighs with Shallots &
   Spinach, 143
Family-Favorite Caramelized Onions, 310
Gnocchi with Mushrooms & Onion, 49
Grilled Zucchini with Onions, 275
Quinoa with Peas & Onion, 31
Sweet Onion Pimiento Cheese
   Deviled Eggs, 272

ORANGES & ORANGE JUICE

Grandmother's Orange Salad, 40
Orange Cornmeal Cake, 305
Orange-Pecan Salmon, 89
Orange Tilapia in Parchment, 136
Simple Orange-Glazed Beets, 41

PASTA & NOODLES

Angel Hair Shrimp Bake, 130
Buffalo Shrimp Mac & Cheese, 227
Chicken Orzo Skillet, 154
Chicken with Couscous, 166
Chili-ghetti, 174
Couscous Tabbouleh with Fresh Mint &
   Feta, 269
Creamy Pasta Primavera, 146
Creamy Tomato Fettuccine with
   Zucchini, 99
Easy Beef Stroganoff, 151
Easy Lazy Lasagna, 92
Favorite Hamburger Noodle Bake, 177
Fettuccine with Black Bean Sauce, 167
Garlic Shrimp Spaghetti, 157
Gnocchi with Mushrooms & Onion, 49
Grilled Jerk Shrimp Orzo Salad, 243
Ground Beef Spaghetti Skillet, 101
Hurry-Up Ham & Noodles, 122
Macaroni Coleslaw, 252
Makeover Traditional Lasagna, 159
Nutty Cheese Tortellini, 90
One-Pan Rotini with Tomato Cream
   Sauce, 170
Orzo with Caramelized Butternut
   Squash & Bacon, 45
Orzo with Feta & Arugula, 40
Pasta Fagioli Soup, 60
Penne with Veggies & Black Beans, 115
Pesto Shrimp Pasta, 268

Pork & Bok Choy Udon Soup, 62
Pork Chops & Pierogies, 100
Quick Sausage Tortellini Soup, 58
Sausage & Swiss Chard Pasta, 105
Shrimp & Noodle Bowls, 144
Skewered Ravioli with Creamy Tomato
   Dipping Sauce, 16
Skillet Tacos, 118
Smoked Sausage with Pasta, 148
Springtime Penne, 113
Tuna Noodle Casserole, 128
Turkey Couscous Salad, 165
Turkey Sausage with Pasta, 157
Weeknight Ravioli Lasagna, 95
Zucchini Pasta, 47

PEACHES

Grilled Chicken with Peach Sauce, 236
Overnight Peach Oatmeal, 223
Peach Caprese, 30
Peach Cobbler Cookies, 292
Peachy Keen Pepper Sauce, 312

PEANUTS & PEANUT BUTTER

Chocolate-Peanut Butter
   Dump Cake, 321
Miniature Peanut Butter Treats, 177
Peanut Turkey Satay, 166
Thai Butternut Squash Peanut Soup, 221

PEARS

Caramelized Pear & Walnut Bread
   Pudding, 298
Grilled Cranberry Pear Crumble, 240
Orchard Pear Pie, 293
Warm Cabbage, Fennel & Pear Salad, 279

PEAS & SNAP PEAS

Quinoa with Peas & Onion, 31
Vegetarian Pea Soup, 219
Zesty Sugar Snap Peas, 53

PEPPERS & CHILES

Bacon-Wrapped Stuffed Jalapenos, 252
Cheesy Stuffed Peppers, 126
Chipotle Berry Fruit Salsa, 266
Chipotle Citrus-Glazed Turkey
   Tenderloins, 106
Chipotle Mexican Street Corn Dip with
   Goat Cheese, 267
Cod with Sweet Peppers, 158
Grilled Pork & Poblano Peppers, 241
Pork & Green Chile Casserole, 135
Potato & Pepper Sausage Bake, 317
Roasted Peppers & Cauliflower, 52
Sassy Chicken & Peppers, 148
Tara's Spanish Chicken, 316
Tex-Mex Pork Chops, 151

PESTO

Artichoke Chicken Pesto Pizza, 86
Cranberry Pesto, 313
Pesto Crostini with Grilled Nectarines &
   Burrata, 231
Pesto Shrimp Pasta, 268
Tomatoes with Parsley Pesto, 37

PIES & TARTS

Easy Fresh Strawberry Pie, 301
Easy Strawberry Lemonade
   Freezer Pie, 293
Gingerbread-Spiced Pumpkin Pie, 289
Granny's Rhubarb Pie, 303
Key Lime Cream Pie, 298
Maple Pecan Pie, 285
Nantucket Cranberry Tart, 278
Orchard Pear Pie, 293
Root Beer Float Pie, 275
Squash Custard Pie, 292

PIES—SAVORY

Mini Ham Quiches, 184
Mini Sausage Quiches, 258
Old-Fashioned Chicken Potpie, 134
Roadside Diner Cheeseburger
   Quiche, 136
Tomato Potpie, 127
Turkey Lattice Pie, 315

PINEAPPLE

Blueberry, Apple & Pineapple
   Dump Cake, 319
Grilled Pineapple with Lime Dip, 232
Makeover Pineapple
   Upside-Down Cake, 294
Tropical Pineapple Coleslaw, 176

PIZZA & FLATBREADS

Artichoke Chicken Pesto Pizza, 86
Creamy Chicken Enchilada Pizza, 27
Deluxe Deep-Dish Pizza, 134
Italian-Style Pizzas, 19
Mini Pizza Cups, 249
Steakhouse Pizza, 135

PORK

(also see Bacon & Pancetta; Ham &
   Proscuitto; Sausage & Pepperoni)
Apples & Onion Topped Chops, 162
Banh Mi Skewers, 13
Cuban Pulled Pork Sandwiches, 211
Curried Pork & Green Tomatoes, 108
Easy Chili Verde, 88
Garden Pork Stir-Fry, 163
Gingered Pork Tenderloin, 111
Grandma Edna's Cajun Pork, 214
Grilled Pork & Poblano Peppers, 241

Hawaiian Pulled Pork Lettuce Wraps, 225
Herbed Pork Medallions, 122
Herbed Pork with Mushroom Sauce, 95
Honey Mustard Pork, 123
Lime & Garlic Grilled Pork Chops, 233
Parmesan Pork Medallions, 84
Pecan Pork Chops, 155
Pork & Bok Choy Udon Soup, 62
Pork & Green Chile Casserole, 135
Pork Chops & Pierogies, 100
Pork Chops with Cumin Rice, 107
Pork Chops with Parmesan Sauce, 160
Pork Tenderloin Fajitas, 264
Pork with Mustard Sauce, 106
Ribs with Plum Sauce, 82
Rosemary Pork with Cherry Topping, 133
Saucy Grilled Pork Chops, 231
Tex-Mex Pork Chops, 151

POTATOES
(also see Sweet Potatoes)
Main Dishes
German Potato Omelet, 187
Ham & Scalloped Potatoes, 99
Makeover Hash & Eggs, 186
Makeover Tater-Topped Casserole, 126
Potato & Pepper Sausage Bake, 317
Potato Omelet, 182
Potato Sausage Frittata, 190
Pressure-Cooker Potato-Cheddar
    Frittata, 214
Tater-Topped Italian Casserole, 137
Tuna Potato Supper, 98
Salads, Side Dishes & Soup
Cream of Potato & Cheddar Soup, 211
Fried Potato Salad, 274
Grilled Potato Fans with Onions, 230
Herbed Potato Packs, 241
Mini Meat Loaf Sheet-Pan Meal, 316
Olive Oil Mashed Potatoes with
    Pancetta, 276
Pressure-Cooker Lemon
    Red Potatoes, 210
Red Potatoes with Beans, 51
Super Simple Scalloped Potatoes, 282

PRESSURE-COOKER RECIPES
25-Minute Turkey Chili, 226
Cheddar Bacon Beer Dip, 226
Buffalo Shrimp Mac & Cheese, 227
Cuban Pulled Pork Sandwiches, 211
Pressure-Cooker Chicken
    Cacciatore, 224
Pressure-Cooker Flan in a Jar, 219
Pressure-Cooker Lemon
    Red Potatoes, 210
Pressure-Cooker Potato-Cheddar
    Frittata, 214

Pressure-Cooker Pumpkin Spice
    Oatmeal, 220
Saucy Italian Chicken, 218
Pressure-Cooker Sausage &
    Waffle Bake, 227
Pressure-Cooker Spiced Short Ribs, 212

PUMPKIN
Cardamom Pumpkin Pudding Cake, 320
Gingerbread-Spiced Pumpkin Pie, 289
Moist Pumpkin Scones, 200
Pressure-Cooker Pumpkin Spice
    Oatmeal, 220
Pumpkin Pecan Custard, 319
Quick & Easy Pumpkin Crescents, 198

QUICK BREADS
(see Muffins & Quick Breads)

RHUBARB
Danish Rhubarb Pudding, 299
Easy Rhubarb Relish, 310
Granny's Rhubarb Pie, 303
Nut-Topped Strawberry Rhubarb
    Muffins, 207
Rhubarb Torte, 256

RICE & GRAINS
Broccoli Rice Casserole, 47
Cabbage Barley Soup, 79
Cheddar Broccoli Quinoa, 115
Cherry & Spice Rice Pudding, 320
Creamy Chicken Rice Soup, 69
Cumin Quinoa Patties, 149
Ginger Chicken & Quinoa Stew, 212
Hearty Asian Lettuce Salad, 163
Pork Chops with Cumin Rice, 107
Quinoa Arancini, 23
Quinoa with Peas & Onion, 31
Rice with Collard Greens Relish, 37
Sausage Rice Dinner, 102
Slow-Cooked Vegetable Wild Rice
    Soup, 223
Southwestern Beef & Rice Skillet, 112
Southwestern Beef Barley Stew, 142

SALADS
Fruit Salads
Apricots with Herbed Goat Cheese, 45
Coconut Tropical Fruit Salad, 191
Cottage Cheese Cantaloupe Salad, 39
Peach Caprese, 30
Gelatin Salads
Apricot Fluff, 51
Grandmother's Orange Salad, 40
Green Salads
Blackberry Balsamic Spinach Salad, 46
Cranberry & Roasted Beet Salad, 36

Perfect Winter Salad, 282
Red, White & Blue Summer Salad, 273
Strawberry Arugula Salad, 53
Tangerine Tossed Salad, 48
Main Dish Salads
Balsamic-Salmon Spinach Salad, 164
Couscous Tabbouleh with
    Fresh Mint & Feta, 269
Crab-Stuffed Avocados, 271
Flat Iron Steak Salad, 234
Grilled Jerk Shrimp Orzo Salad, 243
Grilled Steak Bruschetta
    Salad for Two, 245
Hearty Asian Lettuce Salad, 163
Honeydew Shrimp Salad, 31
Meatless Taco Salad, 107
Nectarine Chicken Salad, 147
Refreshing Shrimp Salad, 162
Sausage Spinach Salad, 83
Slow-Cooker Buffalo Chicken Salad, 220
Steak Frites Salad, 155
Tarragon Tuna Salad, 154
Turkey Couscous Salad, 165
Zesty Steak Salad, 140
Vegetable Salads
Chipotle Sweet Potato Salad, 35
Fresh Ginger Carrot Salad, 53
Fried Potato Salad, 274
Garden Bounty Panzanella Salad, 256
Warm Cabbage, Fennel & Pear Salad, 279

SANDWICHES & WRAPS
(also see Burgers)
Sandwiches
Avocado Egg Salad Toast, 85
Cajun Chicken Club, 70
Champion Roast Beef Sandwiches, 69
Cheddar French Dip Sandwiches, 63
Cherry Chicken Croissants, 64
Crabmeat Boats, 74
Cuban Pulled Pork Sandwiches, 211
Curried Beef Pita Pockets, 66
Dilly Chicken Sandwiches, 78
Gourmet Barbecue Beef Sandwiches, 74
Grilled Bacon-Tomato Sandwiches, 72
Ham & Cheese Pockets, 71
Ham & Swiss with a Twist, 79
Hot Dog Sliders with Mango-Pineapple
    Salsa, 274
Makeover Deluxe Grilled Cheese, 60
Moroccan Chicken Tagine Pockets, 25
Open-Faced Turkey Phillies, 71
Pizza Sloppy Joes, 76
Quick Sloppy Joes, 176
Party Pitas, 251
Sliders
California Turkey Sliders, 19
Chicken Parmesan Slider Bake, 172

Hot Dog Sliders with Mango-Pineapple Salsa, 274

Wraps
Chicken Caesar Wraps, 66
Cobb Salad Wraps, 70
Deli Turkey Lettuce Wraps, 67
Greek Veggies Egg Wraps, 117
Hawaiian Pulled Pork Lettuce Wraps, 225
Indian-Spiced Beefy Lettuce Wraps, 78
Spicy Buffalo Chicken Wraps, 76

SAUSAGE & PEPPERONI
Cheddar & Chorizo Strata, 186
Cheese & Sausage Appetizers, 255
Chorizo & Chickpea Soup, 65
Hot Dog Sliders with Mango-Pineapple Salsa, 274
Easy Sausage & Vegetable Skillet, 109
Mini Sausage Quiches, 258
Pepperoni Pinwheels, 13
Potato & Pepper Sausage Bake, 317
Potato Sausage Frittata, 190
Pressure-Cooker Sausage & Waffle Bake, 227
Quick Sausage Tortellini Soup, 58
Roasted Kielbasa & Vegetables, 315
Sausage & Sauerkraut, 86
Sausage & Swiss Chard Pasta, 105
Sausage Breakfast Burritos, 192
Sausage Rice Dinner, 102
Sausage Spinach Salad, 83
Sausage-Tomato Coconut Curry, 104
Smoked Sausage with Pasta, 148

SCONES
Cranberry Gingerbread Scones, 287
Hazelnut Chocolate Chip Scones, 202
Moist Pumpkin Scones, 200

SIDE DISHES
Miscellaneous
Grandma's Poultry Dressing, 38
Macaroni Coleslaw, 252
Orzo with Caramelized Butternut Squash & Bacon, 45
Orzo with Feta & Arugula, 40
Sauteed Garlic Mushrooms, 33
Spicy Refried Beans, 265
Tomatoes with Parsley Pesto, 37
Warm Garlicky Grape Tomatoes, 51

Potatoes & Sweet Potatoes
Gnocchi with Mushrooms & Onion, 49
Grilled Potato Fans with Onions, 230
Herbed Potato Packs, 241
Pressure-Cooker Lemon Red Potatoes, 210
Red Potatoes with Beans, 51
Roasted Sweet Potato Wedges, 48

Super Simple Scalloped Potatoes, 282
Rice & Grains
Broccoli Rice Casserole, 47
Quinoa with Peas & Onion, 31
Rice with Collard Greens Relish, 37

Vegetables
Baked Vidalia Onions, 30
Black-Eyed Peas with Collard Greens, 32
Cabbage & Rutabaga Slaw, 47
Caribbean Island Coleslaw, 33
Citrus Peach Carrots, 39
Cornbread Pudding Casserole, 278
Fried Cabbage, 39
Garlic Oregano Zucchini, 41
Green Beans Amandine, 35
Grilled Cabbage, 237
Grilled Spicy Corn on the Cob, 230
Grilled Zucchini with Onions, 275
Kale & Fennel Skillet, 38
Makeover Creamed Corn, 42
Maple & Bacon Glazed Brussels Sprouts, 280
Mashed Cauliflower, 284
Old-Fashioned Green Beans, 279
Oregano Green Beans with Toasted Pine Nuts, 46
Roasted Asparagus & Tomatoes, 42
Roasted Peppers & Cauliflower, 52
Simple Orange-Glazed Beets, 41
Special Scalloped Corn, 32
Tuscan-Style Roasted Asparagus, 285
Zesty Sugar Snap Peas, 53

SLOW COOKER RECIPES
All-In-One Breakfast, 195
Artichoke Spread with Garlic Bread, 12
Bacon Breakfast Casserole, 188
Butter Pecan Syrup, 302
Cabbage Barley Soup, 79
Cheesy Bruschetta Spread, 16
Cherry & Spice Rice Pudding, 320
Chicken Tomatillo Soup, 64
Chorizo & Chickpea Soup, 65
Cream of Potato & Cheddar Soup, 211
Easy Chili Verde, 88
Ginger Chicken & Quinoa Stew, 212
Gourmet Barbecue Beef Sandwiches, 74
Grandma Edna's Cajun Pork, 214
Greek Shrimp Canapes, 14
Greek-Style Lentil Soup, 213
Hawaiian Pulled Pork Lettuce Wraps, 225
Honey-Glazed Ham, 210
Marinara-Mozzarella Dip, 21
Moroccan Chicken Tagine Pockets, 25
New England Indian Pudding, 318
Oregano Green Beans with Toasted Pine Nuts, 46

Overnight Peach Oatmeal, 223
Potluck Enchilada Meatballs, 250
Shredded Chicken Tostadas, 216
Slow-Cooked Black Bean Soup, 218
Slow-Cooked Vegetable Wild Rice Soup, 223
Slow-Cooker Buffalo Chicken Salad, 220
Slow-Cooker Cinnamon Roll, 192
Slow-Cooker Honey Nut Granola, 185
Slow-Cooker Honey Teriyaki Chicken, 217
Slow-Cooker Oatmeal, 195
Slow-Cooker Strawberry Pudding Cake, 302
Thai Butternut Squash Peanut Soup, 221
So-Easy Sticky Chicken Wings, 252
Spiced Lime & Cilantro Chicken, 224
Tomato Apple Chutney, 312
Vegetarian Pea Soup, 219

SOUPS
(also see Chili; Stews)
Bean Counter Chowder, 56
Borscht with Garden Vegetables, 56
Broccoli Chowder, 58
Cabbage Barley Soup, 79
Chicken Alphabet Soup, 173
Chicken Tomatillo Soup, 64
Chickpea Tortilla Soup, 73
Chorizo & Chickpea Soup, 65
Cream of Potato & Cheddar Soup, 211
Creamy Chicken Rice Soup, 69
Curried Chicken Soup, 72
Easy Clam Chowder, 71
Greek-Style Lentil Soup, 213
Pasta Fagioli Soup, 60
Pork & Bok Choy Udon Soup, 62
Quick Sausage Tortellini Soup, 58
Rich Seafood Chowder, 75
Slow-Cooked Black Bean Soup, 218
Slow-Cooked Vegetable Wild Rice Soup, 223
Super Fast Mexican Soup, 57
Thai Butternut Squash Peanut Soup, 221
Vegetarian Pea Soup, 219
Zesty Turkey Tomato Soup, 73

SPINACH
Sausage Spinach Salad, 83
Spanakopita Spring Rolls, 20
Spinach & Shrimp Fra Diavolo, 160

SQUASH
(also see Zucchini & Summer Squash)
Maple-Roasted Chicken & Acorn Squash, 83
Orzo with Caramelized Butternut Squash & Bacon, 45

Squash Custard Pie, 292
Thai Butternut Squash Peanut
 Soup, 221
Turkey Squash Casserole, 133

STEWS
Ginger Chicken & Quinoa Stew, 212
One-Pot Salsa Chicken, 149
Southwestern Beef Barley Stew, 142
Spicy Chicken Stew, 144
Tuscan Portobello Stew, 150

STRAWBERRIES
Easy Fresh Strawberry Pie, 301
Easy Strawberry Lemonade
 Freezer Pie, 293
Homemade Strawberry Ice Cream, 172
Nut-Topped Strawberry Rhubarb
 Muffins, 207
Slow-Cooker Strawberry
 Pudding Cake, 302
Strawberry Arugula Salad, 53
Strawberry Bliss Omelet, 193

SWEET POTATOES
Apple-Sweet Potato
 Pecan Dump Cake, 321
Chipotle Sweet Potato Salad, 35
Grandma's Sweet Potato Biscuits, 205
One-Pot Salsa Chicken, 149
Roasted Sweet Potato Wedges, 48
Sweet Potato Spice Bread, 202

TOMATOES
10-Minute Zesty Salsa, 264
Cacciatore Chicken Breasts, 152
Grilled Bacon-Tomato Sandwiches, 72
Chocolate Tomato Spice Cake, 307
Chunky Ketchup, 313
Curried Pork & Green Tomatoes, 108
Feta Tomato-Basil Fish, 156
One-Pan Rotini with Tomato Cream
 Sauce, 170
Roasted Asparagus & Tomatoes, 42
Saucy Italian Chicken, 218
Sausage-Tomato Coconut Curry, 104
Tomato Apple Chutney, 312
Tomato Potpie, 127
Tomatoes with Parsley Pesto, 37
Warm Garlicky Grape Tomatoes, 51
Zesty Turkey Tomato Soup, 73

TORTILLAS
Black Bean Tortilla Pinwheels, 19
Chicken Veggie Fajitas, 314
Chickpea Tortilla Soup, 73
Cranberry Chipotle Chicken
 Enchiladas, 165

Easy Roast Beef Roll-Ups, 15
Fish Tacos, 150
Grilled Vegetable Quesadillas, 232
Lentil Taco Cups, 152
Pork Tenderloin Fajitas, 264
Sausage Breakfast Burritos, 192
Southwest Tortilla-Turkey Skillet, 121
Turkey Enchilada Stack, 141
The Ultimate Fish Tacos, 266

TURKEY & TURKEY SAUSAGE
25-Minute Turkey Chili, 226
California Turkey Sliders, 19
Chipotle Citrus-Glazed Turkey
 Tenderloins, 106
Deli Turkey Lettuce Wraps, 67
Easy Turkey Schnitzel, 114
Herb-Glazed Turkey Slices, 158
Herbed Roast Turkey Breast, 277
Open-Faced Turkey Phillies, 71
Peanut Turkey Satay, 166
Skillet Tacos, 118
Southwest Tortilla-Turkey Skillet, 121
TLC (Thanksgiving Leftover
 Casserole), 276
Turkey Couscous Salad, 165
Turkey Dinner Muffins, 111
Turkey Enchilada Stack, 141
Turkey Lattice Pie, 315
Turkey Sandwich with Raspberry-
 Mustard Spread, 57
Turkey Sausage with Pasta, 157
Turkey Scallopini, 111
Turkey Squash Casserole, 133
Zesty Turkey Tomato Soup, 73

VEGETABLES
(*also see specific kinds*)
Black-Eyed Peas with Collard
 Greens, 32
Cabbage & Rutabaga Slaw, 47
Chicken Thighs with
 Shallots & Spinach, 143
Chicken Veggie Fajitas, 314
Creamy Pasta Primavera, 146
Easy Sausage & Vegetable Skillet, 109
Garden Bounty Panzanella Salad, 256
Grilled Vegetable Quesadillas, 232
Kale & Fennel Skillet, 38
Maple & Bacon Glazed Brussels
 Sprouts, 280
Penne with Veggies & Black Beans, 115
Pork & Bok Choy Udon Soup, 62
Rice with Collard Greens Relish, 37
Roasted Kielbasa & Vegetables, 315
Sausage & Swiss Chard Pasta, 105
Sliced Ham with Roasted
 Vegetables, 314

Slow-Cooked Vegetable Wild Rice
 Soup, 223
Warm Cabbage, Fennel & Pear
 Salad, 279

YEAST BREADS
Best Ever Breadsticks, 198
Herbed Bubble Bread, 207
Italian Herb & Cheese Breadsticks, 254
Rosemary Walnut Bread, 199

ZUCCHINI
Creamy Tomato Fettuccine with
 Zucchini, 99
Flounder Zucchini Bundles, 120
Garlic Oregano Zucchini, 41
Grilled Zucchini with Onions, 275
Zucchini Honey Relish, 311
Zucchini-Parmesan Bake, 93
Zucchini Pasta, 47

Alphabetical Recipe Index

This index lists every recipe in alphabetical order so you can easily find all of your favorites.

10-Minute Zesty Salsa, 264
25-Minute Turkey Chili, 226

A

All-American Hamburgers, 272
All-In-One Breakfast, 195
Almond-Topped Fish, 144
Angel Hair Shrimp Bake, 130
Appetizer Blue Cheese Logs, 27
Apple Butter Biscuit Breakfast
    Bake, 187
Apple-Sweet Potato Pecan
    Dump Cake, 321
Apple Wonton Bundles, 257
Apples & Onion Topped Chops, 162
Apricot Fluff, 51
Apricots with Herbed Goat Cheese, 45

Artichoke Chicken Pesto Pizza, 86
Artichoke Spread with Garlic Bread, 12
Asian Chicken Dinner, 164
Asparagus Beef Teriyaki, 120
Aunt Frances' Lemonade, 250
Avocado Egg Salad Toast, 85

B

Baby Swiss Christmas Cheesecake, 281
Bacon & Egg Bundles, 193
Bacon Breakfast Casserole, 188
Bacon-Wrapped Stuffed
    Jalapenos, 252
Baked Asparagus Dip, 261
Baked Banana French Toast, 188
Baked Breaded Cod, 91
Baked Vidalia Onions, 30

Balsamic-Goat Cheese
    Grilled Plums, 239
Balsamic-Salmon Spinach Salad, 164
Banana Nut Bread, 205
Banh Mi Skewers, 13
Barbecue Seasoning, 239
Bean Counter Chowder, 56
Beef Steaks with Blue Cheese, 88
Best Ever Breadsticks, 198
Black Bean Tortilla Pinwheels, 19
Black-Eyed Peas with
    Collard Greens, 32
Black Forest Dump Cake, 319
Black Russian, 15
Blackberry Balsamic Spinach Salad, 46
Blue Cheese-Stuffed
    Steaks for Two, 92
Blueberry, Apple & Pineapple
    Dump Cake, 319
Blueberry-Dijon Chicken, 118
Borscht with Garden Vegetables, 56
Breakfast in a Pan, 186
Broccoli Chowder, 58
Broccoli Rice Casserole, 47
Brunch Casserole, 195

APRICOT FLUFF, 51

Buffalo Shrimp Mac & Cheese, 227
Butter Pecan Syrup, 302
Buttermilk Pound Cake, 259
Buttermilk Vegetable Dip, 261

C

Cabbage & Rutabaga Slaw, 47
Cabbage Barley Soup, 79
Cacciatore Chicken Breasts, 152
Cajun Chicken Club, 70
Cajun Shrimp, 146
California Roast Lamb, 280
California Turkey Sliders, 19
Caramel Creme Brulee, 271
Caramelized Pear & Walnut Bread
    Pudding, 298
Cardamom Pumpkin Pudding
    Cake, 320
Caribbean Island Coleslaw, 33
Champion Roast Beef Sandwiches, 69
Cheddar & Chorizo Strata, 186
Cheddar Bacon Beer Dip, 226
Cheddar Bacon Toasts, 18
Cheddar Broccoli Quinoa, 115
Cheddar French Dip Sandwiches, 63
Cheese & Sausage Appetizers, 255
Cheese-Stuffed Burgers for Two, 62
Cheesecake Berry Parfaits, 275
Cheesy Bruschetta Spread, 16
Cheesy Hamburger Supper, 116
Cheesy Stuffed Peppers, 126
Cherry & Spice Rice Pudding, 320
Cherry Chicken Croissants, 64
Cherry Pudding Cake, 318
Cherry Rhubarb Crunch, 305
Chicken Alphabet Soup, 173
Chicken & Broccoli Cups, 21
Chicken Caesar Wraps, 66
Chicken Cordon Bleu in Pastry, 89
Chicken Cordon Bleu Puffs, 127
Chicken Orzo Skillet, 154
Chicken Parmesan Slider Bake, 172
Chicken Piccata Pockets, 270
Chicken Skillet Supper, 122
Chicken Thighs with Shallots &
    Spinach, 143
Chicken Tomatillo Soup, 64
Chicken Veggie Fajitas, 314
Chicken with Couscous, 166
Chickpea Tortilla Soup, 73
Chili-ghetti, 174
Chipotle Berry Fruit Salsa, 266
Chipotle Citrus-Glazed Turkey
    Tenderloins, 106
Chipotle Mexican Street Corn Dip
    with Goat Cheese, 267
Chipotle Sweet Potato Salad, 35

Chocolate Bread Pudding, 269
Chocolate-Caramel Rum Coffee, 22
Chocolate Cheesecake Bars, 296
Chocolate-Dipped Caramel Apple
    Slices, 306
Chocolate Eclair Delight, 301
Chocolate-Peanut Butter
    Dump Cake, 321
Chocolate Tomato Spice Cake, 307
Chorizo & Chickpea Soup, 65
Chunky Fruit & Nut Relish, 313
Chunky Ketchup, 313
Cinnamon Apple Coffee Cake, 183
Cinnamon Monkey Bread, 204
Citrus Cider Punch, 248
Citrus Peach Carrots, 39
Coastal Carolina Muffin-Tin
    Frittatas, 191
Cobb Salad Wraps, 70
Coconut Tropical Fruit Salad, 191
Cod with Sweet Peppers, 158
Cola Burgers, 179
Cold Chicken-Cheese Kabobs, 14
Cornbread Pudding Casserole, 278
Cornmeal Oven-Fried Chicken, 128
Cottage Cheese Cantaloupe Salad, 39
Couscous Tabbouleh with Fresh Mint
    & Feta, 269
Crab-Stuffed Avocados, 271
Crab-Stuffed Portobellos, 105
Crab-Topped Fish Fillets, 102
Crabmeat Boats, 74
Cranberry & Roasted Beet Salad, 36
Cranberry Chipotle Chicken
    Enchiladas, 165
Cranberry Gingerbread Scones, 287
Cranberry Maple Chicken, 91
Cranberry Pesto, 313
Cream of Potato & Cheddar Soup, 211
Creamy Chicken & Thyme, 152
Creamy Chicken Enchilada Pizza, 27
Creamy Chicken Rice Soup, 69
Creamy Curried Chicken, 116
Creamy Pasta Primavera, 146
Creamy Tomato Fettuccine with
    Zucchini, 99
Crumb-Topped Sole, 132
Cuban Pulled Pork Sandwiches, 211
Cumin Quinoa Patties, 149
Curried Beef Pita Pockets, 66
Curried Chicken Soup, 72
Curried Pork & Green
    Tomatoes, 108

D

Danish Rhubarb Pudding, 299
Deli Turkey Lettuce Wraps, 67

Deluxe Deep-Dish Pizza, 134
Deviled Chicken Thighs, 137
Dill Bloody Marys, 25
Dilly Chicken Sandwiches, 78
Dinner in a Bag, 102
Double Cranberry Banana Bread, 201
Dr Pepper BBQ Sauce, 311

E

Easy Beef Stroganoff, 151
Easy Cheesy Biscuits, 277
Easy Chili Verde, 88
Easy Clam Chowder, 71
Easy Fresh Strawberry Pie, 301
Easy Lazy Lasagna, 92
Easy Rhubarb Relish, 310
Easy Roast Beef Roll-Ups, 15
Easy Salisbury Steak, 121
Easy Sausage & Vegetable Skillet, 109
Easy Strawberry Lemonade
    Freezer Pie, 293
Easy Turkey Schnitzel, 114
Enchilada Chicken, 85

F

Family-Favorite Caramelized
    Onions, 310
Fast Fruit Salsa, 18
Favorite Hamburger Noodle
    Bake, 177
Favorite Irish Soda Bread, 199
Feta Tomato-Basil Fish, 156
Fettuccine with Black Bean Sauce, 167
Finnish Mulled Wine, 283
Fish Tacos, 150
Flat Iron Steak Salad, 234
Flounder Zucchini Bundles, 120
Fluffy Biscuits, 206
Fresh Ginger Carrot Salad, 53
Fried Cabbage, 39
Fried Ice Cream Dessert Bars, 296
Fried Potato Salad, 274
Frosted Gingerbread Nut Cookies, 286
Fruit Dip, 261
Fruit on a Stick, 25

G

Garden Bounty Panzanella Salad, 256
Garden Pork Stir-Fry, 163
Garlic Herbed Beef Tenderloin, 257
Garlic Oregano Zucchini, 41
Garlic-Pepper Rub, 239
Garlic Shrimp Spaghetti, 157
German Potato Omelet, 187
Ginger Chicken & Quinoa Stew, 212

Ginger-Glazed Grilled Honeydew, 244
Gingerbread Cutout Cookies, 288
Gingerbread-Spiced Pumpkin Pie, 289
Gingerbread Truffles, 289
Gingerbread Waffles, 288
Gingered Pork Tenderloin, 111
Glazed Salmon, 86
Gnocchi with Mushrooms & Onion, 49
Gourmet Barbecue Beef
    Sandwiches, 74
Grandma Edna's Cajun Pork, 214
Grandma's Christmas Cake, 283
Grandma's English Trifle, 307
Grandma's Poultry Dressing, 38
Grandma's Sweet Potato Biscuits, 205
Grandmother's Orange Salad, 40
Granny's Rhubarb Pie, 303
Greek Shrimp Canapes, 14
Greek-Style Lentil Soup, 213
Greek Veggies Egg Wraps, 117
Green Beans Amandine, 35
Grilled Bacon-Tomato Sandwiches, 72
Grilled Cabbage, 237
Grilled Chicken with Peach Sauce, 236
Grilled Cranberry Pear Crumble, 240

Grilled Glazed Drummies, 248
Grilled Jerk Shrimp Orzo Salad, 243
Grilled Peppered Steaks, 244
Grilled Pineapple with Lime Dip, 232
Grilled Pork & Poblano Peppers, 241
Grilled Potato Fans with Onions, 230
Grilled Spicy Corn on the Cob, 230
Grilled Steak Bruschetta Salad
    for Two, 245
Grilled Tilapia with Mango, 234
Grilled Vegetable Quesadillas, 232
Grilled Zucchini with Onions, 275
Ground Beef Spaghetti Skillet, 101

H

Ham & Cheese Pockets, 71
Ham & Scalloped Potatoes, 99
Ham & Swiss with a Twist, 79
Hawaiian Pulled Pork Lettuce
    Wraps, 225
Hazelnut Chocolate Chip Scones, 202
Hearty Asian Lettuce Salad, 163
Herb Buttermilk Dinner Rolls, 200
Herb Focaccia Rolls, 284

Herb-Glazed Turkey Slices, 158
Herbed Bubble Bread, 207
Herbed Pork Medallions, 122
Herbed Pork with Mushroom
    Sauce, 95
Herbed Potato Packs, 241
Herbed Roast Turkey Breast, 277
Homemade Strawberry Ice Cream, 172
Honey Cornbread, 204
Honey-Glazed Chicken, 95
Honey-Glazed Ham, 210
Honey Mustard Pork, 123
Honey Walleye, 100
Honeydew Shrimp Salad, 31
Hot Dog Sliders with Mango-Pineapple
    Salsa, 274
Hurry-Up Ham & Noodles, 122

I

Indian-Spiced Beefy Lettuce Wraps, 78
Irresistible Apple Blackberry
    Crumble, 299
Italian Herb & Cheese Breadsticks, 254
Italian-Style Pizzas, 19

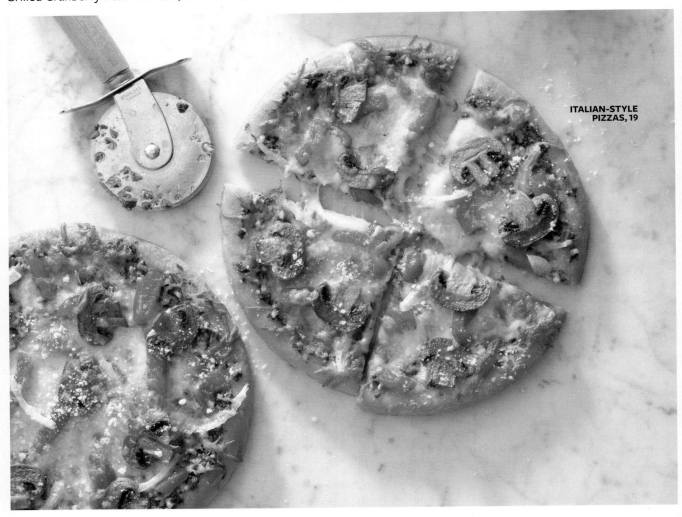

ITALIAN-STYLE
PIZZAS, 19

K

Kale & Fennel Skillet, 38
Key Lime Cream Pie, 298

L

Lemon Feta Chicken, 84
Lemon Mushroom Chicken, 156
Lemony Grilled Salmon Fillets with
    Dill Sauce, 243
Lime & Garlic Grilled Pork Chops, 233
Lentil Taco Cups, 152
Little Cheddar Meat Loaves, 173
Luscious Almond Cheesecake, 249

M

Macaroni Coleslaw, 252
Makeover Creamed Corn, 42
Makeover Deluxe Grilled Cheese, 60
Makeover Hash & Eggs, 186
Makeover Pineapple Upside-Down
    Cake, 294
Makeover Tater-Topped Casserole, 126
Makeover Traditional Cheesecake, 295
Makeover Traditional Lasagna, 159
Mama's Blackberry Cobbler, 306
Maple & Bacon Glazed Brussels
    Sprouts, 280
Maple-Glazed Salmon, 236
Maple Pecan Pie, 285
Maple-Roasted Chicken & Acorn
    Squash, 83
Margarita Sangria, 265
Marinara-Mozzarella Dip, 21
Marshmallow Berry Pancakes, 171
Mashed Cauliflower, 284
Meatless Taco Salad, 107
Mini Ham Quiches, 184
Mini Meat Loaf Sheet-Pan Meal, 316
Mini Pizza Cups, 249
Mini Sausage Quiches, 258
Miniature Peanut Butter Treats, 177
Moist Pumpkin Scones, 200
Monkey Bread, 178
Moroccan Chicken Tagine Pockets, 25
Mushroom-Blue Cheese
    Tenderloin, 130

N

Nacho Pie, 114
Nana's Rocky Road Fudge, 255
Nantucket Cranberry Tart, 278
Nectarine Chicken Salad, 147
New England Indian Pudding, 318
No-Churn Gingerbread Ice Cream, 286

Nut-Topped Strawberry Rhubarb
    Muffins, 207
Nutty Cheese Tortellini, 90
Nutty Chicken Fingers, 171

O

Old-Fashioned Applesauce, 179
Old-Fashioned Chicken Potpie, 134
Old-Fashioned Corn Relish, 311
Old-Fashioned Green Beans, 279
Olive Oil Mashed Potatoes with
    Pancetta, 276
One-Pan Rotini with Tomato Cream
    Sauce, 170
One-Pot Salsa Chicken, 149
Open-Faced Turkey Phillies, 71
Orange Blossom Mint Tea, 268
Orange Cornmeal Cake, 305
Orange-Pecan Salmon, 89
Orange Razzletini, 12
Orange Tilapia in Parchment, 136
Orchard Pear Pie, 293
Oregano Green Beans with Toasted
    Pine Nuts, 46
Orzo with Caramelized Butternut
    Squash & Bacon, 45
Orzo with Feta & Arugula, 40
Overnight Peach Oatmeal, 223

P

Palmiers, 300
Pan-Fried Scallops with White Wine
    Reduction, 141
Parmesan Chicken Breasts, 91
Parmesan Pork Medallions, 84
Party Pitas, 251
Pasta Fagioli Soup, 60
Peach Caprese, 30
Peach Cobbler Cookies, 292
Peachy Keen Pepper Sauce, 312
Peanut Turkey Satay, 166
Pecan Pork Chops, 155
Penne with Veggies & Black Beans, 115
Pepperoni Pinwheels, 13
Perfect Winter Salad, 282
Pesto Crostini with Grilled Nectarines
    & Burrata, 231
Pesto Shrimp Pasta, 268
Pizza Sloppy Joes, 76
Pork & Bok Choy Udon Soup, 62
Pork & Green Chile Casserole, 135
Pork Chops & Pierogies, 100
Pork Chops with Cumin Rice, 107
Pork Chops with Parmesan Sauce, 160
Pork Tenderloin Fajitas, 264
Pork with Mustard Sauce, 106

Potato & Pepper Sausage Bake, 317
Potato Omelet, 182
Potato Sausage Frittata, 190
Potluck Enchilada Meatballs, 250
Pressure-Cooker Chicken
    Cacciatore, 224
Pressure-Cooker Flan in a Jar, 219
Pressure-Cooker Lemon
    Red Potatoes, 210
Pressure-Cooker Potato-Cheddar
    Frittata, 214
Pressure-Cooker Pumpkin Spice
    Oatmeal, 220
Pressure-Cooker Sausage & Waffle
    Bake, 227
Pressure-Cooker Spiced
    Short Ribs, 212
Prosciutto-Pepper Pork Chops, 93
Pull-Apart Garlic Bread, 251
Pumpkin Pecan Custard, 319

Q

Quick & Easy Pumpkin Crescents, 198
Quick Cilantro Chicken, 114
Quick Icebox Sandwiches, 174
Quick Sausage Tortellini Soup, 58
Quick Sloppy Joes, 176
Quinoa Arancini, 23
Quinoa with Peas & Onion, 31

R

Raspberry-Coconut French Toast, 184
Raspberry Coleslaw, 52
Red, White & Blue Summer Salad, 273
Reese's Chocolate Snack Cake, 261
Refreshing Shrimp Salad, 162
Red Potatoes with Beans, 51
Rhubarb Torte, 256
Ribs with Plum Sauce, 82
Rice with Collard Greens Relish, 37
Rich Seafood Chowder, 75
Roadside Diner Cheeseburger
    Quiche, 136
Roasted Asparagus & Tomatoes, 42
Roasted Kielbasa & Vegetables, 315
Roasted Peppers & Cauliflower, 52
Roasted Sweet Potato Wedges, 48
Root Beer Float Pie, 275
Rosemary & Thyme Lemon
    Cocktail, 25
Rosemary Beef Roast over Cheesy
    Polenta, 225
Rosemary Pork with Cherry
    Topping, 133
Rosemary-Thyme Lamb Chops, 92
Rosemary Walnut Bread, 199

S

Sassy Chicken & Peppers, 148
Saturday Afternoon Oven
   Pot Roast, 129
Saucy Grilled Pork Chops, 231
Saucy Italian Chicken, 218
Sausage & Sauerkraut, 86
Sausage & Swiss Chard Pasta, 105
Sausage Breakfast Burritos, 192
Sausage Rice Dinner, 102
Sausage Spinach Salad, 83
Sausage-Tomato Coconut Curry, 104
Sauteed Garlic Mushrooms, 33
Savory Steak Rub, 239
Scallops in Sage Cream, 82
Scrambled Egg Muffins, 187
Sensational Spiced Salmon, 127
Sheet-Pan Lemon Garlic Chicken, 317
Shredded Chicken Tostadas, 216
Shrimp & Noodle Bowls, 144
Simple Orange-Glazed Beets, 41
Skewered Ginger Shrimp with
   Plums, 237
Skewered Ravioli with Creamy
   Tomato Dipping Sauce, 16
Skillet Tacos, 118
Sliced Ham with Roasted
   Vegetables, 314
Slow-Cooked Black Bean Soup, 218
Slow-Cooked Vegetable Wild Rice
   Soup, 223
Slow-Cooker Buffalo Chicken
   Salad, 220
Slow-Cooker Cinnamon Roll, 192
Slow-Cooker Honey Nut
   Granola, 185
Slow-Cooker Honey Teriyaki
   Chicken, 217
Slow-Cooker Oatmeal, 195
Slow-Cooker Strawberry Pudding
   Cake, 302
Smoked Sausage with Pasta, 148
So-Easy Sticky Chicken Wings, 252
Sopaipillas, 267
Southern Shrimp & Grits, 123
Southwest Tortilla-Turkey Skillet, 121
Southwestern Beef & Rice Skillet, 112
Southwestern Beef Barley Stew, 142
Spanakopita Spring Rolls, 20
Special Scalloped Corn, 32
Spiced Lime & Cilantro Chicken, 224
Spiced Rum Fruitcake, 294
Spicy Buffalo Chicken Wraps, 76
Spicy Chicken Stew, 144
Spicy Flank Steak, 240
Spicy Refried Beans, 265
Spinach & Shrimp Fra Diavolo, 160

Springtime Penne, 113
Squash Custard Pie, 292
Standing Rib Roast, 281
Steak Frites Salad, 155
Steak Sandwich Kabobs, 245
Steakhouse Pizza, 135
Stir-Fried Shrimp & Mushrooms, 140
Strawberry Arugula Salad, 53
Strawberry Bliss Omelet, 193
Sugar Cookie S'mores, 170
Sugar-Glazed Ham, 90
Summertime Watermelon Punch
   for a Crowd, 258
Super Fast Mexican Soup, 57
Super Simple Scalloped Potatoes, 282
Sweet & Sour Burgers, 69
Sweet Onion Pimiento Cheese
   Deviled Eggs, 272
Sweet Potato Spice Bread, 202
Swiss Mushroom Chicken, 108
Szechuan Burgers with Bok Choy
   Slaw, 63

T

Taco Burgers, 59
Tangerine Tossed Salad, 48
Tangy Sweet & Sour Meatballs, 117
Tara's Spanish Chicken, 316
Tarragon Chicken with Apples
   for Two, 113
Tarragon Tuna Salad, 154
Tater-Topped Italian Casserole, 137
Teriyaki Glazed Chicken, 98
Tex-Mex Pork Chops, 151
Thai Butternut Squash Peanut
   Soup, 221
Thai Salad with Cilantro Lime
   Dressing, 44
Tilapia with Cucumber Relish, 142

TLC (Thanksgiving Leftover
   Casserole), 276
Tomato Apple Chutney, 312
Tomato Basil Tortellini Soup, 217
Tomato Potpie, 127
Tomatoes with Parsley Pesto, 37
Triple Bean Bake with Bacon, 275
Triple-Citrus Steaks with Jicama &
   Mango, 147
Tropical Pineapple Coleslaw, 176
Tuna Artichoke Melts, 65
Tuna Noodle Casserole, 128
Tuna Potato Supper, 98
Turkey Couscous Salad, 165
Turkey Dinner Muffins, 111
Turkey Enchilada Stack, 141
Turkey Lattice Pie, 315

Turkey Sandwich with Raspberry-
   Mustard Spread, 57
Turkey Sausage with Pasta, 157
Turkey Scallopini, 111
Turkey Squash Casserole, 133
Tuscan Portobello Stew, 150
Tuscan-Style Roasted Asparagus, 285

U

The Ultimate Fish Tacos, 266
Ultimate Fruity Granola, 183

V

Vanilla Bean Fizz, 20
Vegetarian Pea Soup, 219

W

Warm Cabbage, Fennel & Pear
   Salad, 279
Warm Garlicky Grape Tomatoes, 51
Weeknight Ravioli Lasagna, 95

Z

Zesty Steak Salad, 140
Zesty Sugar Snap Peas, 53
Zesty Turkey Tomato Soup, 73
Zippy Praline Bacon, 182
Zippy Shrimp Skewers, 22
Zucchini Honey Relish, 311
Zucchini-Parmesan Bake, 93
Zucchini Pasta, 47